BASIC WRITTEN CHINESE

MOVE FROM COMPLETE BEGINNER LEVEL TO BASIC PROFICIENCY

CORNELIUS C. KUBLER

TUTTLE Publishing

Tokyo | Rutland, Vermont | Singapore

The Tuttle Story: "Books to Span the East and West"

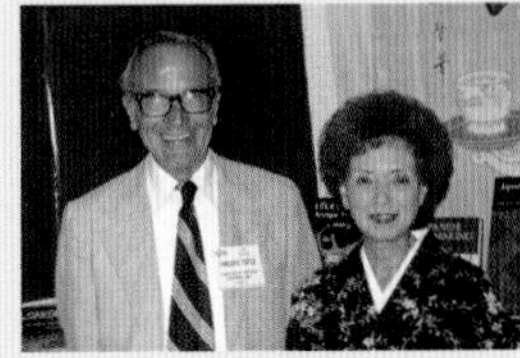

Most people are surprised to learn that the world's largest publisher of books on Asia had its beginnings in the tiny American state of Vermont. The company's founder, Charles E. Tuttle, belonged to a New England family steeped in publishing. And his first love was naturally books—especially old and rare editions.

Immediately after WW II, serving in Tokyo under General Douglas MacArthur, Tuttle was tasked with reviving the Japanese publishing industry, and founded the Charles E. Tuttle Publishing Company, which thrives today as one of the world's leading independent publishers.

Though a westerner, Charles was hugely instrumental in bringing knowledge of Japan and Asia to a world hungry for information about the East. By the time of his death in 1993, Tuttle had published over 6,000 books on Asian culture, history and art—a legacy honored by the Japanese emperor with the "Order of the Sacred Treasure," the highest tribute Japan can bestow upon a non-Japanese.

With a backlist of 1,500 titles, Tuttle Publishing is more active today than at any time in its past—inspired by Charles' core mission to publish fine books to span the East and West and provide a greater understanding of

Published by Tuttle Publishing, an imprint of Periplus Editions (HK) Ltd.

www.tuttlepublishing.com

ISBN 978-0-8048-4016-3
Interior design: Anne Bell Carter

Assistance received from the following in the filming of conversations is gratefully acknowledged:
Unit 2, Part 1: The Mandarin Training Center, National Taiwan Normal University, Taipei; Part 3: Shangrila Hotel, Beijing; Part 4: Hilton Hotel, Taipei. Unit 3, Part 4: Beijing West Railway Station, Beijing. Unit 4, Part 1: The Mandarin Training Center, National Taiwan Normal University, Taipei; Part 2: Jianquan Clinic, Taipei; Part 3: Swisshotel, Beijing. Unit 5, Part 3: Yuelong Restaurant, Beijing. Unit 7, Part 4: Fortune Garden Restaurant, North Adams, Massachusetts.

Library of Congress Cataloging-in-Publication Data for this title is on record.

Distributed by:

North America, Latin America & Europe
Tuttle Publishing
364 Innovation Drive
North Clarendon, VT 05759-9436 U.S.A.
Tel: 1 (802) 773-8930 Fax: 1 (802) 773-6993
info@tuttlepublishing.com
www.tuttlepublishing.com

Japan
Tuttle Publishing
Yaekari Building, 3rd Floor
5-4-12 Osaki Shinagawa-ku Tokyo 141 0032
Tel: (81) 3 5437-0171 Fax: (81) 3 5437-0755
sales@tuttle.co.jp
www.tuttle.co.jp

Asia Pacific
Berkeley Books Pte. Ltd.
61 Tai Seng Avenue #02-12, Singapore 534167
Tel: (65) 6280-1330 Fax: (65) 6280-6290
inquiries@periplus.com.sg
www.periplus.com

First edition
14 13 12 11 8 7 6 5 4 3 2 1 1110EP

Printed in Hong Kong

A Note to the Learner

Welcome to this course in written Chinese!

As a native English speaker, your working hard to learn Chinese is not enough; you have to work smart in order to learn this very different language efficiently. No matter why you've chosen to learn Chinese—for business, travel, cultural studies, or another goal—the *Basic Chinese* approach of two separate but integrated tracks in spoken and written Chinese will help you learn this language most efficiently and successfully.

Basic Written Chinese is designed so it can be used in a class with an instructor or by independent learners working on their own.

- *Basic Written Chinese* systematically introduces **288 of the highest-frequency characters** (in both their simplified and traditional forms) and **over 700 common words written with them** in context in sentences and a variety of reading passages, so as to help you master basic Chinese reading and writing.
- The **structure** of each new character is explained in detail to make the learning of characters easier, and "look-alike" characters are compared and contrasted.
- Many lessons include **character differentiation drills** and some lessons include **realia** such as name cards, street signs, or e-mail messages.
- Each lesson introduces 6 new characters and a number of words that are written using them. By dividing the learning into small tasks, you maintain a sense of accomplishment rather than getting bogged down.
- You'll experience both **printed and handwritten forms** of characters, as well as several **different printed fonts**.

Basic Written Chinese should be used in conjunction with the accompanying **Basic Written Chinese Practice Essentials**.

- Either before or at the same time that you study a lesson in *Basic Written Chinese*, you should study the same lesson in **Basic Spoken Chinese** and **Basic Spoken Chinese Practice Essentials**, so that you have access to all the relevant information and practice regarding Chinese pronunciation, grammar, and culture.
- The characters in each lesson are chosen, based on frequency of occurrence, from those used to write the Basic Conversation of the corresponding lesson in *Basic Spoken Chinese*. Thus, when you begin a new lesson of *Basic Written Chinese*, you already know the pronunciations, meanings and usages of the new characters and words, so you need only learn their written representations. This considerably **lightens your learning load**!
- Both **simplified and traditional characters** are taught in the same volume. This means students can learn either or both kinds of characters without having to purchase another book; and instructors have the flexibility to teach a combined class where some students read and write one type of characters and other students the other type.
- Includes an **audio disc** with with over 5 hours of recordings by native speakers of the new vocabulary and reading exercises, to help with pronunciation, phrasing, and comprehension. The disc also includes several useful Appendices.
- The online *Basic Chinese* **Instructor's Guide** (available free from the publisher) contains detailed suggestions for using these materials as well as a wealth of exercises for use by instructors in class or by tutors during practice sessions.

出版和使用说明

《基础中文：读与写》专供读写课使用。这本教材通过各种练习有系统地介绍两百八十八个高频字（简体及繁体）和七百多个高频词。学习者宜与配套的《基础中文：读与写》练习册、《基础中文：听与说》及《基础中文：听与说》练习册一起使用。

出版和使用說明

《基礎中文：讀與寫》專供讀寫課使用。這本教材通過各種練習有系統地介紹兩百八十八個高頻字（簡體及繁體）和七百多個高頻詞。學習者宜與配套的《基礎中文：讀與寫》練習冊、《基礎中文：聽與說》及《基礎中文：聽與說》練習冊一起使用。

Contents

Acknowledgments

I am indebted to a number of people for their assistance in the preparation of this volume. It's not possible to mention everyone who participated, but special thanks are due the following for their contributions:

For assistance in drafting an earlier version of the reading exercises, parts of which survive in the present version: my good friend Qunhu Li, formerly my colleague in the Chinese Program at Williams College and now Director of New Century Language and Culture Center in Tianjin. Student research assistants Jenny Chen and Tron Wang also contributed to the development of the reading exercises.

For assistance with the character presentation sheets and related work: student research assistants Emily Chang, Angie Chien, Andy C. Chiu, Anthang Hoang, and Peter Rankin.

For providing handwriting samples: Zhixin Dong, Shengli Feng, Jerling Guo Kubler, Dongshan Zhang, and Yiqing Zhu.

For corrections to the manuscript and helpful comments of all kinds: Jerling Guo Kubler, Eric Pelzl, Weibing Ye, Shaopeng Zhang, and my most collegial colleagues in the Chinese Program at Williams College, present and past: Cecilia Chang, Bing Han, Yu-yin Hsu, Hao-hsiang Liao, Christopher M. B. Nugent, Cathy Silber, Hsin-I Tseng, Yang Wang, and Li Yu.

For making the accompanying audio recordings: Jerling Guo Kubler, Fei Wang, and Shaopeng Zhang.

For allowing themselves to be photographed for the cover: Williams College students Kevin DeWar and Zachary Whitney.

For providing useful information on the frequency of Chinese words and characters, as well as much appreciated inspiration and encouragement over many years: James E. Dew. I should also acknowledge here my debt to Victor H. Mair for his many stimulating comments over the years concerning the Chinese writing system.

For advice and assistance with computer-related work: Adam Jianjun Wang, Senior Instructional Technology specialist at Williams College, and Peter Leimbigler of Asia Communications Québec Inc. All of the Chinese language content in this volume was processed using the KEY 5.1 Chinese language software that Dr. Leimbigler and his colleagues developed.

For meticulous editing and many other helpful suggestions during the production of this course: Sandra Korinchak, Senior Editor at Tuttle Publishing. I also wish to express my appreciation for their enthusiastic support of the project and its development to Tuttle's Publisher Eric Oey and Vice President Christina Ong; and to Nancy Goh, Loh Sook Fan, and the Tuttle Sales and Marketing team for their expertise and assistance throughout.

Logistical and financial support from the following during the final stage of the preparation of these materials is gratefully acknowledged: Tseng Chin-Chin and staff at the Graduate Institute of Teaching Chinese as a Second Language at National Taiwan Normal University; and Jenny F. So and staff at the Institute of Chinese Studies at the Chinese University of Hong Kong.

Last but not least, I wish to thank the students in the basic Chinese classes at Williams College from 1993 through 2010 for their corrections and suggestions, as well as for their encouragement and inspiration.

Cornelius C. Kubler
Department of Asian Studies
Williams College
Williamstown, Massachusetts, USA

Orientation

About This Course

Basic Spoken Chinese and *Basic Written Chinese* constitute an introductory course in modern Chinese (Mandarin), the language with the largest number of native speakers in the world, which is the official language of mainland China and Taiwan and one of the official languages of Singapore. The focus of this course, which is designed for adult English-speaking learners, is on communicating in Chinese in practical, everyday situations. We have tried to keep in mind the needs of a wide range of users, from college and university students to business people and government personnel. With some adjustments in the rate of progress, high school students may also be able to use these materials to their advantage. By availing themselves of the detailed usage notes and making good use of the *Practice Essentials* books, the video, and the audio, it is even possible for motivated self-learners to work through these materials on their own, though it would be desirable for them to meet with a teacher or native speaker for an hour or two per week, if possible. Although users with specialized needs will, in the later stages of their study, require supplementary materials, we believe this course provides a solid general foundation or "base" (hence the title of the course) that all learners of Chinese need, on which they may build for future mastery.

The course is divided into spoken and written tracks, each with various types of ancillary materials. The following diagram will clarify the organization of the whole course:

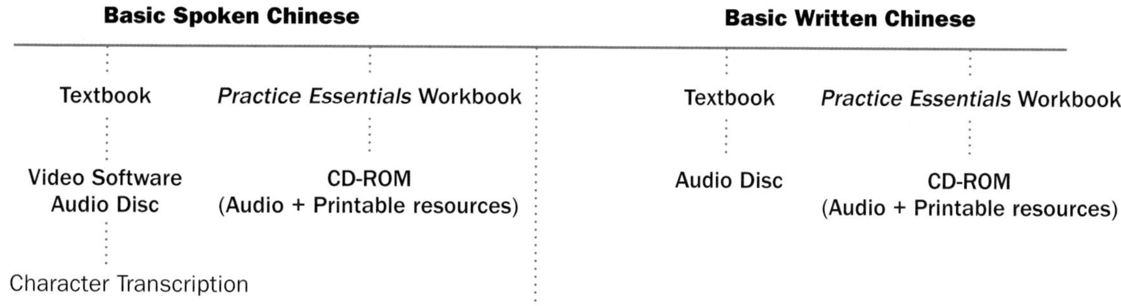

Instructor's Guide for
Basic Spoken Chinese* and *Basic Written Chinese

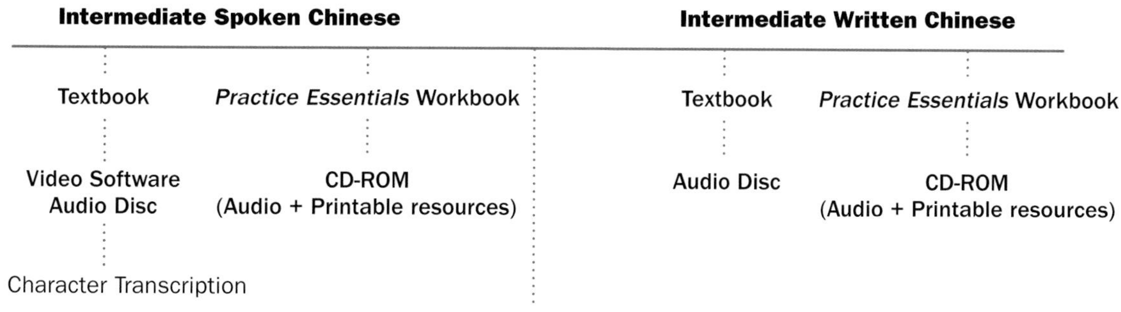

Instructor's Guide for
Intermediate Spoken Chinese* and *Intermediate Written Chinese

Several modes of study are possible for these materials: (1) the spoken series only; (2) a lesson in the spoken series followed a few days, weeks, or months later by the corresponding lesson in the written series; and (3) a lesson in the spoken and written series studied simultaneously. What is not possible is to study the written series first or only, since the written series assumes knowledge of the pronunciation system and relevant grammatical and cultural information, which are introduced in the spoken series.

Students embarking upon the study of Chinese should be aware that, along with Japanese, Korean, and Arabic, Chinese is one of the most difficult languages for native English speakers. This course makes no pretensions of being an "easy" introduction to the language. However, students can be assured that if they make the effort to master thoroughly the material presented here, they will acquire a solid foundation in Chinese.

The proficiency goals in speaking and reading by completion of the *Intermediate Spoken Chinese* and *Intermediate Written Chinese* portions of the course are Intermediate-Mid on the American Council on the Teaching of Foreign Languages (ACTFL) Chinese Proficiency Guidelines, which correlates with S-1/R-1 on the U.S. government Interagency Language Roundtable (ILR) Language Skill Level Descriptions. By the time they attain this level, learners will be able to conduct simple, practical conversations with Chinese speakers on a variety of everyday topics. They will also be able to read simple, connected texts printed in simplified or traditional Chinese characters and recognize about 600 high-frequency characters and common words written with them. Of course, they will not yet be able to conduct conversations on professional topics or read newspapers or novels, skills that in the case of Chinese take a considerably longer time to develop.

Some of the special features of *Basic Spoken Chinese* and *Basic Written Chinese* include:

Separate but integrated tracks in spoken and written Chinese. Most textbooks for teaching basic Chinese teach oral and written skills from the same materials, which are covered at a single rate of progress. Students typically study a dialog, learn how to use in their speech the words and grammar contained in the dialog, and also learn how to read and write every character used to write the dialog. But the fact is that, due to the inherent difficulty of Chinese characters, native English speakers can learn spoken Chinese words much faster than they can learn the characters used to write those words. As East Asian language pedagogues Eleanor H. Jorden and A. Ronald Walton have argued,* why must the rate of progress in spoken Chinese be slowed down to the maximum possible rate of progress in written Chinese? Moreover, in Chinese, more than in most languages, there are substantial differences between standard spoken style and standard written style, with many words and grammar patterns that are common in speech being rare in writing or vice versa. For all these reasons, this course uses separate but related materials for training in spoken and written Chinese. However, reflecting the fact that written Chinese is based on spoken Chinese, and so as to mutually reinforce the four skills (listening, speaking, reading, and writing), the written track is closely integrated with the spoken track. A day's spoken lesson is based on a conversation typically introducing one to three new grammar patterns and 15 to 20 new spoken words, while the corresponding written lesson introduces six new high-frequency characters and a number of words that are written using them, chosen from among (but not including all of) the characters used to write the basic conversation of the corresponding lesson. Experience shows that the learning of written skills in Chinese proceeds more efficiently if learners study for reading and writing the characters for words they have previously learned for speaking and comprehension. Under this approach, when students take up a new lesson in written Chinese, they already know the pronunciations, meanings, and usages of the new words, needing only to learn their written representations—which considerably lightens the learning load. Such an approach also allows students and instructors maximum flexibility concerning at which point, how, and even whether, to introduce reading and writing.

Graduated approach. There is so much to learn to become proficient in Chinese that Chinese language learning can easily become overwhelming. By dividing large tasks into a series of many smaller ones, the learning of Chinese becomes more manageable. Therefore, each spoken lesson consists of only one fairly short (five- to twelve-line) conversation, while each written lesson introduces only six new characters. An added bonus to this approach is the sense of accomplishment learners feel through frequent completion of small tasks, rather than getting bogged down in long lessons that seem never-ending.

Naturalness of the language. A special effort has been made to present natural, idiomatic, up-to-date Chinese as opposed to stilted "textbook style." This will be evident, for example, in the use of interjections, pause fillers,

---

* Cf. Eleanor H. Jorden and A. Ronald Walton, "Truly Foreign Languages: Instructional Challenges" in *The Annals of the American Academy of Political and Social Science*, March 1987.

and final particles, which occur more frequently in this text than in most other Chinese language textbooks. Occasionally, for comprehension practice, we have included recordings of slightly accented Mandarin speech, so as to familiarize learners with some of the more common variations in pronunciation they are likely to encounter.

Authenticity of the language. Chinese, like English, is a language spoken in a number of different societies, with multiple standards and varying usages. Although the emphasis of this course is on the core that is common to Mandarin Chinese wherever it is spoken, linguistic differences among the major Chinese speech communities as well as recent innovations are taken up where appropriate. Of the 96 basic conversations in *Basic Spoken Chinese* and *Intermediate Spoken Chinese*, the audio and video for 56 of them were recorded in Beijing, with another 31 recorded in Taipei, 3 in Hong Kong, one in Macao, 2 in Singapore, 2 in Malaysia, and one in the U.S. The relatively small number of terms that are restricted in use to a particular speech area are so indicated.

Emphasis on the practical and immediately useful. We have tried to present material that is high in frequency and has the most immediate "pay-off value" possible. An effort has been made to include the most useful words, characters, grammar patterns, situations, and functions, based on several published frequency studies as well as research by the author. The units of this course have been arranged in order of general usefulness and practical importance. Although the course is designed to be studied from beginning to end, learners with time for only, say, the first five or ten units will at least be exposed to many of the most useful characters, vocabulary items, and structural patterns.

Eclecticism of approach. We believe that language is so complex and the personalities of learners so different, that no single approach or method can possibly meet the needs of all learners at all times. For this reason, the pedagogical approach we have chosen is purposefully eclectic. This course is proficiency-oriented and situational in approach with a carefully ordered underlying grammatical foundation. We have borrowed freely from the audio-lingual, communicative, functional-notional, and grammar-translation approaches.

Maximum flexibility of use. Student and teacher needs and personalities vary widely, as do the types of programs in which Chinese is taught. We have tried to leave options open whenever possible. This is true, for example, in the question of how to teach pronunciation; whether to teach the spoken skills only or also the written skills; when to introduce reading and writing; whether to teach simplified or traditional characters or both; and which of the exercises to do and in which order to do them. There is detailed discussion of all these and other questions in the Instructor's Guide for *Basic Spoken Chinese* and *Basic Written Chinese*.

Attention to sociolinguistic and cultural features. Knowing how to say something with correct grammar and pronunciation is not sufficient for effective communication. Learners must know what to say and what not to say, when to say it, and how to adjust what they say for the occasion. How do the gender, age, and social position of the speaker and listener affect language? Finally, language does not exist apart from the culture of its speakers. What are the cultural assumptions of Chinese speakers? These are some of the matters to which we have tried to pay attention.

Extensive built-in review. In order to promote long-term retention of the material learned, a great effort has been made to recycle vocabulary and grammar periodically in later units in the textbook and *Practice Essentials* after they have been introduced.

Attention to the needs of learners with prior knowledge of Chinese. While the course is designed for beginners and assumes no prior knowledge of Chinese, it tries to take into account the special situation and needs of learners who possess some prior knowledge of the language acquired from home or residence overseas. Consequently, there are special notes on features of standard Mandarin pronunciation and usage that differ from the Cantonese or Taiwanese-influenced Mandarin to which some learners may have been exposed.

Organization and Use

Basic Written Chinese consists of twelve units. The first two are introductory units not directly related to the material in *Basic Spoken Chinese*.[1] They are followed by ten units, numbered 1 to 10, that parallel the ten units in *Basic Spoken Chinese*. Each of these units in turn consists of four parts, with each part presenting six characters, common words written with them, and reading exercises to help you master the new material.

The twelve units of *Basic Written Chinese* introduce a total of 288 characters and about 700 common words and expressions written with them. Except for the two introductory units, the six characters in each lesson were chosen, based on frequency of occurrence, from the characters used to write the Basic Conversation of the corresponding lesson in *Basic Spoken Chinese*.[2] Since each lesson of *Basic Written Chinese* was designed to be studied after the corresponding lesson of *Basic Spoken Chinese* and *Basic Spoken Chinese Practice Essentials*, when you begin a new lesson of *Basic Written Chinese*, you already know the pronunciations, meanings, and usages of the new words, so you need only learn their written representations. This considerably lightens your learning load!

Our guide in questions of frequency has been the general character list in the 现代汉语频率词典 **Xiàndài Hànyǔ Pínlǜ Cídiǎn** *Frequency Dictionary of Modern Chinese*, published by Beijing Languages Institute in 1985. All of the characters in *Basic Written Chinese* were selected from the top 1,000 (and most from the top 300) characters in that dictionary, with three exceptions: the surname 李 **Lǐ**, the character 湾（灣）in 台湾（台灣）**Táiwān**, and the character 津 in 天津 **Tiānjīn**.

NEW CHARACTERS AND WORDS

The first section of each part or lesson in *Basic Written Chinese* is called "New Characters and Words." It introduces the six new characters of the lesson as well as common words written with them. For each new character, the following information is provided:

1. **Number.** The blue-colored number at the beginning of the section for each new character is the number of the character in this course. Later in the course, characters are sometimes referred to by their number.

2. **Simplified form.** If only one large, blue-colored character is given, then the simplified form is the same as the traditional form.

3. **Traditional form.** If the traditional form of a character is different from the simplified form, it is given next, also in large, blue-colored font, but *enclosed in parentheses*. So that learners are always clear about which characters are simplified and which are traditional, whenever simplified and traditional characters occur together, simplified characters always come first, with traditional characters following, enclosed in parentheses.

4. **Pinyin.** The Pinyin transcription follows on the same line after the character.

5. **English.** The last item on the first line of each new character section is an English translation of the basic meaning of the character. The translation here is for reference only and does not need to be learned. The meaning of the individual character may be different from the meanings of words containing the character. Moreover, the English translation is not meant to be complete and includes only those meanings that are judged to be pedagogically useful for learners at this point in their study of Chinese.

---

1. The two introductory units take up numbers, personal names, and place names and are designed to familiarize learners with the basic strokes of characters while they (in many cases) are learning pronunciation and romanization from *Basic Spoken Chinese*. One advantage of numbers and names, besides their obvious utility, is that they can occur by themselves and require no grammatical knowledge to be understood.

2. On the rare occasions when there were no appropriate characters in the Basic Conversation of the corresponding lesson, characters from the Supplementary Vocabulary of the corresponding lesson were chosen, or characters from previous lessons where there had been an excess of appropriate characters.

6. **Radical.** Beginning on the second line of each new character section, the radical for the new character is given. If the character differs in its simplified and traditional forms, and if those two forms have different radicals, then both radicals are indicated. If the radical has a common colloquial name, that also is given.

7. **Phonetic.** If there is a pedagogically useful phonetic, it is indicated. If the character itself is a common phonetic, examples are given of characters in which the phonetic occurs.

8. **Other components.** Any other components of the character are mentioned and discussed.

9. **Structural explanation.** When something pedagogically useful can be said about the history and development of the character, it is included. Our primary consideration is helping students remember the character, so some explanations that have mnemonic value are mentioned even if they may not be historically accurate. On the other hand, explanations that are excessively complex and would not be helpful to the average learner have been omitted.

10. **Similar characters.** At the end of the new character section are listed any "look-alike" characters with which the new character should be contrasted.

11. **New words written with the character.** Indented under the section for each new character is a list of new words that are written with the character. These are given in simplified characters, traditional characters (if different from simplified), Pinyin transcription, and English translation. They are also recorded on the accompanying audio disc.[3]

12. **New words written with characters you already know.** This section, which is also recorded on the accompanying audio disc, presents new words occurring in the corresponding lesson of *Basic Spoken Chinese* that happen to be written with characters that have already been introduced in connection with other words in previous lessons of *Basic Written Chinese*.

IMPORTANT NOTE TO LEARNERS: What you must learn before beginning the Reading Exercises and proceeding to the next lesson is *those new words in sections (11) and (12) that are followed by word class abbreviations in bolded brackets*. Everything else is for reference only.

READING EXERCISES

The next section of each lesson is the Reading Exercises. These should be the focus of study and practice, since they present the new characters, words, and other features of written Chinese in context. When working with the Reading Exercises, you should practice both oral and silent reading. Be sure to make frequent use of the accompanying audio disc to hear and practice correct pronunciation, phrasing, and intonation.

The Reading Exercises are presented twice: first in simplified characters in horizontal format, and then again in traditional characters in vertical format.[4] This is done to provide learners with practice in reading both types of characters and both formats. Of course, learners may choose to read only one version of the Reading Exercises, or they may read one version first and the other version several months later.

---

3. Be aware that, when reading characters out loud, Chinese readers have a tendency to give syllables their full tone, so that some syllables that are neutral tone in conversation are pronounced with a full tone instead (e.g., 朋友 "friend" may be read off as **péngyǒu** instead of **péngyou**). Our advice in such cases is to follow the pronunciation of your teacher, mentor, or the audio recording that accompanies this text.

4. The main exception to this is Unit A, which is exactly the same in simplified and traditional characters; therefore, it is presented only once, in horizontal format. Although in this book simplified characters are presented in horizontal format and traditional characters are usually presented in vertical format, which reflects general practice in the Chinese "real world," learners should be aware that simplified characters can also be printed or handwritten in vertical format, and traditional characters can also be (and not infrequently are) printed or handwritten in horizontal format.

The Reading Exercises for Units 1 to 10 consist of the following components:

1. **Sentences.** These illustrate the use of the new characters and words in context. There are always ten sentences in this section, and they exemplify all the new characters and most of the new words of the lesson.

2. **Conversations.** The conversations are in spoken style. The name or role of each person speaking is included and should be studied along with the conversation itself. During class or practice sessions, you should find a partner or partners, and each of you should take a role. Then switch roles, so you get practice reading all of the lines.

3. **Character Differentiation Drills.** In the same way that drills can be useful for teaching spoken language, they can also help teach written language. The purpose of the character differentiation drills is to give you practice in differentiating "look-alike" characters that learners new to Chinese might confuse. Pronounce each drill out loud and think of the meaning of the character you're pronouncing.

4. **Narratives.** The purpose of the narratives is to give you practice in reading connected prose, which is different in a number of ways from a series of independent sentences. A few of the narratives include some elements of written-style Chinese. The first time you read a narrative, you should read it out loud; the second time, read silently and try gradually to increase your reading speed. Always think of the meaning of what you're reading.

5. **Notes.** These are miscellaneous comments to help you understand the meaning, structure, and cultural background of the material in the Reading Exercises. No attempt is made to provide systematic treatment of grammar, since that is provided in *Basic Spoken Chinese*.

Some of the lessons include additional sections on special topics such as numbers, personal and place names, money, times, and dates. There are also a total of 18 supplements presenting examples of popular culture and realia ranging from tongue twisters and riddles to tables and handwritten notes.

An Overview of the Chinese Writing System

Most people equate the Chinese writing system with Chinese characters. Characters are certainly the most prominent feature of written Chinese, but the Chinese writing system actually consists of a whole lot more. In addition to simplified characters, traditional characters, and unofficial but often encountered alternate characters, the Chinese writing system also includes the uppercase and lowercase letters of the Roman alphabet (as in X光 "X-ray," B型肝炎 "Hepatitis B," 卡拉OK "Karaoke," and e世代 "digital generation"); the Pinyin romanization system (for computer entry or to indicate the pronunciations of rare characters); the Arabic numbers plus the Chinese symbol 〇; mathematical symbols such as + − × ÷ = and % ; the Chinese currency sign ¥; the reduplication sign 々; punctuation; use of smaller characters for humility; and spacing conventions. Of course, as an educated reader and writer of English, you already know some of the preceding, so not everything will be new for you.

Chinese characters are variously termed "ideograms," "ideographs," "logographs," or "graphs." In this book, we shall simply call them "Chinese characters" or just "characters." It's important to keep in mind that, as is true of all languages, in Chinese speech is primary, the standard Chinese writing system of today essentially being a set of written symbols for recording Chinese speech; Chinese characters certainly do not, as claimed by some, constitute a "language-independent system of logical symbols." It's best to think of a Chinese character as standing for a meaningful syllable of a spoken word, a little as if in English we had one symbol for "auto," another for "bio," and yet another for "graph," so that we could then put them together in different combinations like "autograph," "biography," and "autobiographer."

ORIGIN OF THE CHARACTERS

Until quite recently, Chinese children were taught in school that the Chinese characters were the invention of one man, Cang Jie, an official in the court of the Yellow Emperor around 2600 BCE. According to one version of this legend, Cang Jie got the idea for characters from the tracks which he saw birds and other animals make in the ground. However, scholars today agree that Chinese characters are not the invention of any one person but are rather the cumulative product of many individuals over a long period of time. The characters are quite clearly pictographic in origin. The prototypes for the characters are simple drawings of animals and other natural objects which can be found etched on fragments of ancient pottery dating back to before 2000 BCE. Recently, there have been reports of thousands of pictorial symbols dating back even earlier that have been found carved on cliff faces in northwest China.

The earliest examples of fully developed Chinese writing we have today are the so-called 甲骨文 **Jiǎgǔwén** or oracle bone inscriptions, dating from the late Shang Dynasty (ca. 1300 BCE). To divine the future for the Shang rulers, priests would hold ox collar bones and tortoise shells over a fire until they developed cracks and then interpret the meanings of the cracks, making predictions about weather, religion, politics, and war. The interpretations and predictions would then be recorded on the bones and shells in a few lines of text written in the characters of the day (see the photos on this page and page 15). Over 100,000 pieces of **Jiǎgǔwén** are extant, containing over 3,000 different characters, roughly half of which can be read today.

Oracle bone

The story of the discovery of the **Jiǎgǔwén** is a colorful chapter in the history of Chinese paleography. The oracle bones, which had been discovered in the vicinity of Anyang, Henan, had for some time been regarded as "dragon bones" and had been sold and ground up for Chinese medicine in pharmacies in the Beijing area. In 1899, a scholar by the name of Wang Yirong, who was taking the dragon bones for malaria, examined the characters on the bones and started researching them with his friend Liu E. They concluded that the inscriptions on the bones were older than any other characters known at the time. Wang died the next year, but Liu published a book on his and Wang's collection of bones in 1903, which made their discovery known to the world.

Both the forms of the characters and the total number of characters multiplied greatly during the succeeding Zhou Dynasty (11th century to 221 BCE), differing widely from place to place. The characters from this period, most extant specimens of which are inscribed on various kinds of bronze vessels, are collectively known as 大篆 **Dàzhuàn** or Great Seal Script.

In 221 BCE, Qin Shi Huang, the First Emperor, unified the country and made mandatory throughout all of China the use of the Qin script. This script, known as 小篆 **Xiǎozhuàn** or Small Seal Script, is ancestral to all later forms of Chinese writing and is still sometimes used today for ornamental purposes and in the making of seals. At about the same time as the official **Xiǎozhuàn** script, there developed among the common people a much simplified form of **Xiǎozhuàn** called 隶书 (隸書) **Lìshū** or Clerical Script, which was characterized by a straightening out of round strokes and a generally much less pictographic appearance. By the latter part of the Han Dynasty (ca. 200 CE), **Lìshū** had been further simplified into 楷书 (楷書) **Kǎishū** or Standard Script, which has served ever since as the standard for both printed and carefully handwritten characters.

The table below summarizes the development of two characters from their **Jiǎgǔwén** to their **Kǎishū** forms (but keep in mind that it is of necessity somewhat simplified, and in actual practice there was not a neat and easily dissected progression—two or more types of characters typically coexisted in different locales for decades or even centuries):

Jiǎgǔwén	Dàzhuàn	Xiǎozhuàn	Lìshū	Kǎishū	Pinyin	English
虎	虎	虎	虎	虎	**hǔ**	tiger
龍	龍	龍	龍	龍	**lóng**	dragon

STRUCTURE OF THE CHARACTERS

Every Chinese character is made up of from one to twenty or more separate strokes. The basic strokes are eight in number: **diǎn** (丶), **héng** (一), **shù** (丨), **piě** (丿), **nà** (㇏), **tí** (㇀), **gōu** (亅), and **zhé** (㇕). Some of the basic strokes have several variants, and there are also compound strokes consisting of combinations of the basic strokes. Don't worry, you'll learn all these strokes as you learn Chinese characters made up of them. In case you're curious, the characters with the fewest strokes in the language are 一 **yī** "one" and 乙 **yǐ** "second of the ten Celestial Stems," each of which is composed of only one stroke; while the most complex commonly written character is 鬱 **yù** "melancholy," which consists of 29 strokes (in the simplified character system it has been simplified to 郁). Less common, fortunately for us, is 齉 **nàng**, an onomatopoeic word meaning "nasal twang" that has all of 36 strokes, whether in the traditional or the simplified character system!

According to Chinese tradition, the characters are divided based upon their structure into six types called 六书 (六書) **Liùshū** "Six Categories of Writing." This system of categorization was first employed in a well-known Chinese etymological dictionary known as the 说文解字 (說文解字) **Shuōwén Jiězì** that was completed by a man named Xu Shen in 121 CE. The different categories of characters are as follows:

1. 象形字 **Xiàngxíngzì** "Pictographs." These are more or less stylized drawings of objects in the real world such as elements of the universe, topographical features, flora, fauna, parts of the human body, tools, and architectural structures. Although in the development of the Chinese script, pictographs were the earliest type of character, they now make up only a small fraction of characters. Thus, it's incorrect to consider modern Chinese writing as being primarily pictographic, or to refer to all characters as "pictographs." Some examples of pictographs still in common use today are:

Jiǎgǔwén	Kǎishū	Pinyin	English
	日	**rì**	sun, day
	山	**shān**	mountain
	木	**mù**	tree, wood
	馬	**mǎ**	horse
	口	**kǒu**	mouth

Oracle bone

2. 指事字 **Zhǐshìzì** “Simple Ideographs.” Rather than being pictures of objects, like the pictographs, these are symbolic representations of abstract concepts such as number and position. The proportion of simple ideographs in written Chinese is even smaller than that of pictographs. Examples:

Character	Pinyin	Explanation
一	**yī**	one line = “one”
二	**èr**	two lines = “two”
三	**sān**	three lines = “three”
上	**shàng**	first two strokes above the horizontal line = “above”
中	**zhōng**	line through the middle of the box = “middle”

3. 会意字（會意字）**Huìyìzì** "Compound Ideographs." While simple ideographs are composed of a unified whole and are complete in themselves, compound ideographs rely for their meaning on the combination or interaction of the meanings of two or more separate parts, each of which can occur as an independent character. This category of characters, while more important than the simple ideographs, also accounts for only a small fraction of characters. Examples:

Character	Pinyin	Explanation
从	**cóng**	person + person = "follow"
森	**sēn**	three trees = "forest"
明	**míng**	sun + moon = "bright"
休	**xiū**	person resting next to a tree = "rest"
歪	**wāi**	character for "not" on top of the character for "straight" = "not straight, crooked"

4. 假借字 **Jiǎjièzì** "Borrowed Characters." Although pictographs and ideographs could be devised for some words in the language, there were many other words which did not readily lend themselves to either of these two means of written representation. Frequently, when the Chinese ancients wanted to write something for which they knew no character, they would borrow another character which had the same or a similar sound. For example, in ancient China there were two different words both pronounced somewhat like English "lug": one was the name for growing grain, which was written with the pictograph 來, and the other was the verb "to come," which as yet had no character. Someone came up with the then novel idea of writing "to come" with the borrowed character 來 "grain." Though the original meaning "grain" and the borrowed meaning "to come" coexisted for a period of time, eventually, in this particular case, "to come" won out, with the result that in modern Chinese that is the only possible meaning of the character. After phonetic-semantic compounds (see below), the borrowed characters constitute the second-largest category of characters. They also played an important role in the simplification of characters in the 1950s and 1960s. In fact, along with the phonetic-semantic compounds, they help make the case that even in ancient times, Chinese characters were largely phonetic in nature. But though the context would often clarify the meaning of borrowed characters, sometimes there were ambiguities. The problem of avoiding ambiguities when borrowing characters for their sound gave rise to the next category of characters, which today accounts for the great majority of characters in the language.

5. 形声字（形聲字）**Xíngshēngzì** "Phonetic-Semantic Compounds." In trying to solve the problem of avoiding ambiguities, the ancient Chinese hit upon the idea of combining the sound-borrowing principle

of the **Jiǎjièzì** with the semantic principle of the first three categories of characters to create compound characters, one part of which—called the *phonetic*, often on the right side of a character—would indicate the sound; and the other part of which—called the *semantic*, often on the left side of a character—would indicate the meaning.

Take the common Chinese noun pronounced **mā**, meaning "mom" or "mother." At some point in the past when this word did not yet have a character associated with it, some Chinese writer who wanted to write this word borrowed the character 馬 **mǎ** "horse" to represent the sound of **mā** (the two words are pronounced identically except for tone) but made a crucially important addition: he or she added to the left of 馬 the character 女 **nǚ** "woman" to indicate to the reader, first, that a word different from 馬 was meant; and, second, that the word had something to do with "woman." And so was created the character 媽 **mā** "mom, mother." Similarly, consider 螞 **mǎ** "ant," which is made up of the same phonetic element plus the semantic element 虫 **chóng** "insect"; or the question particle 嗎 **ma**, composed of the same phonetic plus the semantic 口 **kǒu** "mouth," which indicates that this is a word often used in speech.

Here are examples of several groups of phonetic-semantic compounds:

Phonetic	Semantic	Phonetic-Semantic Compound
主 **zhǔ** "main"	亻 **rén** "person" 氵 **shuǐ** "water" 木 **mù** "tree" 馬 **mǎ** "horse"	住 **zhù** "live" 注 **zhù** "pour" 柱 **zhù** "pillar" 駐 **zhù** "station"
里 **lǐ** "mile"	亻 **rén** "person" 玉 **yù** "jade" 魚 **yú** "fish" 金 **jīn** "metal"	俚 **lǐ** "vulgar" 理 **lǐ** "texture" 鯉 **lǐ** "carp" 鋰 **lǐ** "lithium"
占 **zhān** "divine"	米 **mǐ** "rice" 亻 **rén** "person" 戈 **gē** "weapon" 立 **lì** "stand"	粘 **zhān** "glue" 佔 **zhàn** "occupy" 战 **zhàn** "war" 站 **zhàn** "stand"
方 **fāng** "place"	金 **jīn** "metal" 魚 **yú** "fish" 言 **yán** "speak" 糸 **sī** "silk"	鈁 **fāng** "francium (metal)" 魴 **fáng** "bream (fish)" 訪 **fǎng** "visit" 紡 **fǎng** "spin"

In the above examples, which were carefully chosen to illustrate the principle of **Xíngshēngzì**, there are fairly close correlations between the sound of the phonetic and the sound of the compound. Unfortunately, due to sound change and interdialectal borrowing over the course of many centuries, plus the fact that the "fit" for some phonetics was never exact to begin with but only approximate, many of the correlations have become obscured, so that the phonetic information contained in phonetic-semantic compounds today is often inexact.

The phonetics of Chinese characters are a little like different vowel and consonant combinations in English. In English, we have many regular sound-to-writing correspondences, like the combination "-ill" that is pronounced the same way in all words ending in "-ill," for example, "pill," "kill," and "hill." But we also have some irregular correspondences like "-ove" which can have several different pronunciations, for example, "shove," "cove," and "prove." Chinese phonetics are typically like the irregular English correspondences, with one phonetic often representing two or three common pronunciations.

In groups of different characters sharing the same phonetic, the final is the most likely to be similar, the initial is the next most likely to be similar, and the tone is the least likely to be similar. Even when the initials or finals of different characters in a phonetic series are different, they are often still phonetically related, that is, they may all be labial sounds made with the lips like [b p f]; or they may all be sounds made with the velum in the back of the mouth like [g k h]; or they may all end in the same consonant like [-eng -ing].

As for the semantics in phonetic-semantic compounds, they can provide only a hint as to the meaning of the character, for example, "related to water" or "made of metal" or "type of fish." Sometimes the semantic seems illogical, but that may be due to changes in culture and society since the system of semantics was first devised; for example, 枕 **zhěn** "pillow" is written with the semantic 木 **mù** "wood," but that is because formerly Chinese pillows were indeed made of wood. The semantic element of a Chinese character is in English more commonly referred to as the radical of the character, because Chinese dictionaries have traditionally been organized based on a sequence of 214 radicals, arranged in a set order from those with the least number of strokes to those with the most strokes. The radical of a character usually corresponds to its semantic, though there are some exceptions. While the system of phonetics and the system of semantics (or radicals) of Chinese characters are inexact and involve many inconsistencies, they can still be quite useful for guessing the pronunciations and meanings of unfamiliar characters, or for learning and remembering new ones. Native Chinese readers make use of them in their reading, and we'll be exploiting them to their fullest potential in this book.

6. 转注 (轉注) **Zhuǎnzhù** "Mutually Explanatory Characters." The sixth category of characters mentioned in the **Shuōwén Jiězì** is termed 转注 (轉注) **Zhuǎnzhù**. These involve pairs of words that are phonetically and semantically similar, where one word in each pair already had a character associated with it but the other did not. Subsequently, a character was created for the word without a character by modifying the existing character for the other word in the pair. Most **Zhuǎnzhù** characters are no longer in use, but one commonly cited example is the pair 老 **lǎo** "old" and 考 **kǎo** "deceased father." Since the **Zhuǎnzhù** make up the smallest category in the **Liùshū** and since not even specialists are in agreement as to their exact nature, we shall not discuss this category in more detail here.

CURSIVE SCRIPT

In addition to the types of characters discussed above, which are the **Kǎishū** standard printed or carefully handwritten forms of characters, there also exist cursive forms of characters. In the same way that when writing English by hand we normally connect letters (i.e., we don't usually print little but instead write the word with connected strokes as *little*), Chinese writers also usually connect many of the strokes of characters when writing by hand.

Depending on a number of factors such as the formality of the occasion, the educational level of the writer and person written to, the personal preferences of the writer, and how much of a hurry the writer happens to be in, there will be wide variation in the degree of cursiveness of any particular piece of handwriting. Handwritten Chinese containing a moderate degree of cursiveness is quite common and is known as 连笔字 (連筆字) **Liánbǐzì** "Connected Characters" or 行书 (行書) **Xíngshū** "Running Script." We'll be introducing a small amount of slightly cursive handwriting later in this course. A more extreme degree of cursiveness is termed 草书 (草書) **Cǎoshū** "Grass Script" and is, fortunately for the foreign learner of the language, much less common than it used to be. Actually, it's often difficult to determine exactly at what point **Xíngshū** ends and **Cǎoshū** begins. There is a well-known Chinese proverb that says 草书三天不认主 (草書三天不認主) **Cǎoshū sāntiān bú rèn zhǔ** "After three days, something written in **Cǎoshū** will not be recognizable even by the writer." There is an even more divergent type of cursive script known as 狂草 **Kuángcǎo** or "Crazy Grass" but, not to worry, we won't be dealing with anything like that in this course!

Here are some examples of characters written in **Xíngshū** and **Cǎoshū**:

Kǎishū	Xíngshū	Cǎoshū	Pinyin	English
先	先	先	**xiān**	first
生	生	生	**shēng**	give birth
學	學	學	**xué**	learn
後	後	後	**hòu**	after

SIMPLIFIED CHARACTERS

So as to increase literacy, the government of the People's Republic of China began promoting the use of so-called 简体字 (簡體字) **jiǎntǐzì** or "simplified characters" by means of two official lists it promulgated in 1955 and 1964. By the term "simplified" was meant primarily a reduction in the number of strokes of characters, especially of high-frequency characters composed of a higher than average number of strokes. Actually, the history of character simplification in China is a long one, most of the characters on the two lists having been used informally for centuries, much as we in English have long used abbreviations like "nite" for "night" or "thru" for "through" in informal writing. In Chinese, the main difference from before is that, in mainland China and Singapore, the simplified characters have now been standardized and given official status.

There is no doubt that simplified characters, having a reduced number of strokes, can be handwritten more quickly than the traditional characters (though in the past most adult writers did their rapid writing in **Xíngshū**, which is even faster). However, precisely because of the reduction in strokes, the number of points of contrast among characters has been reduced, resulting in an increased number of similar-looking characters. Take the two expressions **shèyǒu** "has established" and **méiyou** "does not have." Written in traditional characters (設有, 沒有), the distinction is clear; but written in simplified characters (设有, 没有), they are easily confused, especially when handwritten rapidly. Other examples of such simplified character look-alikes include 活话 (cf. traditional 活話), 向问 (cf. traditional 向問), and 刷剧 (cf. traditional 刷劇). It could be argued that character simplification has made writing easier, but has in some instances actually made reading harder (not to mention that most readers must now become familiar with *two* sets of characters).

Roughly half of the three thousand or so characters necessary for literacy in Chinese has been affected by the simplification process. Of the 288 characters introduced in *Basic Written Chinese*, a total of 197 are the same in their simplified and traditional forms, with only 91 being different—and a number of those involve very small differences that are hardly noticeable. Learning the distinctions between the simplified characters and the traditional characters is not as burdensome a task as it may at first seem, since in many cases the simplification of one character component—for example, that of the so-called "speech radical" from 言 to 讠—has affected dozens of characters that contain it.

The main methods by which characters were simplified include:

1. Simplified characters already in popular use were given official status. Examples:

過 → 过 **guò** "pass"
當 → 当 **dāng** "serve as"

2. Simpler forms that were originally the standard form of the character but which had later been replaced by more complex forms were reinstituted. Examples:

從 → 从 **cóng** "from"
眾 → 众 **zhòng** "multitude"
雲 → 云 **yún** "cloud"

3. Simpler characters were borrowed to write more complex characters with the same pronunciation, according to the **Jiǎjiè** principle of borrowed characters. While this occasionally creates ambiguities, the context usually makes the meaning clear. Examples:

困 **kùn** "difficulty," 睏 **kùn** "sleepy" → 困 **kùn** "difficulty; sleepy"
谷 **gǔ** "valley," 穀 **gǔ** "grain" → 谷 **gǔ** "valley; grain"

4. Cursive forms of characters were regularized into **Kǎishū** style. Examples:

東 → 东 **dōng** "east"
樂 → 乐 **lè** "happy"
為 → 为 **wéi** "be"

5. Parts of characters were used to substitute for whole characters. Examples:

習 → 习 **xí** "practice"
與 → 与 **yǔ** "and"
雖 → 虽 **suī** "although"
條 → 条 **tiáo** "strip"
飛 → 飞 **fēi** "fly"
電 → 电 **diàn** "electricity"

6. The redundant parts of characters were deleted or simplified. Examples:

蟲 → 虫 **chóng** "insect"
齒 → 齿 **chǐ** "tooth"

7. Wide characters were made narrower, and long characters were made shorter. Examples:

   噸 → 吨 **dūn** "ton"
   蠶 → 蚕 **cán** "silkworm"

8. New characters were constructed based on the **Xíngshēng** principle of phonetic-semantic compounds. Examples:

   藝 → 艺 **yì** "art" (since 乙 **yǐ** is a near homonym of 藝)
   畢 → 毕 **bì** "finish" (since 比 **bǐ** is a near homonym of 畢)

9. Common character components were replaced by simpler components. For example, the common but complex component 雚 was replaced by the much simpler component 又. Examples:

   歡 → 欢 **huān** "happy"
   觀 → 观 **guān** "look"
   勸 → 劝 **quàn** "urge"
   權 → 权 **quán** "authority"

RECENT DEVELOPMENTS IN THE CHINESE WRITING SYSTEM

In the PRC today, all mass media publications such as newspapers and magazines are printed exclusively in simplified characters. So are school textbooks from kindergarten through high school. Scholarly works and university textbooks, especially those dealing with ancient literature and history, are sometimes still printed in traditional characters. Street signs and handwritten materials, such as notes and letters, typically contain a mixture of some simplified and some traditional characters, depending on the age, educational level, and personal preference of the writer. In addition to the official simplified characters, there are also several hundred unofficial simplified characters commonly used in handwritten notes or on signs.

Interestingly, in recent years—even though the government discourages this—it has become fashionable in some parts of China to use traditional characters on the signs of hotels, restaurants, and shops. Professional people often have some traditional characters on their name cards. The reasons for this partial return of traditional characters include that they are considered more formal, more aesthetically pleasing, and more chic, since they are associated with the affluent Chinese societies of Hong Kong and Taiwan. Traditional characters are probably also considered more eye-catching, precisely since they differ from what is normally written. While educated mainland Chinese readers can read most texts printed in traditional characters, they often cannot write traditional characters.

In Taiwan the situation is more or less reversed. With few exceptions, only the traditional characters appear in print. However, as in pre-1949 China, many simplified characters are used in informal handwriting such as in notes, personal letters, and signs. In recent years, with the increased contact between Taiwan and mainland China through the exchange of letters, e-mails, television programming, and personal visits, many people in Taiwan have become familiar with the relatively few simplified characters that are post-1949 innovations. However, while educated Taiwanese typically can recognize most simplified characters, they may not be able to write them.

As for the other Chinese language-using societies, traditional characters are official and widely used in Hong Kong and Macao, but one increasingly sees simplified characters there also, in part due to the influence of the large numbers of visitors from the mainland. In Singapore, simplified characters are official, though it's not uncommon to see traditional characters on store signs. In Malaysian Chinese communities, both simplified and traditional characters are in common use, as is the case in overseas Chinese communities in the rest of the world.

What we have, then, is a single language with multiple written standards—a rather common situation among the major languages of the world, and in essence not so very different from the different spellings and usages prevalent in the various English-speaking countries. The bottom line for you, as a learner of Chinese, is that if you wish to become proficient in reading all kinds of Chinese written today (even just Chinese written in mainland China), you'll eventually need to be able to *read* both simplified and traditional characters. With time and practice, this is all very doable, and the materials you have in your hands right now are designed to help you do that as efficiently and easily as possible, since every lesson is presented first in simplified characters and then again in traditional characters (of course, you can also choose to study only one type of characters). Now, as regards *writing*, since most educated Chinese can recognize both forms of characters and since computer conversion of simplified to traditional or vice versa is easily accomplished, there is really no need for most learners to learn how to write both forms of characters. You'll probably wish to learn how to write the type of characters used in the region where you plan to live or travel most frequently.

Finally, there is the question of the format of the characters. Traditionally, Chinese characters were written from top to bottom, right to left. Since the 1950s, it has become increasingly common to write Chinese according to the Western format, that is, horizontally, from left to right. This is now the standard format in the PRC, though in recent years the vertical style seems to have been making a limited comeback for writings on literary or cultural topics. In Taiwan and Hong Kong, the traditional vertical format is still common, though scientific and technical writings, informal handwritten notes and letters, and the subtitles of movies and television programs are now usually in horizontal style. The option of horizontal or vertical formats—and a third, rarer format with characters written horizontally but from right to left—adds a stylistic variety and versatility to Chinese that is absent from English and most other languages. Since both horizontal and vertical formats are commonly encountered everywhere that Chinese is used, this textbook includes texts in both formats.

What does the future hold in store for the Chinese writing system? That is not so easy to predict. There is no question that, if written as it is spoken, Chinese could be written in Pinyin. It's possible that, someday, Pinyin might replace the characters, something that a number of Chinese intellectuals and political leaders have in the past advocated. The widespread use of computers for processing Chinese characters, for which most people input Pinyin and select the characters they want from their monitor screen, has already had a noticeable effect on the ability of native Chinese to handwrite characters from memory, as have newer communications technologies like e-mail and text messaging. Not only people's ability to write characters has been affected, but also the content of the Chinese they write, which includes many neologisms, simplifications, and abbreviations, and reflects frequent mixing of characters with Pinyin and Roman letters.

On the other hand, Chinese society is, like our own, very conservative and the characters have been an intrinsic part of Chinese culture for thousands of years. Though characters have the disadvantages of being hard to learn and at times cumbersome to work with, they do have certain advantages, including flexibility of format (think of book titles), efficient use of space (one page of English in United Nations documents typically translates to about $^3/_5$ of a page of Chinese), and the fact that one can skim or scan for a specific word or phrase faster in Chinese than in alphabetic languages (since characters tend to stand out more). It must also be acknowledged that the Chinese writing system has stood the test of time and proven to be eminently successful, since it is used today by more people than any other written language in history. The reality is that Chinese characters will be around for the forseeable future, so the only realistic approach for the non-native who wishes to learn Chinese reading and writing is to buckle down and learn them. Indeed, due to simplifications and standardization in the language, better reference tools, and improvements in technology, textbooks, and teaching methods, written Chinese is today easier to learn than ever before. In the next section, we'll take up some practical suggestions for ways to help you learn it better.

Suggested Strategies for Learning to Read and Write Chinese

In learning to read and write Chinese, it's important not only to work hard but also to work smart, that is, to make the most efficient use possible of your time and energy. Many of the strategies suggested in the orientation section of *Basic Spoken Chinese* apply also to written Chinese, so it would be well worth your while to review those strategies now. Below are listed a few additional strategies that apply specifically to reading and writing.

1. Learn to handwrite all the characters in this volume. Being able to handwrite characters is important not only for writing but also for reading, since if you can write a character correctly from memory, you're more likely to be able to recognize it and distinguish it from similar characters. Later on in your study of Chinese, you'll also want to learn how to process Chinese characters using computers, but we feel it's very important for beginning learners to have the experience of learning how to write several hundred of the highest-frequency characters by hand.

2. In learning and reviewing characters, it's important to practice writing each one many times, so that you eventually are able to write it from memory. The character practice sheets in the accompanying volume *Basic Written Chinese Practice Essentials* have been designed to help you learn to do this with the correct stroke order and direction. Don't just "draw" the characters; at the same time you're writing a character, pronounce it out loud and think of its meaning. By combining mechanical, visual, and auditory stimuli in this way, you're more likely to remember the characters you study.

3. Be sure to follow the correct stroke order and direction. If you don't, your characters will not only not look right but you might have difficulty in using dictionaries, since these are traditionally based on the number of strokes in characters or character components. The accuracy of handwriting recognition software might also be affected if strokes are written in the wrong order and direction. And if you're not familiar with correct stroke order, you may in the future have problems reading and writing Chinese cursive script, since which strokes can be connected is closely related to the order and direction of individual strokes.

4. While accuracy is most important, strive to make your characters look as aesthetically pleasing and as "Chinese" as possible. Be aware that, in Chinese society, how you write your characters says a lot about the kind of person you are and the education you've received.

5. Be sensitive to the constituent components of characters, many of which reoccur in other characters. For example, there are many groups of characters that share a component called the *semantic* or *radical*, e.g., the characters 河, 湖, and 海, all of which contain on their left side the so-called "water" radical (氵) and have meanings related to "water" ("river," "lake," and "sea," respectively). And then there are other groups of characters that share a component called the *phonetic*, e.g., 生, 姓, and 星, all of which share the phonetic 生 and have a pronunciation somewhat similar to **shēng**. This textbook provides detailed information on character components, but you would do well to keep your own lists of characters you've studied that share radicals, phonetics, or other components.

6. When you encounter a new character or one you once learned but have forgotten, guess its pronunciation from the phonetic, and guess its meaning from the radical. And always carefully consider the context—the word the character represents or is part of, the sentence in which it occurs, and the overall discourse. This is what native readers do.

7. Watch out for characters that are similar in appearance to other characters. The fact is that there are in Chinese many groups of similar-looking characters such as 干千, 大太, 文交, 可司, 住往, 王五

正, or 差着看. Many of these "look-alike" characters are pointed out and drilled in this textbook, but you may also wish to keep your own collection in a separate notebook.

8. The best method for learning characters is to study several new ones every day. Daily study of a few new characters (and regular review of "old" characters) is far more productive than cramming the night before a test.

9. One of the most effective ways of learning characters is to test yourself frequently. After you've studied several characters and the words written with them, fold a separate sheet of paper down the long end and cover up the left-hand side of the page where the Chinese is. Now test yourself to see if you can write the Chinese by looking at the English. With a pencil, put a small "X" by those items you still have problems with and review them later. Then retest yourself.

10. Wherever you go, take along a couple of dozen Chinese character flashcards from *Basic Written Chinese Practice Essentials*. Use "empty" time you spend waiting in line or before classes begin to study the flashcards. Your goal should be to identify those characters and words you still have problems with and remove them from the larger set for special attention.

11. Both the ability to read Chinese out loud with correct pronunciation and phrasing and the ability to read Chinese silently at a reasonable rate of speed are important. When reading the sentences, conversations, and narratives in this textbook, first read them out loud once or twice, and then read them again silently once or twice.

12. To attain a high level of Chinese reading proficiency, it's important to do two types of reading: *intensive* reading, where you read slowly and carefully, trying to understand and master every new character, word, and grammar pattern; and *extensive* reading, where you read faster and in greater quantity but read only for the general meaning, not bothering to look up every unfamiliar item unless an item is crucial to an understanding of the passage. While the majority of readings in this course will be of the intensive kind, you'll have some opportunities to experience extensive reading also.

13. Having urged you to practice writing characters, we now need to warn you against going to extremes. Some learners are tempted to spend a lot of time "playing" with characters, to the extent that other kinds of class preparation (such as drilling with the audio recordings, memorizing conversations, or studying the grammatical and cultural notes) are neglected. Certainly, Chinese characters are an art form and we encourage you to write them as beautifully as you can, but don't go overboard. Stay aware of your priorities: listening and speaking must come first, then reading. These three skills are almost certain to be more useful to you—and they are easier to develop—than the skill of writing.

14. While it's true that, among the writing systems of the world, Chinese characters are unique in some ways, and while it can be interesting and helpful to study the structure and development of individual characters, it's also important not to become "fixated" on characters. For the most part, Chinese characters are neither more nor less than written symbols used to represent speech, and it's best to take a matter-of-fact attitude toward them. Even more important than learning the individual characters, you need to focus on the other aspects of Chinese that are essential for attaining reading proficiency: the words written using characters, punctuation, written-style vocabulary and grammar, reading fluency, the ability to read between the lines, skimming, scanning, and so forth. Good luck to you in your studies of written Chinese!

Abbreviations

Word Classes*

[A]	Adverb
[AT]	Attributive
[AV]	Auxiliary Verb
[BF]	Bound Form
[CJ]	Conjunction
[CV]	Coverb
[EV]	Equative Verb
[EX]	Expression
[I]	Interjection
[IE]	Idiomatic Expression
[L]	Localizer
[M]	Measure
[MA]	Moveable Adverb
[N]	Noun
[NU]	Number
[P]	Particle
[PH]	Phrase
[PR]	Pronoun
[PT]	Pattern
[PV]	Postverb
[PW]	Place Word
[QW]	Question Word
[RC]	Resultative Compound
[RE]	Resultative Ending
[SN]	Surname
[SP]	Specifier
[SV]	Stative Verb
[TW]	Time Word
[V]	Verb
[VO]	Verb-Object Compound

Other Abbreviations and Symbols

(B)	Beijing
(T)	Taipei
lit.	literally
*	(indicates that what follows is incorrect)
/	(separates alternate forms)

* For explanations of the above word classes, see the section on "Word Classes of Spoken Chinese" at the end of the accompanying volume, *Basic Spoken Chinese.*

Classroom Expressions

Use of the following classroom expressions, along with the Classroom Expressions in the companion volume *Basic Spoken Chinese*, will allow most classes to be run entirely or almost entirely in Chinese. By working with the audio disc, learn how to understand these expressions when you hear them; you needn't learn how to use them yourself just yet. Later on you should also become familiar with the Chinese expressions in the Table of Chinese Punctuation Marks (see the disc).

1. 现在我们听写。(現在我們聽寫。)
   Xiànzài wǒmen tīngxiě. Now we have a dictation quiz.

2. 请你念课文。(請你念課文。)
   Qǐng nǐ niàn kèwén. Please read the text out loud.

3. 请你再念一遍。(請你再念一遍。)
   Qǐng nǐ zài niàn yíbiàn. Please read it again.

4. 这个字怎么念？(這個字怎麼念？)
   Zhèige zì zěnme niàn? How do you pronounce this character?

5. 这个字怎么写？(這個字怎麼寫？)
   Zhèige zì zěnme xiě? How do you write this character?

6. 请你再写一遍。(請你再寫一遍。)
   Qǐng nǐ zài xiě yíbiàn. Please write it again.

7. 请注意笔顺。(請注意筆順。)
   Qǐng zhùyì bǐshùn. Please pay attention to stroke order.

8. 这个字的部首是什么？(這個字的部首是什麼？)
   Zhèige zìde bùshǒu shi shénme? What is this character's radical?

9. 这个字的声符是什么？(這個字的聲符是什麼？)
   Zhèige zìde shēngfú shi shénme? What is this character's phonetic?

10. 这是简体字，那是繁体字。(這是簡體字，那是繁體字。)
    Zhè shi jiǎntǐzì, nà shi fántǐzì. These are simplified characters, those are traditional characters.

11. 请你翻译。(請你翻譯。)
    Qǐng nǐ fānyì. Please translate.

12. 请你们把练习给我。(請你們把練習給我。)
    Qǐng nǐmen bǎ liànxí gěi wǒ. Please you all give me the exercise.

Numbers, Surnames, Personal Names, and Place Names

UNIT A

COMMUNICATIVE OBJECTIVES

Once you've mastered this unit, you'll be able to use Chinese to read and write:

1. The basic numbers from 1 to 10.
2. Telephone numbers.
3. Several common surnames: "He," "Li," "Lin," "Wang," and "Wen."
4. Common personal names like "Daming," "Dashan," "Jingsheng," "Mingming," "Taisheng," "Xiaoming," "Xiaowen," etc.
5. Some common place names in mainland China and Taiwan: "Beijing," "Taichung," "Taipei," "Taishan."
6. The special Chinese punctuation mark called the **dùnhào** that looks like this: 、

PART 1

Numbers from 1 to 5 and the Surname Wáng

New Characters and Words

Study the six characters below and the common words written with them, paying careful attention to each character's pronunciation, meaning, and structure, as well as similar-looking characters. After you've studied a character, turn to the *Practice Essentials* volume and practice writing it on the practice sheet, making sure to follow the correct stroke order and direction as you pronounce it out loud and think of its meaning.

1 一 **yī** one

一 is itself a radical. One line represents "one."

一 **yī** one [NU]

---

2 二 **èr** two

二 is itself a radical. Two lines represent "two." Notice that the top line is shorter than the bottom one.

二 **èr** two [NU]

---

3 三 **sān** three

Radical is 一 **yī** (1). Three lines represent "three." Notice that the middle line is the shortest, that the top line is a little longer than the middle line, and that the bottom line is the longest of the three strokes. Notice also that the Chinese numbers 一二三 are simple ideographs, being symbolic representations of the concepts "one, two, three," much like the Roman numerals I II III turned on their sides. Contrast 三 and 二 **èr** (2).

三 **sān** three [NU]

---

4 四 **sì** four

Radical is 囗 **wéi** "enclose" [BF]. This radical is referred to colloquially as 围字框 (圍字框) **wéizìkuàng** "frame of the character 围 (圍) ."

四 **sì** four [NU]

---

5 五 **wǔ** five

Radical is 二 **èr** (2).

五 **wǔ** five [NU]

---

6 王 **wáng** king

Radical is 玉 **yù** "jade." Contrast 王 and 五 **wǔ** (5).

王 **Wáng** Wang, Wong, Ong [SN]

Reading Exercises (Simplified and Traditional Characters)

Now practice reading the new characters and words for this lesson in context. Be sure to refer to the Notes at the end of this lesson, and make use of the accompanying audio disc to hear and practice correct pronunciation, phrasing, and intonation.

A. SINGLE DIGITS

Read out loud each of the following numbers.

1. 三
2. 一
3. 五
4. 二
5. 四
6. 一
7. 三
8. 二
9. 四
10. 五

Pinyin is sometimes added to characters on signs but is often, as here, incorrect

B. TELEPHONE NUMBERS

Read out loud each of the following telephone numbers.

1. 三 二 一 二 五
2. 一 一 四 二
3. 三 五 一 三 四
4. 五 二 一 一 一
5. 三 三 二 四 三
6. 五 五 四 三
7. 四 四 二 一 五 三 四 二
8. 一 一 三 五 一 二 三 四
9. 三 五 二 三 四 四 一 四
10. 二 五 二 三 四 二 三 一

C. SURNAMES

Read out loud the following common Chinese surname.

1. 王

D. CHARACTER DIFFERENTIATION DRILLS

Distinguish carefully the following similar-looking characters, pronouncing each one out loud and thinking of its meaning.

1. 三 三 三 二 二 二
2. 二 二 二 三 三 三
3. 王 王 王 五 五 五
4. 五 五 五 王 王 王

Notes

A1a. **A NOTE ON CHINESE FONTS.** To help you attain proficiency in reading printed Chinese, this textbook has been designed to expose you to several different printed fonts. The Reading Exercises for units A, B, and 1-4 have been set in Kai font, which is the font closest to handwriting. Beginning with Unit 5, Song font—the most common font for books and periodicals—is employed. In the New Characters and Words sections at the beginning of each lesson, Kai font is used for the characters in blue type, with Song font used for the characters in black type; Song font is also used for the characters in the Notes at the end of each lesson. You may notice minor variations in how some strokes are written in these different fonts, but be assured you'll gradually become accustomed to them. Though you need to be able to recognize Chinese characters printed in various fonts, for your own handwriting you should follow the models on the character practice sheets in the accompanying *Basic Written Chinese Practice Essentials.*

A1b. **A NOTE ON VARIATION IN WRITTEN CHINESE.** Given the immense population and vast area of China, and the substantial diversity among the various Chinese-speaking societies, it's to be expected that there is a significant amount of variation in written Chinese. Native writers from different areas will at times use different vocabulary and grammar and may have different stylistic preferences. This textbook always offers at least one acceptable alternative, but you shouldn't be surprised if you encounter variation. The best course of action for you is learning at least one correct way of saying or writing something, and then being a careful observer of how native speakers use Chinese in society.

B7. Telephone numbers in the larger cities of China are eight digits in length. In smaller cities and the countryside, telephone numbers may consist of fewer than eight digits. Mobile phone numbers usually have eleven digits.

B10. In formal writing, as on business cards or letterheads, telephone numbers may be indicated using the Chinese numerals, as here. However, telephone numbers are also commonly written with Arabic numerals, as in English, but often without the use of any hyphens, e.g., as 42235151 rather than 4223-5151. The lack of hyphens doesn't seem to bother Chinese people, who are used to reading and memorizing long number sequences, but often creates difficulties for Americans.

C1. For more information on Chinese surnames, cf. note SV5E in BSC 2-3.

Numbers from 6 to 10 and the Surname Lín

New Characters and Words

Study the six characters below and the common words written with them, paying careful attention to each character's pronunciation, meaning, and structure, as well as similar-looking characters. After you've studied a character, turn to the *Practice Essentials* volume and practice writing it on the practice sheet, making sure to follow the correct stroke order and direction as you pronounce it out loud and think of its meaning.

7 六 **liù** six

Radical is 八 **bā** "eight" (9), see below.

六 **liù** six [**NU**]

---

8 七 **qī** seven

Radical is 一 **yī** (1).

七 **qī** seven [**NU**]

---

9 八 **bā** eight

八 is itself a radical.

八 **bā** eight [**NU**]

---

10 九 **jiǔ** nine

Radical is 乙 **yǐ** "second of the ten Celestial Stems." 九 can itself serve as a phonetic, e.g, 究 **jiū** as in 研究 **yánjiū** "research" or 鸠 (鳩) **jiū** as in 斑鸠 (斑鳩) **bānjiū** "turtle dove."

九 **jiǔ** nine [**NU**]

---

11 十 **shí** ten

十 is itself a radical. This character was originally a picture of two hands pressed palm to palm, i.e., "ten" fingers. Contrast 十 and 七 **qī** (8).

十 **shí** ten [**NU**]

---

12 林 **lín** grove, small forest

Radical is the pictograph 木 **mù** "tree" [**BF**]. This radical is referred to colloquially as 木字旁 **mùzìpáng** "side made up of the character 木." Note that when 木 is written at the left of a character as a radical, its last stroke is shortened so that it doesn't collide with the component to its right. "Two" "trees" standing next to each other form a "grove." 林 can itself serve as a phonetic, e.g., 淋 **lín** as in 淋湿 (淋濕) **línshī** "soaked, drenched."

林 **Lín** Lin, Lam, Lum, Lim (also Lim, Im, or Rim, a common Korean surname) [**SN**]

Reading Exercises (Simplified and Traditional Characters)

Now practice reading the new characters and words for this lesson in context. Be sure to refer to the Notes at the end of this lesson, and make use of the accompanying audio disc to hear and practice correct pronunciation, phrasing, and intonation.

A. SINGLE DIGITS

Read out loud each of the following numbers.

1. 十
2. 七
3. 六
4. 九
5. 八
6. 六
7. 七
8. 十
9. 九
10. 八

Automobile license plate from Taipei

B. TELEPHONE NUMBERS

Read out loud each of the following telephone numbers.

一、三 九 五 九 四 一 三 九
二、八 六 一 二 四
三、七 一 九 二 六 八 七 九
四、五 七 八 九 二 六
五、九 六 八 四 一 八 七 三
六、二 二 八 五 六 七 八 五

C. MISCELLANEOUS NUMBERS

Read out loud each of the following series of numbers. Some of them have special meanings and usages, for which you can consult the Notes at the end of this lesson.

一、一 三 五
二、二 四 六

三、一 二 三 四 五
四、五 四 三 二 一
五、六 七 八 九 十
六、十 九 八 七 六
七、一 二 三 四 五 六 七 八 九 十
八、十 九 八 七 六 五 四 三 二 一
九、二 四 六 八 十
十、一 三 五 七 九

D. SURNAMES

Read out loud each of the following common Chinese surnames.

一、林
二、王

Notes

B1. **CHINESE PUNCTUATION.** While Chinese, like Latin, was originally written without any punctuation marks, and later in its history only with a kind of period (。) that served as an all-purpose punctuation mark, it has over the last 150 years adopted the punctuation system of Western languages, even though there exist a few differences in usage. Indeed, China has gone the West one better by creating several additional punctuation marks that do not exist in Western languages. One of these is a kind of inverted comma called the 顿号 (頓號) **dùnhào** that looks like this: 、 One use of the **dùnhào** is after numbers, for example: 一、二、三、

C1. 一三五 could either represent the numbers 1 3 5 or stand for the first, third, and fifth days of the week, much like the English abbreviation "MWF."

C2. 二四六 could either represent the numbers 2 4 6 or stand for the second, fourth, and sixth days of the week, like English "T Th Sat."

The characters in red are in written Cantonese, which is quite different from written Mandarin

PART 3

Some Common Personal Names and Place Names

New Characters and Words

Study the six characters below and the common words written with them, paying careful attention to each character's pronunciation, meaning, and structure, as well as similar-looking characters. After you've studied a character, turn to the *Practice Essentials* volume and practice writing it on the practice sheet, making sure to follow the correct stroke order and direction as you pronounce it out loud and think of its meaning.

13 大 **dà** big, large, great

大 is itself a radical. 大 is a picture of a person with the head, arms, and legs all outstretched to make her or him look as "big" as possible. 大 can also serve as a phonetic, e.g., 达 (達) **dá** "reach." Contrast 大 and 六 **liù** (7).

大 **dà** big, large, great [SV]

14 山 **shān** mountain

山 is itself a radical. It is a picture of a mountain range, where the middle line represents the highest peak. 山 can itself serve as a phonetic in some rather rare characters such as 疝 **shàn** as in 疝气 (疝氣) **shànqì** "hernia."

山 **shān** mountain [N]

15 明 **míng** bright

Radical is 日 **rì** "sun" [BF]. The colloquial name for this radical is 日字旁 **rìzìpáng** "side made up of the character 日." The right-hand component is 月 **yuè** "moon" [BF]. Together, the "sun" and "moon" are very "bright."

明 **míng** bright [BF]

16 北 **běi** north

Radical is 匕 **bǐ** "ladle" [BF].

17 京 **jīng** capital

Radical is 亠 **tóu** "head" [BF]. 京 itself can serve as a phonetic, e.g., 鲸 (鯨) **jīng** as in 鲸鱼 (鯨魚) **jīngyú** "whale" or 景 **jǐng** as in 风景 (風景) **fēngjǐng** "scenery."

北京 **Běijīng** Beijing (lit. "northern capital") [PW]

18 台 **tái** terrace; (abbreviation for Taiwan)

Radical is 口 **kǒu** "mouth." This radical is referred to colloquially as 口字底 **kǒuzìdǐ** "bottom made up of the character 口." In the traditional character system, there is a much more complex alternate form for 台 that is written 臺, which is sometimes still seen in formal titles like 臺灣銀行 **Táiwān Yínháng** "Bank of Taiwan" (in simplified characters this would be 台湾银行). However, even in the traditional character system, 台 is now much more common than 臺.

台北	**Táiběi**	Taipei (lit. "northern part of Taiwan") [PW]
台山	**Táishān**	Taishan, Toisan (county in Guangdong province from which many Chinese emigrated to the U.S.; was upgraded to a "county-level city" in 1992) [PW]

Reading Exercises (Simplified and Traditional Characters)

Now practice reading the new characters and words for this lesson in context. Be sure to refer to the Notes at the end of this lesson, and make use of the accompanying audio disc to hear and practice correct pronunciation, phrasing, and intonation.

A. PERSONAL NAMES

Read out loud the following Chinese personal names, each of which consists of a surname followed by a one- or two-syllable given name.

一、王大山
二、林京
三、王明山
四、林明明
五、王林
六、王明大
七、林台山
八、王明
九、王山明
十、林大明

B. PLACE NAMES

Read out loud each of the following place names.

一、台山
二、北京
三、台北

C. CHARACTER DIFFERENTIATION DRILLS

Distinguish carefully the following similar-looking characters, pronouncing each one out loud and thinking of its meaning.

一、六 六 六 大 大 大
二、大 大 大 六 六 六

Notes

A4. Reduplicated names like 明明 can be pronounced either with full tones on each syllable (**Míngmíng**), or with a neutral tone on the second syllable (**Míngming**), which is how the speaker in the audio recording pronounces it here.

A5. Some characters can occur both as surnames and in given names. For example, the character 林 is a common surname but can also occur in a one or two-syllable given name.

Kiosk in Hong Kong selling telephone calling cards and other items

More Common Personal Names and Place Names

PART 4

New Characters and Words

Study the six characters below and the common words written with them, paying careful attention to each character's pronunciation, meaning, and structure, as well as similar-looking characters. After you've studied a character, turn to the *Practice Essentials* volume and practice writing it on the practice sheet, making sure to follow the correct stroke order and direction as you pronounce it out loud and think of its meaning.

19 何 **hé** who, what, how

Radical is 人 **rén** "person," which is written 亻 when occurring at the left side of a character so as not to get in the way of the component at the right. The colloquial name for this radical is 人字旁 **rénzìpáng** "side made up of the character 人." The phonetic in 何 is 可 **kě** "may" [BF].

何	**Hé**	He, Ho [SN]

20 李 **lǐ** plum

Radical is 木 **mù** "tree" [BF]. The other component is 子 **zǐ** "son" [BF]. The "plum" is the "son" (or fruit) of the plum "tree."

李	**Lǐ**	Li, Lee (also Lee, Rhee, or Yi, the second-most-common Korean surname) [SN]

21 文 **wén** writing, literature

文 is itself a radical. 文 also serves as a phonetic, e.g., 蚊 **wén** as in 蚊子 **wénzi** "mosquito" and 纹 (紋) **wén** as in 指纹 (指紋) **zhǐwén** "fingerprint." Be sure to contrast 文 and 六 **liù** (7).

文	**Wén**	Wen [SN]

22 生 **shēng** be born, give birth to

生 is itself a radical. 生 also serves as a phonetic, e.g., 星 **xīng** as in 星期 **xīngqī** "week" and 甥 **shēng** as in 外甥 **wàishēng** "sister's son" or "nephew." The character 生 is made up of 土 **tǔ** "soil" and 屮 (an ancient character for "grass"). The etymology is: "Grass" is "given birth to" in the "soil." Be careful to contrast 生 and 王 **wáng** (6).

生	**shēng**	be born, give birth to [V]

23 中 **zhōng** middle, among

Radical is 丨 **kǔn** "vertical line." The whole character 中 can serve as a phonetic in other characters, e.g., 忠 **zhōng** as in 忠于 (忠於) **zhōngyú** "be loyal to" or 钟 (鐘) **zhōng** "clock." 中 is a picture of an arrow that has pierced the "middle" of a square target.

台中	**Táizhōng**	Taichung (city in central Taiwan) [PW]

24 小 **xiǎo** small, little, young

小 is itself a radical. 小 can also serve as a phonetic, e.g., in 削 **xiāo** "peel", in 消 **xiāo** as in 消息 **xiāoxi** "news", and in 少 **shǎo** "few." The character 小 represents 八 **bā** "eight" made "smaller" by a vertical line (丨) that divides the character into two parts. Contrast 小 and 六 **liù** (7).

小 **xiǎo** be small, little, young **[sv]**

Reading Exercises (Simplified and Traditional Characters)

Now practice reading the new characters and words for this lesson in context. Be sure to refer to the Notes at the end of this lesson, and make use of the accompanying audio disc to hear and practice correct pronunciation, phrasing, and intonation.

A. TWO-CHARACTER PERSONAL NAMES

Read out loud the following personal names, each of which consists of a surname followed by a one-syllable given name.

一、何文
二、李京
三、王文
四、李明
五、林山
六、王生
七、文山
八、林中

B. THREE-CHARACTER PERSONAL NAMES

Read out loud the following personal names, each of which consists of a surname followed by a two-syllable given name.

一、李大一
二、林台生
三、王小文
四、何明明
五、王京生
六、文大中
七、何小山

八、李大林
九、林明生
十、李小明

C. PLACE NAMES

Read out loud each of the following place names.

一、台山
二、北京
三、台中
四、台北

D. CHARACTER DIFFERENTIATION DRILLS

Distinguish carefully the following similar-looking characters, pronouncing each one out loud and thinking of its meaning.

一、六 六 六 文 文 文
二、文 文 文 六 六 六
三、王 王 王 生 生 生
四、生 生 生 王 王 王
五、小 小 小 六 六 六
六、六 六 六 小 小 小
七、小 小 六 六 文 文

Notes

B2. When choosing personal names, Chinese people sometimes choose names that describe some aspect of a person. Consider the name 林台生; the character 台 can stand for Taiwan and 生 means "be born." Thus, 林台生 could mean "a person with the family name 林 who was born in Taiwan."

B5. Look carefully at the name 王京生. Keeping in mind note B2 above and the fact that the literal meaning of the character 京 is "capital" (which refers to 北京), what do you think 王京生 could mean?

Entrance to the Forbidden City in Beijing. The characters on the left mean "Long live the People's Republic of China"; the characters on the right mean "Long live the great unity of the world's peoples."

People, Places, Streets, and Roads

UNIT B

COMMUNICATIVE OBJECTIVES

Once you've mastered this unit, you'll be able to use Chinese to read and write:

1. More Chinese surnames: "An," "Du," "Jin," "Lu," "Nan."
2. More Chinese personal names: "Antian," "Guanghai," "Haiwen," "Xiaochuan," "Tianhu," etc.
3. More place names in mainland China and Taiwan: "Chengdu," "Guangzhou," "Hong Kong," "Nanjing," "Shanghai," "Taitung," "Tainan," "Tianjin," "Xian."
4. The names of a number of Chinese provinces: "Guangdong," "Guangxi," "Hainan," "Hebei," "Henan," "Hubei," "Hunan," "Shandong," "Shanxi," "Sichuan."
5. The names of two important Japanese cities that are written with Chinese characters: "Tokyo," "Kyoto."
6. People's places of origin: "native of Beijing," "native of Guangdong," "native of Taiwan," etc.
7. Names of roads, streets, and avenues: "Tianjin East Road," "Zhongshan South Road," "Chengdu Street," "Tianjin Avenue," etc.

PART 1

Personal Names, Place Names, People and Their Places of Origin

New Characters and Words

Study the six characters below and the common words written with them, paying careful attention to each character's pronunciation, meaning, and structure, as well as similar-looking characters. After you've studied a character, turn to the *Practice Essentials* volume and practice writing it on the practice sheet, making sure to follow the correct stroke order and direction as you pronounce it out loud and think of its meaning.

25 上 **shàng** above

The radical, located at the very bottom of the character, is 一 **yī** (1), which here represents a base. The two strokes "above" that base signify "above."

26 海 **hăi** ocean, sea

Radical is 水 **shuĭ** "water." Notice that this radical is written 氵 and is referred to colloquially as 三点水 (三點水) **sāndiăn shuĭ** "three drops of water" when it occurs at the left-hand side of a character. The other component is 每 **mĕi** "each."

上海 **Shànghăi** Shanghai [PW]

27 广(廣) **guăng** broad

Radical is 广 **yăn** "eaves" [BF]. This radical is referred to colloquially as 广字头 (廣字頭) **guăngzìtóu** "top made up of the character 广." Phonetic is 黃 **huáng** "yellow." 广 (廣) can itself serve as a phonetic, e.g., in 矿 (礦) **kuàng** as in 煤矿 (煤礦) **méikuàng** "coal mine."

28 州 **zhōu** state, district

Radical is 川 **chuān** "river" [BF] (38). 州 can itself serve as a phonetic, e.g., in 洲 **zhōu** "continent" [BF] as in 亚洲 (亞洲) **Yàzhōu** "Asia."

广州 (廣州) **Guăngzhōu** Guangzhou (capital of Guangdong Province, formerly spelled "Canton") [PW]

29 东(東) **dōng** east

Radical of the simplified form is 一 **yī** "one" (1). Radical of the traditional form is 木 **mù** "tree" [BF], which is a picture of a tree and its branches. The other component in the traditional form is 日 **rì** "sun" [BF], a squared-off picture of the sun with a sun spot in it. Traditional character 東 is a compound ideograph, the explanation being that the "sun" can be seen through the "trees" as it rises in the "east." 东 (東) can serve as a phonetic in other characters, e.g., 冻 (凍) **dòng** "freeze" and 栋 (棟) **dòng** (measure for houses).

广东 (廣東) **Guăngdōng** Guangdong (province) [PW]
山东 (山東) **Shāndōng** Shandong (province) [PW]

台东（台東）	**Táidōng**	Taitung (city on east coast of Taiwan) [PW]
东京（東京）	**Dōngjīng**	Tokyo (capital of Japan) [PW]

30 人 **rén** person

人 is itself a very common radical. It is a pictograph showing the two legs of a human being. The printed form of this character often appears with the two "legs" connected at the top, whereas in the handwritten form the left "leg" curves down from top to bottom but the right "leg" joins the left "leg" half of the way down. The word 人 can be added to many place words to indicate "a person from ..." or "a native of ...." Contrast 人 with 八 **bā** (9), 大 **dà** (13), and 文 **wén** (21).

人	**rén**	person [N]
北京人	**Běijīng rén**	person from Beijing [PH]
广东人（廣東人）	**Guǎngdōng rén**	person from Guangdong [PH]
上海人	**Shànghǎi rén**	person from Shanghai [PH]

Reading Exercises (Simplified Characters)

Now practice reading the new characters and words for this lesson in context. Be sure to refer to the Notes at the end of this lesson, and make use of the accompanying audio disc to hear and practice correct pronunciation, phrasing, and intonation.

A. PERSONAL NAMES

Read out loud each of the following personal names.

一、林广海　　三、李东山　　五、文明明
二、王文　　四、何海文

B. PLACE NAMES

Read out loud each of the following place names.

一、上海　　三、广东　　五、东京
二、广州　　四、山东　　六、台东

C. PEOPLE AND THEIR PLACES OF ORIGIN

Read out loud each of the following expressions, thinking of the meaning as you say it.

一、北京人　　五、台中人　　九、山东人
二、广东人　　六、台东人　　十、台山人
三、台北人　　七、东京人
四、上海人　　八、广州人

D. CHARACTER DIFFERENTIATION DRILLS

Distinguish carefully the following similar-looking characters, pronouncing each one out loud and thinking of its meaning.

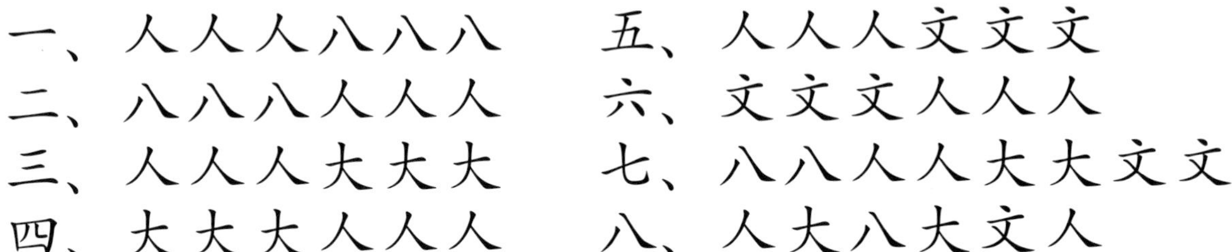

一、人人人八八八
二、八八八人人人
三、人人人大大大
四、大大大人人人
五、人人人文文文
六、文文文人人人
七、八八人人大大文文
八、人大八大文人

Reading Exercises (Traditional Characters)

A. PERSONAL NAMES

Read out loud each of the following personal names.

一、林廣海
二、王文
三、李東山
四、何海文
五、文明明

B. PLACE NAMES

Read out loud each of the following place names.

一、上海
二、廣州
三、廣東
四、山東
五、東京
六、台東

C. PEOPLE AND THEIR PLACES OF ORIGIN

Read out loud each of the following expressions, thinking of the meaning as you say it.

一、北京人
二、廣東人
三、台北人
四、上海人
五、台中人
六、台東人
七、東京人
八、廣州人
九、山東人
十、台山人

D. CHARACTER DIFFERENTIATION DRILLS

Distinguish carefully the following similar-looking characters, pronouncing each one out loud and thinking of its meaning.

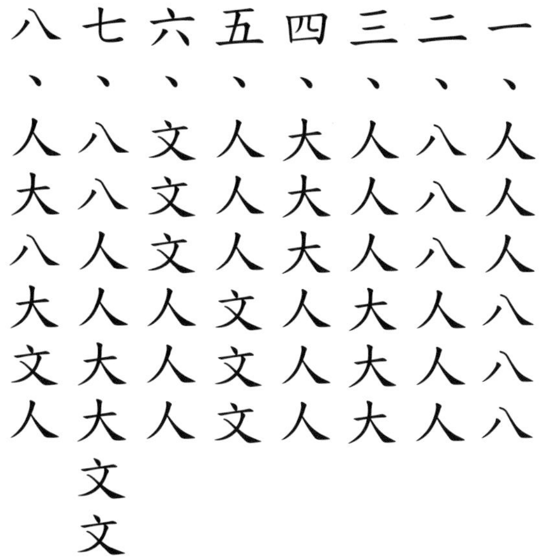

一、人人人八八八
二、八八八人人人
三、人人人大大大
四、大大大人人人
五、人人人文文文
六、文文文人人人
七、八八人人大大文文
八、人大八大文人

Notes

C2. Since Chinese nouns are often not marked for number (that is, don't indicate singular or plural), an expression like 北京人 could mean either "a person from Beijing" or "people from Beijing." The context would often make the meaning clear. In the case of 北京人, given an appropriate context, an additional interpretation is actually possible: "Peking man," that is, Homo erectus pekinensis.

Restaurant sign in Macau (large characters read from right to left)

PART 2

Personal Names, Place Names, People and Their Places of Origin, and Names of Roads

New Characters and Words

Study the six characters below and the common words written with them, paying careful attention to each character's pronunciation, meaning, and structure, as well as similar-looking characters. After you've studied a character, turn to the *Practice Essentials* volume and practice writing it on the practice sheet, making sure to follow the correct stroke order and direction as you pronounce it out loud and think of its meaning.

31 成 **chéng** become

Radical is 戈 **gē** "spear" [BF]. 成 is itself a phonetic, e.g., in 城 **chéng** "city" and in 诚 (誠) **chéng** as in 诚实 (誠實) **chéngshí** "honest."

32 都 **dū** large city, capital

Radical is 邑 **yì** "city" [BF], which is written 阝 when occurring at the right-hand side of a character. This radical is referred to colloquially as 右耳旁 **yòu'ěrpáng** "side made up of a right ear." The component on the left side of 都 is 者 **zhě**, a nominalizing suffix that often means "one who does something." A mnemonic for remembering this character is: "Cities" are where "those who do things" assemble.

都	**Dū**	Du [SN]
成都	**Chéngdū**	Chengdu (capital of Sichuan Province) [PW]
京都	**Jīngdū**	Kyoto (major city in Japan) [PW]

33 天 **tiān** sky, heaven

Radical is 大 **dà** "big" (13). No matter how "big" people are (大), there is always something above them (the stroke on top: 一), which is the sky or heaven. 天 can serve as a phonetic in other characters, e.g., 添 **tiān** "add" and 舔 **tiǎn** "lick." Contrast 天 with 大 **dà** (13), 文 **wén** (21), and 人 **rén** (30).

34 津 **jīn** ford; (abbreviation for Tianjin)

Radical is 水 **shuǐ** "water." Notice that this radical is written 氵 and is referred to colloquially as 三点水 (三點水) **sāndiǎn shuǐ** "three drops of water" when it occurs at the left-hand side of a character.

天津	**Tiānjīn**	Tianjin (major port in north China) [PW]

35 西 **xī** west

西 is itself a radical. It can also serve as a phonetic, e.g., 牺 (犧) **xī** as in 牺牲 (犧牲) **xīshēng** "sacrifice." The top stroke of this character represents a bird and the rest of the character represents the bird's nest. When the sun sets in the west, it's time for the birds to return to their nests, hence this character indicates "west." Contrast 西 and 四 **sì** (4).

广西 (廣西)	**Guǎngxī**	Guangxi (province) [PW]

山西	**Shānxī**	Shanxi (province) [**PW**]

36 路 **lù** road

Radical is 足 **zú** "foot" [**BF**], which at the left side of a character is referred to colloquially as 足字旁 **zúzìpáng** "side made up of the character 足." Note that when this character is written as a radical, its last two strokes are different, with the last stroke curving up so as to make room for the component on the right. The other component of 路 is 各 **gè** "each." Perhaps the following mnemonic will help you remember this character: Put "each" "foot" on the "road." Note that 路 is often added to place words or personal names to create the names of roads.

路	**Lù**	Lu (also Ro or Rho, a common Korean surname) [**SN**]
路	**lù**	road [**N**]
上海路	**Shànghǎi Lù**	Shanghai Road
成都西路	**Chéngdū Xī Lù**	Chengdu West Road
天津东路 (天津東路)	**Tiānjīn Dōng Lù**	Tianjin East Road

Reading Exercises (Simplified Characters)

Now practice reading the new characters and words for this lesson in context. Be sure to refer to the Notes at the end of this lesson, and make use of the accompanying audio disc to hear and practice correct pronunciation, phrasing, and intonation.

A. PERSONAL NAMES

Read out loud each of the following personal names.

一、路广天　　三、林天生　　五、王海
二、李成　　四、文明成　　六、都明海

B. PLACE NAMES

Read out loud each of the following place names.

一、成都　　四、广西　　七、山东
二、上海　　五、天津　　八、京都
三、广东　　六、广州　　九、东京

C. PEOPLE AND THEIR PLACES OF ORIGIN

Read out loud each of the following expressions, thinking of the meaning as you say it.

一、台中人　　四、山西人　　七、成都人
二、台东人　　五、天津人　　八、北京人
三、广西人　　六、台北人　　九、台山人

D. NAMES OF ROADS

Read out loud the names of each of these streets or roads in mainland China and Taiwan.

一、北京路
二、上海路
三、广州路
四、山西东路
五、成都西路
六、天津东路
七、广西西路
八、台中路
九、山东西路
十、台山东路

E. CHARACTER DIFFERENTIATION DRILLS

Distinguish carefully the following similar-looking characters, pronouncing each one out loud and thinking of its meaning.

一、天 天 天 大 大 大
二、大 大 大 天 天 天
三、天 天 天 文 文 文
四、文 文 文 天 天 天
五、天 天 天 人 人 人
六、人 人 人 天 天 天
七、西 西 西 四 四 四
八、四 四 四 西 西 西
九、人 大 天 文 西 四

Reading Exercises (Traditional Characters)

A. PERSONAL NAMES

Read out loud each of the following personal names.

一、路廣天
二、李成
三、林天生
四、文明成
五、王海
六、都明海

B. PLACE NAMES

Read out loud each of the following place names.

一、成都
二、上海
三、廣東
四、廣西
五、天津
六、廣州
七、山東
八、京都
九、東京

C. PEOPLE AND THEIR PLACES OF ORIGIN

Read out loud each of the following expressions, thinking of the meaning as you say it.

一、台中人
二、台東人
三、廣西人
四、山西人
五、天津人
六、台北人
七、成都人
八、北京人
九、台山人

D. NAMES OF ROADS

Read out loud the names of each of these streets or roads in mainland China and Taiwan.

一、北京路
二、上海路
三、廣州路
四、山西東路
五、成都西路
六、天津東路
七、廣西西路
八、台中路
九、山東西路
十、台山東路

E. CHARACTER DIFFERENTIATION DRILLS

Read out loud the names of each of these streets or roads in mainland China and Taiwan.

一、天天天大大大
二、大大大天天天
三、天天天文文文
四、文文文天天天
五、天天天人人人
六、人人人天天天
七、西西西四四四
八、四四四西西西
九、人大天文西四

Notes

D1. As in the West, Chinese roads may be named after famous cities, provinces, or people.

PART 3

Personal Names, Place Names, People and Their Places of Origin, and Names of Streets and Roads

New Characters and Words

Study the six characters below and the common words written with them, paying careful attention to each character's pronunciation, meaning, and structure, as well as similar-looking characters. After you've studied a character, turn to the *Practice Essentials* volume and practice writing it on the practice sheet, making sure to follow the correct stroke order and direction as you pronounce it out loud and think of its meaning.

37 安 **ān** peace

Radical is 宀 **mián** "roof" [BF]. This radical is referred to colloquially as 宝盖头 (寶蓋頭) **bǎogàitóu** "top made up of a canopy." The other component is 女 **nǚ** "woman" [BF], which in ancient times had a secondary pronunciation similar to **ān**, so here it serves as a phonetic. The traditional—and very sexist—explanation is that if the "woman" of the house stayed under the "roof" (i.e., stayed at home rather than going out), there would be "peace." 安 is itself a common phonetic, e.g., in 鞍 **ān** as in 马鞍 (馬鞍) **mǎ'ān** "saddle," 按 **àn** "according to," and 案 **àn** as in 案子 **ànzi** "legal case."

安	**Ān**	An (also An or Ahn, a common Korean surname) [SN]
西安	**Xī'ān**	Xian (capital of Shaanxi Province) [PW]

38 川 **chuān** river

川 is itself a radical. 川 is a pictograph showing three separate streams converging to form a "river," which is even more apparent in an alternate form of this character: 巛. The character 川 can also serve as a phonetic in other characters, e.g., in 巡 **xún** as in 巡逻 (巡邏) **xúnluó** "patrol," 训 (訓) **xùn** as in 教训 (教訓) **jiàoxùn** "a lesson learned," and 顺 (順) **shùn** "smooth." Contrast 川 with 三 **sān** (3) and 州 **zhōu** (28).

四川	**Sìchuān**	Sichuan (province) [PW]

39 香 **xiāng** fragrant

This character is itself a radical. Contrast 香 and 东 (東) **dōng** (29).

香山	**Xiāng Shān**	Fragrant Hills (suburb to the northwest of Beijing) [PW]

40 港 **gǎng** harbor

Radical is 水 **shuǐ** "water." Notice that this radical is written 氵 and is referred to colloquially as 三点水 (三點水) **sāndiǎn shuǐ** "three drops of water" when it occurs at the left-hand side of a character. Phonetic is 巷 **xiàng** as in 巷子 **xiàngzi** "lane."

香港	**Xiānggǎng**	Hong Kong [PW]

41 南 **nán** south

Radical is 十 **shí** (11). This character is itself a phonetic and occurs as a phonetic in a few other characters, e.g., 腩 **nán** as in 牛腩 **niúnán** "sirloin beef."

南	**Nán**	Nan (also Nam, a common Korean surname) [SN]
南京	**Nánjīng**	Nanjing (capital of Jiangsu Province; formerly spelled Nanking) [PW]
台南	**Táinán**	Tainan (city in southern Taiwan) [PW]
海南	**Hǎinán**	Hainan (province) [PW]
中山南路	**Zhōngshān Nán Lù**	Zhongshan South Road

42 街 **jiē** street

Radical is 行 **xíng** "go" [BF]. Inserted into the middle of 行 are two 土 **tǔ** "earth." One "goes" on the "street," which is made of much "earth." Note that 街 is often added to place words or personal names to create street names.

街	**jiē**	street [N]
大街	**dàjiē**	main street, avenue [PW]
西安街	**Xī'ān Jiē**	Xian Street
香港街	**Xiānggǎng Jiē**	Hong Kong Street
天津大街	**Tiānjīn Dàjiē**	Tianjin Avenue

Reading Exercises (Simplified Characters)

Now practice reading the new characters and words for this lesson in context. Be sure to refer to the Notes at the end of this lesson, and make use of the accompanying audio disc to hear and practice correct pronunciation, phrasing, and intonation.

A. PERSONAL NAMES

Read out loud each of the following personal names.

一、安小明　　三、何安天　　五、南山
二、李南　　四、林小川　　六、王海香

B. PLACE NAMES

Read out loud each of the following place names.

一、成都　　四、西安　　七、山东
二、台南　　五、天津　　八、南京
三、广东　　六、香山　　九、香港

C. PEOPLE AND THEIR PLACES OF ORIGIN

Read out loud each of the following expressions, thinking of the meaning as you say it.

一、南京人
二、台东人
三、广西人
四、山西人
五、四川人
六、香港人
七、成都人
八、台南人
九、台北人

D. NAMES OF STREETS AND ROADS

Read out loud the names of each of these Chinese streets or roads.

一、四川街
二、中山南路
三、广州街
四、山西东街
五、南京东路
六、天津大街
七、香港街
八、上海街
九、山东西街

E. CHARACTER DIFFERENTIATION DRILLS

Distinguish carefully the following similar-looking characters, pronouncing each one out loud and thinking of its meaning.

一、川 川 川 三 三 三
二、三 三 三 川 川 川
三、川 川 川 州 州 州
四、州 州 州 川 川 川
五、三 川 州 州 川 三

Reading Exercises (Traditional Characters)

A. PERSONAL NAMES

Read out loud each of the following personal names.

一、安小明
二、李南
三、何安天
四、林小川
五、南山
六、王海香

B. PLACE NAMES

Read out loud each of the following place names.

一、成都
二、台南
三、廣東
四、西安
五、天津
六、香山
七、山東
八、南京
九、香港

C. PEOPLE AND THEIR PLACES OF ORIGIN

Read out loud each of the following expressions, thinking of the meaning as you say it.

一、南京人
二、台東人
三、廣西人
四、山西人
五、四川人
六、香港人
七、成都人
八、台南人
九、台北人

D. NAMES OF STREETS AND ROADS

Read out loud the names of each of these Chinese streets or roads.

一、四川街
二、中山南路
三、廣州街
四、山西東街
五、南京東路
六、天津大街
七、香港街
八、上海街
九、山東西街

E. CHARACTER DIFFERENTIATION DRILLS

Distinguish carefully the following similar-looking characters, pronouncing each one out loud and thinking of its meaning.

一、川 川 川 三 三 三
二、三 三 三 川 川 川
三、川 川 川 州 州 州
四、州 州 州 川 川 川
五、三 川 州 州 川 三

Notes

D2. 中山 here refers to Dr. Sun Yat-sen, the founder of the Republic of China.

PART 4

More Personal and Place Names, People and Their Places of Origin, and Names of Streets and Roads

New Characters and Words

Study the six characters below and the common words written with them, paying careful attention to each character's pronunciation, meaning, and structure, as well as similar-looking characters. After you've studied a character, turn to the *Practice Essentials* volume and practice writing it on the practice sheet, making sure to follow the correct stroke order and direction as you pronounce it out loud and think of its meaning.

43 河 **hé** river

Radical is 水 **shuǐ** "water." Notice that this radical is written 氵 and is referred to colloquially as 三点水 (三點水) **sāndiǎn shuǐ** "three drops of water" when it occurs at the left-hand side of a character. Phonetic is 可 **kě** "may" [**BF**]. Contrast 河 with 何 **Hé** (19).

河南	**Hé'nán**	Henan (province) [**PW**]
河北	**Héběi**	Hebei (province) [**PW**]

44 湖 **hú** lake [**N**]

Radical is 水 **shuǐ** "water." Again, this radical is written 氵 and is referred to colloquially as 三点水 (三點水) **sāndiǎn shuǐ** "three drops of water" when it occurs at the left-hand side of a character. Phonetic is 胡 **Hú** [**SN**].

湖南	**Hú'nán**	Hunan (province) [**PW**]
湖北	**Húběi**	Hubei (province) [**PW**]
五大湖	**Wǔ Dà Hú**	Great Lakes (lit. "five great lakes") [**PW**]

45 湾 (灣) **wān** bay

Radical is 水 **shuǐ** "water." Notice that this radical is written 氵 and is referred to colloquially as 三点水 (三點水) **sāndiǎn shuǐ** "three drops of water" when it occurs at the left-hand side of a character. Phonetic is 弯 (彎) **wān** "bend." Land "bends" around "water," creating a "bay."

台湾 (台灣)	**Táiwān**	Taiwan [**PW**]

46 金 **jīn** gold, metal

金 is itself a common radical. Incidentally, 金 is the character that represents the syllable "kum" in the word "kumquat" (this word was borrowed into English from Cantonese, in which language **jīn** is pronounced "kum" or, more accurately, **gām**).

金	**Jīn**	Jin, Chin (also Kim, the most common Korean surname) [**SN**]
金山	**Jīnshān**	large district in Shanghai; town in northern Taiwan famous for its hot springs [**PW**]

47 **市** **shì** market, city

Radical is 巾 **jīn** "cloth" [BF]. 市 serves as a phonetic in 柿 **shì** as in 柿子 **shìzi** "persimmon."

市	**shì**	city, municipality [BF]
北京市	**Běijīng Shì**	Beijing City [PH]
广州市 (廣州市)	**Guǎngzhōu Shì**	Guangzhou City [PH]
台北市	**Táiběi Shì**	Taipei City [PH]

48 **省** **shěng** province

Radical is 目 **mù** "eye" [BF], which is a pictograph representing two eyes set upright. The other component is 少 **shǎo** "few." 省 is often added to the names of the various Chinese provinces.

省	**shěng**	province [N]
河南省	**Hé'nán Shěng**	Henan Province [PH]
河北省	**Héběi Shěng**	Hebei Province [PH]
湖南省	**Hú'nán Shěng**	Hunan Province [PH]
湖北省	**Húběi Shěng**	Hubei Province [PH]
山西省	**Shānxī Shěng**	Shanxi Province [PH]
四川省	**Sìchuān Shěng**	Sichuan Province [PH]

Reading Exercises (Simplified Characters)

Now practice reading the new characters and words for this lesson in context. Be sure to refer to the Notes at the end of this lesson, and make use of the accompanying audio disc to hear and practice correct pronunciation, phrasing, and intonation.

A. PERSONAL NAMES

Read out loud each of the following personal names.

一、王金海
二、金广
三、林安河
四、李南川
五、李天湖

B. PLACE NAMES

Read out loud each of the following place names.

一、台湾省台东市
二、上海市
三、广西省
四、北京市
五、广东省广州市
六、四川省成都市
七、河北省
八、河南省
九、湖北省
十、湖南省

C. PEOPLE AND THEIR PLACES OF ORIGIN

Read out loud each of the following expressions, thinking of the meaning as you say it.

一、河北人
二、河南省人
三、台湾省台北市人
四、山西人
五、四川人
六、香港人
七、成都市人
八、北京市人
九、天津市人
十、西安市人

D. NAMES OF STREETS AND ROADS

Read out loud the names of each of these streets or roads in mainland China and Taiwan.

一、天津街
二、台南路
三、广州街
四、湖北街
五、河北路
六、四川大街
七、香港街
八、河南街
九、台湾东路
十、湖南东街

Reading Exercises (Traditional Characters)

A. PERSONAL NAMES

Read out loud each of the following personal names.

一、王金海
二、金廣
三、林安河
四、李南川
五、李天湖

B. PLACE NAMES

Read out loud each of the following place names.

一、台灣省台東市
二、上海市
三、廣西省
四、北京市
五、廣東省廣州市
六、四川省成都市
七、河北省
八、河南省
九、湖北省
十、湖南省

C. PEOPLE AND THEIR PLACES OF ORIGIN

Read out loud each of the following expressions, thinking of the meaning as you say it.

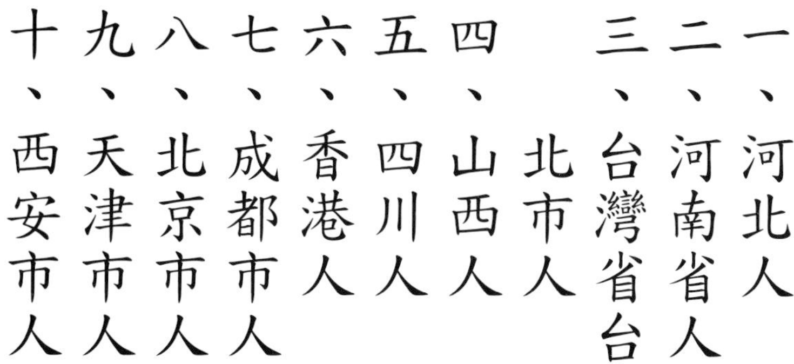

一、河北人
二、河南省人
三、台灣省台北市人
四、山西人
五、四川人
六、香港人
七、成都市人
八、北京市人
九、天津市人
十、西安市人

D. NAMES OF STREETS AND ROADS

Read out loud the names of each of these Chinese streets or roads.

一、天津街
二、台南路
三、廣州街
四、湖北街
五、河北路
六、四川大街
七、香港街
八、河南街
九、台灣東路
十、湖南東街

Notes

B1. When mentioning a series of categories, the Chinese language always proceeds from larger or more general to smaller or more specific. That is why, in this item and several others in parts B and C, the province is mentioned before the city. This is also why, as we have already seen, Chinese people's surnames are mentioned before their given names.

The name of a famous street in Beijing

沒有他就沒有iPhone

上街!

中央人民广播电台
中国之声
北京 FM106.1
携手北京晨报
共同打造有声的报纸《早报早读》

香港中文大學

10月28日~10月31日

8年，416次

十个人中一个姓王

北京人姓王的最多

我们在一起

最後7天

北京市北方中学

上海时间

為什麼不去金門

是誰？

从开始到现在

一年，只要1,290元

中国工人

道知不能不你

《從A到A+》

These are titles, headlines, and other snippets of printed Chinese taken from newspapers and magazines published in mainland China, Hong Kong, and Taiwan. All of the characters in them are introduced in this book. (*See last page for English translations.*)

Greetings and Useful Phrases

UNIT 1

COMMUNICATIVE OBJECTIVES

Once you've mastered this unit, you'll be able to use Chinese to read and write:

1. Common greetings and useful phrases such as "How are you?", "Thank you," "Please sit down," and "I'll be on my way."
2. Questions about how people are, who is or is not going where, relative heights of people from different parts of China, the difficulty of Chinese, and changes that have taken place.
3. Common Chinese surnames: "He," "Gao," "Li," "Lin," "Wang," "Xie."
4. Common Chinese titles: "Mr.," "Mrs.," "Miss," "Ms.," "Old Wang," "Little Li."
5. Chinese personal pronouns: "I," "you," "he," "she," "we," "they."
6. Some Chinese punctuation marks that are different from English.

PART 1

"Where Are You Going?"

New Characters and Words

Study the six characters below and the common words written with them, paying careful attention to each character's pronunciation, meaning, and structure, as well as similar-looking characters. After you've studied a character, turn to the *Practice Essentials* volume and practice writing it on the practice sheet, making sure to follow the correct stroke order and direction as you pronounce it out loud and think of its meaning.

49 你 **nǐ** you

Radical is 人 **rén** "person," which is written 亻 when occurring at the left side of a character so as not to get in the way of the component to the right. The colloquial name for this radical is 人字旁 **rénzìpáng** "side made up of the character 人." The other component of 你 is 尔 **ěr**, which in Classical Chinese means "you."

你 **nǐ** you [**PR**]

---

50 好 **hǎo** good

Radical is 女 **nǚ** "woman" [**BF**]. This radical is referred to colloquially as 女字旁 **nǚzìpáng** "side made up of the character 女." Note that when 女 is written at the left of a character as a radical, its last stroke is shortened so that it doesn't collide with the component to its right. The other component of 好 is 子 **zǐ** "son" [**BF**]. The traditional explanation is that for a "woman" to be together with her "son" is "good."

你好 **nǐ hǎo** "how are you?," "hi" [**IE**]

---

51 我 **wǒ** I

In this character, note that the radical, 戈 **gē** "dagger-axe" [**BF**], is on the right side. The whole character 我 consists of the verb 找 **zhǎo** "look for" plus a small hat (the stroke 丿) at the very top of the character that represents "I" or "me." The verb 找 in turn is composed of 扌 **shǒu** "hand" and 戈 **gē** "dagger-axe." So the

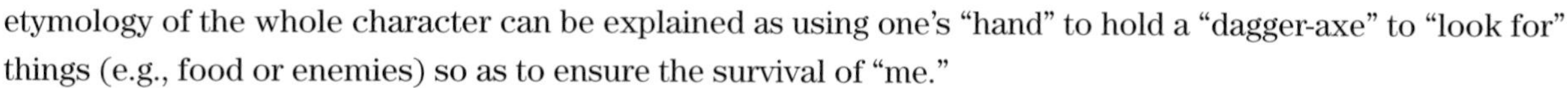

etymology of the whole character can be explained as using one's "hand" to hold a "dagger-axe" to "look for" things (e.g., food or enemies) so as to ensure the survival of "me."

我 **wǒ** I, me [PR]

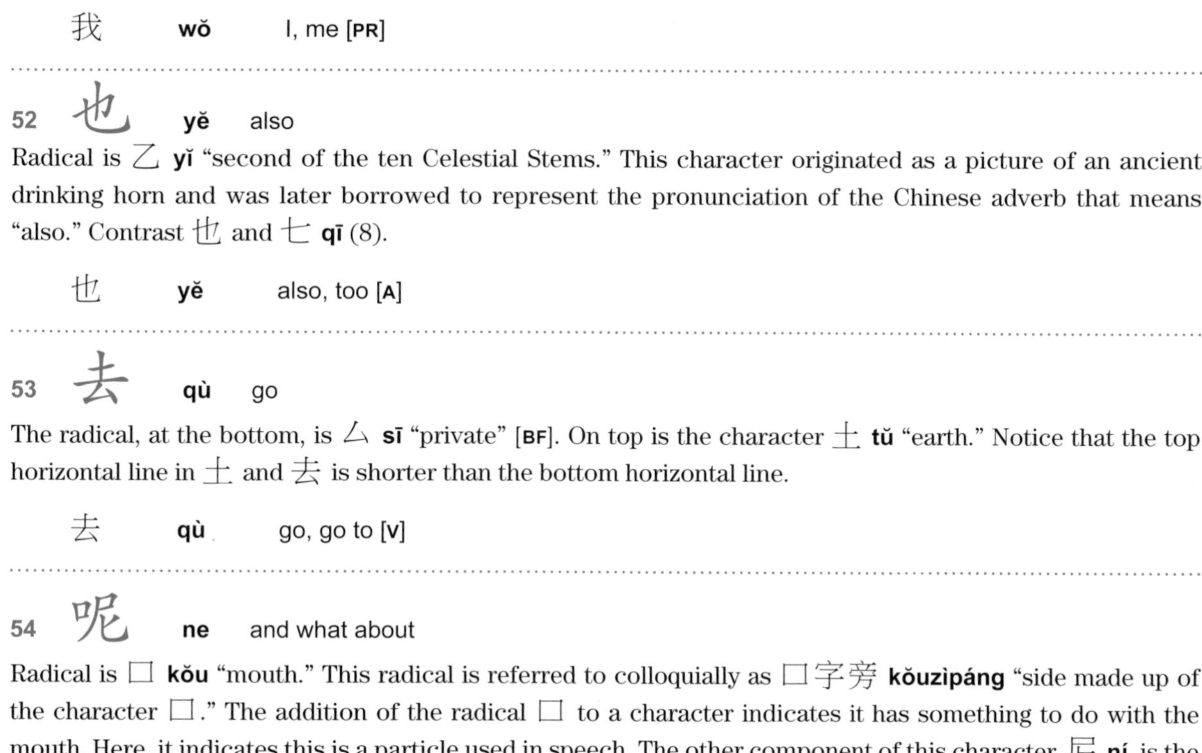

52 也 **yě** also

Radical is 乙 **yǐ** "second of the ten Celestial Stems." This character originated as a picture of an ancient drinking horn and was later borrowed to represent the pronunciation of the Chinese adverb that means "also." Contrast 也 and 七 **qī** (8).

也 **yě** also, too [A]

53 去 **qù** go

The radical, at the bottom, is 厶 **sī** "private" [BF]. On top is the character 土 **tǔ** "earth." Notice that the top horizontal line in 土 and 去 is shorter than the bottom horizontal line.

去 **qù** go, go to [V]

54 呢 **ne** and what about

Radical is 口 **kǒu** "mouth." This radical is referred to colloquially as 口字旁 **kǒuzìpáng** "side made up of the character 口." The addition of the radical 口 to a character indicates it has something to do with the mouth. Here, it indicates this is a particle used in speech. The other component of this character, 尼 **ní**, is the phonetic; by itself, it means "Buddhist nun" [BF].

呢	**ne**	and what about, and how about [P]
我去，你呢？	**Wǒ qù, nǐ ne?**	I'm going, and what about you?

New Words in BSC 1-1 Written with Characters You Already Know

王 **Wáng** Wang [SN]

Reading Exercises (Simplified Characters)

Now practice reading the new characters and words for this lesson in context in sentences, conversations, and narratives. Be sure to refer to the Notes at the end of this lesson, and make use of the accompanying audio disc to hear and practice correct pronunciation, phrasing, and intonation.

A. SENTENCES

Read out loud each of the following sentences, which include all the new characters of this lesson. The first time you read a sentence, focus special attention on the characters and words that are new to you, reminding yourself of their pronunciation and meaning. The second time, aim to comprehend the overall meaning of the sentence.

一、何大山，你好！文中生，你好！

二、我去山东，你去山西。

三、李小山去河北，王大文去河南。
四、你去南京，我也去南京，李大明也去南京。
五、去，去，去，去北京！
六、何台生去台北，王大明呢？
七、王京生去台山，林台生也去台山。
八、你去广东，我也去广东。
九、何大海，你去香港，我也去。
十、我去北京，王大海也去北京。

B. CONVERSATIONS

Read out loud the following conversations, including the name or role of the person speaking. If possible, find a partner or partners and each of you play a role. Then switch roles, so you get practice reading all of the lines.

一、
王京生：我去北京，也去香山。你呢？
文小山：我去天津。

二、
李中　：林生，你好！我去香港，你呢？
林生　：我去东京。文京明，你呢？
文京明：我也去东京。

三、
李京生：北京好！
王台生：台北好！
何大海：北京好，台北也好。

C. CHARACTER DIFFERENTIATION DRILLS

Distinguish carefully the following similar-looking characters, pronouncing each one out loud and thinking of its meaning.

一、也 也 也 七 七 七
二、七 七 七 也 也 也
三、也 七 也 七 也 也 七

D. NARRATIVES

Read the following narratives, paying special attention to punctuation and overall structure. The first time you read a narrative, read it out loud; the second time, read silently and try to gradually increase your reading speed. Always think of the meaning of what you're reading.

一、何大海去西安，李中山也去西安。林文生去台中，也去台北。我去北京，也去上海。你呢？

二、文中去四川省成都市。李大山去广东省广州市。你呢？

三、王安湖去东京。东京好！金明去上海。上海也好。李京去香港，我也去香港。何小文，你呢？

Reading Exercises (Traditional Characters)

A. SENTENCES

Read out loud each of the following sentences, which include all the new characters of this lesson. The first time you read a sentence, focus special attention on the characters and words that are new to you, reminding yourself of their pronunciation and meaning. The second time, aim to comprehend the overall meaning of the sentence.

一、何大山，你好！文中生，你好！

二、我去山東，你去山西。

三、李小山去河北，王大文去河南。

四、你去南京，我也去南京，李大明也去南京。

五、去，去，去，去，去北京！

六、何台生去台北，王大明呢？

七、王京生去台山，林台生也去台山。

八、你去廣東，我也去廣東。

九、何大海，你去香港，我也去。

十、我去北京，王大海也去北京。

B. CONVERSATIONS

Read out loud the following conversations, including the name or role of the person speaking. If possible, find a partner or partners and each of you play a role. Then switch roles, so you get practice reading all of the lines.

一、王京生：我去北京，也去香山。你呢？
文小山：我去天津。

二、李中：林生，你好！我去香港，你呢？
林生：我去東京。文京明，你呢？
文京明：我也去東京。

三、李京生：北京好！
王台生：台北好！
何大海：北京好，台北也好。

C. CHARACTER DIFFERENTIATION DRILLS

Distinguish carefully the following similar-looking characters, pronouncing each one out loud and thinking of its meaning.

一、也也也七七七

二、七七七也也也

三、也七也七也也七

Typical street scene in Hong Kong

D. NARRATIVES

Read the following narratives, paying special attention to punctuation and overall structure. The first time you read a narrative, read it out loud; the second time, read silently and try to gradually increase your reading speed. Always think of the meaning of what you're reading.

一、何大海去西安，李中山也去西安。林文生去台中，也去台北。我去北京，也去上海。你呢？

二、文中去四川省成都市。李大山去廣東省廣州市。你呢？

三、王安湖去東京。東京好！金明去上海。上海也好。李京去香港，我也去香港。何小文，你呢？

Notes

A1. The Chinese comma, called 逗号 (逗號) **dòuhào** (，), and the Chinese exclamation mark, called 叹号 (嘆號) **tànhào** (！), are often used as in English.

A2A. Take the clause 我去山东 (我去山東) **Wǒ qù Shāndōng** "I go to Shandong." It clearly consists of three separate words: 我 + 去 + 山东 (山東), yet it's written all together. As you've probably realized by now, the Chinese writing system does not leave spaces between words (except on rare occasions when a space before a word can indicate deep respect). This feature of the Chinese writing system explains why the average Chinese person has little concept of the "word." Instead, he or she will typically speak of **zì** or "characters," since these are the basic unit of the Chinese writing system.

A2B. Examine this sentence: 我去山东，你去山西 (我去山東，你去山西) "I go to Shandong; you go to Shanxi" or "I go to Shandong and you go to Shanxi." Consider this translation strategy: a Chinese comma between two clauses is often best translated in English as a semicolon (；) or by the word "and."

A2C. Notice the "Chinese period" at the end of this sentence. The Chinese period is called 句号 (句號) **jùhào**. Instead of a dot as in English, a Chinese period is a small circle, like this: 。 In horizontal writing, the Chinese period is placed to the bottom right of the last character of the sentence. In vertical writing, it is usually placed underneath the last character. In either case, it occupies the same amount of space as any other character.

A5. Verbs, such as the 去 in this sentence, are sometimes repeated for emphasis.

A6. Note the name 何台生. Where do you think this person, who has the surname 何, might have been born? (ANSWER: 台 could here stand for 台湾 (台灣), and 生 could mean "be born," so 台生 could be an abbreviated way to indicate "born in Taiwan.")

A7. Considering the information in the previous note, where do you think 王京生 was probably born?

A8. This sentence has two possible interpretations. In addition to "You go to Guangdong, and I also go to Guangdong," it could also be interpreted as "If you go to Guangdong, then I will also go to Guangdong." Although there are in Chinese explicit words for "if," be aware that "if" must sometimes be inferred from the context and be supplied in the English translation. Sentence A9 is in this regard similar to sentence A8.

B1A. Notice the colon (：) after the speaker's name. The Chinese word for colon is 冒号 (冒號) **màohào**. Chinese colons are used much as in English.

B1B. Notice the question mark (？) at the end of the first line. In Chinese, question marks are called 问号 (問號) **wènhào**. Chinese question marks are used much as in English (occasionally, Chinese question marks are used not only in direct questions but also in indirect questions, which is different from English).

B3. 好 here functions as a stative verb meaning "be good." Thus, 北京好 means "Beijing is good" or "Beijing is better." 台北好 works exactly the same way.

Hong Kong restaurant (characters read from right to left)

"Long Time No See!"

PART 2

New Characters and Words

Study the six characters below and the common words written with them, paying careful attention to each character's pronunciation, meaning, and structure, as well as similar-looking characters. After you've studied a character, turn to the *Practice Essentials* volume and practice writing it on the practice sheet, making sure to follow the correct stroke order and direction as you pronounce it out loud and think of its meaning.

55 他 **tā** he

Radical is 人 **rén** "person," which is written 亻 when occurring at the left side of a character so as not to get in the way of the component at the right. The colloquial name for this radical is 人字旁 **rénzìpáng** "side made up of the character 人." The rest of the character 他 consists of 也 **yě** "also" (52).

他	**tā**	he, him **[PR]**

---

56 她 **tā** she

Radical is 女 **nǚ** "woman" **[BF]**. This radical is referred to colloquially as 女字旁 **nǚzìpáng** "side made up of the character 女." Note that when 女 is written at the left of a character as a radical, its last stroke is shortened so that it doesn't collide with the component to its right. The rest of the character 她 consists of 也 **yě** "also" (52). This character didn't exist in Chinese until the early twentieth century, when it was created under the influence of Western languages to distinguish the gender of the third person pronoun **tā**. Of course, in spoken Chinese there is still no difference. Be aware that in some older writings by more traditional authors, 他 may still be used to mean "she." Contrast 她 with 他 **tā** (55).

她	**tā**	she, her **[PR]**

57 们 (們) **men** (plural marker for pronouns)

Radical is 人 **rén** "person," which is written 亻 when occurring at the left side of a character so as not to get in the way of the component at the right. The colloquial name for this radical is 人字旁 **rénzìpáng** "side made up of the character 人 ." Phonetic is 门 (門) **mén** "door." Contrast 们 (們) and 很 **hěn** (58).

他们 (他們)	**tāmen**	they, them (males only, or males and females together) [**PR**]
她们 (她們)	**tāmen**	they, them (females only) [**PR**]

58 很 **hěn** very

Radical is 彳 **chì** "short and slow step" [**BF**]. This radical is referred to colloquially as 双立人 (雙立人) **shuānglìrén** "double standing person, two people with one following the other." Phonetic is 艮 **gèn** (name of one of the eight trigrams in the *Book of Changes*). Contrast 很 and 们 (們) (57).

很	**hěn**	very [**A**]

59 忙 **máng** busy

Radical is 心 **xīn** "heart." When at the left side of a character, this radical is referred to colloquially as 心字旁 **xīnzìpáng** "side made up of the character 心" and is written as 忄. The radical 心 is frequently used for characters having to do with emotions or states of mind. Phonetic is 亡 **wáng** "lose" [**BF**]. Perhaps this mnemonic will help you remember this character: When you are really "busy" (忙), you occasionally "lose" (亡) track of what's really in your "heart" (忄).

忙	**máng**	be busy [**SV**]

60 吗 (嗎) **ma** (particle that indicates questions)

Radical is 口 **kǒu** "mouth." This radical is referred to colloquially as 口字旁 **kǒuzìpáng** "side made up of the character 口." As is the case here, 口 often indicates that a word containing it is a particle used in speech. Phonetic is 马 (馬) **mǎ** "horse."

吗 (嗎)	**ma**	(particle that indicates questions) [**P**]

New Words in BSC 1-2 Written with Characters You Already Know

都	**dōu**	all, both [**A**] (都 is here pronounced **dōu**, not **dū** as in the city name 成都 **Chéngdū**)
好	**hǎo**	be good [**SV**]

Reading Exercises (Simplified Characters)

Now practice reading the new characters and words for this lesson in context in sentences, conversations, and narratives. Be sure to refer to the Notes at the end of this lesson, and make use of the accompanying audio disc to hear and practice correct pronunciation, phrasing, and intonation.

A. SENTENCES

Read out loud each of the following sentences, which include all the new characters of this lesson. The first time you read a sentence, focus special attention on the characters and words that are new to you, reminding yourself of their pronunciation and meaning. The second time, aim to comprehend the overall meaning of the sentence.

一、北京很好，香港、台北也都很好。
二、我很忙，他们也很忙。你呢？你忙吗？
三、我很好。李小明、何台生他们也都很好。
四、金中、何大生他们都去上海吗？
五、王明，你好！你去天津吗？
六、她们去台山。他呢？他也去台山吗？
七、我去东京，文文去京都。他们呢？
八、我去上海，他们也都去上海。
九、广东人去广西，广西人去广东！
十、王大海去台北，我也去台北。你呢？你也去台北吗？

B. CONVERSATIONS

Read out loud the following conversations, including the name or role of the person speaking. If possible, find a partner or partners and each of you play a role. Then switch roles, so you get practice reading all of the lines.

一、
王大中：林小文，你好！
林小文：王大中，你好！
王大中：你忙吗？
林小文：很忙。你呢？
王大中：我也很忙。

二、
林广海：何台生好吗？
王中　：他很好。
林广海：何小明呢？
王中　：他也很好。

林广海：王文生、王山生他们呢？
王中　：王文生、王山生他们也都很好。

三、
何京生：林一明，你好！
林一明：何京生，你好！我去山西。你呢？
何京生：我去山东。
林一明：她们呢？
何京生：她们也去山东。

C. CHARACTER DIFFERENTIATION DRILLS

Distinguish carefully the following similar-looking characters, pronouncing each one out loud and thinking of its meaning.

一、他 他 他 也 也 也
二、她 她 她 也 也 也
三、他 也 她 也 七 也 他 她

D. NARRATIVES

Read the following narratives, paying special attention to punctuation and overall structure. The first time you read a narrative, read it out loud; the second time, read silently and try to gradually increase your reading speed. Always think of the meaning of what you're reading.

一、李文、王京生他们去南京。我也去南京。金明明也去南京。李文、王京生他们都很忙。我也很忙。金明明也很忙。你呢？你也去南京吗？你也很忙吗？

二、林文生去河北，也去河南。他很忙。李京去湖北，也去湖南，她也很忙。我去广东，也去广西。我也很忙。

Reading Exercises (Traditional Characters)

A. SENTENCES

Read out loud each of the following sentences, which include all the new characters of this lesson. The first time you read a sentence, focus special attention on the characters and words that are new to you, reminding yourself of their pronunciation and meaning. The second time, aim to comprehend the overall meaning of the sentence.

一、北京很好，香港、台北也都很好。

二、我很忙，他們也很忙。你呢？你忙嗎？

三、我很好。李小明、何台生他們也都很好。

四、金中、何大生他們都去上海嗎？

五、王明，你好！你去天津嗎？

六、她們去台山。他呢？他也去台山嗎？

七、我去東京，文文去京都。他們呢？

八、我去上海，他們也都去上海。

九、廣東人去廣西，廣西人去廣東！

十、王大海去台北，我也去台北。你呢？你也去台北嗎？

B. CONVERSATIONS

Read out loud the following conversations, including the name or role of the person speaking. If possible, find a partner or partners and each of you play a role. Then switch roles, so you get practice reading all of the lines.

一、

王大中：林小文，你好！

林小文：王大中，你好！

王大中：你忙嗎？

林小文：很忙。你呢？

王大中：我也很忙。

二、

林廣海：何台生好嗎？

王中　：他很好。

林廣海：何小明呢？

王中　：他也很好。

林廣海：王文生、王山生他們呢？

王中　：王文生、王山生他們也都很好。

三、

何京生：林一明，你好！

林一明：何京生，你好！我去山西。你呢？

何京生：我去山東。

林一明：她們呢？

何京生：她們也去山東。

C. CHARACTER DIFFERENTIATION DRILLS

Distinguish carefully the following similar-looking characters, pronouncing each one out loud and thinking of its meaning.

一、他他他也也也

二、她她她也也也

三、他也她也七也他她

"She" and "he" beauty salon

D. NARRATIVES

Read the following narratives, paying special attention to punctuation and overall structure. The first time you read a narrative, read it out loud; the second time, read silently and try to gradually increase your reading speed. Always think of the meaning of what you're reading.

一、李文、王京生他們去南京。我也去南京。金明明也去南京。李文、王京生他們都很忙。我也很忙。金明明也很忙。你呢？你也去南京嗎？你也很忙嗎？

二、林文生去河北，也去河南。他很忙。李京去湖北，也去湖南，她也很忙。我去廣東，也去廣西。我也很忙。

Notes

A1A. Another use of the 顿号 (頓號) **dùnhào** (、) is to separate items in a series that stand in unmarked coordination, somewhat like the English conjunction "and." Thus, 香港、台北也都很好 could mean "Hong Kong and Taipei would also both be fine." The **dùnhào** would be used, for example, between the names of differerent items that you wish to purchase, between each of the names in a series of personal names that is mentioned within a sentence, or between the names of different countries in a sentence. For this reason, the **dùnhào** is in English sometimes referred to as the "enumerative comma" or "listing comma." In spoken Chinese, there would be a brief pause wherever a **dùnhào** occurs. Note how the **dùnhào** and the regular comma, called 逗号 (逗號) **dòuhào**, differ in appearance:

DÙNHÀO: 、	DÒUHÀO: ，

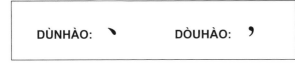

As you see above, the **dùnhào** slants down toward the *right* and is rounded at the *bottom*, as distinguished from the **dòuhào**, which is rounded *at the top* and then slants down toward the left.

A1B. Notice that the character 都 can represent two different words with two different pronunciations. Pronounced **dū** (as in 成都 **Chéngdū**) it means "city," but pronounced **dōu** it is an adverb meaning "all, both." Context will usually make the intended meaning and pronunciation clear. There are in Chinese a number of common characters that can represent several different spoken words with different pronunciations. Of course, in English we also have cases where one written form represents several different spoken forms; for example, consider the word "read" in "What will you read?" as opposed to in "What have you read?"

A3. After a listing of names in a series, the appropriate plural pronoun is often added so as to "sum up" and clarify or emphasize the group of people concerned. Thus, in this sentence, 李小明、何台生他们 (李小明、何台生他們) would literally mean "Li Xiaoming and He Taisheng, they...." Normally, the "they" would be omitted in an English translation.

B2, B3.

Note that while 她们 (她們) always refers to "they" in the sense of two or more women, 他们 (他們) can be used both for groups of men and for mixed groups consisting of men and women. Of course, this distinction exists only in the written language, since the spoken language has only one term (**tāmen**), which is not marked for gender.

D1, D2.

Note that in Chinese, if you come to the end of a line (in either horizontal or vertical format) and are in the middle of a multisyllabic word, you write as many syllables as will fit on that line and then just continue on the next line. Chinese has nothing equivalent to the English hyphen at the end of a line to indicate that the preceding syllable is normally written together with the syllable that follows in the next line.

PART 3

Chance Encounter on the Street

New Characters and Words

Study the six characters below and the common words written with them, paying careful attention to each character's pronunciation, meaning, and structure, as well as similar-looking characters. After you've studied a character, turn to the *Practice Essentials* volume and practice writing it on the practice sheet, making sure to follow the correct stroke order and direction as you pronounce it out loud and think of its meaning.

61 老 **lǎo** old

老 is itself a radical. 老 can also serve as a phonetic, e.g., in 姥 **lǎo** as in 姥姥 **lǎolao** "maternal grandmother." The character 老 was originally a picture of an "old" man with a walking stick. Contrast 老 and 去 **qù** (53).

老	**Lǎo**	Lao, Lau [**SN**]
老	**lǎo**	be old [**SV**]
老王	**Lǎo Wáng**	Old Wang

62 高 **gāo** tall, high

高 is itself a radical. 高 can also serve as a phonetic in other characters, e.g., in 膏 **gāo** as in 牙膏 **yágāo** "toothpaste," 搞 **gǎo** "do, make," and 稿 **gǎo** as in 稿子 **gǎozi** "manuscript." As a mnemonic, think of the character 高 as depicting a "tall" pavilion or tower.

高	**gāo**	be tall, high [**SV**]
高	**Gāo**	Gao, Kao (also Go, Ko, or Koh, a common Korean surname) [**SN**]
老高	**Lǎo Gāo**	Old Gao

63 不 **bù** not

Radical is 一 **yī** (1). This character can be explained as showing the sky (represented by 一) and a bird flying up to it but "not" being able to get there. In handwriting, the first two strokes of this character are often connected. Contrast 不 and 上 **shàng** (25).

不	**bù**	not [A]
不忙	**bù máng**	not busy
不高	**bù gāo**	not tall

64 太 **tài** excessively

Radical is 大 **dà** (13). 太 is itself a phonetic, e.g., in 钛（鈦）**tài** "titanium," 态（態）as in 态度（態度）**tàidu** "attitude," and 汰 as in 淘汰 **táotài** "eliminate." The character 太 is formed by adding a stroke under the character 大, which itself already means "big," and so 太 has the meaning "excessively" or "too" something. Contrast 太 with 人 **rén** (30), 大 **dà** (13), and 不 **bù** (63).

太	**tài**	excessively, too [A]
太忙	**tài máng**	too busy
不太高	**bú tài gāo**	not too tall

65 难（難） **nán** difficult

Radical is 隹 **zhuī** "short-tailed bird" [BF]. The whole character can serve as a phonetic, e.g., in 摊（攤）as in 摊子（攤子）**tānzi** "vendor's stall" or in 滩（灘）as in 海滩（海灘）**hǎitān** "beach."

难（難）	**nán**	be difficult, hard [SV]

66 谢（謝） **xiè** thank

Radical is 讠（言）**yán** "speech" [BF]. The colloquial name for this radical is 言字旁 **yánzìpáng** "side made up of the character 言." The rest of 谢（謝）consists of the character 射 **shè** "shoot forth," which is here also the phonetic. The idea is that "words" of "thanks" are "shooting forth" from the mouth of the person saying them.

谢（謝）	**Xiè**	Xie, Hsieh [SN]
谢谢（謝謝）	**xièxie**	"thank you" [IE]

New Words in BSC 1-3 Written with Characters You Already Know

小	**xiǎo**	be small, little, young [SV]
何	**Hé**	He, Ho [SN]
小何	**Xiǎo Hé**	Little He
中文	**Zhōngwén**	Chinese language [N]

Reading Exercises (Simplified Characters)

Now practice reading the new characters and words for this lesson in context in sentences, conversations, and narratives. Be sure to refer to the Notes at the end of this lesson, and make use of the accompanying audio disc to hear and practice correct pronunciation, phrasing, and intonation.

A. SENTENCES

Read out loud each of the following sentences, which include all the new characters of this lesson. The first time you read a sentence, focus special attention on the characters and words that are new to you, reminding yourself of their pronunciation and meaning. The second time, aim to comprehend the overall meaning of the sentence.

一、老高，谢谢！小何，谢谢！
二、林文生很高吗？
三、小何很高，你也很高。
四、林一明，香山好不好？去香山难不难？
五、你不去台湾吗？我也不去台湾。
六、她们太忙，她们不去。你呢？你去不去？
七、她很老，她们都很老。
八、小明太小吗？他不小！
九、中文难不难？
十、王大海不太忙。

B. CONVERSATIONS

Read out loud the following conversations, including the name or role of the person speaking. If possible, find a partner or partners and each of you play a role. Then switch roles, so you get practice reading all of the lines.

一、
小高：老李！
老李：小高！你忙不忙？
小高：不忙，不忙。你呢？
老李：我也不太忙。

二、
小何：老王，你好！
老王：小何，你好！
小何：你忙不忙？

老王：我很忙。
小何：你去不去北京？
老王：我太忙，不去。你去不去？
小何：我也不去。

三、
王大山：林京生！
林京生：王大山！
王大山：你好吗？
林京生：我很好，谢谢！你呢？
王大山：我很忙。我去西安，你去不去？
林京生：我也去西安。去西安难不难？
王大山：去西安不太难。
林京生：很好，很好。

C. CHARACTER DIFFERENTIATION DRILLS

Distinguish carefully the following similar-looking characters, pronouncing each one out loud and thinking of its meaning.

一、老 老 老 去 去 去
二、老 去 去 老 去 老 老
三、太 太 太 大 大 大
四、太 太 太 人 人 人
五、太 大 人 太 大 大 太 人

D. NARRATIVES

Read the following narratives, paying special attention to punctuation and overall structure. The first time you read a narrative, read it out loud; the second time, read silently and try to gradually increase your reading speed. Always think of the meaning of what you're reading.

一、小金，去天津街难不难？不太难吗？好。去上海路难不难？很难吗？好，我去天津街，不去上海路。小金，你很好，谢谢！

二、北京人很高吗？北京人很高。山东人呢？山东人也很高。上海人高不高？上海人不太高。广东人、台湾人呢？广东人、台湾人也都不太高。

Reading Exercises (Traditional Characters)

A. SENTENCES

Read out loud each of the following sentences, which include all the new characters of this lesson. The first time you read a sentence, focus special attention on the characters and words that are new to you, reminding yourself of their pronunciation and meaning. The second time, aim to comprehend the overall meaning of the sentence.

一、老高，謝謝！小何，謝謝！

二、林文生很高嗎？

三、小何很高，你也很高。

四、林一明，香山好不好？去香山難不難？

五、你不去台灣嗎？我也不去台灣。

六、她們太忙，她們不去。你呢？你去不去？

七、她很老，她們都很老。

八、小明太小嗎？他不小！

九、中文難不難？

十、王大海不太忙。

B. CONVERSATIONS

Read out loud the following conversations, including the name or role of the person speaking. If possible, find a partner or partners and each of you play a role. Then switch roles, so you get practice reading all of the lines.

一、

小高：老李！

老李：小高！你忙不忙？

小高：不忙，不忙。你呢？

老李：我也不太忙。

二、

小何：老王，你好！

老王：小何，你好！

小何：你忙不忙？

老王：我很忙。

小何：你去不去北京？

老王：我太忙，不去。你去不去？

小何：我也不去。

三、

王大山：林京生！

林京生：王大山！

王大山：你好嗎？

林京生：我很好，謝謝！你呢？

王大山：我很忙。我去西安，你去不去？

林京生：我也去西安。去西安難不難？

王大山：去西安不太難。

林京生：很好，很好。

C. CHARACTER DIFFERENTIATION DRILLS

Distinguish carefully the following similar-looking characters, pronouncing each one out loud and thinking of its meaning.

一、老老老去去去

二、老去去老去老老

三、太太太大大大

四、太太太人人人

五、太大人太大大太人

D. NARRATIVES

Read the following narratives, paying special attention to punctuation and overall structure. The first time you read a narrative, read it out loud; the second time, read silently and try to gradually increase your reading speed. Always think of the meaning of what you're reading.

一、小金，去天津街難不難？不太難嗎？好。去上海路難不難？很難嗎？好，我去天津街，不去上海路。小金，你很好，謝謝！

二、北京人很高嗎？北京人很高。山東人呢？山東人也很高。上海人高不高？上海人不太高。廣東人、台灣人呢？廣東人、台灣人也都不太高。

Notes

A10. The expression 不太好 here means "is not doing very well."

B3. Note that the first two lines of this conversation consist of nothing other than each speaker's name: 林京生！王大山！ Calling out someone's name in this manner is a common type of informal greeting.

D1. This description of the relative heights of Chinese people from different regions is greatly simplified due to vocabulary limitations.

PART 4

Visiting an Acquaintance at Her Home

谢太太，请坐，请坐。
(謝太太，請坐，請坐。)
谢谢，谢谢！
(謝謝，謝謝！)

New Characters and Words

Study the six characters below and the common words written with them, paying careful attention to each character's pronunciation, meaning, and structure, as well as similar-looking characters. After you've studied a character, turn to the *Practice Essentials* volume and practice writing it on the practice sheet, making sure to follow the correct stroke order and direction as you pronounce it out loud and think of its meaning.

67 请(請) **qǐng** invite; "please"

Radical is 讠(言) **yán** "speech" [BF]. The colloquial name for this radical is 言字旁 **yánzìpáng** "side made up of the character 言." Phonetic is 青 **qīng** "green." Note the connection between the meaning of the radical 讠(言) **yán** "speech" and the basic meaning of the whole character 请(請): When you "invite" someone to do something, you usually do so by "speaking." Also, note the connection between the primary meaning "invite" and the extended meaning "please": when you politely ask someone to "please" do something, you are, in a manner of speaking, "inviting" them to do something.

请(請)	**qǐng**	"please" [IE]

---

68 坐 **zuò** sit

Radical is 土 **tǔ** "earth." The colloquial name for this radical is 土字底 **tǔzìdǐ** "bottom made up of the character 土." Notice that the top horizontal line of 土 is shorter than the bottom line. 坐 is a picture of two "people" (人) "sitting" on the "earth" (土). Contrast 坐 with 生 **shēng** (22) and 上 **shàng** (25).

坐	**zuò**	sit [V]
请坐(請坐)	**qǐng zuò**	"please sit down" [IE]

69 先 **xiān** first

Radical is 儿 **ér**, which is the simplified character for "son" [BF]. Contrast 先 with 去 **qù** (53) and 老 **lǎo** (61).

先	**xiān**	first, before someone else [A]
先生	**xiānsheng**	Mr. (as a title; lit. "first born") [N]

70 走 **zǒu** leave, depart

The character 走 **zǒu** "walk" is itself a radical. The colloquial name for this radical is 走字旁 **zǒuzìpáng** "side made up of the character 走." Note that when 走 serves as the radical in another character, its last stroke is lengthened, with the component on the right side placed above the last stroke of 走 (e.g., 起 **qǐ** "rise"). Contrast 走 with 去 **qù** (53), 老 **lǎo** (61), and 先 **xiān** (69).

走	**zǒu**	leave, depart [V]

71 了 **le** (indicates changed status or situation)

Radical is 亅 **jué** "vertical hook." (However, in some dictionaries of simplified characters, 了 is arranged under the radical 乙 **yǐ** "second of the ten Celestial Stems").

了	**le**	(indicates changed status or situation) [P]
我走了。	**Wǒ zǒule.**	"I'll be leaving now."
先走了。	**Xiān zǒule.**	"I'll be leaving now (first, before you)."
她不去了。	**Tā bú qùle.**	"She's no longer going."
他好了吗？(他好了嗎？)	**Tā hǎole ma?**	"Is he well now?"

72 姐 **jiě** older sister

Radical is 女 **nǚ** "woman" [BF]. This radical is referred to colloquially as 女字旁 **nǚzìpáng** "side made up of the character 女." Note that when 女 is written at the left of a character as a radical, its last stroke is shortened so that it doesn't collide with the component to its right. Phonetic is 且 **qiě** as in 而且 **érqiě** "moreover."

小姐	**xiáojie**	Miss, Ms. (as a title) [N]

New Words in BSC 1-4 Written with Characters You Already Know

我们 (我們)	**wǒmen**	we, us [PR]
你们 (你們)	**nǐmen**	you (plural) [PR]
谢谢 (謝謝)	**xièxie**	thank [V]
太太	**tàitai**	Mrs. (as a title) [N]
李	**Lǐ**	Li [SN]
林	**Lín**	Lin [SN]
谢 (謝)	**Xiè**	Xie, Hsieh [SN]

Reading Exercises (Simplified Characters)

Now practice reading the new characters and words for this lesson in context in sentences, conversations, and narratives. Be sure to refer to the Notes at the end of this lesson, and make use of the accompanying audio disc to hear and practice correct pronunciation, phrasing, and intonation.

A. SENTENCES

Read out loud each of the following sentences, which include all the new characters of this lesson. The first time you read a sentence, focus special attention on the characters and words that are new to you, reminding yourself of their pronunciation and meaning. The second time, aim to comprehend the overall meaning of the sentence.

一、王先生、王太太，你们好！请坐，请坐。
二、我好了，他也好了，你也好了吗？
三、我老了，你们也老了，我们都老了！
四、安小姐太忙了，她不去了。
五、李小姐、金小姐她们都去台湾了。
六、文小姐，你不坐吗？
七、我谢谢你，我也谢谢他。
八、何小姐很忙，她先走了。你不太忙，你先请坐。
九、老李，我请你去香港，好不好？
十、我们不去东京了。王大海，你呢？你去不去东京？

B. CONVERSATIONS

Read out loud the following conversations, including the name or role of the person speaking. If possible, find a partner or partners and each of you play a role. Then switch roles, so you get practice reading all of the lines.

一、
谢大文：何大海，你好吗？请坐，请坐。
何大海：谢大文，你好！谢谢！
谢大文：何大海，我们都老了……
何大海：你老，我不老！

二、
王先生：林小姐，你好！
林小姐：王先生，你好！
王先生：林小姐，你忙吗？请坐，请坐。
林小姐：王先生，谢谢你，我不坐了。我很忙，我先走了。

C. CHARACTER DIFFERENTIATION DRILLS

Distinguish carefully the following similar-looking characters, pronouncing each one out loud and thinking of its meaning.

一、走 走 走 先 先 先
二、走 走 走 去 去 去
三、走 走 走 老 老 老
四、先 先 先 去 去 去
五、先 先 先 老 老 老
六、走 先 老 去 走 老 去 先

D. NARRATIVES

Read the following narratives, paying special attention to punctuation and overall structure. The first time you read a narrative, read it out loud; the second time, read silently and try to gradually increase your reading speed. Always think of the meaning of what you're reading.

一、王太太很忙。她去北京、天津、上海、香港、台北，也去东京。她太忙了！请她坐很难。王先生不太忙。请王先生坐不难。

二、何先生、林太太、谢小姐，你们好！请坐，请坐！你们去西安吗？太忙了，不去了吗？我也很忙，我也不去西安了。

Reading Exercises (Traditional Characters)

A. SENTENCES

Read out loud each of the following sentences, which include all the new characters of this lesson. The first time you read a sentence, focus special attention on the characters and words that are new to you, reminding yourself of their pronunciation and meaning. The second time, aim to comprehend the overall meaning of the sentence.

一、王先生、王太太，你們好！請坐，請坐。

二、我好了，他也好了，你也好了嗎？

三、我老了，你們也老了，我們都老了！

四、安小姐太忙了，她不去了。

五、李小姐、金小姐她們都去台灣了。

六、文小姐，你不坐嗎？

七、我謝謝你，我也謝謝他。

八、何小姐很忙，她先走了。你不太忙，你先請坐。

九、老李，我請你去香港，好不好？

十、我們不去東京了。王大海，你呢？你去不去東京？

B. CONVERSATIONS

Read out loud the following conversations, including the name or role of the person speaking. If possible, find a partner or partners and each of you play a role. Then switch roles, so you get practice reading all of the lines.

一、謝大文：何大海，你好嗎？請坐，請坐。
何大海：謝大文，你好！謝謝！
謝大文：何大海，我們都老了……
何大海：你老，我不老！

二、王先生：林小姐，你好！
林小姐：王先生，你好！
王先生：林小姐，你忙嗎？請坐，請坐。
林小姐：王先生，謝謝你，我不坐了。我很忙，我先走了。

C. CHARACTER DIFFERENTIATION DRILLS

Distinguish carefully the following similar-looking characters, pronouncing each one out loud and thinking of its meaning.

一、走走走先先先
二、走走走去去去
三、走走走老老老
四、先先先去去去
五、先先先老老老
六、走先老去走老去先

D. NARRATIVES

Read the following narratives, paying special attention to punctuation and overall structure. The first time you read a narrative, read it out loud; the second time, read silently and try to gradually increase your reading speed. Always think of the meaning of what you're reading.

一、王太太很忙。她去北京、天津、上海、香港、台北，也去東京。她太忙了！請她坐很難。王先生不太忙。請王先生坐不難。

二、何先生、林太太、謝小姐，你們好！請坐，請坐！你們去西安嗎？太忙了，不去了嗎？我也很忙，我也不去西安了。

Notes

A8. The phrase 你先请坐 (你先請坐) here means something like "you first please sit down (for a while, before you do the other things you need to do)."

A9. In the clause 我请你去香港 (我請你去香港) "I invite you to go to Hong Kong," the verb 请 (請) is used in its basic sense of "invite."

B1. In the third line of this dialog, …… is a Chinese punctuation mark called 省略号 (省略號) **shěnglüèhào**. In English this can be called an "ellipsis mark." This punctuation mark indicates that a sentence has suddenly been cut off or that some part has been omitted. Presumably, in this line, the person speaking—who had just said "We've both gotten old"—was going to say something like "Soon we're going to die" but decided at the last minute it would be better to omit this (since in traditional Chinese culture, it's considered very inauspicious to talk about death).

D1. As we saw in note A9 above, besides meaning "please," 请 (請) can also be used in its basic sense of "invite." This is how the two 请 (請) in this first narrative are used. So 请她坐很难 (請她坐很難) could be translated as "To invite her to sit is hard" and 请王先生坐不难 (請王先生坐不難) could be translated as "To invite Mr. Wang to sit is not hard." Actually, in idiomatic English, we could also translate this kind of 请 (請) as "ask" (e.g., "To ask her to sit is hard."), but it's important to distinguish this kind of "ask" that involves an invitation or request from English "ask" as in "ask a question," for which a completely different Chinese verb is used.

D2. Note that in the question 太忙了，不去了吗？(太忙了，不去了嗎？), the understood but deleted subject is 你们 (你們) "you (all)." So this question could be translated as "Are you all too busy and no longer going?" In Chinese, when a subject or topic is clear from the context (and in this case the subject is clear, since it was mentioned in the first sentence of the paragraph), it is often omitted later in the discourse.

UNIT 2

Introductions

COMMUNICATIVE OBJECTIVES

Once you've mastered this unit, you'll be able to use Chinese to read and write:

1. The names of different countries and regions: China, America, Guizhou, Hong Kong, Taiwan.
2. Different nationalities and ethnic origins: American, Chinese, Taiwanese.
3. Questions and responses about where someone is from.
4. Questions and responses about what someone's last name, first name, and full name are.
5. Questions and responses about whether something is a certain way or not.
6. Sentences that express suppositions: "I would suppose that...," "They must not be...."
7. Sentences involving the terms for "both," "all," "not all," and "none."
8. Sentences involving possession: "my," "your," "her," "his," "our," "their," etc.
9. Sentences that express negative past actions: "didn't go," "didn't bring," etc.
10. Negative imperative sentences that request that people not do something: "Don't...."
11. Polite ways to express "you" and ask what someone's last name is.

PART 1

Asking About Name and Nationality

New Characters and Words

Study the six characters below and the common words written with them, paying careful attention to each character's pronunciation, meaning, and structure, as well as similar-looking characters. After you've studied a character, turn to the *Practice Essentials* volume and practice writing it on the practice sheet, making sure to follow the correct stroke order and direction as you pronounce it out loud and think of its meaning.

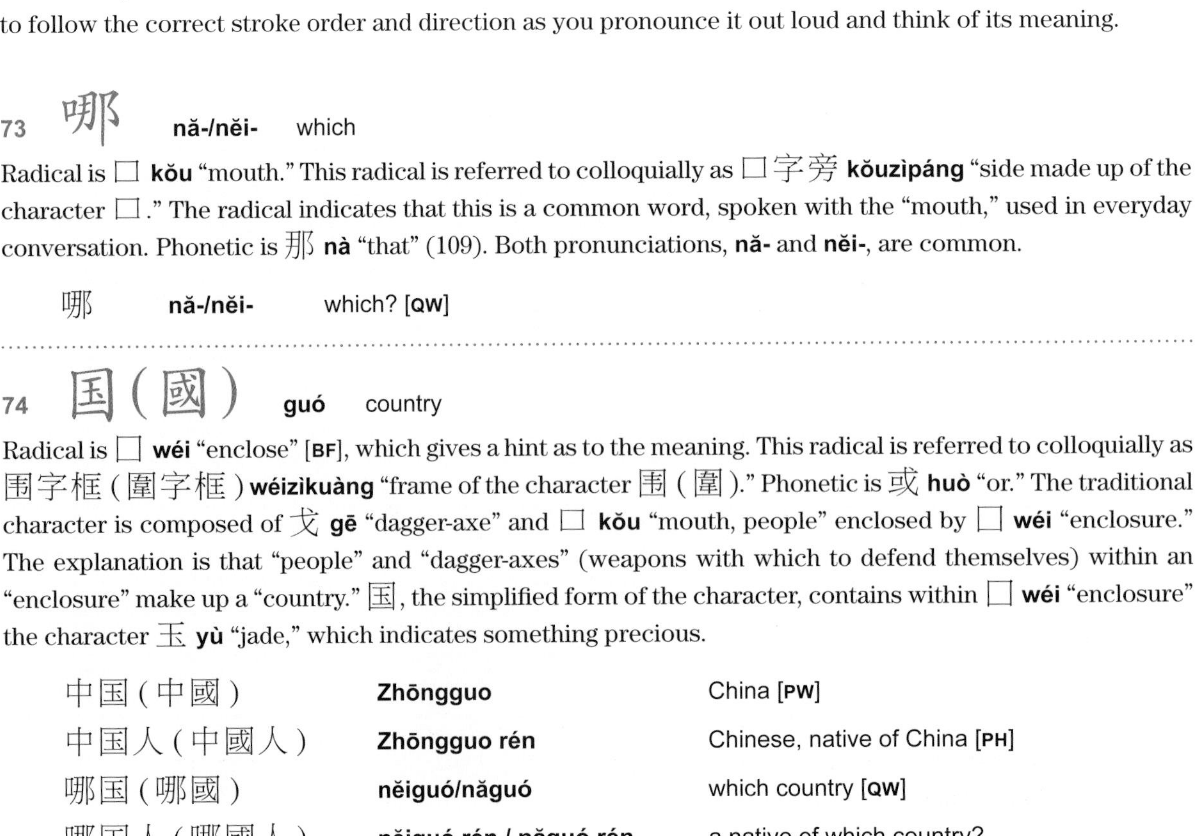

73 哪 **nǎ-/něi-** which

Radical is 口 **kǒu** "mouth." This radical is referred to colloquially as 口字旁 **kǒuzìpáng** "side made up of the character 口." The radical indicates that this is a common word, spoken with the "mouth," used in everyday conversation. Phonetic is 那 **nà** "that" (109). Both pronunciations, **nǎ-** and **něi-**, are common.

哪	**nǎ-/něi-**	which? [QW]

74 国(國) **guó** country

Radical is 囗 **wéi** "enclose" [BF], which gives a hint as to the meaning. This radical is referred to colloquially as 围字框(圍字框) **wéizìkuàng** "frame of the character 围(圍)." Phonetic is 或 **huò** "or." The traditional character is composed of 戈 **gē** "dagger-axe" and 口 **kǒu** "mouth, people" enclosed by 囗 **wéi** "enclosure." The explanation is that "people" and "dagger-axes" (weapons with which to defend themselves) within an "enclosure" make up a "country." 国, the simplified form of the character, contains within 囗 **wéi** "enclosure" the character 玉 **yù** "jade," which indicates something precious.

中国(中國)	**Zhōngguo**	China [PW]
中国人(中國人)	**Zhōngguo rén**	Chinese, native of China [PH]
哪国(哪國)	**něiguó/nǎguó**	which country [QW]
哪国人(哪國人)	**něiguó rén / nǎguó rén**	a native of which country?

75 问(問) **wèn** ask

Radical is 口 **kǒu** "mouth." This radical is referred to colloquially as 口字旁 **kǒuzìpáng** "side made up of the character 口." Phonetic is 门 (門) **mén** "door" (123). Put your head in the "door" way and, with your "mouth," "ask" a question.

问(問)	**wèn**	ask [V]
请问(請問)	**qǐng wèn**	"excuse me," "may I ask" [IE]
请你问她。(請你問她。)	**Qǐng nǐ wèn tā.**	Please ask her.

76 是 **shì** be

Radical is 日 **rì** "sun" [BF] (132). Contrast 是 with 去 **qù** (53), 老 **lǎo** (61), 先 **xiān** (69), and 走 **zǒu** (70).

是	**shì**	be, is, are, was, were, would be [EV]
不是	**bú shi**	is not, are not
是不是	**shì bu shi**	is it or is it not

77 美 **měi** beautiful

Radical is 羊 **yáng** "sheep." The other component is 大 **dà** (13). The idea is that a "big" "sheep" is "beautiful." The character 美 is used to refer to America because of the similarity in its pronunciation to the sound "me" in "America" and because of the positive meaning "beautiful."

美国(美國)	**Měiguo**	America [PW]
美国人(美國人)	**Měiguo rén**	American, native of America [PH]

78 叫 **jiào** call, be called

Radical is 口 **kǒu** "mouth." This radical is referred to colloquially as 口字旁 **kǒuzìpáng** "side made up of the character 口." This radical gives an indication of the meaning, since one "calls" with one's "mouth." In handwriting, this character is occasionally written as 呌.

叫	**jiào**	be called or named [EV]

New Words in BSC 2-1 Written with Characters You Already Know

人	**rén**	person [N]
不都	**bù dōu**	not all [PT]
都不	**dōu bù**	all not, none [PT]
台湾 (台灣)	**Táiwān**	Taiwan [PW]

Reading Exercises (Simplified Characters)

Now practice reading the new characters and words for this lesson in context in sentences, conversations, and narratives. Be sure to refer to the Notes at the end of this lesson, and make use of the accompanying audio disc to hear and practice correct pronunciation, phrasing, and intonation.

A. SENTENCES

Read out loud each of the following sentences, which include all the new characters of this lesson. The first time you read a sentence, focus special attention on the characters and words that are new to you, reminding yourself of their pronunciation and meaning. The second time, aim to comprehend the overall meaning of the sentence.

一、你是你，我是我。
二、请问，李先生，你是哪国人？
三、李先生、林太太、谢小姐都不是中国人。
四、你叫林国文，是不是？请问，你去哪国？
五、我叫金山，他叫李文。
六、你叫李台生吗？你是台湾人吗？
七、我们都是美国人。你呢？你也是美国人吗？
八、请问，老高、小何他们都是北京人吗？
九、我们不都是美国人。小高是，我不是。
十、王大海是美国人，也是中国人。

B. CONVERSATIONS

Read out loud the following conversations, including the name or role of the person speaking. If possible, find a partner or partners and each of you play a role. Then switch roles, so you get practice reading all of the lines.

一、

李文　：你是哪国人？
王台生：我是中国人。
李文　：你们都是中国人吗？
王台生：我们不都是中国人。他是美国人。

二、

中国人：你好！你是哪国人？
美国人：我是美国人。你呢？
中国人：我是中国人。你是不是叫王国先？
美国人：不是。他叫王国先。我叫何高文。

三、
中国人：请问，他们都是河北人吗？
美国人：湖北人？他们都不是湖北人。
中国人：不是"湖北"，是"河北"！他们都是河北人吗？
美国人：他们不都是河北人。小高、小李是河北人，小林、小王是河南人。

C. CHARACTER DIFFERENTIATION DRILLS

Distinguish carefully the following similar-looking characters, pronouncing each one out loud and thinking of its meaning.

一、是 是 是 走 走 走
二、是 是 是 先 先 先
三、是 是 是 老 老 老
四、是 是 是 去 去 去
五、是 走 先 是 老 去 是

D. NARRATIVES

Read the following narratives, paying special attention to punctuation and overall structure. The first time you read a narrative, read it out loud; the second time, read silently and try to gradually increase your reading speed. Always think of the meaning of what you're reading.

一、王先生、王太太都是中国人。王先生叫王大明，他是山西人。王太太叫李小文，她是广东人。王先生、王太太都很忙。何文生先生是美国人，他请王先生、王太太去香港，他们不去。"何先生，我们太忙了。"他请他们去东京，他们也不去。"何先生，谢谢你，我们太忙，太忙了！"。

二、金小姐、谢小姐、林小姐她们不都是美国人，也不都是中国人。金小姐是美国人，谢小姐、林小姐是中国人。你呢？你是哪国人？

Reading Exercises (Traditional Characters)

A. SENTENCES

Read out loud each of the following sentences, which include all the new characters of this lesson. The first time you read a sentence, focus special attention on the characters and words that are new to you, reminding yourself of their pronunciation and meaning. The second time, aim to comprehend the overall meaning of the sentence.

一、你是你，我是我。

二、請問，李先生，你是哪國人？

三、李先生、林太太、謝小姐都不是中國人。

四、你叫林國文，是不是？請問，你去哪國？

五、我叫金山，他叫李文。

六、你叫李台生嗎？你是台灣人嗎？

七、我們都是美國人。你呢？你也是美國人嗎？

八、請問，老高、小何他們都是北京人嗎？

九、我們不都是美國人。小高是，我不是。

十、王大海是美國人，也是中國人。

The Pinyin for some of the characters is incorrect and reflects Kunming dialect

B. CONVERSATIONS

Read out loud the following conversations, including the name or role of the person speaking. If possible, find a partner or partners and each of you play a role. Then switch roles, so you get practice reading all of the lines.

一、
李文　：你是哪國人？
王台生：我是中國人。
李文　：你們都是中國人嗎？
王台生：我們不都是中國人。他是美國人。

二、
中國人：你好！你是哪國人？
美國人：我是美國人。你呢？
中國人：我是中國人。你是不是叫王國先？
美國人：不是。他叫王國先。我叫何高文。

三、
中國人：請問，他們都是河北人嗎？
美國人：湖北人？他們都不是湖北人。
中國人：不是「湖北」，是「河北」！他們都是河北人嗎？
美國人：他們不都是河北人。小高、小李是河北人，小林、小王是河南人。

C. CHARACTER DIFFERENTIATION DRILLS

Distinguish carefully the following similar-looking characters, pronouncing each one out loud and thinking of its meaning.

一、是是是走走走

二、是是是先先先

三、是是是老老老

四、是是是去去去

五、是走先是老去是

D. NARRATIVES

Read the following narratives, paying special attention to punctuation and overall structure. The first time you read a narrative, read it out loud; the second time, read silently and try to gradually increase your reading speed. Always think of the meaning of what you're reading.

一、王先生、王太太都是中國人。王先生叫王大明，他是山西人。王太太叫李小文，她是廣東人。王先生、王太太都很忙。何文生先生是美國人，他請王先生、王太太去香港，他們不去。「何先生，我們太忙了。」他請他們去東京，他們也不去。「何先生，謝謝你，我們太忙，太忙了！」

二、金小姐、謝小姐、林小姐她們不都是美國人，也不都是中國人。金小姐是美國人，謝小姐、林小姐是中國人。你呢？你是哪國人？

Notes

A2. **CHARACTERS WITH ALTERNATE PRONUNCIATIONS.** As you know, some English words have alternate pronunciations; for example, the word "aunt" can be pronounced so it rhymes with the name of the insect the "ant" or so it rhymes with the verb "want." Similarly, some Chinese words and the characters with which they are written have alternate pronunciations. Your first example of this is the character 哪, which can be pronounced either **nǎ-** or **něi-**. So the expression 哪国人 (哪國人) "a person from which country?" can be pronounced either **nǎguó rén** or **něiguó rén**.

A10. In this sentence, consider the pronunciation of 美国人 (美國人) and 中国人 (中國人). In normal conversation, northern Chinese speakers would pronounce these two expressions as **Měiguo rén** and **Zhōngguo rén**, with a neutral tone on 国 (國). However, you should be aware that when reading Chinese text out loud—especially when they read slowly, Chinese people tend to give a full tone to many characters that in speech would have a neutral tone. Therefore, many Chinese readers would pronounce these two expressions as **Měiguó rén** and **Zhōngguó rén**. This is because readers are looking at the individual characters and, quite literally, have the pronunciations of the individual characters in mind. Because of this tendency to try to pronounce a character with its full tone, some readers will even pronounce a word like 他们 (他們) **tāmen** as nonexistent **tāmén**, probably because of the visual influence of the phonetic 门 (門), which is indeed pronounced **mén**. What should you do? In the case of 美国人 (美國人) and 中国人 (中國人), either pronunciation is correct. The best advice is to imitate your teacher's pronunciation or the pronunciation on the accompanying recordings.

B2. Note the question 你是不是叫王国先？(你是不是叫王國先？) This literally means "(As regards) you, is (it the case or) not is (it the case that you) are called Wang Guoxian?" A smoother English translation would be "Is your name Wang Guoxian?" 是不是 is often used in this way to create questions.

B3. In line 3 of this dialog, notice the quotation marks around the quoted place names 湖北 and 河北. In Chinese, quotation marks are called 引号 (引號) **yǐnhào**. In horizontal text written in simplified characters, quotation marks look like this: " ". In vertical text written in traditional characters, quotation marks look like this: ﹂ ﹁. In horizontal text written in traditional characters, quotation marks look like this: 「 」. Chinese quotation marks are used much as in English.

D1. In this narrative, 请 (請) has the meaning "invite" or "ask" (not "please").

D2. Always be sensitive to the difference between the Chinese enumerative comma 顿号 (頓號) **dùnhào** (、) and the Chinese regular comma 逗号 (逗號) **dòuhào** (，). For example, the meaning of the first clause in this narrative would be very different if a **dòuhào** had been used instead of a **dùnhào**. Compare:

金小姐、谢小姐、林小姐她们不都是美国人 (金小姐、謝小姐、林小姐她們不都是美國人)
"Ms. Jin, Ms. Xie, and Ms. Lin are not all Americans..." (meaning not all three of them are Americans)

金小姐，谢小姐、林小姐她们不都是美国人 (金小姐，謝小姐、林小姐她們不都是美國人)
"Ms. Jin, Ms. Xie and Ms. Lin are not both Americans..." (meaning that the speaker of this sentence is telling a certain Ms. Jin that Ms. Xie and Ms. Lin are not both Americans)

PART 2

Introducing a Roommate

New Characters and Words

Study the six characters below and the common words written with them, paying careful attention to each character's pronunciation, meaning, and structure, as well as similar-looking characters. After you've studied a character, turn to the *Practice Essentials* volume and practice writing it on the practice sheet, making sure to follow the correct stroke order and direction as you pronounce it out loud and think of its meaning.

79 的 **-de** (indicates possession)

Radical is 白 **bái** "white." The other component is 勺 **sháo** "spoon."

的	**-de**	(indicates possession) [**P**]
我的名字	**wǒde míngzi**	my name
她的同屋	**tāde tóngwū**	her roommate

80 同 **tóng** same

Radical is 口 **kǒu** "mouth." The other components are 一 **yī** and 冂 **jiōng** "wide." Perhaps this mnemonic will help you remember the character 同: "one" and the "same" "person" (represented by his/her 口 "mouth") in a "wide" space. 同 is itself a phonetic in 铜 (銅) **tóng** "copper," 筒 **tǒng** as in 筒子 **tǒngzi** "tube", and 洞 **dòng** "hole." Contrast 同 with 问 (問) **wèn** (75) and 国 (國) **guó** (74).

81 屋 **wū** room

Radical is 尸 **shī** "corpse" [**BF**]. The other element is 至 **zhì** "arrive" [**BF**]. Here's a macabre explanation of 屋 that you'll be sure to remember: the "corpse" "arrives" in the "room."

同屋	**tóngwū**	roommate [**N**]

82 别(別) **bié** don't

Radical is 刀 **dāo** "knife," which is written 刂 when occurring at the right-hand side of a character. This radical is referred to colloquially as 立刀 **lìdāo** "standing knife." The other component of the simplified character is 另 **lìng** "another." Notice the small difference and (on the character practice sheets in *Practice Essentials*) the different stroke order between the simplified and traditional characters for this word; however, many native writers of Chinese don't pay attention to such details.

别(別) **bié** don't [AV]

83 名 **míng** name

Radical is 口 **kǒu** "mouth." This radical is referred to colloquially as 口字底 **kǒuzìdǐ** "bottom made up of the character 口." The other part is 夕 **xī** "evening" [BF]. The idea is that in the "evening," everyone should call out (with their "mouths") their "names," so that others might know who approaches.

84 字 **zì** Chinese character

Radical is 宀 **mián** "roof" [BF]. This radical is referred to colloquially as 宝盖头(寶蓋頭) **bǎogàitóu** "top made up of a canopy." Phonetic is 子 **zǐ** "son" [BF]. To the ancient Chinese, "characters" were as precious as a "son" under a "roof."

名字 **míngzi** name [N]

New Words in BSC 2-2 Written with Characters You Already Know

好 **hǎo** "all right," "O.K." [IE]
叫 **jiào** call someone a name [V]

Reading Exercises (Simplified Characters)

Now practice reading the new characters and words for this lesson in context. Be sure to refer to the Notes at the end of this lesson, and make use of the accompanying audio disc to hear and practice correct pronunciation, phrasing, and intonation.

A. SENTENCES

Read out loud each of the following sentences, which include all the new characters of this lesson. The first time you read a sentence, focus special attention on the characters and words that are new to you, reminding yourself of their pronunciation and meaning. The second time, aim to comprehend the overall meaning of the sentence.

一、请问，你同屋的名字是不是林小明？

二、我的同屋是中国人，老谢的同屋是美国人，你的同屋是哪国人？

三、金小姐、谢小姐是同屋，我的同屋是林大一，你的同屋是……？

四、金山街很难去，别去了，我们去南京东路好了。
五、她叫金香川。她的名字很难叫！
六、老林，你别走，你先请坐。
七、请你别叫我王先生，叫我京生好了。
八、你别去台北。谢小姐、李小姐她们都很忙。
九、台湾是不是中国的一个省？
十、“王大海”是中国人的名字吗？

B. CONVERSATIONS

Read out loud the following conversations, including the name or role of the person speaking. If possible, find a partner or partners and each of you play a role. Then switch roles, so you get practice reading all of the lines.

一、
小高：你好！我叫高大明。
小文：你好！我叫文中。
小高：你是我的同屋吗？
小文：是，我们是同屋。

二、
金先生：王先生，你好！
王先生：别叫我王先生，叫我小王好了。
金先生：好，小王。你的名字是不是叫王明？
王先生：不是，我的名字叫王太中。

三、
李大山：你好！我叫李大山。你的名字是……？
林京生：我叫林京生，你叫我小林好了。
李大山：小林，你是哪国人？
林京生：我是中国人，你呢？
李大山：我是美国人。

C. CHARACTER DIFFERENTIATION DRILLS

Distinguish carefully the following similar-looking characters, pronouncing each one out loud and thinking of its meaning.

一、同 同 同 问 问 问
二、同 同 同 国 国 国
三、同 问 国 同 国 同 问

D. NARRATIVES

Read the following narratives, paying special attention to punctuation and overall structure. The first time you read a narrative, read it out loud; the second time, read silently and try to gradually increase your reading speed. Always think of the meaning of what you're reading.

一、我的名字叫李小明，你们叫我小明好了。我是香港人。我的同屋是美国人，很高，名字叫高大山，我们都叫他“老高”。我请我的同屋去广州，他不去，他太忙了。

二、我的名字叫何大海。你们别叫我“何先生”，你们叫我“小何”好了。我是中国人，中国四川省成都市人。

Reading Exercises (Traditional Characters)

A. SENTENCES

Read out loud each of the following sentences, which include all the new characters of this lesson. The first time you read a sentence, focus special attention on the characters and words that are new to you, reminding yourself of their pronunciation and meaning. The second time, aim to comprehend the overall meaning of the sentence.

一、請問，你同屋的名字是不是林小明？

二、我的同屋是中國人，老謝的同屋是美國人，你的同屋是哪國人？

三、金小姐、謝小姐是同屋，我的同屋是林大一，你的同屋是……？

四、金山街很難去，別去了，我們去南京東路好了。

五、她叫金香川。她的名字很難叫！

六、老林，你別走，你先請坐。

七、請你別叫我王先生，叫我京生好了。

八、你別去台北。謝小姐、李小姐她們都很忙。

九、台灣是不是中國的一個省？

十、「王大海」是中國人的名字嗎？

B. CONVERSATIONS

Read out loud the following conversations, including the name or role of the person speaking. If possible, find a partner or partners and each of you play a role. Then switch roles, so you get practice reading all of the lines.

一、小高：你好！我叫高大明。
小文：你好！我叫文中。
小高：你是我的同屋嗎？
小文：是，我們是同屋。

二、金先生：王先生，你好！
王先生：別叫我王先生，叫我小王好了。
金先生：好，小王。你的名字是不是叫王明？
王先生：不是，我的名字叫王太中。

三、李大山：你好！我叫李大山。你的名字是……？
林京生：我叫林京生，你叫我小林好了。
李大山：小林，你是哪國人？
林京生：我是中國人，你呢？
李大山：我是美國人。

C. CHARACTER DIFFERENTIATION DRILLS

Distinguish carefully the following similar-looking characters, pronouncing each one out loud and thinking of its meaning.

一、同同同問問問

二、同同同國國國

三、同問國同國同問

Street scene in Kowloon, Hong Kong

D. NARRATIVES

Read the following narratives, paying special attention to punctuation and overall structure. The first time you read a narrative, read it out loud; the second time, read silently and try to gradually increase your reading speed. Always think of the meaning of what you're reading.

一、我的名字叫李小明，你們叫我小明好了。我是香港人。我的同屋是美國人，很高，名字叫高大山，我們都叫他「老高」。我請我的同屋去廣州，他不去，他太忙了。

二、我的名字叫何大海。你們別叫我「何先生」，你們叫我「小何」好了。我是中國人，中國四川省成都市人。

Notes

A1. In this sentence, look at the phrase 你同屋的名字 "your roommate's name." Normally, to say "your roommate" you would say 你的同屋, so why is this not *你的同屋的名字？The answer is that, in general, Chinese people do not like the "sound" of several 的 in a row, so they usually delete all the 的 except the last one. In other words, we could say the deeper structure of this phrase was originally 你的同屋的名字 but, when it became a surface structure, the first 的 was deleted, so that the phrase became 你同屋的名字.

A3. In 你的同屋是……？, the 省略号 (省略號) **shěnglüèhào** (……) at the end of the sentence indicates an incomplete question. An English translation would be "Your roommate is...?" Incomplete questions like this are often used in Chinese when one doesn't wish to ask too directly ("Who is your roommate?") but still wants, in a more "gentle" manner, to put one's interlocutor into a situation where he or she is almost forced to complete one's sentence. Compare similar usage in B3.

A5. Note how 叫 is used in this sentence. The literal meaning of 她的名字很难叫 (她的名字很難叫) is "Her name is hard to call out." In more idiomatic English, we would say "Her name is hard to say" or "Her name is hard to pronounce." This is because to a native speaker of Mandarin, the syllables 金香川 **Jīn Xiāngchuān** do not sound pleasant when pronounced one right after another (they are all in Tone One and they all end in nasal finals).

A9. Look at this sentence: 台湾是不是中国的一个省？(台灣是不是中國的一個省？) Literally, the sentence means "Taiwan is it or is it not China's a province?" In good English, of course, we would translate this as "Is Taiwan a province of China?"

D1. Pay attention to the construction 不去 in 我请我的同屋去广州，他不去 (我請我的同屋去廣州，他不去). Here, 不去 means "didn't want to go" or "couldn't go." The whole sentence could be translated as "I asked my roommate to go to Guangzhou, but he didn't want to go." (To express past negative "didn't," another word, that we will be taking up in BWC 2-4, would be used.)

PART 3

Inquiring Formally as to Name and Place of Work

您贵姓？
(您貴姓？)
我姓高。
他是您的先生吧？

New Characters and Words

Study the six characters below and the common words written with them, paying careful attention to each character's pronunciation, meaning, and structure, as well as similar-looking characters. After you've studied a character, turn to the *Practice Essentials* volume and practice writing it on the practice sheet, making sure to follow the correct stroke order and direction as you pronounce it out loud and think of its meaning.

85 贵(貴) **guì** precious, expensive, honorable

Radical is 贝(貝) **bèi** "cowry shell" [**BF**], a "precious" commodity which was used for money in ancient China. The traditional form of the character is a phonetic in 柜(櫃) **guì** as in 柜子(櫃子) **guìzi** "cabinet."

贵(貴)	**Guì**	Gui [**SN**]
贵州(貴州)	**Guìzhōu**	Guizhou (province) [**PW**]

86 姓 **xìng** surname, be surnamed

Radical is 女 **nǚ** "woman" [**BF**]. This radical is referred to colloquially as 女字旁 **nǚzìpáng** "side made up of the character 女." Note that when 女 is written at the left of a character as a radical, its last stroke is shortened so that it doesn't collide with the component to its right. Phonetic is 生 **shēng** "be born." The combination of radical and phonetic seems to indicate that, at one period in Chinese history, there was a matriarchal society where children received the "surname" of their mother ("woman") when they were "born."

姓	**xìng**	be surnamed [**SV**]
贵姓(貴姓)	**guìxìng**	"what's your honorable surname?" [**IE**]

87 个(個) **ge** (general measure)

Radical of both the simplified and the traditional forms is 人 **rén** "person," which is called 人字头(人字頭) **rénzìtóu** "top made up of the character 人" when occurring at the top of a character and 人字旁 **rénzìpáng** "side made up of the character 人" when occurring at the left side of a character. Phonetic of the traditional form is 固 **gù** "solid" [BF]. Contrast the simplified form 个 with 不 **bù** (63), 人 **rén** (30), 八 **bā** (9), 大 **dà** (13) and 太 **tài** (64).

个(個)	**ge**	(general measure) [M]
哪个(哪個)	**něige/năge**	which one?, which?

---

88 您 **nín** you (polite)

Radical is 心 **xīn** "heart." This radical is referred to colloquially as 心字底 **xīnzìdǐ** "bottom made up of the character 心." The rest of the character is 你 **nǐ** "you" (49). The idea is that when you say the word 您 you show respect, which comes from the "heart." Contrast 您 with 你 (49). Use of this pronoun always expresses respect. It is usually singular in meaning but can occasionally refer to plural "you."

您	**nín**	you (polite) [PR]

---

89 吧 **ba** (indicates supposition)

Radical is 口 **kǒu** "mouth" [BF]. The radical 口 is referred to colloquially as 口字旁 **kǒuzìpáng** "side made up of the character 口." As we saw before with 呢 **ne** (54) and 吗(嗎) **ma** (60), the addition of the radical 口 to a character indicates it has something to do with the mouth and often indicates it is a particle used in speech. Phonetic is 巴 **Bā**, the name of an ancient state in Sichuan.

吧	**ba**	(indicates supposition) [P]
她是香港人吧?	**Tā shi Xiānggăng rén ba?**	She must be from Hong Kong?

---

90 兴(興) **xìng** interest, excitement

The radical of the simplified form is 八 **bā** (9). The radical of the traditional form is 臼 **jiù** "mortar" [BF].

高兴(高興)	**gāoxìng**	be happy [SV]

New Words in BSC 2-3 Written with Characters You Already Know

一	**yī**	one, a [NU]
先生	**xiānsheng**	husband [N]
太太	**tàitai**	wife [N]
香港	**Xiānggăng**	Hong Kong [PW]

Reading Exercises (Simplified Characters)

Now practice reading the new characters and words for this lesson in context in sentences, conversations, and narratives. Be sure to refer to the Notes at the end of this lesson, and make use of the accompanying audio disc to hear and practice correct pronunciation, phrasing, and intonation.

A. SENTENCES

Read out loud each of the following sentences, which include all the new characters of this lesson. The first time you read a sentence, focus special attention on the characters and words that are new to you, reminding yourself of their pronunciation and meaning. The second time, aim to comprehend the overall meaning of the sentence.

一、小姐，请问，您贵姓？
二、我先生是美国人，他姓高，他的名字叫高明。
三、我姓林，您是不是姓王？
四、谢大明是您先生的名字吧？
五、"王小姐"？哪个王小姐？我们都姓王！
六、哪个人好？哪个人不好？他呢？他是不是好人？
七、哪个名字好，哪个名字不好？
八、李小姐不是好人，她走了，我们都很高兴。
九、我去中国，很高兴。你去中国，也很高兴吧？
十、你的老同屋是哪个？是不是他？是不是王大海？

B. CONVERSATIONS

Read out loud the following conversations, including the name or role of the person speaking. If possible, find a partner or partners and each of you play a role. Then switch roles, so you get practice reading all of the lines.

一、
王先生：我很高兴。你也很高兴吧？
李小姐：别问！你是你，我是我。

二、
何一国：您是李先生吧？
王先明：不是。我姓王，不姓李。
何一国：高小文是您的太太吧？
王先明：也不是。高小文是李先国的太太。我太太叫林美中。

三、
王先生：请问，您贵姓？
何小姐：我姓何，你叫我小何好了。
王先生：小何，你是中国人吧？
何小姐：我不是中国人，我是美国人。
王先生：中文很难吧？
何小姐：中文不太难。

C. CHARACTER DIFFERENTIATION DRILLS

Distinguish carefully the following similar-looking characters, pronouncing each one out loud and thinking of its meaning.

一、你 你 你 您 您 您
二、个 个 个 人 人 人
三、个 个 个 大 大 大
四、个 个 个 太 太 太
五、个 人 太 大 人 个 个 人

Address plate on Beijing building

D. NARRATIVES

Read the following narratives, paying special attention to punctuation and overall structure. The first time you read a narrative, read it out loud; the second time, read silently and try to gradually increase your reading speed. Always think of the meaning of what you're reading.

一、李文是美国人，她的同屋是中国人，也姓李，名字叫李同。李文很高兴她的同屋是中国人，李同也很高兴她的同屋是美国人。

二、您好！我的名字叫谢中文，我是美国人。我的先生叫何台生，他是台湾人。我们都很忙。请问，您贵姓？您是哪国人？您也很忙吗？哪个是您的先生？是他吧？请问，他叫……请您别走，好不好？您是不是不高兴了？

Reading Exercises (Traditional Characters)

A. SENTENCES

Read out loud each of the following sentences, which include all the new characters of this lesson. The first time you read a sentence, focus special attention on the characters and words that are new to you, reminding yourself of their pronunciation and meaning.

The second time, aim to comprehend the overall meaning of the sentence.

一、小姐，請問，您貴姓？

二、我先生是美國人，他姓高，他的名字叫高明。

三、我姓林，您是不是姓王？

四、謝大明是您先生的名字吧？

五、「王小姐」？哪個王小姐？我們都姓王！

六、哪個人好？哪個人不好？他呢？他是不是好人？

七、哪個名字好，哪個名字不好？

八、李小姐不是好人，她走了，我們都很高興。

九、我去中國，很高興。你去中國，也很高興吧？

十、你的老同屋是哪個？是不是他？是不是王大海？

B. CONVERSATIONS

Read out loud the following conversations, including the name or role of the person speaking. If possible, find a partner or partners and each of you play a role. Then switch roles, so you get practice reading all of the lines.

一、王先生：我很高興。你也很高興吧？
王台生：別問！你是你，我是我。

二、何一國：您是李先生吧？
王先明：不是。我姓王，不姓李。
何一國：高小文是您的太太吧？
王先明：也不是。高小文是李先生國的太太。我太太叫林美中。

三、王先生：請問，您貴姓？
何小姐：我姓何，你叫我小何好了。
王先生：小何，你是中國人吧？
何小姐：我不是中國人，我是美國人。
王先生：中文很難吧？
何小姐：中文不太難。

C. CHARACTER DIFFERENTIATION DRILLS

Distinguish carefully the following similar-looking characters, pronouncing each one out loud and thinking of its meaning.

一、你你你您您您

二、個個個人人人 (simplified only)

三、個個個大大大 (simplified only)

四、個個個太太太 (simplified only)

五、個人太大人個個人 (simplified only)

D. NARRATIVES

Read the following narratives, paying special attention to punctuation and overall structure. The first time you read a narrative, read it out loud; the second time, read silently and try to gradually increase your reading speed. Always think of the meaning of what you're reading.

一、李文是美國人，她的同屋是中國人，也姓李，名字叫李同。李文很高興她的同屋是中國人，李同也很高興她的同屋是美國人。

二、您好！我的名字叫謝中文，我是美國人。我的先生叫何台生，他是台灣人。我們都很忙。請問，您貴姓？您是哪國人？您也很忙嗎？哪個是您的先生？是他吧？請問，他叫……請您別走，好不好？您是不是不高興了？

Notes

D1. Notice in this narrative that 高兴 (高興) "be happy" sometimes takes an object and then means "be happy that...."

D2. 您是不是不高兴了？(您是不是不高興了？) "Is it the case that you've become unhappy?" or "Have you gotten angry?" or "Are you upset?"

PART 4

A Self-introduction

New Characters and Words

Study the six characters below and the common words written with them, paying careful attention to each character's pronunciation, meaning, and structure, as well as similar-looking characters. After you've studied a character, turn to the *Practice Essentials* volume and practice writing it on the practice sheet, making sure to follow the correct stroke order and direction as you pronounce it out loud and think of its meaning.

91 片 **piàn** flat and thin piece of something

This character is itself a radical.

名片	**míngpiàn**	name card **[N]**

---

92 没(沒) **méi** (indicates past negative of action verbs)

Radical is 水 **shuǐ** "water." Notice that this radical is written 氵 and is referred to colloquially as 三点水 (三點水) **sāndiǎn shuǐ** "three drops of water" when it occurs at the left-hand side of a character. Though 没 is now the official simplified character and 沒 is the official traditional character, historically these two characters are alternate versions of the same character. Thus, many writers of traditional characters write this character as in the simplified form.

没(沒)	**méi**	(indicates past negative of action verbs) **[AV]**
没问(沒問)	**méi wèn**	didn't ask
没带名片(沒帶名片)	**méi dài míngpiàn**	didn't bring name cards

93 带(帶) **dài** take, bring; belt, band, ribbon

Radical is 巾 **jīn** "cloth" [BF]. Though "take" or "bring" is the meaning introduced in this lesson, another meaning of this character is "belt." The top part of this character looks like a belt (一) with various items hanging off it, which someone is "bringing" with him or her.

带(帶)	**dài**	take along, take, bring [V]

94 公 **gōng** public, official

Radical is 八 **bā** "eight." The component at the bottom is 厶 **sī** "private" [BF]. Contrast 公 with 去 **qù** (53), which also contains 厶 **sī**.

95 司 **sī** bureau, department

Radical is 口 **kǒu** "mouth." The whole character is itself a phonetic, e.g., in 饲(飼) **sì** as in 饲养(飼養) **sìyǎng** "feed (animals)" and in 伺 **cì** as in 伺候 **cìhou** "serve." Contrast 司 with 同 (80) and 问(問) (75).

司	**Sī**	Si [SN]
公司	**gōngsī**	company, firm [N]

96 这(這) **zhè/zhèi-** this

Radical is 辶 **chuò** "walk, go" [BF]. The colloquial name for this radical is 走之 **zǒu zhī** "the walking 之," because of its meaning "walk" and its resemblance to the particle 之. Note that, depending on the particular font, this may be written as 辶 or 辶.The other component of the simplified character is 文 **wén** "writing" (21), while the other component of the traditional character is 言 **yán** "word, speech" [BF]. The idea is that "this" "writing" (or, in the case of the traditional character, "this" "word") "goes."

这(這)	**zhè/zhèi-**	this [PR/SP]
这个(這個)	**zhèige**	this, this one

New Words in BSC 2-4 Written with Characters You Already Know

先生	**xiānsheng**	gentleman [N]
太太	**tàitai**	married woman, lady [N]
小姐	**xiáojie**	young lady, unmarried lady [N]
中美	**Zhōng-Měi**	Sino-American [AT]
了	**-le**	(indicates completed action) [P]
的	**-de**	(indicates that what precedes describes what follows) [P]

Reading Exercises (Simplified Characters)

Now practice reading the new characters and words for this lesson in context in sentences, conversations, and narratives. Be sure to refer to the Notes at the end of this lesson, and make use of the accompanying audio disc to hear and practice correct pronunciation, phrasing, and intonation.

A. SENTENCES

Read out loud each of the following sentences, which include all the new characters of this lesson. The first time you read a sentence, focus special attention on the characters and words that are new to you, reminding yourself of their pronunciation and meaning. The second time, aim to comprehend the overall meaning of the sentence.

一、你好！我叫林山。这是我们公司的名片。
二、美国人不都带名片，中国人也不都带名片吧？
三、李小姐是哪个公司的？她是不是中美公司的？
四、先生，这是您的名片吧？您是不是叫王国中？
五、这是美国 IBM 公司的 CEO 安先生。
六、这是我们公司的谢先生。
七、这是台北中山公司的王小姐。
八、小李没去，小林也没去，他们都没去。
九、我没问，她也没问，我们都没问；你问了吗？
十、大海，请你带我们去你的公司，好吗？

B. CONVERSATIONS

Read out loud the following conversations, including the name or role of the person speaking. If possible, find a partner or partners and each of you play a role. Then switch roles, so you get practice reading all of the lines.

一、

司先生：您好！我姓司。请问，您贵姓？
高先生：我姓高，叫高二明。这是我的名片。
司先生：谢谢！
高先生：司先生，您带名片了吗？
司先生：带了，带了。...... 我的名片呢？

二、

美国人：李大文，你好！请坐，请坐。
中国人：谢谢，谢谢！我叫林大文，不叫李大文。
美国人：我没叫你李大文。
中国人：这是我们公司的名片。
美国人：谢谢，这是我的名片。你的公司叫“大山公司”，是吗？

中国人: 不是。我们公司叫"太山公司"。中文很难吧?
美国人: 不难，中文不难!

三、
何先生: 小李，这是台生公司的高小姐。
李先生: 高小姐，您好!我姓李。这是我的名片。
高小姐: 谢谢李先生。我叫高京文。我没带名片。
李先生: 高小姐，你们公司很忙吧?
高小姐: 是，我们公司很忙。你们公司也很忙吧?
何先生: 高小姐，李先生，我先走了!

C. CHARACTER DIFFERENTIATION DRILLS

Distinguish carefully the following similar-looking characters, pronouncing each one out loud and thinking of its meaning.

一、司 司 司 同 同 同
二、司 司 司 问 问 问
三、司 同 问 同 问 司 同

D. NARRATIVES

Read the following narratives, paying special attention to punctuation and overall structure. The first time you read a narrative, read it out loud; the second time, read silently and try to gradually increase your reading speed. Always think of the meaning of what you're reading.

一、我姓李，名字叫李文。我是中国人。我的公司的名字叫美山公司。美山公司是一个很大的美国公司。这是我们公司的名片。老王也是美山公司的，小何也是我们公司的。请你去美山公司，好吗?我带你去我们公司，好不好?

二、我是一个北京人。我先生不太好。他不带我去上海，也不带我去香港、台湾。他带我去他的公司，中美公司，我很不高兴。小高是我先生的老同屋。这个人很好，他带我去天津，也带我去广州，也带我去美国。小高人太好了！

Reading Exercises (Traditional Characters)

A. SENTENCES

Read out loud each of the following sentences, which include all the new characters of this lesson. The first time you read a sentence, focus special attention on the characters and words that are new to you, reminding yourself of their pronunciation and meaning. The second time, aim to comprehend the overall meaning of the sentence.

一、你好！我叫林山。這是我們公司的名片。

二、美國人不都帶名片，中國人也不都帶名片吧？

三、李小姐是哪個公司的？她是不是中美公司的？

四、先生，這是您的名片吧？您是不是叫王國中？

五、這是美國IBM公司的CEO安先生。

六、這是我們公司的謝先生。

七、這是台北中山公司的王小姐。

八、小李沒去，小林也沒去，他們都沒去。

九、我沒問，她也沒問，我們都沒問；你問了嗎？

十、大海，請你帶我們去你的公司，好嗎？

B. CONVERSATIONS

Read out loud the following conversations, including the name or role of the person speaking. If possible, find a partner or partners and each of you play a role. Then switch roles, so you get practice reading all of the lines.

一、司先生：您好！我姓司。請問，您貴姓？
高先生：我姓高，叫高二明。這是我的名片。
司先生：謝謝！
高先生：司先生，您帶名片了嗎？
司先生：帶了，帶了。……我的名片呢？

二、美國人：李大文，你好！請坐，請坐。
中國人：謝謝，謝謝！我叫林大文，不叫李大文。
美國人：我沒叫你李大文。
中國人：這是我們公司的名片。
美國人：謝謝，這是我的名片。你的公司叫「大山公司」，是嗎？
中國人：不是。我們公司叫「太山公司」。中文很難吧？
美國人：不難，中文不難！

三、何先生：小李，這是台生公司的高小姐。
李先生：高小姐，您好！我姓李。這是我的名片。
高小姐：謝謝李先生。我叫高京文。我沒帶名片。
李先生：高小姐，你們公司很忙吧？
高小姐：是，我們公司很忙。你們公司也很忙吧？
何先生：高小姐，李先生，我先走了！

C. CHARACTER DIFFERENTIATION DRILLS

Distinguish carefully the following similar-looking characters, pronouncing each one out loud and thinking of its meaning.

一、司司司同同同

二、司司司問問問

三、司同問同問司同

D. NARRATIVES

Read the following narratives, paying special attention to punctuation and overall structure. The first time you read a narrative, read it out loud; the second time, read silently and try to gradually increase your reading speed. Always think of the meaning of what you're reading.

一、我姓李，名字叫李文。我是中國人。我的公司的名字叫美山公司。美山公司是一個很大的美國公司。這是我們公司的名片。老王也是美山公司的，小何也是我們公司的。請你去美山公司，好嗎？我帶你去我們公司，好不好？

二、我是一個北京人。我先生不太好。他不帶我去上海，也不帶我去香港、台灣。他帶我去他的公司，中美公司，我很不高興。小高是我先生的老同屋。這個人很好，他帶我去天津，也帶我去廣州，也帶我去美國。小高人太好了！

Entrance to the natatorium at National Taiwan Normal University in Taipei. Notice that the word 游泳馆 (游泳館) **yóuyǒngguǎn** "natatorium" is here written from right to left.

Notes

A3. 李小姐是哪个公司的？她是不是中美公司的？(李小姐是哪個公司的？她是不是中美公司的？) Literally this means "Ms. Li is one from which company? Is she one from Zhongmei Company?" Presumably, in the deep structure of this sentence, there was a noun meaning "person" or "employee," so that the sentence originally may have been something like "Ms. Li is an employee from which company? Is she an employee from Zhongmei Company?" However, that noun was deleted in the surface structure, leaving only 的 to mean "one from." In smoother English, we could translate these two questions as "Ms. Li is with which company? Is she with Zhongmei Company?" Instead of "with" you could also say "from": "Ms. Li is from which company? Is she from Zhongmei Company?"

A5. **ORTHOGRAPHIC REPRESENTATION OF FOREIGN BORROWINGS IN CHINESE.** This sentence should be rather easy for you to comprehend: 这是美国 IBM 公司的 CEO (這是美國 IBM 公司的 CEO) "This is the CEO of the American IBM company." Modern Chinese, as written by and for younger urbanites in newspapers, magazines, menus, signs, e-mails, blogs, text messages and so forth, is replete with borrowings from English and other languages that are represented by the letters of the Roman alphabet, sometimes in combination with Arabic numbers. Here are some common examples: CD, DIY, DNA, DVD, ID, IQ, IT, KTV, MP3, MTV, OK, PVC. Some such terms can occur by themselves, but others may be combined with Chinese characters, e.g., B型 **B xíng** "blood type B," 3D银幕 (3D銀幕) **3D yínmù** "3D screen," 维生素C (維生素C) **wéishēngsù C** "vitamin C." Usually, only upper-case letters are used, but there are a few common borrowings in lower-case letters (e.g., n 次 **n cì** "an infinite number of times"). Note that, when borrowed into Chinese, each Roman letter or number is considered a separate unit, equivalent to a Chinese character. Obviously, such borrowings are all terms related to modern, foreign-influenced society, not traditional Chinese culture. For that reason, government authorities, Chinese teachers, and other purists often criticize such usage. However, the fact is that most writers of Chinese pay them little heed and go right on using these foreign borrowings. We certainly don't encourage you to make frequent use of such borrowings in your own written (or, for that matter, spoken) Chinese. However, since this textbook attempts to present written Chinese as actually used today, we do include a few such borrowings in the reading exercises.

A6. 这是我们公司的谢先生 (這是我們公司的謝先生) "This is Mr. Xie from our company."

A10. 请你带我们去你的公司 (請你帶我們去你的公司) "Please take us to your company." Note that the verb 带 (帶) can be used to mean "take" or "bring" *things* or, as here, *people*.

B1. 您带名片了吗？(您帶名片了嗎？) "Did you bring a name card?"

B2. Examine the last line by the Chinese speaker: 我们公司叫 "太山公司" (我們公司叫「太山公司」) "Our company is called 'Taishan Company.'" In this sentence, 我们公司 (我們公司) means "our company," but why is there no 的 between 我们 (我們) and 公司？ The answer is that, though it would not be grammatically incorrect to say 我们的公司 (我們的公司), very often in Chinese a 的 is dropped when there is an especially close connection between a pronoun and a noun, especially when it involves a phrase that is said with high frequency. This holds true for body parts ("my hand"), for relatives ("my mother"), and—as we see here—for institutions to which there is a strong sense of belonging ("our company," "our school," etc.). Also, note that the speaker says not "my company" but, rather, "our company." This is related to the strong sense of group affiliation in Chinese society as compared to the more individual outlook in Western society.

B3. 你们公司 (你們公司) "your company." Grammatically, this is like 我们公司 (我們公司) in B2 above.

D1. 老王也是美山公司的，小何也是我们公司的 (老王也是美山公司的，小何也是我們公司的) "Old Wang is also with Meishan Company, and Little He is also with our company." Grammatically, these two clauses are like A3 above.

D2. Look at the word 人 in 小高人太好了. This 人 here means not just "person" but "as a person" or, even more specifically, "the manner in which a person conducts herself or himself." We could translate the whole sentence as "Little Gao, as a person, is too good" or, in better English, "As a person, Little Gao is wonderful." Of course, given the context of this paragraph, we would have to conclude that this is a very subjective view of Little Gao!

Numbers, Dates, Time, and Money (I)

UNIT 3

COMMUNICATIVE OBJECTIVES

Once you've mastered this unit, you'll be able to use Chinese to read and write:

1. How many of something there are.
2. How many people there are (both in the regular way and politely).
3. People's ages.
4. Sums of money.
5. Clock times.
6. Amounts of time.
7. Larger numbers in the hundreds and thousands.
8. Expressions containing the Chinese symbol 〇 **líng** "zero."
9. The so-called "long forms" of the numbers 1-10, 100, and 1,000 that are used on financial records and currency to prevent alteration and fraud.
10. A Chinese tongue twister.
11. Chinese characters printed in a smaller font size.

PART 1

"How Many Students in Your Class?"

New Characters and Words

Study the six characters below and the common words written with them, paying careful attention to each character's pronunciation, meaning, and structure, as well as similar-looking characters. After you've studied a character, turn to the *Practice Essentials* volume and practice writing it on the practice sheet, making sure to follow the correct stroke order and direction as you pronounce it out loud and think of its meaning.

97 几(幾) **jǐ-** how many

Radical of the simplified form is 几, which is itself a radical. Radical of the traditional form is 幺 **yāo** "small" [**BF**]. The whole character can serve as a phonetic, e.g., in 机(機) **jī** as in 机会(機會) **jīhui** "opportunity," 讥(譏) **jī** as in 讥笑(譏笑) **jīxiào** "ridicule," and 饥(饑) **jī** as in 饥饿(饑餓) **jī'è** "hunger." Contrast simplified 几 with 九 **jiǔ** (10).

几(幾)	**jǐ-**	how many? [**QW**]
几个(幾個)	**jǐge**	how many? (people or things)

---

98 位 **wèi** (polite measure for people)

Radical is 人 **rén** "person," which is written 亻 when occurring at the left side of a character so as not to get in the way of the component at the right. The colloquial name for this radical is 人字旁 **rénzìpáng** "side made up of the character 人." The right-hand component is 立 **lì** "establish" [**BF**].

位	**wèi**	(polite measure for people) [**M**]
哪位	**něiwèi/nǎwèi**	which one? (polite)
几位(幾位)	**jǐwèi**	how many? (people; polite)
三位	**sānwèi**	three (persons; polite)

99 两(兩) **liǎng-** two

Radical of the simplified form is 一 **yī** (1). Radical of the traditional form is 入 **rù** "enter" [BF]; distinguish 入 from 人 **rén** "person" (30). The whole character may serve as a phonetic, e.g., in 辆(輛) **liàng** (measure for vehicles). The "two" instances of 人 contained within the simplified form of this character (or the "two" instances of 入 contained in the traditional form) make it easy to remember the meaning of "two." Contrast 两(兩) with 西 **xī** (35).

两(兩)	**liǎng-**	two [NU]
两个(兩個)	**liǎngge**	two (people or things)
两位(兩位)	**liǎngwèi**	two (persons; polite)

100 男 **nán** male, man

Radical is 田 **tián** "field" [BF]. The other component is 力 **lì** "strength" [BF]. The traditional explanation, even if not entirely in accord with the facts, is that the "male" is the one who exerts his "strength" in the "fields." Contrast 男 with 别(別) **bié** (82).

男的	**nánde**	man, male [N]
男生	**nánshēng**	male student [N]

101 女 **nǚ** female, woman

This character, which is itself both a radical and a phonetic, is a picture of a woman's two breasts. You have seen it used as a radical in these characters: 好 **hǎo** (50), 她 **tā** (56), 姐 **jiě** (72) as in 小姐 **xiáojie**, and 姓 **xìng** (86). It occurs as a phonetic in 奴 **nú** as in 奴隶(奴隸) **núlì** "slave," 努 **nǔ** as in 努力 **nǔlì** "try hard," and 怒 **nù** as in 发怒(發怒) **fā'nù** "get angry." When 女 is used as a radical, the last stroke is shortened (e.g. 好).

女的	**nǚde**	woman, female [N]
女生	**nǚshēng**	female student [N]

102 师(師) **shī** teacher

Radical is 巾 **jīn** "cloth" [BF]. The whole character serves as a phonetic, e.g., in 狮(獅) **shī** as in 狮子(獅子) **shīzi** "lion."

老师(老師)	**lǎoshī**	teacher [N]
男老师(男老師)	**nánlǎoshī**	male teacher [N]
女老师(女老師)	**nǚlǎoshī**	female teacher [N]

New Words in BSC 3-1 Written with Characters You Already Know

二	**èr**	two [NU]
三	**sān**	three [NU]
四	**sì**	four [NU]
五	**wǔ**	five [NU]
六	**liù**	six [NU]

七	**qī**	seven [**NU**]
八	**bā**	eight [**NU**]
九	**jiǔ**	nine [**NU**]
十	**shí**	ten [**NU**]

Reading Exercises (Simplified Characters)

Now practice reading the new characters and words for this lesson in context in sentences, conversations, and narratives. Be sure to refer to the Notes at the end of this lesson, and make use of the accompanying audio disc to hear and practice correct pronunciation, phrasing, and intonation.

A. NUMBERS AND MEASURES

Read out loud each of the following number and measure expressions, making sure to think carefully of the meaning of what you're reading.

一、几个？一个、两个、三个。
二、几个？四个、五个、六个。
三、几个？七个、八个、九个、十个！
四、几位？一位、两位、三位。
五、几位？四位、五位、六位。
六、几位？七位、八位、九位、十位！

B. SENTENCES

Read out loud each of the following sentences, which include all the new characters of this lesson. The first time you read a sentence, focus special attention on the characters and words that are new to you, reminding yourself of their pronunciation and meaning. The second time, aim to comprehend the overall meaning of the sentence.

一、这位女生的名字是金小山吗？
二、他们不都是男生。八个是男生，两个是女生。
三、请问，小安是男的吧？小金呢？小金是女的吧？
四、请问，几位去成都，几位去广州？
五、这个男生是美国人。请问，哪个女生是台湾人？
六、这是高老师先生的公司吗？不是吗？哪个是？
七、她的先生姓李，是一位很好的老师。
八、两位男老师去天津街了，三位女老师去上海路了。
九、我的中文老师是男老师，你的中文老师也是男的吗？
十、王大海是男生，他的同屋也是男的吧？

C. CONVERSATIONS

Read out loud the following conversations, including the name or role of the person speaking. If possible, find a partner or partners and each of you play a role. Then switch roles, so you get practice reading all of the lines.

一、
中国人：先生，您好！请问，几位？
美国人：两位。

二、
老师：几个男生，几个女生？
男生：一个男生，两个女生。

三、
男的：请问，先生，您......
女的：我不是男的，我是女的！

四、
师先生：他们都是中国人吧？
李小姐：不，他们不都是中国人。六位是中国人，两位是美国人。
师先生：几个男的，几个女的？
李小姐：三个男的，五个女的。

D. CHARACTER DIFFERENTIATION DRILLS

Distinguish carefully the following similar-looking characters, pronouncing each one out loud and thinking of its meaning.

一、两 两 两 西 西 西
二、男 男 男 别 别 别
三、西 两 别 男 两 西 男 别
四、几 几 几 九 九 九
五、几 九 九 几 几 九 几

E. NARRATIVE

Read the following narrative, paying special attention to punctuation and overall structure. The first time you read the narrative, read it out loud; the second time, read silently and try to gradually increase your reading speed. Always think of the meaning of what you're reading.

这位老师是我们的中文老师。他姓高，叫高国公，我们都叫他高老师。高老师是北京人。他的太太也是我们的老师，她的名字叫何文香。何老师不是北京人，她是四川人。高老师、何老师他们两位都很忙。这是高老师的名片，何老师的名片我没带。他们两位老师都很好，我们很高兴他们都是我们的老师。

Reading Exercises (Traditional Characters)

A. NUMBERS AND MEASURES

Read out loud each of the following number and measure expressions, making sure to think carefully of the meaning of what you're reading.

一、幾個？一個、兩個、三個。

二、幾個？四個、五個、六個。

三、幾個？七個、八個、九個、十個！

四、幾位？一位、兩位、三位。

五、幾位？四位、五位、六位。

六、幾位？七位、八位、九位、十位！

"I love my city, always maintain cleanliness"

B. SENTENCES

Read out loud each of the following sentences, which include all the new characters of this lesson. The first time you read a sentence, focus special attention on the characters and words that are new to you, reminding yourself of their pronunciation and meaning. The second time, aim to comprehend the overall meaning of the sentence.

一、這位女生的名字是金小山嗎？

二、他們不都是男生。八個是男生，兩個是女生。

三、請問，小安是男的吧？小金呢？小金是女的吧？

四、請問，幾位去成都，幾位去廣州？

五、這個男生是美國人。請問，哪個女生是台灣人？

六、這是高老師先生的公司嗎？不是嗎？哪個是？

七、她的先生姓李，是一位很好的老師。

八、兩位男老師去天津街了，三位女老師去上海路了。

九、我的中文老師是男老師，你的中文老師也是男的嗎？

十、王大海是男生，他的同屋也是男的吧？

C. CONVERSATIONS

Read out loud the following conversations, including the name or role of the person speaking. If possible, find a partner or partners and each of you play a role. Then switch roles, so you get practice reading all of the lines.

一、中國人：先生，您好！請問，幾位？
美國人：兩位。

二、老師：幾個男生，幾個女生？
男生：一個男生，兩個女生。

三、男的：請問，先生，您……
女的：我不是男的，我是女的！

四、師先生：他們都是中國人吧？
李小姐：不，他們不都是中國人。六位是中國人，兩位是美國人。
師先生：幾個男的，幾個女的？
李小姐：三個男的，五個女的。

D. CHARACTER DIFFERENTIATION DRILLS

Distinguish carefully the following similar-looking characters, pronouncing each one out loud and thinking of its meaning.

一、兩兩兩西西西

二、男男男別別別

三、西兩別男兩西男別

四、幾幾幾九九九 (simplified only)

五、幾九九幾幾九幾 (simplified only)

厕所 (廁所) **cèsuǒ** "toilet"

E. NARRATIVE

Read the following narrative, paying special attention to punctuation and overall structure. The first time you read the narrative, read it out loud; the second time, read silently and try to gradually increase your reading speed. Always think of the meaning of what you're reading.

這位老師是我們的中文老師。他姓高，叫高國公，我們都叫他高老師。高老師是北京人。他的太太也是我們的老師，她的名字叫何文香。何老師不是北京人，她是四川人。高老師、何老師他們兩位都很忙。這是高老師的名片，何老師的名片我沒帶。他們兩位老師都很好，我們很高興他們都是我們的老師。

Notes

A1. As you may have noticed, beginning with this lesson the Chinese font size has been reduced. This textbook has been designed to provide you with practice in reading printed and handwritten Chinese text with characters in a variety of sizes and styles.

B6. Look at the phrase 高老师先生的公司 (高老師先生的公司) "Teacher Gao's husband's company." We could say that, at a deeper level, the grammatical structure of this phrase was originally 高老师的先生的公司 (高老師的先生的公司), with two 的 in it, but that according to the rule we mentioned in 2-2, note A1, about Chinese people not liking the "sound" of several 的 in a row and usually deleting all 的 except the last one, this phrase became 高老师先生的公司 (高老師先生的公司), with only one 的 in it.

B7. L ook at this sentence: 她的先生姓李，是一位很好的老师(她的先生姓李，是一位很好的老師) "Her husband's last name is Li; he's a very good teacher." First, we note that the Chinese comma is sometimes equivalent to an English semicolon (translating as "Her husband's last name is Li, he's a very good teacher" would create an English run-on sentence). Second, we note that in the Chinese there is no subject for the second clause (literally it says "is a very good teacher"). You should be aware that if the subject or topic has already been made clear (as is the case here, in the previous clause), it's perfectly normal not to repeat it in later clauses or sentences. In fact, excessive repetition of the subject or topic is considered poor, Western-influenced style.

B8. Depending on the context, 两位男老师…… 三位女老师…… (兩位男老師…… 三位女老師……) could mean either "Two male teachers...three female teachers..." or "The two male teachers...the three female teachers..."

C1. This dialog may well have taken place in a restaurant.

E1. As we saw in the previous unit, 高兴 (高興) sometimes functions as a verb taking a following clause as object and means "be happy that..." So the sentence 我们很高兴他们都是我们的老师 (我們很高興他們都是我們的老師) could be translated as "We are very happy that they are both our teachers."

PART 2

Inquiring About Age

这是你姐姐，对不对？
(這是你姐姐，對不對？)
对，她今年二十三岁了。
(對，她今年二十三歲了。)

New Characters and Words

Study the six characters below and the common words written with them, paying careful attention to each character's pronunciation, meaning, and structure, as well as similar-looking characters. After you've studied a character, turn to the *Practice Essentials* volume and practice writing it on the practice sheet, making sure to follow the correct stroke order and direction as you pronounce it out loud and think of its meaning.

103 多 **duō** much, many, more; how

Radical is 夕 **xī** "evening" [**BF**]. The repetition of 夕 in 多 suggests the meaning of "many." Contrast 多 with 名 **míng** (83). In the sense of "how," the official pronunciation of 多 is **duō** in mainland China but **duó** in Taiwan.

多	**duō/duó**	how [**QW**]
多大	**duō dà/duó dà**	how old?

104 年 **nián** year

Radical is 干 **gān** "shield" [**BF**]. Contrast 年 with 生 **shēng** (22).

年	**Nián**	Nian [**SN**]

105 纪(紀) **jì** to record

Radical is 丝(絲) **sī** "silk." When at the left side of a character, this radical is referred to colloquially as 绞丝旁(絞絲旁) **jiǎosīpáng** "side made up of twisted silk" and is written as 纟(糹). Phonetic is 己 **jǐ** "self" [**BF**].

年纪(年紀)	**niánji**	age [**N**]
多大年纪(多大年紀)	**duō dà niánji**	how many years old?

106 今 **jīn** now

Radical is 人 **rén** "person," which is here written with its two legs spread out across the top of the character and known as 人字头 (人字頭) **rénzìtóu** "top made up of the character 人." Contrast 今 with 公 **gōng** (94).

今年	**jīnnián**	this year [TW]

107 岁(歲) **suì** year of age

Radical of the simplified form is 山 **shān** "mountain" (14). Radical of the traditional form is 止 **zhǐ** "stop" [BF].

岁 (歲)	**suì**	year of age [M]
几岁 (幾歲)	**jǐsuì**	how many years old? (of a child)
八岁 (八歲)	**bāsuì**	eight years old

108 对(對) **duì** correct

Radical is 寸 **cùn** "inch." The other component in the simplified form is 又 **yòu** "again" (210).

对 (對)	**duì**	be correct [SV]
对不对 (對不對)	**duì bu dui**	correct or not correct, "right?"

New Words in BSC 3-2 Written with Characters You Already Know

大	**dà**	be big; old (of people) [SV]
姐姐	**jiějie**	older sister [N]
上	**shàng-**	last [SP]

Reading Exercises (Simplified Characters)

Now practice reading the new characters and words for this lesson in context in sentences, conversations, and narratives. Be sure to refer to the Notes at the end of this lesson, and make use of the accompanying audio disc to hear and practice correct pronunciation, phrasing, and intonation.

A. NUMBERS AND AGES

Read out loud each of the following numbers or age expressions, making sure to think carefully of the meaning of what you're reading.

1. 三十五
2. 六十八
3. 九十二
4. 四十
5. 七十五
6. 八十三
7. 二十一
8. 三十

9. 五十六
10. 十九
11. 四十五岁
12. 七十一岁
13. 五十七岁
14. 十四岁
15. 四十岁
16. 十二岁
17. 两岁
18. 九十九岁
19. 十八岁
20. 二十二岁

B. SENTENCES

Read out loud each of the following sentences, which include all the new characters of this lesson. The first time you read a sentence, focus special attention on the characters and words that are new to you, reminding yourself of their pronunciation and meaning. The second time, aim to comprehend the overall meaning of the sentence.

一、这是你的姐姐吗？她今年多大年纪了？

二、我姐姐的先生是美国人，他的中文很好，他是中文老师。

三、我的名字叫司小文，今年十九岁，我姐姐叫司文香。

四、你几岁了？五岁了，对不对？

五、你的同屋是中国人吧？他今年多大了？二十岁，对不对？

六、李老师的两个姐姐也都是老师，对不对？她们的年纪都不小了吧？

七、我们今年的中文老师是上海人，不是吗？

八、这个公司的人都是男的吗？这是不对的！

九、小何的两位老师都是美国人，年纪都不大。

十、王大海的两位中文老师年纪都很大，一位八十岁，一位七十五岁。

C. CONVERSATIONS

Read out loud the following conversations, including the name or role of the person speaking. If possible, find a partner or partners and each of you play a role. Then switch roles, so you get practice reading all of the lines.

一、
老先生：老太太，您多大年纪了？
老太太：我年纪不小了，今年八十三岁了。老先生，您呢？
老先生：我今年八十四岁了！

二、
高金美小姐：香香，你多大了？
林文香小姐：我三十岁了。老了！
高金美小姐：不老，不老。我姐姐四十五岁了，她也不老。

三、
李太太：谢太太，这是您的姐姐，对吧？
谢太太：不是！我姐姐五十岁，这位老太太八十岁了！

四、
大海：你多大年纪了？
文山：我二十一岁了。你呢？你多大了？
大海：请你别问，好不好！

D. CHARACTER DIFFERENTIATION DRILLS

Distinguish carefully the following similar-looking characters, pronouncing each one out loud and thinking of its meaning.

一、多 多 多 名 名 名
二、多 名 名 多 多 名 多
三、今 今 今 公 公 公
四、今 公 公 今 公 公 今
五、年 年 年 生 生 生
六、年 生 年 年 生 生 年

E. NARRATIVES

Read the following narratives, paying special attention to punctuation and overall structure. The first time you read a narrative, read it out loud; the second time, read silently and try to gradually increase your reading speed. Always think of the meaning of what you're reading.

一、我的名字叫李小明，今年二十九岁了。我的姐姐叫李中明，今年三十六岁了。我们两个都是湖北人。我的姐姐是一位中文老师，她的先生也是中文老师。我姐姐的先生叫王中山，他是河南人，今年四十岁了。这是他们两位的名片。

二、我的名字叫安东山，今年六岁，他们都叫我“东东”。我是男生，北京人。我姐姐叫安东文，今年九岁，他们都叫她“文文”。

F. SUPPLEMENT: A TONGUE TWISTER

Read out loud each of the lines of the following Chinese tongue twister. When you've read each line separately, say all three lines together as fast as you can!

一、四是四，十是十。
二、十四是十四，四十是四十。
三、十四不是四十，四十也不是十四！

Reading Exercises (Traditional Characters)

A. NUMBERS AND AGES

Read out loud each of the following numbers or age expressions, making sure to think carefully of the meaning of what you're reading.

1. 三十五
2. 六十八
3. 九十二
4. 四十
5. 七十五
6. 八十三
7. 二十一
8. 三十
9. 五十六
10. 十九
11. 四十五歲
12. 七十一歲
13. 五十七歲
14. 十四歲
15. 四十歲
16. 十二歲
17. 兩歲
18. 九十九歲
19. 十八歲
20. 二十二歲

B. SENTENCES

Read out loud each of the following sentences, which include all the new characters of this lesson. The first time you read a sentence, focus special attention on the characters and words that are new to you, reminding yourself of their pronunciation and meaning. The second time, aim to comprehend the overall meaning of the sentence.

一、這是你的姐姐嗎？她今年多大年紀了？

二、我姐姐的先生是美國人，他的中文很好，他是中文老師。

三、我的名字叫司小文，今年十九歲，我姐姐叫司文香。

四、你幾歲了？五歲了，對不對？

五、你的同屋是中國人吧？他今年多大了？二十歲，對不對？

六、李老師的兩個姐姐也都是老師，對不對？她們的年紀都不小了吧？

七、我們今年的中文老師是上海人，不是嗎？

八、這個公司的人都是男的嗎？這是不對的！

九、小何的兩位老師都是美國人，年紀都不大。

十、王大海的兩位中文老師年紀都很大，一位八十歲，一位七十五歲。

C. CONVERSATIONS

Read out loud the following conversations, including the name or role of the person speaking. If possible, find a partner or partners and each of you play a role. Then switch roles, so you get practice reading all of the lines.

一、老先生：老太太，您多大年紀了？
老太太：我年紀不小了，今年八十三歲了。老先生，您呢？
老先生：我今年八十四歲了！

二、高金美小姐：香香，你多大了？
林文香小姐：我三十歲了。老了！
高金美小姐：不老，不老。我姐姐四十五歲了，她也不老。

三、李太太：謝太太，這是您的姐姐，對吧？
謝太太：不是，我姐姐五十歲，這位老太太八十歲了！

四、大海：你多大年紀了？
文山：我二十一歲了。你呢？你多大了？
大海：請你別問，好不好！

D. CHARACTER DIFFERENTIATION DRILLS

Distinguish carefully the following similar-looking characters, pronouncing each one out loud and thinking of its meaning.

一、多多多名名名
二、多名名多多名多
三、今今今公公公
四、今公公今公公今
五、年年年生生生
六、年生年年生生年

E. NARRATIVES

Read the following narratives, paying special attention to punctuation and overall structure. The first time you read a narrative, read it out loud; the second time, read silently and try to gradually increase your reading speed. Always think of the meaning of what you're reading.

一、我的名字叫李小明，今年二十九歲了。我的姐姐叫李中明，今年三十六歲了。我們兩個都是湖北人。我的姐姐是一位中文老師，她的先生也是中文老師。我姐姐的先生叫王中山，他是河南人，今年四十歲了。這是他們兩位的名片。

二、我的名字叫安東山，今年六歲，他們都叫我「東東」。我是男生，北京人。我姐姐叫安東文，今年九歲，他們都叫她「文文」。

F. SUPPLEMENT: A TONGUE TWISTER

Read out loud each of the lines of the following Chinese tongue twister. When you've read each line separately, say all three lines together as fast as you can!

一、四是四，十是十。

二、十四是十四，四十是四十。

三、十四不是四十，四十也不是十四！

Notes

B6. 她们的年纪都不小了吧？(她們的年紀都不小了吧？) literally means "Their age is not small, I suppose?" In good English, we could translate as "I guess they're not so young, huh?" or "I guess they must be rather old?"

B7. In the question 我们今年的中文老师是上海人，不是吗？(我們今年的中文老師是上海人，不是嗎？), the tag question 不是吗 (不是嗎) literally means "is it not so?" In smoother English, we could translate the whole question as "Our Chinese teacher this year is from Shanghai, right?"

B8. In this sentence, 这是不对的！(這是不對的！) means "This isn't right!" (in the sense of "This isn't as it should be!").

B9. In this sentence, 年纪都不大 (年紀都不大) literally means "age both not big." In better English, we could translate "neither of them is very old" or "both of them are rather young."

C1. Note that in Chinese, addressing an elderly woman as 老太太, lit. "old lady," is considered quite polite and respectful, not at all rude as it would be in English.

C3. The context for this conversation is as follows: the first speaker is looking at several photographs and is guessing who the person in the photograph might be. The second speaker comments on the accuracy of the first speaker's guess.

E1. In the sentence 这是他们两位的名片 (這是他們兩位的名片), the pronoun 这 (這) means "these" rather than "this." How do we know this? From the context, because it would not make sense to interpret the sentence as "This is the name card of the two of them," since two people would not normally share one name card.

F. This tongue twister would be especially challenging for the hundreds of millions of native Chinese speakers who have non-standard Mandarin pronunciation and pronounce **sh-** as **s-**.

Stand in southern Taiwan selling coconuts

Purchasing a Tea Cup

那个多少钱？
(那個多少錢？)
一百九十八块。
(一百九十八塊。)

New Characters and Words

Study the six characters below and the common words written with them, paying careful attention to each character's pronunciation, meaning, and structure, as well as similar-looking characters. After you've studied a character, turn to the *Practice Essentials* volume and practice writing it on the practice sheet, making sure to follow the correct stroke order and direction as you pronounce it out loud and think of its meaning.

109 那 **nà/nèi-** that

Radical is 邑 **yì** "city" [BF], which is written 阝 when occurring at the right-hand side of a character. This radical is referred to colloquially as 右耳旁 **yòu'ěrpáng** "side made up of a right ear." The other component of 那 is said to have meant "fur." Originally, 那 was the name of a "city" in the west of Sichuan whose inhabitants wore "furs." The character was later used to represent the sound of the word for "that," which had no character of its own. 那 itself can serve as a phonetic in a few characters, e.g., in 哪 **něi-/nǎ-** (73) and in 娜 **Nà** (female personal name). Contrast 那 with 明 **míng** (15) and 哪 **něi-/nǎ-** (73). While the characters 那 and 哪 are now usually distinguished, be aware that in older texts and even now in the writing of some Chinese, 那 may represent either 那 or 哪. Therefore, if a sentence or phrase seems puzzling and it doesn't make sense to interpret 那 as "that," examine the punctuation and context and consider the possibility that 那 is being used in place of 哪 to mean "which?" or a related question word.

那	**nà/nèi-**	that [PR/SP]; in that case, so [CJ]
那个 (那個)	**nèige**	that one, that
那位	**nèiwèi**	that (person; polite)

110 少 shǎo few

Radical is 小 **xiǎo** "small," which gives an idea of the meaning "few." However, distinguish carefully between 少 and 小 "small" (24). The whole character 少 can serve as a phonetic, e.g., in 沙 **shā** "sand," 纱 (紗) **shā** "gauze," 吵 **chǎo** "noisy," 炒 **chǎo** "stir-fry." Contrast 少 with 小 **xiǎo** (24).

多少	**duōshǎo**	how much, how many [**QW**]

111 钱(錢) qián money

Radical is 金 **jīn** "gold, metal" [**BF**] since money, in the form of coins, is often made from metal. The radical 金 **jīn** is referred to colloquially as 金字旁 **jīnzìpáng** "side made up of the character 金." When used as a radical in writing simplified characters, the sixth and seventh strokes of 金 are deleted, so that the radical is simplified to 钅. When writing traditional characters, the last stroke of 金 as a left-side radical slants up toward the right, so as not to get in the way of the other component(s). The phonetic in 钱(錢) is 戋(戔) **jiān** "small" [**BF**], which occurs as a phonetic in many characters and represents the sound **jian**, **qian**, or **zhan** (in various tones).

钱(錢)	**qián**	money [**N**]
钱(錢)	**Qián**	Qian (also Jeon, Cheon, or Chon, a common Korean surname) [**SN**]
多少钱(多少錢)	**duōshǎo qián**	how much money?

112 块(塊) kuài piece, lump, dollar

Radical is 土 **tǔ** "earth." The colloquial name for this radical is 土字旁 **tǔzìpáng** "side made up of the character 土." Notice that the top horizontal line of 土 is shorter than the bottom line. Also, notice that when used as a radical, the bottom line of 土 slants up toward the right, so as not to get in the way of the other component. Phonetic of the simplified form is 夬 **kuài**, a rare character meaning "fork." Phonetic of the traditional form is 鬼 **guǐ** "devil." 块(塊) has acquired the meaning "dollar" because before there was a standardized currency, people used "pieces" of gold or silver to barter for goods just as "dollars" are used today.

块(塊)	**kuài**	dollar (monetary unit) [**M**]
两块钱(兩塊錢)	**liǎngkuài qián**	two dollars

113 百 -bǎi hundred

Radical is 白 **bái** "white," which in this character also serves as the phonetic.

百	**-bǎi**	hundred [**N**]
一百	**yìbǎi**	one hundred
两百块钱（兩百塊錢）	**liǎngbǎikuài qián**	two hundred dollars

114 千 -qiān thousand

Radical is 十 **shí** (11). 千 itself can serve as a phonetic in some characters, e.g., in 迁(遷) **qiān** "move" and in 纤(纖) **xiān** as in 纤维(纖維) **xiānwéi** "fiber." Contrast 千 with 十 **shí** (11).

千	**-qiān**	thousand [**NU**]
一千	**yìqiān**	one thousand
五千块钱(五千塊錢)	**wǔqiānkuài qián**	five thousand dollars

New Words in BSC 3-3 Written with Characters You Already Know

吧	**ba**	(indicates suggestions) [P]
贵(貴)	**guì**	be expensive [SV]
〇	**líng**	zero [NU]

Reading Exercises (Simplified Characters)

Now practice reading the new characters and words for this lesson in context in sentences, conversations, and narratives. Be sure to refer to the Notes at the end of this lesson, and make use of the accompanying audio disc to hear and practice correct pronunciation, phrasing, and intonation.

A. LARGER NUMBERS AND SUMS OF MONEY

Read out loud each of the following larger numbers and money expressions, making sure to think carefully of the meaning of what you're reading.

1. 三百二十一
2. 五百七十七
3. 两千
4. 九百九十八
5. 六千七百二十一
6. 九千九百九十九
7. 四千三百三十
8. 两百七十七
9. 四千两百二十
10. 六千七百五十五
11. 六百块钱
12. 五百五十五块
13. 九千块
14. 三块五
15. 五千六百八十八块钱
16. 两千三百块钱
17. 一百〇一
18. 一千〇一
19. 两千〇五十个
20. 八百〇八块钱

B. SENTENCES

Read out loud each of the following sentences, which include all the new characters of this lesson. The first time you read a sentence, focus special attention on the characters and words that are new to you, reminding yourself of their pronunciation and meaning. The second time, aim to comprehend the overall meaning of the sentence.

一、这位男老师姓高，那位女老师姓钱。
二、五十块钱？太贵了！那，这个多少钱？
三、中国多少人姓王？美国多少人姓 Smith？
四、先生，两个人去中国，两千块钱，太贵了！
五、我们的公司很大，七百人。你的公司多少人？

六、九十九岁的那位中国老太太姓安，对不对？
七、她不是香港人？那，她是台湾人吧？
八、他叫李南，今年四岁了，你们叫他“南南”吧。
九、谢太太，今年去不好，您今年别去了！
十、小王，你要的这个太贵了，你要那个吧！

C. CONVERSATIONS

Read out loud the following conversations, including the name or role of the person speaking. If possible, find a partner or partners and each of you play a role. Then switch roles, so you get practice reading all of the lines.

一、
美国人：那个多少钱？
中国人：哪个？
美国人：那个。
中国人：是这个吗？
美国人：不是这个，是那个！

二、
美国人：小姐，请问，这个多少钱？
香港人：这个……一百九十九块。
美国人：太贵了。那个呢？那个多少钱？
香港人：那个二十三块五。

三、
那先生：请问，这个多少钱？
钱小姐：这个……两千块。
那先生：两千块太贵了吧！
钱小姐：那，一千九百块，好不好？

D. CHARACTER DIFFERENTIATION DRILLS

Distinguish carefully the following similar-looking characters, pronouncing each one out loud and thinking of its meaning.

一、那 那 那 哪 哪 哪

二、那 哪 哪 那 那 哪 那
三、少 少 少 小 小 小
四、少 小 少 少 小 小 少
五、千 千 千 十 十 十
六、千 十 千 千 十 十 千

Taiwan currency

E. NARRATIVE

Read the following narrative, paying special attention to punctuation and overall structure. The first time you read the narrative, read it out loud; the second time, read silently and try to gradually increase your reading speed. Always think of the meaning of what you're reading.

你问我去北京一个人多少钱？好，去北京一个人一百二十块。去香山多少钱？去香山两百八十块。去天津呢？去天津四百五十块。去上海呢？去上海一个人一千四百块。去美国一个人多少钱？这个你别问我；请你问那个人吧！

Reading Exercises (Traditional Characters)

A. LARGER NUMBERS AND SUMS OF MONEY

Read out loud each of the following larger numbers and money expressions, making sure to think carefully of the meaning of what you're reading.

1. 三百二十一
2. 五百七十七
3. 兩千
4. 九百九十八
5. 六千七百二十一
6. 九千九百九十九
7. 四千三百三十
8. 兩百七十七
9. 四千兩百二十
10. 六千七百五十五
11. 六百塊錢
12. 五百五十五塊
13. 九千塊
14. 三塊五
15. 五千六百八十八塊錢
16. 兩千三百塊錢
17. 一百〇一
18. 一千〇一
19. 兩千〇五十個
20. 八百〇八塊錢

B. SENTENCES

Read out loud each of the following sentences, which include all the new characters of this lesson. The first time you read a sentence, focus special attention on the characters and words that are new to you, reminding yourself of their pronunciation and meaning. The second time, aim to comprehend the overall meaning of the sentence.

一、這位男老師姓高，那位女老師姓錢。

二、五十塊錢？太貴了！那，這個多少錢？

三、中國多少人姓王？美國多少人姓Smith？

四、先生，兩個人去中國，兩千塊錢，太貴了！

五、我們的公司很大，七百人。你的公司多少人？

六、九十九歲的那位中國老太太姓安，對不對？

七、她不是香港人？那，她是台灣人吧？

八、他叫李南，今年四歲了，你們叫他「南南」吧。

九、謝太太，今年去不好，您今年別去了！

十、小王，你要的這個太貴了，你要那個吧！

C. CONVERSATIONS

Read out loud the following conversations, including the name or role of the person speaking. If possible, find a partner or partners and each of you play a role. Then switch roles, so you get practice reading all of the lines.

一、美國人：那個多少錢？
中國人：哪個？
美國人：那個。
中國人：是這個嗎？
美國人：不是這個，是那個！

二、美國人：小姐，請問，這個多少錢？
香港人：這個……一百九十九塊。
美國人：太貴了。那個呢？那個多少錢？
香港人：那個二十三塊五。

三、那先生：請問，這個多少錢？
錢小姐：這個……兩千塊。
那先生：兩千塊太貴了吧！
錢小姐：那，一千九百塊，好不好？

D. CHARACTER DIFFERENTIATION DRILLS

Distinguish carefully the following similar-looking characters, pronouncing each one out loud and thinking of its meaning.

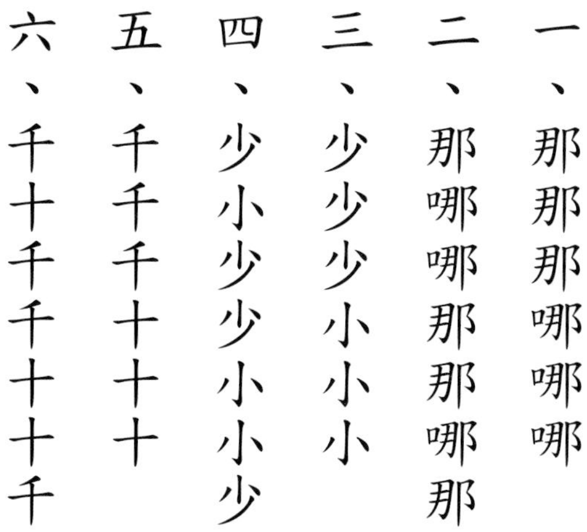

一、那那那哪哪哪
二、那哪哪那那哪那
三、少少少小小小
四、少小少少小小少
五、千千千十十十
六、千十千千十十千

Chinese currency

E. NARRATIVE

Read the following narrative, paying special attention to punctuation and overall structure. The first time you read the narrative, read it out loud; the second time, read silently and try to gradually increase your reading speed. Always think of the meaning of what you're reading.

你問我去北京一個人多少錢？好，去北京一個人一百二十塊。去香山多少錢？去香山兩百八十塊。去天津呢？去天津四百五十塊。去上海呢？去上海一個人一千四百塊。去美國一個人多少錢？這個你別問我；請你問那個人吧！

Notes

A10. Given the context, the last phrase means "Why don't you buy that one?"

A17-20.

The Chinese number 〇 **líng** "zero" is written rounder than in English; it would not be considered correct to write it with the Arabic numeral 0. **Líng** can also be written with the Chinese character 零, but nowadays 〇 is even more common, especially when writing years, room numbers, telephone numbers, and page numbers.

A20. **LONG FORMS OF THE NUMBERS.** (The following is for reference only; you don't need to learn this information now.) Since the Chinese characters 一二三四五六七八九十 are quite simple, consisting of only a few strokes, the potential exists for dishonest people to try to alter them, for example, to add two strokes and create a 三 out of a 一, or to add one stroke and create a 十 out of a 一 . Therefore, to prevent alteration or confusion and to make the numbers appear more "official," on financial records and on currency, the numbers are often written in more complex "long forms." If you open a bank account in mainland China, Taiwan, or Hong Kong, you will need to write these long forms of the numbers on withdrawal slips and other official forms. The long forms have the same pronunciations as the ordinary forms. The long forms of the numbers from 1 to 10, plus 100 and 1,000, are as follows:

ORDINARY FORM	LONG FORM
一	壹
二	贰 (貳)
三	叁
四	肆
五	伍
六	陆 (陸)

ORDINARY FORM	LONG FORM
七	柒
八	捌 (捌)
九	玖
十	拾
百	佰
千	仟

B2. 五十块钱？(五十塊錢？) "Fifty dollars?" is an Intonation Question (cf. BSC 2-3: 1c).

B4. 两个人去中国，两千块钱，太贵了！(兩個人去中國，兩千塊錢，太貴了！) "$2,000 for two people to go to China is too expensive!"

B5. 七百人 means the same as 七百个人 (七百個人). In writing and sometimes in speaking, measures can be omitted between 百 or 千 and 人.

E. 你问我去北京一个人多少钱？(你問我去北京一個人多少錢？) "You're asking me how much it costs for one person to go to Beijing?" This sentence involves the Question Word Question 去北京一个人多少钱？(去北京一個人多少錢？) being embedded within the Intonation Question 你问我？(你問我？).

Buying a Train Ticket

PART 4

十一块五。
(十一塊五。)
天津，十点半的，多少钱？
(天津，十點半的，多少錢？)

New Characters and Words

Study the six characters below and the common words written with them, paying careful attention to each character's pronunciation, meaning, and structure, as well as similar-looking characters. After you've studied a character, turn to the *Practice Essentials* volume and practice writing it on the practice sheet, making sure to follow the correct stroke order and direction as you pronounce it out loud and think of its meaning.

115 点(點) **diǎn** point, dot, o'clock

Radical of the simplified form is 火 **huǒ** "fire." Notice that this radical is written 灬 and is referred to colloquially as 四点火(四點火) **sìdiǎn huǒ** "four dots of fire" when it occurs at the bottom of a character. Radical of the traditional form is 黑 **hēi** "black." The phonetic is 占 **zhān** "practice divination."

点(點)	**diǎn**	o'clock [M]
一点(一點)	**yīdiǎn/yìdiǎn**	one o'clock; a little, some [NU + M]
几点(幾點)	**jǐdiǎn**	what time?
五点(五點)	**wǔdiǎn**	five o'clock

116 刻 **kè** short period of time, quarter of an hour

Radical is 刀 **dāo** "knife," which is written 刂 when occurring at the right-hand side of a character. This radical is referred to colloquially as 立刀 **lìdāo** "standing knife." Phonetic is 亥 **hài**.

刻	**kè**	quarter of an hour [M]
一刻	**yíkè**	a quarter of an hour
三刻	**sānkè**	three quarters of an hour

117 半 **bàn** half

Radical is 十 **shí** (11). Notice how this character neatly divides into two "halves." Contrast 半 with 十 **shí** (11).

半	**bàn**	half [NU]
十点半（十點半）	**shídiǎn bàn**	half past ten, 10:30
一半	**yíbàn**	one-half
一半一半	**yíbàn yíbàn**	half and half

118 差（差） **chà** lack

Radical is 工 **gōng** "work." Note the slight difference—a reduction by one stroke—in the simplified version 差 as compared with the traditional version 差. In practice, most people when handwriting the traditional version write it identically with the simplified version. Contrast 差（差）with 美 **měi** (77).

差（差）	**chà**	lack [V]
差一刻六点（差一刻六點）	**chà yíkè liùdiǎn**	a quarter to six (lit. "lacking a quarter of an hour six o'clock")
差不多（差不多）	**chàbuduō**	almost, about [MA]

119 钟（鐘） **zhōng** bell; clock

Radical is 金 **jīn** "gold, metal" [BF], since bells are made of metal. This radical is referred to colloquially as 金字旁 **jīnzìpáng** "side made up of the character 金." When used as a radical in writing simplified characters, the sixth and seventh strokes of 金 are deleted, so that the radical is then simplified to 钅. When writing traditional characters, the last stroke of 金 slants up toward the right, so as not to get in the way of the other component. Phonetic of the traditional form is 童 **tóng** "child" [BF].

钟（鐘）	**zhōng**	bell; clock [N]
几点钟？（幾點鐘？）	**Jǐdiǎn zhōng?**	What time (of the clock) is it?
三点钟（三點鐘）	**sāndiǎn zhōng**	three o'clock

120 头（頭） **tóu** head; (common noun suffix)

Radical of the simplified form is 大 **dà** (13). Radical of the traditional form is 頁 **yè** "page." Phonetic of the traditional form is 豆 **dòu** "bean." Contrast simplified 头 with 大 **dà** (13) and simplified 兴 **xìng** (90).

钟头（鐘頭）	**zhōngtóu**	hour [N]
半个钟头（半個鐘頭）	**bàn'ge zhōngtóu**	half an hour
一个半钟头（一個半鐘頭）	**yíge bàn zhōngtóu**	an hour and a half

New Words in BSC 3-4 Written with Characters You Already Know

坐	**zuò**	travel by, take [V]
天津	**Tiānjīn**	Tianjin [PW]

Reading Exercises (Simplified Characters)

Now practice reading the new characters and words for this lesson in context in sentences, conversations, and narratives. Be sure to refer to the Notes at the end of this lesson, and make use of the accompanying audio disc to hear and practice correct pronunciation, phrasing, and intonation.

A. CLOCK TIMES AND AMOUNTS OF TIME

Read out loud each of the following time expressions. Be sure you're clear whether what you're reading is a clock time (e.g., "4:00") or an amount of time (e.g., "4 hours").

1. 一点半
2. 十二点三刻
3. 两点钟
4. 六点半
5. 五点钟
6. 八点一刻
7. 十点半
8. 差一刻九点
9. 二十三点二十
10. 十五点半
11. 九点五十
12. 二十点
13. 十八点四十
14. 四个钟头
15. 六个半钟头
16. 半个钟头
17. 一个半钟头
18. 两个半钟头
19. 二十四个钟头
20. 七十二个钟头

B. SENTENCES

Read out loud each of the following sentences, which include all the new characters of this lesson. The first time you read a sentence, focus special attention on the characters and words that are new to you, reminding yourself of their pronunciation and meaning. The second time, aim to comprehend the overall meaning of the sentence.

一、这位先生，请问，几点钟了？
二、九点一刻了，我不坐了，我先走了。
三、差一刻六点了，我们走吧！
四、别太高兴，这个钟很贵，一千六百块钱！
五、我的四位老师，一半是男的，一半是女的。
六、三个是男生，三个是女生，一半一半。
七、你也去成都吗？我坐三点的，你坐几点的？
八、五点钟去台北的那位老先生姓文，不姓王。

九、名字叫李京生的那个女的是小李的姐姐，不是我的姐姐。

十、没带钱的那个男生是王大海，不是我！

C. CONVERSATIONS

Read out loud the following conversations, including the name or role of the person speaking. If possible, find a partner or partners and each of you play a role. Then switch roles, so you get practice reading all of the lines.

一、

老李：几点了？

老谢：十一点三刻了。

老李：十一点三刻了吗？！

老谢：不对，不对。十点三刻。

二、

美国人：上海，两个人。多少钱？几个钟头？

中国人：一个人一百五十五块五。去上海……差不多一个半钟头。

美国人：半个钟头？

中国人：不是半个钟头，是一个半钟头。

美国人：这是钱。谢谢您！

三、

美国人：天津，十点半的。多少钱？

中国人：十一块五。

美国人：好，这是钱，十一块五。去天津几个钟头？

中国人：差不多两个半钟头。

美国人：好，谢谢您！

D. CHARACTER DIFFERENTIATION DRILLS

Distinguish carefully the following similar-looking characters, pronouncing each one out loud and thinking of its meaning.

一、差 差 差 美 美 美

二、差 美 差 差 美 美 美 差
三、头 头 头 兴 兴 兴
四、头 兴 兴 头 兴 兴 头

E. NARRATIVE

Read the following narrative, paying special attention to punctuation and overall structure. The first time you read the narrative, read it out loud; the second time, read silently and try to gradually increase your reading speed. Always think of the meaning of what you're reading.

老高是我的同屋，小何是小李的同屋。我们四个人三点半去北京的“中美公司”。去北京不太难，差不多一个半钟头，一个人差不多十五块钱。老高很高兴，他带了他的名片，也带了一点钱，差不多两百块吧。小李也很高兴，他也带了一点钱，差不多一百块，没带名片。我太忙了，没带名片，也没带钱。没带钱不太好吧？

Reading Exercises (Traditional Characters)

A. LARGER NUMBERS AND SUMS OF MONEY

Read out loud each of the following time expressions. Be sure you're clear whether what you're reading is a clock time (e.g., “4:00”) or an amount of time (e.g., “4 hours”).

1. 一點半
2. 十二點三刻
3. 兩點鐘
4. 六點半
5. 五點鐘
6. 八點一刻
7. 十點半
8. 差一刻九點
9. 二十三點二十
10. 十五點半
11. 九點五十
12. 二十點
13. 十八點四十
14. 四個鐘頭
15. 六個半鐘頭
16. 半個鐘頭
17. 一個半鐘頭
18. 兩個半鐘頭
19. 二十四個鐘頭
20. 七十二個鐘頭

Hong Kong currency

B. SENTENCES

Read out loud each of the following sentences, which include all the new characters of this lesson. The first time you read a sentence, focus special attention on the characters and words that are new to you, reminding yourself of their pronunciation and meaning. The second time, aim to comprehend the overall meaning of the sentence.

一、這位先生，請問，幾點鐘了？

二、九點一刻了，我不坐了，我先走了。

三、差一刻六點了，我們走吧！

四、別太高興，這個鐘很貴，一千六百塊錢！

五、我的四位老師，一半是男的，一半是女的。

六、三個是男生，三個是女生，一半一半。

七、你也去成都嗎？我坐三點的，你坐幾點的？

八、五點鐘去台北的那位老先生姓文，不姓王。

九、名字叫李京生的那個女的是小李的姐姐，不是我的姐姐。

十、沒帶錢的那個男生是王大海，不是我！

C. CONVERSATIONS

Read out loud the following conversations, including the name or role of the person speaking. If possible, find a partner or partners and each of you play a role. Then switch roles, so you get practice reading all of the lines.

一、老李：幾點了？
老謝：十一點三刻了。
老李：十一點三刻了嗎？！
老謝：不對，不對。十點三刻。

二、美國人：上海，兩個人。多少錢？幾個鐘頭？
中國人：一個人一百五十五塊五。去上海……差不多一個半鐘頭。
美國人：半個鐘頭？
中國人：不是半個鐘頭，是一個半鐘頭。
美國人：這是錢。謝謝您！

三、美國人：天津，十點半的。多少錢？
中國人：十一塊五。
美國人：好，這是錢，十一塊五。去天津幾個鐘頭？
中國人：差不多兩個半鐘頭。
美國人：好，謝謝您！

D. CHARACTER DIFFERENTIATION DRILLS

Distinguish carefully the following similar-looking characters, pronouncing each one out loud and thinking of its meaning.

一、差差差美美美
二、差美差差美美美差
三、頭頭頭興興興 (simplified only)
四、頭興興頭興興頭 (simplified only)

These characters can be read in any direction to mean "(National Taiwan) Normal University" or "great teacher"

E. NARRATIVE

Read the following narrative, paying special attention to punctuation and overall structure. The first time you read the narrative, read it out loud; the second time, read silently and try to gradually increase your reading speed. Always think of the meaning of what you're reading.

老高是我的同屋，小何是小李的同屋。我們四個人三點半去北京的「中美公司」。去北京不太難，差不多一個半鐘頭，一個人差不多十五塊錢。老高很高興，他帶了他的名片，也帶了一點錢，差不多兩百塊吧。小李也很高興，他也帶了一點錢，差不多一百塊，沒帶名片。我太忙了，沒帶名片，也沒帶錢。沒帶錢不太好吧？

Notes

B1. In this sentence, 这位先生 (這位先生), lit. "This gentleman," is used as a vocative expression to address the person that this question is addressed to. It's probably best translated as "Sir."

B4. 别太高兴 (別太高興) "Don't be too happy" or "Don't get too happy."

B7. 我坐三点的，你坐几点的？(我坐三點的，你坐幾點的？) "I'm taking the 3:00 one, which one are you taking?" In this question, it's understood from the context that some means of transportation—most likely a train, possibly a plane—is being talked about.

B8. 五点钟去台北的那位老先生姓文，不姓王 (五點鐘去台北的那位老先生姓文，不姓王) "That old gentleman who went/is going to Taipei at five o'clock has the last name Wen, not Wang."

B9. 名字叫李京生的那个女的是小李的姐姐，不是我的姐姐 (名字叫李京生的那個女的是小李的姐姐，不是我的姐姐) "That woman who's named Li Jingsheng is Little Li's older sister, not my older sister."

E. 没带钱不太好吧？(沒帶錢不太好吧？) literally means "Didn't bring money, not too good, I suppose?" We could translate this into more colloquial English as "Not to have brought money wasn't such a cool thing to do, huh?"

UNIT 4

Numbers, Dates, Time, and Money (II)

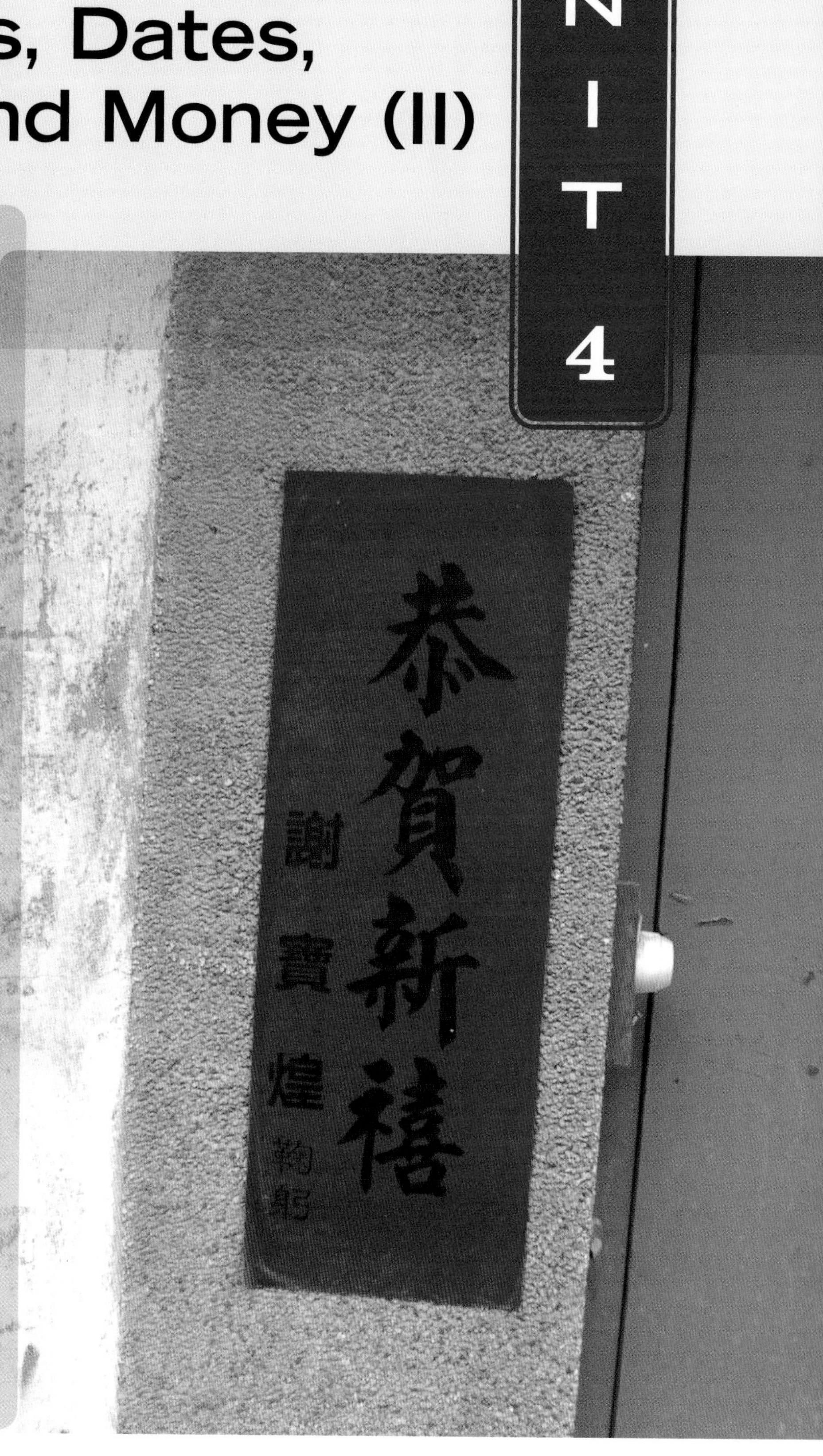

COMMUNICATIVE OBJECTIVES

Once you've mastered this unit, you'll be able to use Chinese to read and write:

1. Dates.
2. Days of the week.
3. Months of the year.
4. Years.
5. Time words like "today," "tomorrow," "this year," "last year," and "next year."
6. Ordinal numbers: "first," "second," "third," etc.
7. Very large numbers: ten thousand through ninety-nine million.
8. Sentences about how much things cost.
9. Opening and closing times of establishments.
10. About the population of various countries, provinces, and cities.
11. Questions and responses about whether someone has ever been to a certain place. If they have been there before, how many times? If they have never been there, do they want to go? When? How long do they want to stay?
12. A Chinese joke.
13. A life insurance table.
14. A number of important dates in Chinese and Southeast Asian history.
15. Some expressions that differ in spoken-style vs. written-style Chinese.

PART 1

Inquiring About Opening and Closing Times

星期六开不开？
(星期六開不開？)
星期六开半天。
(星期六開半天。)

New Characters and Words

Study the six characters below and the common words written with them, paying careful attention to each character's pronunciation, meaning, and structure, as well as similar-looking characters. After you've studied a character, turn to the *Practice Essentials* volume and practice writing it on the practice sheet, making sure to follow the correct stroke order and direction as you pronounce it out loud and think of its meaning.

121 谁(誰) **shéi** who

Radical is 讠(言) **yán** "speech" [**BF**]. The colloquial name for this radical is 言字旁 **yánzìpáng** "side made up of the character 言." The radical indicates that the word "who" is a word frequently used in "speech." The phonetic is 隹 **zhuī** "short-tailed bird" [**BF**], which gives a hint at the pronunciation (since **zhuī** is really an abbreviation of Pinyin **zhueī**, which better shows the rhyme with **shéi**). Some Beijing speakers pronounce this word as **shuí**, in which case the resemblance of the final to **zhuī** is even closer.

谁(誰) **shéi** who, whom [**QW**]

---

122 开(開) **kāi** open; depart (of a train, bus, ship)

Radical for the simplified form is 廾 **gǒng** "two hands." Radical for the traditional form is 门(門) **mén** "door" (123). This radical is referred to colloquially as 门字框(門字框) **ménzìkuàng** "frame of the character 门(門)." 开 originally represented two hands "opening" a bolt inside a "door" (門). Contrast 开(開) with 门(門) **mén** (123), 问(問) **wèn** (75), and 同 **tóng** (80).

开(開) **kāi** open; depart (of a train, bus, ship) [**V**]

123 门(門) **mén** door, gate

This character is a picture of a two-leaved door, as in saloons in the American Old West, and itself serves as a radical for many characters. It can also serve as a phonetic, e.g., in 们(們) **men** (57) as in 我们(我們) **wǒmen** and 问(問) **wèn** (75). Contrast 门(門) with 问(問) **wèn** (75), 开(開) **kāi** (122), 关(關) **guān** (124), and 同 **tóng** (80).

门(門)	**mén**	door, gate [N]
门(門)	**Mén**	Men (also Mun or Moon, a common Korean surname) [SN]
开门(開門)	**kāimén**	open a door, open [VO]
金门(金門)	**Jīnmén**	Quemoy (island off the coast of Fujian Province in southeastern China that is administered by Taiwan) [PW]

124 关(關) **guān** close

Radical of the simplified form is 八 **bā** "eight" (9). Radical of the traditional form is 门(門) **mén** "door." This radical is referred to colloquially as 门字框(門字框) **ménzìkuàng** "frame of the character 门(門)." To save strokes, the traditional form of the character is often handwritten as 関, which is the source of the simplified form 关. Contrast 关(關) with 开(開) **kāi** (122) and 美 **měi** (77).

关(關)	**guān**	close [V]
关(關)	**Guān**	Guan [SN]
关门(關門)	**guānmén**	close a door, close [VO]

125 星 **xīng** star

Radical is 日 **rì** "sun" [BF]. Phonetic is 生 **shēng** "be born." A "star" is a new "sun" that has been "born."

126 期 **qī/qí** period of time

Radical is 月 **yuè** "moon." The colloquial name for this radical is 月字旁 **yuèzìpáng** "side made up of the character 月." Phonetic is 其 **qí** "his, her, its, their." Together these two components literally mean "its moons," which refers to the ancient method of marking "periods of time" by counting "moons." The official pronunciation of 期 is **qī** in mainland China but **qí** in Taiwan.

星期	**xīngqī/xīngqí**	week [N]
星期几(星期幾)	**xīngqījǐ**	which day of the week? [QW]
星期一	**xīngqīyī**	Monday [TW]
星期二	**xīngqī'èr**	Tuesday [TW]
星期三	**xīngqīsān**	Wednesday [TW]
星期四	**xīngqīsì**	Thursday [TW]
星期五	**xīngqīwǔ**	Friday [TW]
星期六	**xīngqīliù**	Saturday [TW]
星期天	**xīngqītiān**	Sunday [TW]
上个星期(上個星期)	**shàngge xīngqī**	last week
这个星期(這個星期)	**zhèige xīngqī**	this week

New Words in BSC 4-1 Written with Characters You Already Know

天 **tiān** day [M]

Reading Exercises (Simplified Characters)

Now practice reading the new characters and words for this lesson in context in sentences, conversations, and narratives. Be sure to refer to the Notes at the end of this lesson, and make use of the accompanying audio disc to hear and practice correct pronunciation, phrasing, and intonation.

A. SENTENCES

Read out loud each of the following sentences, which include all the new characters of this lesson. The first time you read a sentence, focus special attention on the characters and words that are new to you, reminding yourself of their pronunciation and meaning. The second time, aim to comprehend the overall meaning of the sentence.

一、请问，星期一去北京的那位小姐是谁？

二、这个星期请你们别开这个门，请你们开那个门，好吗？

三、请问，台北的公司几点钟开门，几点钟关门？

四、金门多大？多少人？金门人都是中国人，对不对？

五、钱老师去湖南，去了两天半了。

六、这个门很难开，请老王开吧。

七、台湾的公司星期六开半天，星期天关门。

八、今天星期几？你姐姐去北京几天了？

九、请问，那个女的是谁？是小王的姐姐吗？

十、王大海上个星期天去中国了，很高兴。

B. CONVERSATIONS

Read out loud the following conversations, including the name or role of the person speaking. If possible, find a partner or partners and each of you play a role. Then switch roles, so you get practice reading all of the lines.

一、

老师：是谁开了门？你别开门，好不好？

女生：我没开门，也没关门。

老师：我问你，那个女生是谁？

女生：她是我的同屋，她叫关小星。

二、
何小山：您星期六去公司吗？
王大中：去。香港的公司星期六开半天。
何小山：那，星期天您不去公司吧？
王大中：对，星期天我不去。星期天公司不开门。

C. CHARACTER DIFFERENTIATION DRILLS

Distinguish carefully the following similar-looking characters, pronouncing each one out loud and thinking of its meaning.

一、门 门 门 问 问 问
二、门 门 门 同 同 同
三、门 问 同 问 门 问 同
四、门 门 门 开 开 开
五、门 门 门 关 关 关
六、门 问 同 门 开 门 关 门

D. NARRATIVES

Read the following narratives, paying special attention to punctuation and overall structure. The first time you read a narrative, read it out loud; the second time, read silently and try to gradually increase your reading speed. Always think of the meaning of what you're reading.

一、小谢的公司是中国公司，叫“大安公司”。星期一、二、三、四、五八点钟开门，五点钟关门。星期六开半天，八点开门，十二点半关门。星期天不开。小谢星期一八点钟去了公司，公司没开门。他不太高兴，走了。

二、上个星期我们的两位中文老师带我们去了台湾。去台湾不太贵，差不多一千多块钱，差不多十八个钟头。我们去台湾去了五天：星期一去了台中、星期二去了台南、星期三去了台东、星期四去了台北、星期五去了金门。那五天，我们都很高兴！

Reading Exercises (Traditional Characters)

A. SENTENCES

Read out loud each of the following sentences, which include all the new characters of this lesson. The first time you read a sentence, focus special attention on the characters and words that are new to you, reminding yourself of their pronunciation and meaning. The second time, aim to comprehend the overall meaning of the sentence.

一、請問，星期一去北京的那位小姐是誰？

二、這個星期請你們別開這個門，請你們開那個門，好嗎？

三、請問，台北的公司幾點鐘開門，幾點鐘關門？

四、金門多大？多少人？金門人都是中國人，對不對？

五、錢老師去湖南，去了兩天半了。

六、這個門很難開，請老王開吧。

七、台灣的公司星期六開半天，星期天關門。

八、今天星期幾？你姐姐去北京幾天了？

九、請問，那個女的是誰？是小王的姐姐嗎？

十、王大海上個星期天去中國了，很高興。

B. CONVERSATIONS

Read out loud the following conversations, including the name or role of the person speaking. If possible, find a partner or partners and each of you play a role. Then switch roles, so you get practice reading all of the lines.

一、

老師：是誰開了門？你別開門，好不好？

女生：我沒開門，也沒關門。

老師：我問你，那個女生是誰？

女生：她是我的同屋，她叫關小星。

二、

何小山：您星期六去公司嗎？

王大中：去。香港的公司星期六開半天。

何小山：那，星期天您不去公司吧？

王大中：對，星期天我不去。星期天公司不開門。

C. CHARACTER DIFFERENTIATION DRILLS

Distinguish carefully the following similar-looking characters, pronouncing each one out loud and thinking of its meaning.

一、門門門問問問
二、門門門同同同
三、門問同問門問同
四、門門門開開開
五、門門門關關關
六、門問同門開門關門

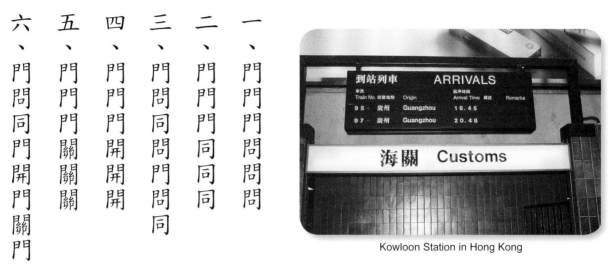

Kowloon Station in Hong Kong

D. NARRATIVES

Read the following narratives, paying special attention to punctuation and overall structure. The first time you read a narrative, read it out loud; the second time, read silently and try to gradually increase your reading speed. Always think of the meaning of what you're reading.

一、小謝的公司是中國公司，叫「大安公司」。星期一、二、三、四、五八點鐘開門，五點鐘關門。星期六開半天，八點開門，十二點半關門。星期天不開。小謝星期一八點鐘去了公司，公司沒開門。他不太高興，走了。

二、上個星期我們的兩位中文老師帶我們去了台灣。去台灣不太貴，差不多一千多塊錢，差不多十八個鐘頭。我們去台灣去了五天：星期一去了台中、星期二去了台南、星期三去了台東、星期四去了台北、星期五去了金門。那五天，我們都很高興！

Notes

A1. 星期一去北京的那位小姐是谁？(星期一去北京的那位小姐是誰？) could be translated as either "Who is that young lady that went to Beijing on Monday?" or "Who is that young lady that is going to Beijing on Monday?" The real world context and prior knowledge that the speaker and listener bring to the task would make the meaning clear.

A5. 钱老师去湖南，去了两天半了（錢老師去湖南，去了兩天半了）means "Teacher Qian has gone to Hunan for two and a half days now" or "Teacher Qian has been in Hunan for two and a half days now." The implication is that this situation is continuing up to the present and that Teacher Qian is still in Hunan. In sentences indicating duration of time, a sentence-final particle 了 at the end of the sentence indicates that the action of the verb has been continuing for a period of time up to and including the present. This use of 了 will be taken up formally at a later time.

A8a. The question 今天星期几？(今天星期幾？) means "What day of the week is it today?" No verb 是 is needed after 今天, though it would not be wrong to add one.

A8b. 你姐姐去北京几天了？(你姐姐去北京幾天了？) "For how many days now has your older sister been in Beijing?" (lit. "Your older sister went to Beijing for how many days now?"). Cf. note A5 above.

Personal Information

PART 2

几月几号？
(幾月幾號？)
四月十三号。
(四月十三號。)

New Characters and Words

Study the six characters below and the common words written with them, paying careful attention to each character's pronunciation, meaning, and structure, as well as similar-looking characters. After you've studied a character, turn to the *Practice Essentials* volume and practice writing it on the practice sheet, making sure to follow the correct stroke order and direction as you pronounce it out loud and think of its meaning.

127 什 **shén** (first syllable of the word for "what")

Radical is 人 **rén** "person," which is written 亻 when occurring at the left side of a character so as not to get in the way of the component at the right. The colloquial name for this radical is 人字旁 **rénzìpáng** "side made up of the character 人." The other component is 十 **shí** (11). In the traditional character system, there exists a more complex form 甚 that is also sometimes used in place of 什. Contrast 什 with 十 **shí** (11), 千 **qiān** (114), and 他 **tā** (55).

---

128 么(麼) **me** (occurs as second syllable of several common words)

Radical of the simplified form is 丿 **piě** "left-falling stroke." Radical of the traditional form is 麻 **má** "hemp," which is also the phonetic. The other component is 幺 **yāo** "tiny, small." A common variant of traditional 麼 is 麽, the last three strokes of which are the origin of the simplified character.

什么(什麼)	**shénme**	what (pronounced **shémme**; note the common traditional variant 甚麼) [QW]
这么(這麼)	**zhème**	like this, in this way, so (pronounced **zhèmme**) [A]
那么(那麼)	**nàme**	then, in that case, so (pronounced **nèmme**) [A]

129 就 **jiù** then; precisely, exactly; only

Radical is 尢 **Yóu** (a rare surname). Phonetic is 尤 **yóu** as in 尤其 **yóuqí** "especially." The other component is 京 **jīng** (17) as in 北京 **Běijīng**. Contrast 就 with 京 **jīng**.

就	**jiù**	then; precisely, exactly [A]
就是	**jiù shi**	be precisely, be exactly, be none other than

130 月 **yuè** moon; month

This character, which is itself a radical, is a pictograph; it is a picture of a crescent moon with two moon spots in it. It has also come to mean "month," since counting full "moons" was formerly a method for keeping track of the number of "months." Be careful to distinguish the names of the months, e.g., 三月 **sānyuè** "March," from amounts of time involving months, e.g., 三个月 (三個月) **sān'ge yuè** "three months." Contrast 月 with 名 **míng** (83) and 多 **duō** (103).

月	**yuè**	month [N]
几月 (幾月)	**jǐyuè**	which month? [QW]
一月	**yīyuè**	January [TW]
二月	**èryuè**	February [TW]
三月	**sānyuè**	March [TW]
四月	**sìyuè**	April [TW]
五月	**wǔyuè**	May [TW]
六月	**liùyuè**	June [TW]
七月	**qīyuè**	July [TW]
八月	**bāyuè**	August [TW]
九月	**jiǔyuè**	September [TW]
十月	**shíyuè**	October [TW]
十一月	**shíyīyuè**	November [TW]
十二月	**shí'èryuè**	December [TW]
上个月 (上個月)	**shàngge yuè**	last month

131 号 (號) **hào** number; day of the month

Radical of the simplified form is 口 **kǒu** "mouth." Radical of the traditional form is 虍 **hǔ** "tiger." In either form, note the presence of 口 **kǒu** "mouth," since "numbers" are often called out with one's "mouth."

号 (號)	**hào**	number; day of the month (in speech) [M]
几号 (幾號)	**jǐhào**	which day of the month? [QW]
十三号 (十三號)	**shísānhào**	13th day of the month (in speech)
五〇四号 (五〇四號)	**wǔ líng sì hào**	number 504

132 日 **rì** sun; day, day of the month; Japan

This character, which can itself serve as a radical, is a squared-off picture of the sun with a sunspot in it. Contrast 日 with 明 **míng** (15), 是 **shì** (76), and 百 **bǎi** (113).

日	**rì**	day; day of the month (in writing) [BF]
十三日	**shísānrì**	13th day of the month (in writing)
星期日	**xīngqīrì**	Sunday [TW]
生日	**shēngrì**	birthday [N]
日文	**Rìwén**	Japanese (especially written Japanese) [N]

New Words in BSC 4-2 Written with Characters You Already Know

今天	**jīntiān**	today [TW]
明天	**míngtiān**	tomorrow [TW]
年	**nián**	year [M]
明年	**míngnián**	next year [TW]
去年	**qùnián**	last year [TW]
东(東)	**dōng**	east [L]
路	**lù**	road [N]
是...的	**shì...de**	(indicates time or place of known past actions) [PT]

Reading Exercises (Simplified and Traditional Characters)

Now practice reading the new characters and words for this lesson in context in sentences, conversations, and narratives. Be sure to refer to the Notes at the end of this lesson, and make use of the accompanying audio disc to hear and practice correct pronunciation, phrasing, and intonation.

A. SOME IMPORTANT DATES IN CHINESE AND SOUTHEAST ASIAN HISTORY

Read out loud each of the following historic dates.

1. 一八六六年十一月十二日，一九二五年三月十二日
   (Sun Yat-sen's birth and death)
2. 一八八七年十月三十一日，一九七五年四月五日
   (Chiang Kai-shek's birth and death)
3. 一八九三年十二月二十六日，一九七六年九月九日
   (Mao Zedong's birth and death)
4. 一八九八年三月五日，一九七六年一月八日
   (Zhou Enlai's birth and death)
5. 一八九八年三月五日，二〇〇三年十月二十三日
   (Madame Chiang Kai-shek's birth and death)

6. 一九一一年十月十日
(founding of the Republic of China)

7. 一九一二年二月十二日
(abdication of the last Qing Dynasty emperor)

8. 一九一九年五月四日
(May Fourth Movement to promote cultural reforms, commonly referred to as 五四)

9. 一九四五年十月二十五日
(end of 50 years of Japanese colonial rule in Taiwan)

10. 一九四七年二月二十八日
(2/28 Incident in Taiwan, commonly referred to as 二二八)

11. 一九四九年十月一日
(founding of the People's Republic of China)

12. 一九六五年八月九日
(founding of the Republic of Singapore)

13. 一九六六年五月十六日
(Mao Zedong launches the Cultural Revolution, which continues until his death ten years later)

14. 一九七八年十二月
(announcement of the policy of 改革开放 (改革開放) **Gǎigé Kāifàng** "Reforms and Openness" that set the stage for the rapid growth of China's economy in the last two decades of the 20th century)

15. 一九八九年六月四日
(June 4th Incident at Tiananmen Square, commonly referred to as 六四)

16. 一九九六年三月二十三日
(first direct presidential election in Taiwan)

17. 一九九七年七月一日
(transfer of sovereignty over Hong Kong from Britain to China)

18. 一九九九年十二月二十日
(transfer of sovereignty over Macau from Portugal to China)

19. 2001年7月13日
(announcement that China was awarded the right to host the 2008 Olympic Games)

20. 2001年12月11日，2002年1月1日
(China's and Taiwan's respective entries into the World Trade Organization)

21. 北京，2008年 8月8日
(place and date of opening ceremony of Chinese Olympic Games)

22. 上海，2010年5月1日
(place and date of opening of Expo 2010)

Reading Exercises (Simplified Characters)

B. SENTENCES

Read out loud each of the following sentences, which include all the new characters of this lesson. The first time you read a sentence, focus special attention on the characters and words that are new to you, reminding yourself of their pronunciation and meaning. The second time, aim to comprehend the overall meaning of the sentence.

一、对，那就是你问的我们公司的名片。
二、你高兴，我就高兴；你不高兴，我就不高兴。
三、钱老师，请问，“五月八日”就是“五月八号”，对不对？
四、明天，也就是五月五号，是我的生日；我明天就不去公司了，好吗？
五、请你们别这么叫她，好不好？她很不高兴。
六、去年是一九九九年，今年是两千年，明年是二〇〇一年，是不是？
七、你们是哪年几月几号去中国的？
八、你去年的日文老师是谁？是不是中川先生？
九、今天是六月十三号星期五。十三号星期五不好吗？
十、王大海上个月去了河南，这个月去湖北，明年二月去四川。

C. CONVERSATIONS

Read out loud the following conversations, including the name or role of the person speaking. If possible, find a partner or partners and each of you play a role. Then switch roles, so you get practice reading all of the lines.

一、
安先生：何小姐，你好！
何小姐：安先生，你好！你这个星期不去台南吗？
安先生：六号是我的生日，我就不去了。
何小姐：六号？明天就是六号。那，明天你多大了？
安先生：我明天三十岁了，老了！

二、
男生：老师，请问，这个中文叫什么？

老师：这个中文叫“钟”。
男生：那个中文叫什么？叫“门”，是吧？
老师：对，那个就叫“门”。中文不难吧？
男生：不太难。谢谢老师！

三、
美国人：哪位是李老师？
中国人：年纪很大的那位男老师就是李老师。
美国人：什么？他就是李老师？那么，这位老师姓什么？
中国人：这位老师姓路。

四、
老高：小金，你是哪年去中国的？是去年吗？
小金：什么？谁去中国了？
老高：不是，不是。我问你，你是去年去中国的，对不对？
小金：不是。我是今年一月去的。

五、
美国男生：中文难？日文难？
美国女生：中文、日文都很难！

六、
美国女生：这是谁？
李先生　：这是小明。
美国女生：小明，你好！你今年几岁了？
小明　　：我四岁。明天是我的生日。明天我就五岁了！

七、
中国小姐：先生，您好！我姓钱。您贵姓？
美国先生：我姓王，我叫王大明。王是“国王”的王，大是“大小”的大，明是“日”、“月”明。

八、
关中山：小金，你坐几点的？
李大安：我坐 …… 七点的。
关中山：七点的？你坐八点的就OK。

D. CHARACTER DIFFERENTIATION DRILLS

Distinguish carefully the following similar-looking characters, pronouncing each one out loud and thinking of its meaning.

一、什 什 什 十 十 十 千 千 千
二、什 什 什 他 他 他
三、什 他 什 十 什 千 什 他
四、月 月 月 多 多 多
五、月 月 月 名 名 名
六、月 名 多 名 月 多 名
七、日 日 日 明 明 明
八、日 日 日 是 是 是
九、日 日 日 百 百 百
十、日 明 是 日 百 日 明

E. NARRATIVE

Read the following narrative, paying special attention to punctuation and overall structure. The first time you read the narrative, read it out loud; the second time, read silently and try to gradually increase your reading speed. Always think of the meaning of what you're reading.

我的先生年纪很大，他明年就八十岁了。我的姐姐年纪也不小，她今年七十六岁了。我今年七十四岁了。我先生的生日是一九三〇年六月十号，我姐姐的生日是一九三三年六月十号。我的生日是一九三五年六月十号。我、我先生、我姐姐， 我们三个人的生日都是六月十号！

Reading Exercises (Traditional Characters)

B. SENTENCES

Read out loud each of the following sentences, which include all the new characters of this lesson. The first time you read a sentence, focus special attention on the characters and words that are new to you, reminding yourself of their pronunciation and meaning. The second time, aim to comprehend the overall meaning of the sentence.

一、對，那就是你問的我們公司的名片。

二、你高興，我就高興；你不高興，我就不高興。

三、錢老師，請問，「五月八日」就是「五月八號」，對不對？

四、明天，也就是五月五號，是我的生日；我明天就不去公司了，好嗎？

五、請你們別這麼叫她，好不好？她很不高興。

六、去年是一九九九年，今年是兩千年，明年是二〇〇一年，是不是？

七、你們是哪年幾月幾號去中國的？

八、你去年的日文老師是誰？是不是中川先生？

九、今天是六月十三號星期五。十三號星期五不好嗎？

十、王大海上個月去了河南，這個月去湖北，明年二月去四川。

C. CONVERSATIONS

Read out loud the following conversations, including the name or role of the person speaking. If possible, find a partner or partners and each of you play a role. Then switch roles, so you get practice reading all of the lines.

一、安先生：何小姐，你好！
何小姐：安先生，你好！你這個星期不去台南嗎？
安先生：六號是我的生日，我就不去了。
何小姐：六號？明天就是六號。那，明天你多大了？
安先生：我明天三十歲了，老了！

二、男生：老師，請問，這個中文叫什麼？
老師：這個中文叫「鐘」。
男生：那個中文叫什麼？叫「門」，是吧？
老師：對，那個就叫「門」。中文不難吧？
男生：不太難。謝謝老師！

三、美國人：哪位是李老師？
中國人：年紀很大的那位男老師就是李老師。
美國人：什麼？他就是李老師？那麼，這位老師姓什麼？
中國人：這位老師姓路。

四、老高：小金，你是哪年去中國的？是去年嗎？
小金：什麼？誰去中國了？
老高：不是，不是。我問你，你是去年去中國的，對不對？
小金：不是。我是今年一月去的。

五、美國男生：中文難？日文難？
美國女生：中文、日文都很難！

六、美國女生：這是誰？
李先生　：這是小明。
美國女生：小明，你好！你今年幾歲了？
小明　　：我四歲。明天是我的生日。明天我就五歲了！

七、中國小姐：先生，您好！我姓錢。您貴姓？
美國先生：我姓王，我叫王大明。王是「國王」的王。大是「大小」的大，明是「日」、「月」明。

八、關中山：小金，你坐幾點的？
李大安：我坐……七點的。
關中山：七點的？你坐八點的就OK。

D. CHARACTER DIFFERENTIATION DRILLS

Distinguish carefully the following similar-looking characters, pronouncing each one out loud and thinking of its meaning.

一、什什什十十十千千千
二、什什什他他他
三、什他什十什千什他
四、月月月多多多
五、月月月名名名
六、月名多名月多名
七、日日日明明明
八、日日日是是是
九、日日日百百百
十、日明是日百日明

E. NARRATIVE

Read the following narrative, paying special attention to punctuation and overall structure. The first time you read the narrative, read it out loud; the second time, read silently and try to gradually increase your reading speed. Always think of the meaning of what you're reading.

我的先生年紀很大，他明年就八十歲了。我的姐姐年紀也不小，她今年七十六歲了。我今年七十四歲了。我先生的生日是一九三〇年六月十號，我姐姐的生日是一九三三年六月十號。我的生日是一九三五年六月十號。我、我先生、我姐姐，我們三個人的生日都是六月十號！

Notes

A1. **WRITTEN-STYLE CHINESE.** In all languages, writing tends to differ in a number of respects from speech. Written style typically involves longer and more complex sentences while spoken style tends to consist of shorter, simple sentences that often refer to the physical context of the speech and may be full of false starts, rewordings, repetitions, and pauses. Vocabulary and grammar may also differ between writing and speech; consider English "illumination" vs. "light," or the grammar structure "were Mary still here" vs. "if Mary was still here."

This difference between written and spoken language is especially great in the case of Chinese. Modern written Chinese has been strongly influenced by Classical Chinese in both vocabulary and grammar. There are many words and structures common in written-style Chinese (as written in newspapers, business letters, or on street signs) that would seldom if ever be used in ordinary conversation. Written-style Chinese is usually referred to as 书面语 (書面語) **shūmiànyǔ**, while spoken Chinese is referred to as 口头语 (口頭語) **kǒutóuyǔ**. Understand that these distinctions are not absolute and that, given an appropriate context, some **shūmiànyǔ** can be spoken and some **kǒutóuyǔ** can be written.

Your first example of written-style Chinese is the word 日 **rì** in the meaning "day of the month." As you know, in spoken Chinese the word 号 (號) **hào** would be used instead. Study the following table:

SPOKEN STYLE	WRITTEN STYLE	ENGLISH
号 (號) **hào**	日 **rì**	day of the month

For example, the date "October 20" would in written-style Chinese be given as 十月二十日, but in spoken Chinese (as in direct quotations in novels, film scripts, or comics), this would be 十月二十号 (十月二十號). Be very careful not to use in your spoken Chinese words and expressions that are written style, since they would sound quite stilted and might not even be understood.

A19. While it's considered more formal to write dates with Chinese characters, Arabic numbers are also commonly used. So for "October 20, 1993," you could write either 一九九三年十月二十日 or 1993 年 10 月 20 日.

B2. 你高兴，我就高兴；你不高兴，我就不高兴 (你高興，我就高興；你不高興，我就不高興) "If you're happy, then I'm happy; if you're unhappy, then I'm unhappy." Notice the implied conditional "if." In Chinese, when there are two clauses in succession, the first one often expresses the condition under which the second clause applies. This is especially likely when the second clause contains a 就 "then."

B6a. 去年是一九九九年，今年是两千年，明年是二〇〇一年 (去年是一九九九年，今年是兩千年，明年是二〇〇一年) "Last year was 1999, this year is 2000, next year will be 2001." The equative verb 是 here has three different English equivalents! As a translation strategy, always check dates and timewords in a sentence before deciding on the tense of any verbs in the translation.

B6b. For "the year 2000," some Chinese say 二〇〇〇年 and others say 两千年 (兩千年).

C1. Since this is a conversation between two people that consists of direct quotations, 六號 is used rather than written-style 六日.

C3. 年纪很大的那位男老师 (年紀很大的那位男老師) "That male teacher who is very old."

C7. 王是 "国王" 的王，大是 "大小" 的大，明是 "日"、"月" 明 (王是「國王」的王，大是「大小」的大，明是「日」、「月」明) "**Wáng** as in the word for 'king,' **Dà** as in the word for 'size,' and **míng** as in the character 明 that is made up of the characters 日 and 月." The noun 国王 (國王) means "king,"and 大小 can mean either "big or small" or "size."

C8. 你坐八点的就OK (你坐八點的就OK) "If you take the 8:00 one you'll be O.K." The implication is that the 8:00 train is early enough and there is no need to take the 7:00 train.

Second Trip to China

PART 3

New Characters and Words

Study the six characters below and the common words written with them, paying careful attention to each character's pronunciation, meaning, and structure, as well as similar-looking characters. After you've studied a character, turn to the *Practice Essentials* volume and practice writing it on the practice sheet, making sure to follow the correct stroke order and direction as you pronounce it out loud and think of its meaning.

133 第 **dì-** (forms ordinal numbers)

Radical is ⺮ **zhú** "bamboo" [**BF**]. The colloquial name for this radical is 竹字头 (竹字頭) **zhúzìtóu** "top made up of the character 竹." Notice that, when 竹 is a radical, its third and sixth strokes are shortened. Phonetic is 弟 **dì** as in 弟弟 **dìdi** "younger brother."

第	**dì-**	(forms ordinal numbers) [**SP**]
第一，第二，第三	**dìyī, dì'èr, dìsān**	first, second, third
第一个 (第一個)	**dìyíge**	the first one
第一位	**dìyíwèi**	the first one (of people; polite)

134 次 **cì** time

Radical is 冫 **bīng** "ice." This radical is referred to colloquially as 两点水 (兩點水) **liǎngdiǎn shuǐ** "two drops of water." The other component is 欠 **qiàn** "owe." Contrast 次 with 你 **nǐ** (49).

次	**cì**	time [**M**]
几次 (幾次)	**jǐcì**	how many times?
一次	**yícì**	one time

第几次(第幾次)	**dìjǐcì**	the number what time?
第一次	**dìyícì**	the first time
上次	**shàngcì**	last time

135 来(來) **lái** come

Radical of the simplified form is 木 **mù** "tree" [BF]. Radical of the traditional form is 人 **rén** "person." The rest of the traditional character is another 人 plus the character 木 **mù** "tree" [BF]. Contrast 来(來) with 东(東) **dōng** (29) and 年 **nián** (104).

来(來)	**lái**	come [V]

136 过(過) **-guo** pass; (indicates past experience)

Radical is 辶 **chuò** "walk, go" [BF]. The colloquial name for this radical is 走之 **zǒu zhī** "the walking 之," because of its meaning "walk" and its resemblance to the particle 之. The other component of the simplified character is 寸 **cùn** "Chinese inch." The other component of the traditional character is 咼, which is the abbreviated form of 渦 **wō** "whirlpool." The character 過 is often printed as 過 (notice the small difference between 咼 and 咼).

过(過)	**-guo**	(indicates experience) [P]
来过(來過)	**láiguo**	have come to some place before
去过(去過)	**qùguo**	have gone to some place before

137 要 **yào** want, need, cost, take; will, be going to

Radical is 西 **xī** "west" (35). The other component is 女 **nǚ** "woman" (101).

要	**yào**	want, need, cost, take [V]; will, be going to [AV]
不要	**búyào**	don't [AV]

138 住 **zhù** live (in), stay (in)

Radical is 人 **rén** "person," which is written 亻 when occurring at the left side of a character so as not to get in the way of the component at the right. The colloquial name for this radical is 人字旁 **rénzìpáng** "side made up of the character 人." Phonetic is 主 **zhǔ** as in 主人 **zhǔrén** "master, host." The "person" who is "master" always has a place to "live" or "stay." Contrast 住 with 位 **wèi** (98).

住	**zhù**	live (in), stay (in) [V]

Reading Exercises (Simplified Characters)

Now practice reading the new characters and words for this lesson in context in sentences, conversations, and narratives. Be sure to refer to the Notes at the end of this lesson, and make use of the accompanying audio disc to hear and practice correct pronunciation, phrasing, and intonation.

A. SENTENCES

Read out loud each of the following sentences, which include all the new characters of this lesson. The first time

you read a sentence, focus special attention on the characters and words that are new to you, reminding yourself of their pronunciation and meaning. The second time, aim to comprehend the overall meaning of the sentence.

一、那次我太忙，没去北京，这次我要去。
二、请问，这是你第几次来中国？你要住几天？
三、她的第一个先生是台湾人，第二个先生是香港人。
四、来，来，来，公司开门了，八点就开了。今天第一天开，不要走！
五、我问你，他姓什么，叫什么名字？他要来台北住几天？
六、林先生要来我们的公司问什么？你要带他来吗？
七、我要坐三点的，去南京。您呢？您要坐几点的？
八、钱先生住广东大街，钱太太住四川路。
九、我们住二〇六，他们住三〇八。是谁来了？我去开门。
十、王大海去过北京、香港、台北，没去过东京。

B. CONVERSATIONS

Read out loud the following conversations, including the name or role of the person speaking. If possible, find a partner or partners and each of you play a role. Then switch roles, so you get practice reading all of the lines.

一、
中国男生：这是你第一次来中国吗？
美国女生：不，这是第二次。我去年来过一次。
中国男生：你这次要住几天？
美国女生：差不多半个月吧。

二、
台湾人：你来过台湾几次？
美国人：我来过两次。第一次是去年三月。
台湾人：你去过北京吗？
美国人：去过。北京，我去过五、六次。
台湾人：北京好？台北好？
美国人：北京、台北都很好！

C. CHARACTER DIFFERENTIATION DRILLS

Distinguish carefully the following similar-looking characters, pronouncing each one out loud and thinking of its meaning.

一、次 次 次 你 你 你
二、次 你 次 次 次 你 你 次
三、来 来 来 东 东 东
四、来 来 来 年 年 年
五、来 东 来 年 来 东 年
六、住 住 住 位 位 位
七、住 位 位 住 住 位 住

D. NARRATIVE

Read the following narrative, paying special attention to punctuation and overall structure. The first time you read the narrative, read it out loud; the second time, read silently and try to gradually increase your reading speed. Always think of the meaning of what you're reading.

我去过中国，去过两次。第一次是二〇〇八年，第二次是二〇一〇年。二〇一〇年那次我十九岁，中文也不太好。我们先去上海住了两、三天，也去了北京、西安、成都、广州、香港。我们是四个男生、十个女生，我们的中文老师王老师也去了。我们很高兴，明年一月王老师要带我们去台湾。我们都没去过台湾。我们要住台北，要住差不多两个星期。

E. SUPPLEMENT: A LIFE INSURANCE TABLE

Read out loud the information contained in the life insurance table below. Be prepared to answer questions from your instructor and/or classmates on what the insurance premiums are each month, half year, or whole year for a male or female of a given age. (excerpt from a Taiwanese life insurance table)

		男	女
	月	143	117
12岁～30岁	半年	847	695
	年	1,692	1,389
	月	227	186
31岁～40岁	半年	1,335	1,099
	年	2,666	2,194
	月	324	271
41岁～50岁	半年	1,898	1,593

	年	3,788	3,181
	月	420	356
51岁～55岁	半年	2,458	2,087
	年	4,905	4,164
	月	513	435
56岁～60岁	半年	2,988	2,543
	年	5,960	5,074
	月	630	535
61岁～65岁	半年	3,654	3,117
	年	7,285	6,216

Reading Exercises (Traditional Characters)

A. SENTENCES

Read out loud each of the following sentences, which include all the new characters of this lesson. The first time you read a sentence, focus special attention on the characters and words that are new to you, reminding yourself of their pronunciation and meaning. The second time, aim to comprehend the overall meaning of the sentence.

一、那次我太忙，沒去北京，這次我要去。

二、請問，這是你第幾次來中國？你要住幾天？

三、她的第一個先生是台灣人，第二個先生是香港人。

四、來，來，來，公司開門了，八點就開了。今天第一天開，不要走！

五、我問你，他姓什麼，叫什麼名字？他要來台北住幾天？

六、林先生要來我們的公司問什麼？你要帶他來嗎？

七、我要坐三點的，去南京。您呢？您要坐幾點的？

八、錢先生住廣東大街，錢太太住四川路。

九、我們住二〇六，他們住三〇八。是誰來了？我去開門。

十、王大海去過北京、香港、台北，沒去過東京。

B. CONVERSATIONS

Read out loud the following conversations, including the name or role of the person speaking. If possible, find a partner or partners and each of you play a role. Then switch roles, so you get practice reading all of the lines.

一、中國男生：這是你第一次來中國嗎？
美國女生：不，這是第二次。我去年來過一次。
中國男生：你這次要住幾天？
美國女生：差不多半個月吧。

二、台灣人：你來過台灣幾次？
美國人：我來過兩次。第一次是去年三月。
台灣人：你去過北京嗎？
美國人：去過。北京，我去過五、六次。
台灣人：北京好？台北好？
美國人：北京、台北都很好！

C. CHARACTER DIFFERENTIATION DRILLS

Distinguish carefully the following similar-looking characters, pronouncing each one out loud and thinking of its meaning.

一、次次次你你你
二、次你次次次你你次
三、來來來東東東
四、來來來年年年
五、來東來年來東年
六、住住住位位位
七、住位位住住位住

D. NARRATIVE

Read the following narrative, paying special attention to punctuation and overall structure. The first time you read the narrative, read it out loud; the second time, read silently and try to gradually increase your reading speed. Always think of the meaning of what you're reading.

我去過中國，去過兩次。第一次是二○○八年，第二次是二○一○年。二○一○年那次我十九歲，中文也不太好。我們先去上海住了兩、三天，也去了北京、西安、成都、廣州、香港。我們四個男生、十個女生，我們的中文老師王老師也去了。我們很高興，明年一月王老師要帶我們去台灣。我們都沒去過台灣。我們要住台北，要住差不多兩個星期。

E. SUPPLEMENT: A LIFE INSURANCE TABLE

Read out loud the information contained in the life insurance table below. Be prepared to answer questions from your instructor and/or classmates on what the insurance premiums are each month, half year, or whole year for a male or female of a given age. (excerpt from a Taiwanese life insurance table)

		男	女
	月	143	117
12歲～30歲	半年	847	695
	年	1,692	1,389
	月	227	186
31歲～40歲	半年	1,335	1,099
	年	2,666	2,194
	月	324	271
41歲～50歲	半年	1,898	1,593
	年	3,788	3,181
	月	420	356
51歲～55歲	半年	2,458	2,087
	年	4,905	4,164
	月	513	435
56歲～60歲	半年	2,988	2,543
	年	5,960	5,074
	月	630	535
61歲～65歲	半年	3,654	3,117
	年	7,285	6,216

Notes

B2a. 五、六次 means "five or six times."

B2b. 北京好？台北好？ means "Is Beijing better, or is Taipei better?" One of the most common ways to indicate alternatives is simply by listing them, one directly after another. Such questions, which are called Choice-type Questions with Choice Implied, will be taken up formally in a later lesson.

Beijing Railway Station

Asking About Population

PART 4

请问，南京有多少人？
（請問，南京有多少人？）
好像有八百万。
（好像有八百萬。）

New Characters and Words

Study the six characters below and the common words written with them, paying careful attention to each character's pronunciation, meaning, and structure, as well as similar-looking characters. After you've studied a character, turn to the *Practice Essentials* volume and practice writing it on the practice sheet, making sure to follow the correct stroke order and direction as you pronounce it out loud and think of its meaning.

139 有 **yǒu** have; there is, there are

Radical is 月 **yuè** "moon" (130).

有	**yǒu**	have; there is, there are [V]
没有（沒有）	**méiyou**	not have; there is not, there are not [V]
有没有（有沒有）	**yǒu méiyou**	have or not have? is there or isn't there?

140 口 **kǒu** mouth

This character, which is itself a common radical, is a pictograph—a squared-off picture of a person's mouth. 口 can also serve as a phonetic, e.g., in 扣 **kòu** "button up." Contrast 口 with 日 **rì** (132) and 国（國）**guó** (74).

人口	**rénkǒu**	population (lit. "human mouths") [N]
海口	**Hǎikǒu**	Haikou (capital of Hainan Province) [PW]

141 像 **xiàng** resemble

Radical is 人 **rén** "person," which is written 亻 when occurring at the left side of a character so as not to get in the way of the component at the right. The colloquial name for this radical is 人字旁 **rénzìpáng** "side made up of the character 人." Phonetic is 象 **xiàng** (as in 大象 **dàxiàng** "elephant"), which is a pictograph showing an elephant.

好像	**hǎoxiàng**	apparently, it seems to me [A]

142 万(萬) **-wàn** ten thousand

Radical of the simplified form is 一 **yī** (1). Radical of the traditional form is 艸 **cǎo** "grass" (as an independent word "grass" is written 草). When 艸 occurs as a radical at the top of a character, it is written ⺾ and is then known as 草字头(草字頭) **cǎozìtóu** "top made up of the character 草." However, in the case of 萬, it happens that the meaning of the "grass" radical has no relation to the meaning of this character, since this character was borrowed from another character with the same pronunciation that meant "scorpion." That character was a pictograph, with ⺾ representing the scorpion's feelers. Contrast 万(萬) with 南 **nán** (41).

万(萬)	**-wàn**	ten thousand [NU]
万(萬)	**Wàn**	Wan [SN]
一万(一萬)	**yíwàn**	ten thousand
两万(兩萬)	**liǎngwàn**	twenty thousand
十万(十萬)	**shíwàn**	hundred thousand [NU]
五十万(五十萬)	**wǔshíwàn**	five hundred thousand
百万(百萬)	**-bǎiwàn**	million [NU]
三百万(三百萬)	**sānbǎiwàn**	three million
千万(千萬)	**-qiānwàn**	ten million [NU]
两千万(兩千萬)	**liǎngqiānwàn**	twenty million

143 比 **bǐ** compare

This character is itself a radical. 比 is a picture of two people standing next to each other, as if "comparing" their height or strength. 比 is itself also a phonetic, e.g., in simplified 毕 **bì** as in 毕业(畢業) **bìyè** "graduate," 庇 **bì** as in 庇护(庇護) **bìhù** "to shelter," 屁 **pì** as in 屁股 **pìgu** "butt, rear end," and 批 as in 批评(批評) **pīpíng** "criticize." Contrast 比 with 北 **běi** (16).

144 较(較) **jiào** compare

Radical is 车(車) **chē** "vehicle." Phonetic is 交 **jiāo** "hand over." Perhaps this mnemonic will help you remember how to write this character: "Hand over" your "vehicle" and let's "compare"!

比较(比較)	**bǐjiào**	comparatively, relatively [A]

New Words in BSC 4-4 Written with Characters You Already Know

多	**duō**	be many, much, more [SV]
少	**shǎo**	be few, less [SV]
北京	**Běijīng**	Beijing [PW]
南京	**Nánjīng**	Nanjing [PW]
西安	**Xī'ān**	Xian [PW]

上海	**Shànghǎi**	Shanghai [PW]
广州 (廣州)	**Guǎngzhōu**	Guangzhou, Canton [PW]
台北	**Táiběi**	Taipei [PW]

Reading Exercises (Simplified Characters)

Now practice reading the new characters and words for this lesson in context in sentences, conversations, and narratives. Be sure to refer to the Notes at the end of this lesson, and make use of the accompanying audio disc to hear and practice correct pronunciation, phrasing, and intonation.

A. LARGE NUMBERS

Read out loud each of the following large numbers. Be especially careful when you get to the ones written in Arabic numbers.

1. 一万七千五百
2. 两万八千一百二十
3. 五万九千四百一十七
4. 十万两千三百六十八
5. 一百万
6. 四百六十六万三千二百
7. 两千多万
8. 五千五百万
9. 100,000,000
10. 1,300,000,000

B. SENTENCES

Read out loud each of the following sentences, which include all the new characters of this lesson. The first time you read a sentence, focus special attention on the characters and words that are new to you, reminding yourself of their pronunciation and meaning. The second time, aim to comprehend the overall meaning of the sentence.

一、一年有十二个月，一个月有四个多星期，一个星期有七天。

二、您好像是第一次来中国吧？中文难不难？

三、那个大街我好像去过，是不是叫南京大街？

四、好像九月去北京比较好；七月不太好，别七月去。

五、谁比较高？是你？是他？好像是他。

六、这个月公司好像比较忙，星期日也不关门。

七、去香港差不多要八百块。去北京比较贵，对不对？

八、小李有个同屋，姓万，海南人，海口来的。我没有同屋。你有没有？

九、河北省山很少，山西省也很少，广西省山比较多。

十、王大海有一个姐姐，二十六岁，她明年要去广州住。

C. CONVERSATIONS

Read out loud the following conversations, including the name or role of the person speaking. If possible, find a partner or partners and each of you play a role. Then switch roles, so you get practice reading all of the lines.

一、
美国男生：高老师，请问，天津有多少人？
高老师　：天津有一千多万人。
美国男生：那么，南京呢？
高老师　：南京的人口比较少，好像有五百万吧。

二、
美国同屋：小王，你有没有五块钱？
中国同屋：我没有。我今天没带钱。
美国同屋：那，我去问老谢吧。
中国同屋：你别问他，好像他也没带钱。你去问老王比较好，好像他带了很多钱。

三、
关开来：老万那个人，IQ好像不太高。
钱东山：那，你呢？你IQ很高吗？
关开来：我……

D. CHARACTER DIFFERENTIATION DRILLS

Distinguish carefully the following similar-looking characters, pronouncing each one out loud and thinking of its meaning.

一、口 口 口 日 日 日
二、口 口 口 国 国 国
三、口 日 国 日 口 国 日
四、比 比 比 北 北 北
五、比 北 比 比 北 北 比
六、万 万 万 南 南 南 (traditional only)
七、万 南 万 万 南 万 万 万 南 (traditional only)

E. NARRATIVES

Read the following narratives, paying special attention to punctuation and overall structure. The first time you read a narrative, read it out loud; the second time, read silently and try to gradually increase your reading speed. Always think of the meaning of what you're reading.

一、上海人太多。香港人口比较少，七百多万。香港有香港人、广东人、上海人，也有不少美国人。香港有很多公司。有香港人开的公司，有中国人开的公司，也有美国人开的公司。住香港很贵，一个月差不多要两万块钱。香港的人好像都很忙。有很多人去了香港，就不走了。

二、中国有二十多个省，人口差不多有1,300,000,000。广东、河南、山东、四川都是中国的大省。2005年广东有九千五百多万人，河南有九千四百多万人，山东也有差不多九千四百万人，四川有八千一百多万人。

F. SUPPLEMENT: A CHINESE JOKE

Read out loud the following joke, which has appeared in several mainland Chinese compilations of jokes.

老师：东东，我问你，哪个月有二十八天？
东东：老师，一月、二月、三月、四月、五月、六月、七月、八月、九月、十月、十一月、十二月都有二十八天！

A fruit store in Beijing

Reading Exercises (Traditional Characters)

A. LARGE NUMBERS

Read out loud each of the following large numbers. Be especially careful when you get to the ones written in Arabic numbers.

1. 一萬七千五百
2. 兩萬八千一百二十
3. 五萬九千四百一十七
4. 十萬兩千三百六十八
5. 一百萬
6. 四百六十六萬三千二百
7. 兩千多萬
8. 五千五百萬
9. 100,000,000
10. 1,300,000,000

B. SENTENCES

Read out loud each of the following sentences, which include all the new characters of this lesson. The first time you read a sentence, focus special attention on the characters and words that are new to you, reminding yourself of their pronunciation and meaning. The second time, aim to comprehend the overall meaning of the sentence.

一、一年有十二個月，一個月有四個多星期，一個星期有七天。

二、您好像是第一次來中國吧？中文難不難？

三、那個大街我好像去過，是不是叫南京大街？

四、好像九月去北京比較好；七月不太好，別七月去。

五、誰比較高？是你？是他？好像是他。

六、這個月公司好像比較忙，星期日也不關門。

七、去香港差不多要八百塊。去北京比較貴，對不對？

八、小李有個同屋，姓萬，海南人，海口來的。我沒有同屋。你有沒有？

九、河北省山很少，山西省也很少，廣西省山比較多。

十、王大海有一個姐姐，二十六歲，她明年要去廣州住。

C. CONVERSATIONS

Read out loud the following conversations, including the name or role of the person speaking. If possible, find a partner or partners and each of you play a role. Then switch roles, so you get practice reading all of the lines.

一、美國男生：高老師，請問，天津有多少人？

高老師：天津有一千多萬人。

美國男生：那麼，南京呢？

高老師：南京的人口比較少，好像有五百萬吧。

二、美國同屋：小王，你有沒有五塊錢？

中國同屋：我沒有。我今天沒帶錢。

美國同屋：那，我去問老謝吧。

中國同屋：你別問他，好像他也沒帶錢。你去問老王比較好，好像他帶了很多錢。

三、關開來：老萬那個人，IQ好像不太高。

錢東山：那，你呢？你IQ很高嗎？

關開來：我……

D. CHARACTER DIFFERENTIATION DRILLS

Distinguish carefully the following similar-looking characters, pronouncing each one out loud and thinking of its meaning.

一、口口口日日日

二、口口口國國國

三、口日國日口國日

四、比比比北北北

五、比北比比北北比

六、萬萬萬南南南

七、萬南萬萬南萬萬萬南

Customs at Kowloon Station in Hong Kong

E. NARRATIVES

Read the following narratives, paying special attention to punctuation and overall structure. The first time you read a narrative, read it out loud; the second time, read silently and try to gradually increase your reading speed. Always think of the meaning of what you're reading.

一、上海人太多。香港人口比較少，七百多萬。香港有香港人、廣東人、上海人，也有不少美國人。香港有很多公司。有香港人開的公司，有中國人開的公司，也有美國人開的公司。住香港很貴，一個月差不多要兩萬塊錢。香港的人好像都很忙。有很多人去了香港，就不走了。

二、中國有二十多個省，人口差不多有1，300，000，000。廣東、河南、山東、四川都是中國的大省。2005年廣東有九千五百多萬人，河南有九千四百多萬人，山東也有差不多九千四百萬人，四川有八千一百多萬人。

F. SUPPLEMENT: A CHINESE JOKE

Read out loud the following joke, which has appeared in several mainland Chinese compilations of jokes.

老師：東東，我問你，哪個月有二十八天？
東東：老師，一月、二月、三月、四月、五月、六月、七月、八月、九月、十月、十一月、十二月都有二十八天！

Notes

B5. 是你？是他？ "Is it you or is it him?" is a Choice-type Question with Choice Implied (cf. note B2b in BWC 4-3).

B8. 小李有个同屋，姓万，海南人，海口来的 (小李有個同屋，姓萬，海南人，海口來的) This is informal, conversational style. A literal translation would be "Little Li has a roommate, (he) is surnamed Wan, (he is) from Hainan, (he) has come from Haikou." In good English we could translate "Little Li has a roommate with the last name Wan who is from Haikou, Hainan." Note that in conversational style, measures, subjects or topics, and the equative verb 是 may all sometimes omitted. 有个同屋 (有個同屋) is short for 有一个同屋 (有一個同屋), 海南人 is short for 他是海南人, and 海口来的 (海口來的) is short for 他是海口来的 (他是海口來的).

UNIT 5

Locating Persons, Places, and Things

COMMUNICATIVE OBJECTIVES

Once you've mastered this unit, you'll be able to use Chinese to read and write:

1. Where someone or something is located relative to someone or something else: "here," "there," "right," "left," "top," "bottom," "above," "below," "inside," and "outside."
2. About the direction in which a certain place is located with reference to another place: "north," "south," "east," and "west."
3. About the location of various Chinese provinces relative to each other.
4. A passage discussing the geography and history of Beijing.
5. A passage introducing Sun Yat-sen University in Guangzhou.
6. A passage about National Taiwan University in Taipei.
7. The transcription of an overheard cell phone conversation in a park in Beijing.
8. A handwritten note from one Chinese student to another.
9. A popular Chinese saying from Taiwan in the 1960s.
10. How Chinese people describe the characters used to write their names.

PART 1

Searching for Mary Wang

我找王小姐。请问，她在不在？
(我找王小姐。請問，她在不在？)
王小姐？哪位王小姐？

New Characters and Words

Study the six characters below and the common words written with them, paying careful attention to each character's pronunciation, meaning, and structure, as well as similar-looking characters. After you've studied a character, turn to the *Practice Essentials* volume and practice writing it on the practice sheet, making sure to follow the correct stroke order and direction as you pronounce it out loud and think of its meaning.

145 可 **kě** may, can; but

Radical is 口 **kǒu** "mouth." 可 is itself a common phonetic, e.g, in 苛 **kē** "harsh" and 柯 **Kē** (surname). Giving permission means saying with one's "mouth" that someone "may" do something. Contrast 可 with 何 **hé** (19), 河 **hé** (43), 司 **sī** (95). Note that in 司, the first stroke begins in the top left quadrant and ends in the lower right quadrant, but in 可, the first stroke begins in the top left quadrant and ends in the top right quadrant, with the first and last strokes not being connected.

可是 **kěshi** but [CJ]

---

146 以 **yǐ** take; use; with

Radical is 人 **rén** "person." Contrast 以 with 比 **bǐ** (143) and 北 **běi** (16).

可以 **kéyi** may, can [AV]; be O.K. [SV]

---

147 知 **zhī** know

Radical is 矢 **shǐ** "arrow" [BF]. The other component is 口 **kǒu** "mouth" [BF]. Those who truly "know" can open their "mouth" and speak forth their opinion with the speed of an "arrow."

148 道 **dào** road, way; Taoism

Radical is 辶 **chuò** "walk, go" [BF]. The colloquial name for this radical is 走之 **zǒu zhī** "the walking 之," because of its meaning "walk" and its resemblance to the particle 之. The other component is 首 **shǒu** "head" [BF]. To "go" to the "head" of the line is to lead the "way." 道 is the character romanized as "Tao" in the word "Taoism" (the right "road" or "way" to travel in life). The verb 知道 **zhīdao** "know" literally means "know the way." Contrast 道 with 这 (這) **zhè** (96) and **guò** 过 (過) (136).

知道	**zhīdao**	know [V]
不知道	**bù zhīdào**	not know (here notice Tone Four on **dào**)

---

149 在 **zài** be located in, at, on; be present

Radical is 土 **tǔ** "earth." The colloquial name for this radical is 土字底 **tǔzìdǐ** "bottom made up of the character 土." Notice that the top horizontal line of 土 is shorter than the bottom line. Phonetic is 才 **cái** "then and only then."

在	**zài**	be located in, at, on [V/CV]; be present [V]

---

150 找 **zhǎo** look for

Radical is 手 **shǒu** "hand," which at the left side of a character is written as 扌 and is referred to colloquially as 提手 **tíshǒu** "raised hand." The other component is 戈 **gē** "dagger-axe." In ancient times, there were many wars and one always had to be able to locate one's weapons. So the etymology of the character 找 can be explained as the "hand" "looking for" the "dagger-axe." Contrast 找 with 我 **wǒ** (51).

找	**zhǎo**	look for [V]

New Words in BSC 5-1 Written with Characters You Already Know

要是	**yàoshi**	if [CJ]
不过 (不過)	**búguò**	however [CJ]

Reading Exercises (Simplified Characters)

Now practice reading the new characters and words for this lesson in context in sentences, conversations, and narratives. Be sure to refer to the Notes at the end of this lesson, and make use of the accompanying audio disc to hear and practice correct pronunciation, phrasing, and intonation.

A. SENTENCES

Read out loud each of the following sentences, which include all the new characters of this lesson. The first time you read a sentence, focus special attention on the characters and words that are new to you, reminding yourself of their pronunciation and meaning. The second time, aim to comprehend the overall meaning of the sentence.

一、高先生，请问，您知道今天几月几号吗？

二、我们可不可以去上海住两、三个星期？

三、你知道不知道王太太今天在不在台北？
四、要是她们去湖南省，那我们也要去湖南省。
五、请问，您找谁？是不是找小李的同屋？他今天不在！
六、钱小姐，你知道谢先生在哪个公司吗？
七、我可不可以问您，您今年多大年纪了？
八、您知道广州的人口是多少吗？我不知道。
九、我知道老李的日文不好，可是小关的日文好像也不太好。
十、王大海去找他姐姐，可是他姐姐不在。

B. CONVERSATIONS

Read out loud the following conversations, including the name or role of the person speaking. If possible, find a partner or partners and each of you play a role. Then switch roles, so you get practice reading all of the lines.

一、

美国人：先生贵姓？
中国人：我姓何，我叫何大一。何是“人”、“可”何，大是“大小”的大，一是“一二三”的一。

二、

女：先生，您好！我找王小姐。请问，她在不在？
男：王小姐？哪位王小姐？
女：我是美国人，中文不太好。我不知道她的中文名字。
男：我知道了。是王国金小姐。不过，她不在。她今天没来公司。

三、

何大一：你好！我叫何大一。请问，你叫什么名字？
李京生：我姓李，叫李京生。你可以叫我小李。
何大一：那，小李，我找一个人，叫林文天。他在不在？
李京生：小林就是我的同屋。他今天不在，去天津了。你明天十一点来找他，好吗？

四、
方小姐：请问，你知不知道谁是IBM公司的CEO？
边先生：这个……我不知道。

C. CHARACTER DIFFERENTIATION DRILLS

Distinguish carefully the following similar-looking characters, pronouncing each one out loud and thinking of its meaning.

一、可 可 可 司 司 司
二、可 可 可 何 何 何
三、可 可 可 河 河 河
四、可 司 何 可 河 司 可
五、以 以 以 比 比 比
六、以 以 以 北 北 北
七、以 比 北 以 北 比 以
八、道 道 道 这 这 这
九、道 道 道 过 过 过
十、道 这 过 道 过 这 道
十一、找 找 找 我 我 我
十二、找 我 我 找 我 找 找 我
十三、知 知 知 和 和 和
十四、知 和 知 知 和 和 知

D. NARRATIVES

Read the following narratives, paying special attention to punctuation and overall structure. The first time you read a narrative, read it out loud; the second time, read silently and try to gradually increase your reading speed. Always think of the meaning of what you're reading.

一、今天差不多三点半老万来找我，可是我不在。我去南京的一个公司了，不过我的同屋小王不知道我去了哪个公司。他请老万明天九点来找我。可是，老万明天很忙，他就不来了。

二、我不知道在南京东路的那个公司明天几点开门、几点关门。不过我可以去找我的同屋小金。要是我问她，她也不知道，我就不去了。

Reading Exercises (Traditional Characters)

A. SENTENCES

Read out loud each of the following sentences, which include all the new characters of this lesson. The first time you read a sentence, focus special attention on the characters and words that are new to you, reminding yourself of their pronunciation and meaning. The second time, aim to comprehend the overall meaning of the sentence.

一、高先生，請問，您知道今天幾月幾號嗎？

二、我們可不可以去上海住兩、三個星期？

三、你知道不知道王太太今天在不在台北？

四、要是她們去湖南省，那我們也要去湖南省。

五、請問，您找誰？是不是找小李的同屋？他今天不在！

六、錢小姐，你知道謝先生在哪個公司嗎？

七、我可不可以問您，您今年多大年紀了？

八、您知道廣州的人口是多少嗎？我不知道。

九、我知道老李的日文不好，可是小關的日文好像也不太好。

十、王大海去找他姐姐，可是他姐姐不在。

B. CONVERSATIONS

Read out loud the following conversations, including the name or role of the person speaking. If possible, find a partner or partners and each of you play a role. Then switch roles, so you get practice reading all of the lines.

一、美國人：先生貴姓？

中國人：我姓何，我叫何大一。何是「人」、「可」何，大是「大小」的大，一是「一二三」的一。

二、女：先生，您好！我找王小姐。請問，她在不在？

男：王小姐？哪位王小姐？

女：我是美國人，中文不太好。我不知道她的中文名字。

男：我知道了。是王國金小姐。不過，她不在。她今天沒來公司。

三、何大一：你好！我叫何大一。請問，你叫什麼名字？

李京生：我姓李，我叫李京生。你可以叫我小李。

何大一：那，小李，我找一個人，叫林文天。他在不在？

李京生：小林就是我的同屋。他今天不在，去天津了。你明天十一點來找他，好嗎？

四、方小姐：請問，你知不知道誰是IBM公司的CEO？

邊先生：這個……我不知道。

C. CHARACTER DIFFERENTIATION DRILLS

Distinguish carefully the following similar-looking characters, pronouncing each one out loud and thinking of its meaning.

一、可可可司司司
二、可可可何何何
三、可可可河河河
四、可司何可河司可
五、以以以比比比
六、以以以北北北
七、以比北以北比以
八、道道道這這這
九、道道道過過過
十、道這過道過這道
十一、找找找我我我
十二、找我我找我找找我
十三、知知知和和和
十四、知和知知和和知

D. NARRATIVE

Read the following narratives, paying special attention to punctuation and overall structure. The first time you read a narrative, read it out loud; the second time, read silently and try to gradually increase your reading speed. Always think of the meaning of what you're reading.

一、

今天差不多三點半老萬來找我，可是我不在。我去南京的一個公司了，不過我的同屋小王不知道我去了哪個公司。他請老萬明天九點來找我。可是老萬明天很忙，他就不來了。

二、

我不知道在南京東路的那個公司明天幾點開門、幾點關門。不過我可以去找我的同屋小金。要是我問她，她也不知道，我就不去了。

"(We) welcome male, female, old, young (to) beautify (their) hair"

Notes

A1. The same way that English can be printed in many different fonts, Chinese also can be printed in a variety of fonts. Beginning in this lesson, Chinese text is printed in so-called Song font, which is slightly different from the Kai font you've seen so far. It's important for you to become accustomed to seeing Chinese characters printed in different fonts. While the new font may seem unfamiliar at first, you'll get accustomed to it soon.

A2. 我们可不可以去 (我們可不可以去) "Can we go...?" is an abbreviated form of 我们可以不可以去 (我們可以不可以去), with the same meaning. Review grammar note 8a in BSC 5-1 on the deletion of the second syllable of bisyllabic verbs in the affirmative part of affirmative-negative questions.

A3. It just happens that in this sentence, the full form of the affirmative-negative question is used: 你知道不知道 "Do you know...?" However, the speaker might just as well have asked 你知不知道, with exactly the same meaning.

B1. 先生贵姓？(先生貴姓？) "Sir, what is your honorable surname?" Be aware that this question is being addressed to the person whose last name the speaker wishes to find out; this isn't about a third person. In very polite style, pronouns like 你 and 您 tend to be avoided, people's titles or roles being mentioned instead. So in Chinese it would be very normal to ask questions that would translate literally into English as "Is this the school president's first trip to America?" or "Does the general manager have any areas where he needs me to help?"

B2a. Note that, in the written record of this conversation, 女 and 男 have been used to indicate who is speaking. These are additional examples of written-style Chinese (cf. BWC 4-2: A1b). In speech, 男 and 女 would never be said alone like this. Instead, one would say 男的 or 男人 for "man," and 女的 or 女人 for "woman."

B2b. 我知道了 "Now I know." Initially, the man didn't know which "Ms. Wang" the woman was looking for, but now he knows.

D1. 可是，老万明天很忙，他就不来了 (可是，老萬明天很忙，他就不來了) "But Old Wan is busy tomorrow, so he's not coming."

D2. 要是我问她，她也不知道，我就不去了 (要是我問她，她也不知道，我就不去了) "If I ask her, and if she doesn't know either, then I won't go."

PART 2

Conversation at a Noodle Stand

New Characters and Words

Study the six characters below and the common words written with them, paying careful attention to each character's pronunciation, meaning, and structure, as well as similar-looking characters. After you've studied a character, turn to the *Practice Essentials* volume and practice writing it on the practice sheet, making sure to follow the correct stroke order and direction as you pronounce it out loud and think of its meaning.

151 吃 **chī** eat

Radical is 口 **kǒu** "mouth." This radical is referred to colloquially as 口字旁 **kǒuzìpáng** "side made up of the character 口." Phonetic is 乞 **qǐ** "beg" as in 乞丐 **qǐgài** "beggar." When a person "begs" and points to their "mouth," they want something to "eat."

吃	**chī**	eat [V]

152 饭(飯) **fàn** cooked rice, food

Radical is 食 **shí** "eat" [BF], which is written as 饣(飠) when occurring at the left side of a character as a radical. The colloquial name for this radical is 食字旁 **shízìpáng** "side made up of the character 食." Phonetic is 反 as in 反对(反對) **fǎnduì** "oppose."

饭(飯)	**fàn**	cooked rice, food [N]
吃饭(吃飯)	**chīfàn**	eat food, eat [VO]
中饭(中飯)	**zhōngfàn**	lunch [N]
中国饭(中國飯)	**Zhōngguo fàn**	Chinese food [PH]

153 学(學) **xué** learn, study

Radical is 子 **zǐ** "child" [**BF**]. It is fitting for a "child" to "learn." Contrast 学(學) with 兴(興) **xìng** (90), 字 **zì** (84), and 李 **lǐ** (20).

学(學)	**xué**	learn, study [**V**]
同学(同學)	**tóngxué**	classmate [**N**]
学生(學生)	**xuésheng**	student [**N**]
男学生(男學生)	**nánxuésheng**	male student [**N**]
女学生(女學生)	**nǚxuésheng**	female student [**N**]
大学(大學)	**dàxué**	university, college [**N**]
大学生(大學生)	**dàxuéshēng**	college student [**N**]
香港中文大学(香港中文大學)	**Xiānggǎng Zhōngwén Dàxué**	Chinese University of Hong Kong [**PW**]

154 工 **gōng** work

This character is itself a radical. It is itself also a very common phonetic, e.g., in 功 **gōng** as in 成功 **chénggōng** "succeed," 攻 **gōng** as in 攻打 **gōngdǎ** "attack," 贡(貢) **gòng** as in 贡献(貢獻) **gòngxiàn** "contribution," 缸 **gāng** as in 水缸 **shuǐgāng** "water vat," 江 **jiāng** as in 长江(長江) **Cháng Jiāng** "Chang Jiang (river)," and 红(紅) **hóng** "red." 工 is a picture of an ancient carpenter's tool, with the lower part representing the blade and the other two strokes representing the handle. By extension, 工 acquired the meaning "work." Contrast 工 with 二 **èr** (2) and 王 **wáng** (6).

工人	**gōngrén**	worker, laborer [**N**]

155 子 **zǐ/zi** (common noun suffix)

This character is itself a radical. It also serves as a phonetic, e.g., in 字 **zì** "character" and 仔 **zǎi** as in 牛仔裤(牛仔褲) **níuzǎikù** "jeans." In Classical Chinese, pronounced with a Third Tone as **zǐ**, 子 means "son" or "child." As a noun suffix, 子 is pronounced in the neutral tone. 子 is a pictograph, showing a newborn child swathed so that its arms show but its legs are not visible. Contrast 子 with 了 **le** (71), 千 **qiān** (114), and 字 **zì** (84).

位子	**wèizi**	seat, place [**N**]

156 儿(兒) **ér** (common suffix)

儿 is itself a radical. The traditional form of the character, 兒, has an alternate form, 児. The suffix 儿(兒), while typical of Beijing colloquial speech, is usually dropped in standard written Chinese, except in direct quotations such as in novels, so one says 一点儿(一點兒) but normally writes 一点(一點). Remember that 儿(兒), when functioning as a suffix, combines with the preceding syllable and isn't pronounced by itself, so one pronounces 一点儿(一點兒) as **yìdiǎnr**, not as ***yìdiǎn'ér**. Contrast simplified 儿 with 九 **jiǔ** (10) and simplified 几 **jǐ** (97).

这儿(這兒)	**zhèr**	here [**PW**]
那儿(那兒)	**nàr**	there [**PW**]
哪儿(哪兒)	**nǎr**	where? [**QW**]

一点儿（一點兒）	**yìdiǎnr**	a little, some [NU + M]
门儿（門兒）	**ménr**	door, gate [N]
同屋儿（同屋兒）	**tóngwūr**	roommate [N]
一半儿（一半兒）	**yíbànr**	half [NU + NU]
一半儿一半儿（一半兒一半兒）	**yíbànr yíbànr**	half and half

New Words in BSC 5-2 Written with Characters You Already Know

北大 **Běidà** Peking University [PW]

Reading Exercises (Simplified Characters)

Now practice reading the new characters and words for this lesson in context in sentences, conversations, and narratives. Be sure to refer to the Notes at the end of this lesson, and make use of the accompanying audio disc to hear and practice correct pronunciation, phrasing, and intonation.

A. SENTENCES

Read out loud each of the following sentences, which include all the new characters of this lesson. The first time you read a sentence, focus special attention on the characters and words that are new to you, reminding yourself of their pronunciation and meaning. The second time, aim to comprehend the overall meaning of the sentence.

一、美国人吃美国饭，中国人吃中国饭。你是哪国人？你吃什么饭？

二、这儿很好，也不贵。老师、学生、工人都可以在这儿吃中饭。

三、南京大学也叫南大，在南京市，有32,000个学生，有500多位老师。

四、我们要吃饭了。请男学生坐这儿，请女学生坐那儿。

五、这个位子不太好，那个位子比较好，请您坐那儿吧！

六、我找北京大学。您知道北大在哪儿吗？是不是在这儿？

七、我找高子文，他是我在台大的同学。您知道他在哪儿吗？

八、那个女的好像不是一个大学生，她是一个工人吧。

九、今年在很多美国大学，学中文的女学生多，男学生少。

十、大海，你不要走，先吃一点儿饭吧。

B. CONVERSATIONS

Read out loud the following conversations, including the name or role of the person speaking. If possible, find a partner or partners and each of you play a role. Then switch roles, so you get practice reading all of the lines.

一、
万小姐：李老师，你今年有多少男学生，多少女学生？
李老师：一半儿一半儿吧。
万小姐：你有多少中国学生，多少美国学生？
李老师：也是一半儿一半儿吧。
万小姐：李老师，这儿的学生去哪儿吃饭呢？
李老师：这个 …… 我就不知道了。

二、
美国人："港大"是香港中文大学吧？
香港人：不是，"港大"是香港大学，不是香港中文大学。香港中文大学叫"中大"。
美国人：广州的中山大学不是也叫"中大"吗？
香港人：对，可是 ……

三、
学生：请问，这个位子有人吗？
工人：没有，没有。你坐吧。
学生：谢谢！
工人：你第一次来这儿吃饭吗？
学生：不，我来过很多次。你是学生吗？
工人：不，我是工人。你呢？
学生：我是美国来的大学生，今年在北大学中文。
工人：一点钟了，我走了。
学生：我也走了。

C. CHARACTER DIFFERENTIATION DRILLS

Distinguish carefully the following similar-looking characters, pronouncing each one out loud and thinking of its meaning.

一、工 工 工 二 二 二

二、工 工 工 三 三 三
三、工 工 工 王 王 王
四、工 王 三 工 二 工 王 工
五、子 子 子 了 了 了
六、子 子 子 字 字 字
七、子 子 子 千 千 千
八、子 了 字 子 千 子 了
九、学 学 学 字 字 字
十、学 学 学 兴 兴 兴
十一、学 兴 字 学 兴 字 学
十二、儿 儿 儿 几 几 几
十三、儿 儿 儿 九 九 九
十四、儿 九 几 儿 几 九 儿

D. NARRATIVES

Read the following narratives, paying special attention to punctuation and overall structure. The first time you read a narrative, read it out loud; the second time, read silently and try to gradually increase your reading speed. Always think of the meaning of what you're reading.

一、我们大学在台湾是很好的大学，叫台湾大学，也叫“台大”。台大在台北市。这个大学很大，有差不多三万个学生，有三千多位老师。台大的学生都很好，在那儿要找好的老师也不太难。我是台大的学生，这是我在那儿的第一年。我姐姐也是台大的学生，这是她的第三年。

二、那个美国大学生问我，在哪儿学中文比较好？我知道在北大学中文很好。那儿有很多很好的中国学生，美国学生也不少。那儿的老师也都比较好。美国学生可以在北大住，也可以在那儿吃饭，都不贵。吃、住一个月好像一千多块钱。中文很难，可是你要是要学，在北大学比较好。这是北京大学王国安老师的名片。你明天可以去北大找王老师问问。

E. SUPPLEMENT: A POPULAR SAYING

Read out loud the following saying, which was popular in Taiwan in the 1960s.

来、来、来，来台大，去、去、去，去美国。

Reading Exercises (Traditional Characters)

A. SENTENCES

Read out loud each of the following sentences, which include all the new characters of this lesson. The first time you read a sentence, focus special attention on the characters and words that are new to you, reminding yourself of their pronunciation and meaning. The second time, aim to comprehend the overall meaning of the sentence.

一、美國人吃美國飯，中國人吃中國飯。你是哪國人？你吃什麼飯？

二、這兒很好，也不貴。老師、學生、工人都可以在這兒吃中飯。

三、南京大學也叫南大，在南京市，有三萬兩千個學生，有五百多位老師。

四、我們要吃飯了。請男學生坐這兒，請女學生坐那兒。

五、這個位子不太好，那個位子比較好，請您坐那兒吧！

六、我找北京大學。您知道北大在哪兒嗎？是不是在這兒？

七、我找高子文，他是我在台大的同學。您知道他在哪兒嗎？

八、那個女的好像不是一個大學生，她是一個工人吧。

九、今年在很多美國大學，學中文的女學生多，男學生少。

十、大海，你不要走，先吃一點兒飯吧。

B. CONVERSATIONS

Read out loud the following conversations, including the name or role of the person speaking. If possible, find a partner or partners and each of you play a role. Then switch roles, so you get practice reading all of the lines.

一、

萬小姐：李老師，你今年有多少男學生，多少女學生？

李老師：一半兒一半兒吧。

萬小姐：你有多少中國學生，多少美國學生？

李老師：也是一半兒一半兒吧。

萬小姐：李老師，這兒的學生去哪兒吃飯呢？

李老師：這個……我就不知道了。

二、

美國人：「港大」是香港中文大學吧？

香港人：不是，「港大」是香港大學，不是香港中文大學。香港中文大學叫「中大」。

美國人：廣州的中山大學不是也叫「中大」嗎？

香港人：對，可是……

三、

學生：請問，這個位子有人嗎？

工人：沒有，沒有。你坐吧。

學生：謝謝！

工人：你第一次來這兒吃飯嗎？

學生：不，我來過很多次。你是學生嗎？

工人：不，我是工人。你呢？

學生：我是美國來的大學生，今年在北大學中文。

工人：一點鐘了，我走了。

學生：我也走了。

Campus of Chinese University of Hong Kong

C. CHARACTER DIFFERENTIATION DRILLS

Distinguish carefully the following similar-looking characters, pronouncing each one out loud and thinking of its meaning.

一、工工工二二二
二、工工工三三三
三、工工王王王
四、工王三工二工王工
五、子子子了了了
六、子子字字字
七、子子子千千千
八、子了字子千子了
九、學學學字字字
十、學學學興興興
十一、學興字學興字學
十二、兒兒兒幾幾幾 (simplified only)
十三、兒兒兒九九九 (simplified only)
十四、兒九幾兒幾九兒 (simplified only)

D. NARRATIVES

Read the following narratives, paying special attention to punctuation and overall structure. The first time you read a narrative, read it out loud; the second time, read silently and try to gradually increase your reading speed. Always think of the meaning of what you're reading.

一、

我們大學在台灣是很好的大學，叫台灣大學，也叫「台大」。台大在台北市。這個大學很大，有差不多三萬個學生，有三千多位老師。台大的學生都很好，在那兒要找好的老師也不太難。我是台大的學生，這是我在那兒的第一年。我姐姐也是台大的學生，這是她的第三年。

二、

那個美國大學生問我，在哪兒學中文比較好？我知道在北大學中文很好。那兒有很多很好的中國學生，美國學生也不少。那兒的老師也都比較好。美國學生可以在北大住，也可以在那兒吃飯，都不貴。吃、住一個月好像一千多塊錢。中文很難，可是你要是要學，在北大學比較好。這是北京大學王國安老師的名片。你明天可以去北大找王老師問問。

E. SUPPLEMENT: A POPULAR SAYING

Read out loud the following saying, which was popular in Taiwan in the 1960s.

來、來、來、來台大，去、去、去，去美國。

Notes

A7. 他是我在台大的同学 (他是我在台大的同學) "He's a classmate of mine at Taiwan University."

A9. 学中文的女学生多，男学生少 (學中文的女學生多，男學生少) "There are many female students studying Chinese, but few male students" (lit. "Female students who study Chinese are many, male students are few"). In the case of starkly contrasting clauses like this, in Chinese it's often not necessary to have a 可是 or 不过 (不過). However, a "but" can sometimes be added to the English to make the translation smoother.

B3. 我是美国来的大学生 (我是美國來的大學生) "I'm a college student from America."

D2. 你明天可以去北大找王老师问问 (你明天可以去北大找王老師問問) "Tomorrow you can go to Peking University and look for Teacher Wang and ask." Regarding the verb duplication of 问问 (問問), as was mentioned in BSC 3-3: 5a, some one-syllable verbs are frequently reduplicated (i.e., repeated) so as to give a relaxed, casual sense to the verb and make the sentence they occur in sound smoother and less abrupt. The meaning is the same as when they are not reduplicated. Note that 问问 (問問) is pronounced with a neutral tone on the second syllable as **wènwen**, not as ***wènwèn**.

E. This saying was popular in Taiwan in the 1960s, a time when modern economic development was just beginning and many people wished to go to the U.S. for graduate study. The idea was that if you studied hard and did well on the college entrance exam, you could "come to Taiwan University" and then, after graduation, you could "go to America" for graduate study and, perhaps, to find a well-paying job.

"University Road Farmers' Market"

"Where Are You Staying?"

PART 3

香山在哪儿？
(香山在哪兒？)
在北京的北边儿。
(在北京的北邊兒。)

New Characters and Words

Study the six characters below and the common words written with them, paying careful attention to each character's pronunciation, meaning, and structure, as well as similar-looking characters. After you've studied a character, turn to the *Practice Essentials* volume and practice writing it on the practice sheet, making sure to follow the correct stroke order and direction as you pronounce it out loud and think of its meaning.

157 地 **dì** the ground; place

Radical is 土 **tǔ** "earth." The colloquial name for this radical is 土字旁 **tǔzìpáng** "side made up of the character 土." Notice that the top horizontal line of 土 is shorter than the bottom line. Also notice that when used as a radical, the bottom line of 土 slants up toward the right, so as not to get in the way of the other component. The other component in 地 is 也 **yě** "also." Contrast 地 with 七 **qī** (8), 也 **yě** (52), 他 **tā** (55), and 她 **tā** (56).

158 方 **fāng** square, open space

This character is itself a radical. It also serves as a common phonetic, e.g., in 放 **fàng** "put," 房 **fáng** as in 房子 **fángzi** "house," 防 **fáng** as in 防止 **fángzhǐ** "prevent," and 访（訪）**fǎng** as in 拜访（拜訪）**bàifǎng** "visit." Contrast 方 with simplified 万 **wàn** (142).

方	**Fāng**	Fang (also Bang, Bhang, or Pang, a common Korean surname) **[SN]**
地方	**dìfang**	place **[N]**

159 边(邊) **biān** side

Radical is 辶 **chuò** "walk, go" [BF]. The colloquial name for this radical is 走之 **zǒu zhī** "the walking 之," because of its meaning "walk" and its resemblance to the particle 之. Contrast simplified 边 with simplified 这 **zhè** (96) and simplified 过 **guò** (136).

边(邊)	**Biān**	Bian (also Byeon, Pyon, or Byon, a common Korean surname) [SN]
这边(這邊)	**zhèibian/zhèbian**	this side, here [PW]
那边(那邊)	**nèibian/nàbiān**	that side, there [PW]
哪边(哪邊)	**něibiān/nǎbiān**	what side?, where? [QW]
东边(東邊)	**dōngbiān**	in the east [PW]
南边(南邊)	**nánbiān**	in the south [PW]
西边(西邊)	**xībiān**	in the west [PW]
北边(北邊)	**běibiān**	in the north [PW]

160 事 **shì** matter, thing (abstract)

Radical is 亅 **jué**, which is referred to colloquially as 竖钩儿(豎鉤兒) **shùgōur** "vertical hook." Contrast 事 with 东(東) **dōng** (29) and 来(來) **lái** (135).

事	**shì**	matter, thing (abstract) [N]
一点事(一點事)	**yìdiǎn shì**	a little something to do
没事儿(沒事兒)	**méi shìr**	"it's nothing," "never mind" [IE]
同事	**tóngshì**	colleague [N]

161 回 **huí** go back to; time

Radical is 囗 **wéi** "enclose" [BF]. This radical is referred to colloquially as 围字框(圍字框) **wéizìkuàng** "frame of the character 围(圍)." This character was originally written as a spiral and meant "go back to the origin," but was later squared off. In the traditional character system, 回 has two alternate forms which are sometimes seen, 囘 and 囬. Contrast 回 with 四 **sì** (4), simplified 问 **wèn** (75), 同 **tóng** (80), 口 **kǒu** (140), 日 **rì** (132), and 国(國) **guó**.

回	**huí**	go back to [V]; time [M]
回国(回國)	**huíguó**	return to one's native country [VO]
这回(這回)	**zhèihuí**	this time
那回	**nèihuí**	that time
第一回	**dìyīhuí**	the first time

162 店 **diàn** shop, store

Radical is 广 **yǎn** "eaves" [BF]. This radical is referred to colloquially as 广字头(廣字頭) **guǎngzìtóu** "top made up of the character 广." The phonetic is 占 **zhān** "practice divination," as you encountered previously in **diǎn** 点(點) "o'clock" (115).

饭店(飯店)	**fàndiàn**	hotel [PW]

New Words in BSC 5-3 Written with Characters You Already Know

可	**kě**	indeed, certainly **[A]**
在	**-zài**	at, in, on **[PV]** (e.g., 住在 **zhùzai** "live in")
一	**yāo**	one (on the telephone) **[NU]**
到	**-dào**	to **[A]** (e.g., 坐到 **zuòdao** "take a train or bus to a certain place")
山	**shān**	mountain, hill **[N]**
香	**xiāng**	be fragrant, smell good **[L]**
香山	**Xiāng Shān**	Fragrant Hills (suburb to the northwest of Beijing) **[PW]**

Reading Exercises (Simplified Characters)

Now practice reading the new characters and words for this lesson in context in sentences, conversations, and narratives. Be sure to refer to the Notes at the end of this lesson, and make use of the accompanying audio disc to hear and practice correct pronunciation, phrasing, and intonation.

A. SENTENCES

Read out loud each of the following sentences, which include all the new characters of this lesson. The first time you read a sentence, focus special attention on the characters and words that are new to you, reminding yourself of their pronunciation and meaning. The second time, aim to comprehend the overall meaning of the sentence.

一、香山那个地方不难找，我有两位老同事住在那儿。
二、你的那位同事住在什么地方？他是不是住在南京路？
三、这个地方大学很多，北边有一个大学，南边也有一个大学。
四、你们要是没事儿，五点半回饭店吃饭比较好。
五、你去年是不是回过国？回了几天呢？
六、这回我们回中国，好像饭店都贵了一点儿，人也都老了一点儿。
七、广西省在广东省的西边，海南省在广东省的南边。
八、山东省在河南省的东边，山西省在河南省的北边。
九、这个地方的人口比较多，那个地方的人口比较少。
十、王大海知道，有很多事，第一回很难，第二回、第三回就不难了。

B. CONVERSATIONS

Read out loud the following conversations, including the name or role of the person speaking. If possible, find a partner or partners and each of you play a role. Then switch roles, so you get practice reading all of the lines.

一、
小王：小李，问你一下儿，我星期日带同学来，可以吗？
小李：可以。这个地方星期日不关门。
小王：谢谢你！
小李：没事儿。

二、
高先生：小李，你这回来北京住在哪儿？
李先生：我住在北京饭店，七一五号。
高先生：北京饭店在哪儿呢？
李先生：在北京市的东边儿。你住在老地方？
高先生：对，我们住在香山，你去年去过。
李先生：老高，我这回来北京，有很多事儿谢谢你！
高先生：没事儿，没事儿。

三、
学生　：老师，我们坐在什么地方？
边老师：学生坐在这儿，老师坐在那儿。
学生　：好，谢谢老师！

C. AN OVERHEARD CELL PHONE CONVERSATION

Read out loud the following cell phone conversation, which was overheard by the author in a park in Beijing.

A：什么事？
B：……
A：是，是，是。对，对，对，我知道。
B：……
A：好，好。可以，可以。我知道。
B：……
A：吃饭？可以吧。几号？下星期一？
B：……

A：几点？在哪儿？
B：……
A：好，可以。很好，很好。
B：……
A：没事儿，没事儿。

D. CHARACTER DIFFERENTIATION DRILLS

Distinguish carefully the following similar-looking characters, pronouncing each one out loud and thinking of its meaning.

一、地 地 地 他 他 他
二、地 地 地 她 她 她
三、地 地 地 也 也 也
四、地 他 地 她 也 她 地 他
五、事 事 事 东 东 东
六、事 事 事 来 来 来
七、事 东 事 来 事 东 来
八、回 回 回 日 日 日
九、回 回 回 口 口 口
十、回 回 回 国 国 国
十一、回 回 回 同 同 同
十二、回 日 回 口 回 国 回 同
十三、边 边 边 过 过 过
十四、边 过 过 边 边 过 边
十五、方 方 方 万 万 万
十六、方 万 方 方 万 万 方

"Beijing Hotel"

E. NARRATIVES

Read the following narratives, paying special attention to punctuation and overall structure. The first time you read a narrative, read it out loud; the second time, read silently and try to gradually increase your reading speed. Always think of the meaning of what you're reading.

一、我住的地方在我们公司的东边。公司的南边有一个大学，叫南山大学。有一个美国人在那个大学学中文。他没事儿就来我的公司找我，差不多一个星期来一、两次。要是我不在，他就来找我的同事老王。

二、北京在河北省，在中国的北边。北京市北边、西边都是山，西边的山叫“西山”。北京是一个很老的地方，有三千多年了。2010年北京人口有差不多22,000,000。

Reading Exercises (Traditional Characters)

A. SENTENCES

Read out loud each of the following sentences, which include all the new characters of this lesson. The first time you read a sentence, focus special attention on the characters and words that are new to you, reminding yourself of their pronunciation and meaning. The second time, aim to comprehend the overall meaning of the sentence.

一、香山那個地方不難找，我有兩位老同事住在那兒。

二、你的那位同事住在什麼地方？他是不是住在南京路？

三、這個地方大學很多，北邊有一個大學，南邊也有一个大學。

四、你們要是沒事兒，五點半回飯店吃飯比較好。

五、你去年是不是回過國？回了幾天呢？

六、這回我們回中國，好像飯店都貴了一點兒，人也都老了一點兒。

七、廣西省在廣東省的西邊，海南省在廣東省的南邊。

八、山東省在河南省的東邊，山西省在河南省的北邊。

九、這個地方的人口比較多，那個地方的人口比較少。

十、王大海知道，有很多事，第一回很難，第二回、第三回就不難了。

B. CONVERSATIONS

Read out loud the following conversations, including the name or role of the person speaking. If possible, find a partner or partners and each of you play a role. Then switch roles, so you get practice reading all of the lines.

一、小王：小李，問你一下兒，我星期日帶同學來，可以嗎？
小李：可以。這個地方星期日不關門。
小王：謝謝你！
小李：沒事兒。

二、高先生：小李，你這回來北京住在哪兒？
李先生：我住在北京飯店，七一五號。
高先生：北京飯店在哪兒呢？
李先生：在北京市的東邊兒。你住在老地方？
高先生：對，我們住在香山，你去年去過。
李先生：老高，我這回來北京，有很多事兒，謝謝你！
高先生：沒事兒，沒事兒。

三、學生：老師，我們坐在什麼地方？
邊老師：學生坐在這兒，老師坐在那兒。
學生：好，謝謝老師！

Restaurant façade in Hong Kong

C. AN OVERHEARD CELL PHONE CONVERSATION

Read out loud the following cell phone conversation, which was overheard by the author in a park in Beijing.

A：什麼事？

B：……

A：是，是是，是。對，對，對，我知道。

B：……

A：好，好好。可以，可以。我知道。

B：……

A：吃飯？可以吧。幾號？下星期一？

B：……

A：幾點？在哪兒？

B：……

A：好，可以。很好，很好。

B：……

A：沒事兒，沒事兒。

D. CHARACTER DIFFERENTIATION DRILLS

Distinguish carefully the following similar-looking characters, pronouncing each one out loud and thinking of its meaning.

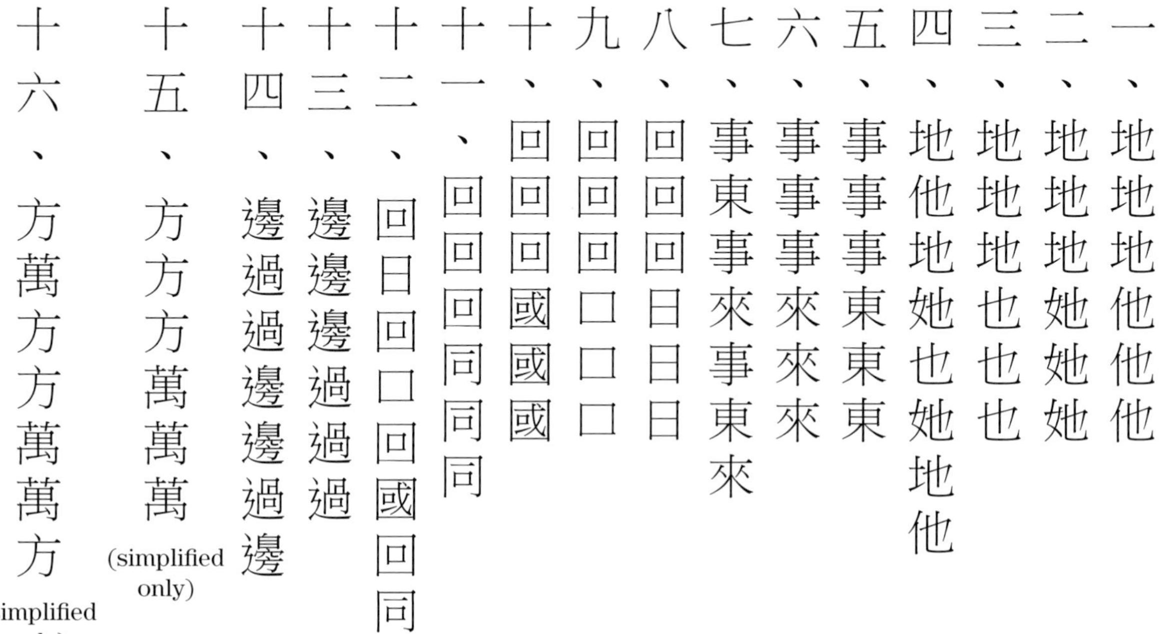

一、地地地他他他

二、地地地她她她

三、地地地也也也

四、地他地她也她地他

五、事事事東東東

六、事事事來來來

七、事東事來事東來

八、回回回日日日

九、回回回口口口

十、回回回國國國

十一、回回回同同同

十二、回日回口回國回同

十三、邊邊邊過過過

十四、邊過過邊邊過邊

十五、方方方萬萬萬 (simplified only)

十六、方萬方方萬萬方 (simplified only)

E. NARRATIVES

Read the following narratives, paying special attention to punctuation and overall structure. The first time you read a narrative, read it out loud; the second time, read silently and try to gradually increase your reading speed. Always think of the meaning of what you're reading.

一、我住的地方在我們公司的南邊。公司的南邊有一個大學，叫南山大學。有一個美國人在那個大學學中文。他沒事兒就來我的公司找我，差不多一個星期來一、兩次。要是我不在，他就來找我的同事老王。

二、北京在河北省，在中國的北邊。北京市北邊、西邊都是山，西邊的山叫「西山」。北京是一個很老的地方，有三千多年了。二〇一〇年北京人口有差不多兩千兩百萬。

Notes

A1a. 香山那个地方（香山那個地方）literally means "Fragrant Hills, that place." In better English, we might translate as "That place called Fragrant Hills" or just "The place called Fragrant Hills." As you have seen before, it's very common in Chinese to add an appositive phrase after a noun that further describes the noun.

A1b. The 老 of 老同事 "old colleagues" refers to colleagues whom you have worked with for a long time, not "aged" colleagues.

A5. 你去年是不是回过国？回了几天呢？（你去年是不是回過國？回了幾天呢？）"Did you return to your native country last year? How many days did you return?" Since 回国（回國）is a Verb-Object Compound, it can be split by grammatical suffixes like 过（過）in this way.

A7. 广西省在广东省的西边（廣西省在廣東省的西邊）. Grammatically, this could mean either "Guangxi Province is to the west of Guangdong Province" or "Guangxi Province is in the west of Guangdong Province." Of course, common sense tells us that the second interpretation isn't possible.

B2. 你住在老地方？"You're living in the same place as before?" (lit. "You live in the old place?") This is an Intonation Question.

B3. 我们坐在什么地方？（我們坐在什麼地方？）"Where do we sit?" The implication is "Where are we supposed to sit?"

E1a. 他没事儿就来我的公司找我（他沒事兒就來我的公司找我）"When he has nothing to do, he comes to my company looking for me." Here 没事儿（沒事兒）retains its literal meaning of "not have matters (that one has to do)" rather than being an idiomatic expression used after someone thanks you that means "never mind" or "don't mention it."

E1b. 差不多一个星期来一、两次（差不多一個星期來一、兩次）"He comes about once or twice a week."

E2. Though Beijing municipality is surrounded on all sides by Hebei Province, administratively it isn't considered part of it.

PART 4

New Computer

对，在右边，
不过请你先不要开。
(對，在右邊，
不過請你先不要開。)
开关在右边吧？
(開關在右邊吧？)

New Characters and Words

Study the six characters below and the common words written with them, paying careful attention to each character's pronunciation, meaning, and structure, as well as similar-looking characters. After you've studied a character, turn to the *Practice Essentials* volume and practice writing it on the practice sheet, making sure to follow the correct stroke order and direction as you pronounce it out loud and think of its meaning.

163 里(裏) **lǐ** in, inside

In the simplified form, this character is its own radical. The radical of the traditional form is 衣 **yī** "clothing" [**BF**]. The phonetic of either the simplified or the traditional form is 里 **lǐ** "mile," which occurs as a phonetic in numerous other characters, e.g., 理 **lǐ** as in 理由 **lǐyóu** "reason," 鲤 **lǐ** as in 鲤鱼（鯉魚）**lǐyú** "carp," 俚 **lǐ** as in 俚语（俚語）**lǐyǔ** "slang," and 裡 **lǐ** (alternate form of traditional 裏). In the traditional form, 里 has been placed "in" or "inside" the character 衣. There is an alternate traditional character 裡 that is also very common; it is composed of the same components as 裏, but they are arranged left/right rather than top/bottom, making 裡 easier to write than 裏.

里(裏)	**lǐ**	in, inside [**L**]
里边(裏邊 or 裡邊)	**lǐbian**	not have; there is not, there are not [**PW**]
里头(裏頭 or 裡頭)	**lǐtou**	in, inside [**PW**]
哪里(哪裏 or 哪裡)	**náli**	not at all [**IE**]

---

164 外 **wài** outside

Radical is 夕 **xī** "evening" [**BF**]. The other component is the character 卜 **bǔ** "to divine" [**BF**]. Here is a mnemonic for remembering this character: "divining" in the "evening" while "outside." Contrast 外 with 名 **míng** (83) and 多 **duō** (103).

外	**wài**	outside [L]
外边 (外邊)	**wàibian**	outside [PW]
外头 (外頭)	**wàitou**	outside [PW]

165 左 **zuǒ** left

Radical is 工 **gōng** "work" (154). 左 itself serves as a phonetic in other characters, e.g., in 佐 **zuǒ** as in 辅佐 (輔佐) **fǔzuǒ** "assist." Contrast 左 with 右 **yòu** (166), 不 **bù** (63), and 在 **zài** (149).

左	**zuǒ**	left [L]
左	**Zuǒ**	Zuo [SN]
左边 (左邊)	**zuǒbian**	left side, left [PW]

166 右 **yòu** right

Radical is 口 **kǒu** "mouth." 右 serves as a phonetic in other characters, e.g., in 佑 **yòu** as in 保佑 **bǎoyòu** "help." Contrast 右 with 左 **zuǒ** (165), 不 **bù** (63), and 在 **zài** (149).

右	**yòu**	right [L]
右边 (右邊)	**yòubian**	right side, right [PW]

167 下 **xià** go down; below, bottom; next

Radical is 一 **yī** "one," which here represents a base. The character 卜 **bǔ** "divine" placed "below" this line signifies "below." Contrast 下 with 上 **shàng** (25) and 不 **bù** (63).

下	**xià**	on the bottom, under, below [L]; next [SP]
下边 (下邊)	**xiàbian**	on the bottom, under, below [PW]
下头 (下頭)	**xiàtou**	on the bottom, under, below [PW]
下次	**xiàcì**	next time
下个月 (下個月)	**xiàge yuè**	next month
一下儿 (一下兒)	**yíxiàr**	(softens the verb; the **-r** suffix is optional); [NU + M]

168 面 **miàn** side, surface; face

This character is itself a radical. It is also a phonetic, e.g., in 面 (麵) **miàn** "flour" and 缅 (緬) **miǎn** as in 缅甸 (緬甸) **Miǎndiàn** "Burma." The character 面 originally meant "face" (cf. the expressions 面子 **miànzi** "face, feelings" and 面孔 **miànkǒng** "facial expression") and only later gained the meaning "side." 面 is a pictograph, showing a person's head and face; notice the nose in the middle of the face! Contrast 面 with 西 **xī** (35), 两 (兩) **liǎng-** (99), and 回 **huí** (161).

里面 (裏面)	**lǐmiàn**	in, inside [PW]
外面	**wàimian**	outside [PW]
上面	**shàngmian**	on top, on, above [PW]
下面	**xiàmian**	on the bottom, under, below [PW]

New Words in BSC 5-4 Written with Characters You Already Know

东西 (東西)	**dōngxi**	thing [N]
开关 (開關)	**kāiguān**	on-off switch [N]
上	**shàng**	on, on top [L]
上头 (上頭)	**shàngtou**	on top, on [PW]
上边 (上邊)	**shàngbian**	on top, on [PW]
台	**tái**	(for computers, etc.) [M]
五八六	**wŭ-bā-liù**	Pentium® (brand of computer) [N]
要	**yào**	want to [AV]

Reading Exercises (Simplified Characters)

Now practice reading the new characters and words for this lesson in context in sentences, conversations, and narratives. Be sure to refer to the Notes at the end of this lesson, and make use of the accompanying audio disc to hear and practice correct pronunciation, phrasing, and intonation.

A. SENTENCES

Read out loud each of the following sentences, which include all the new characters of this lesson. The first time you read a sentence, focus special attention on the characters and words that are new to you, reminding yourself of their pronunciation and meaning. The second time, aim to comprehend the overall meaning of the sentence.

一、那个东西我先去找一下儿，要是没有，我们可以在里面问一下儿。

二、坐在高先生左边的那个小姐是谁？高太太在哪儿呢？

三、你要是找我们，我们不是在上面，就是在下面。

四、我上个星期去西安了，这个星期要去成都，下个星期要回天津。

五、我不知道这个公司里头有多少人，可是我知道不少。

六、你的名片就在你左边的那个位子上。

七、这个饭店里有多少工人？好像今天有很多没来，是不是？

八、那个大钟下头是什么东西？

九、那三个人里头一个是我的老师，一个是我的同学，一个是我的学生。

十、王大海在里边找，在外边找，在上边找，在下边找，在左边找，在右边找，可是都没有。

B. CONVERSATIONS

Read out loud the following conversations, including the name or role of the person speaking. If possible, find a partner or partners and each of you play a role. Then switch roles, so you get practice reading all of the lines.

一、

边外山：这边儿的位子上有东西，我们去右边儿坐吧。

金文明：右边儿的位子上也有东西。我们去哪儿呢？

边外山：里边儿的位子上好像没有东西，我们去里边儿坐吧。

二、

方大年：你去哪儿？

左明生：我去里头找开关。

方大年：开关不是在外头吗？

左明生：我不知道。谢谢你！

方大年：哪里，哪里。

“Cold drinks, food, fruit”

三、

王：小李，我问你一下儿，这是一台五八六吗？里面有多少RAM？

李：对，是一台五八六。里面有一百二十八个。

王：是你的吗？

李：不是我的，是我的同屋小何的。

王：开关在右边吧？

李：好像开关在左边，不过请你不要开。

C. CHARACTER DIFFERENTIATION DRILLS

Distinguish carefully the following similar-looking characters, pronouncing each one out loud and thinking of its meaning.

一、外 外 外 名 名 名

二、外 外 外 多 多 多
三、外 名 外 多 名 外 多
四、左 左 左 右 右 右
五、左 左 左 在 在 在
六、左 左 左 不 不 不
七、左 右 不 在 不 在 左 右
八、下 下 下 不 不 不
九、下 下 下 上 上 上
十、下 不 上 不 上 不 下
十一、面 面 面 回 回 回
十二、面 面 面 两 两 两
十三、面 面 面 西 西 西
十四、面 回 面 西 面 两 面

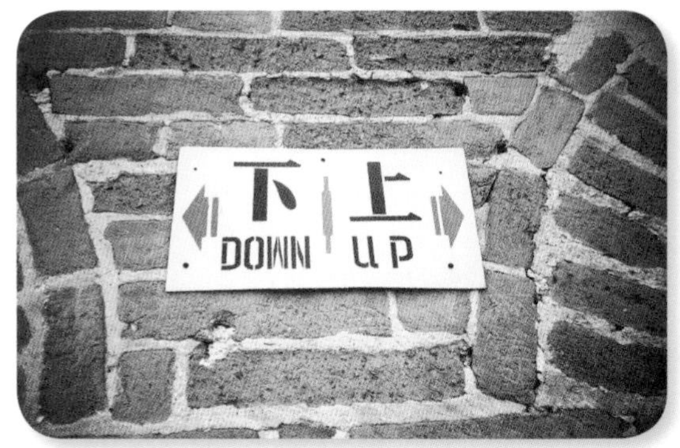

Sign at the Great Wall in Badaling

D. NARRATIVE

Read the following narrative, paying special attention to punctuation and overall structure. The first time you read the narrative, read it out loud; the second time, read silently and try to gradually increase your reading speed. Always think of the meaning of what you're reading.

上个月我的同事老金第一次去广州。在广州他先去了中大，就是中山大学。那边的学生很多，差不多八万四千人，也有不少美国学生。老师有八千一百多位。中大里边、外边都有很多饭店可以住，不过外边的饭店比较贵。吃饭也不难，可以在大学里面吃，也可以在外面吃，可是在中大里面吃比较好。老金很高兴他去了广州，也很高兴他住在中山大学的饭店里。下个月十五号他要第二次去广州，这次他的太太也去。

E. SUPPLEMENT: A HANDWRITTEN NOTE

Read out loud the following handwritten note from one mainland Chinese student to another. Be prepared to answer questions from your instructor and/or classmates on the content of the note.

外山：你好！

我今天三点半来找你，可是你不在。明天是小古的生日，他明天21岁。同学们要请他吃个饭。你明天可以来吗？小李、小王、小何他们都要去。小何也要带他的美国同屋Jason去。好像有两、三个女同学也要去。明天（星期六）6:15在天津西路156号的"成都饭店"。要是你可以去，请带50块钱。

学东

3月8日

Reading Exercises (Traditional Characters)

A. SENTENCES

Read out loud each of the following sentences, which include all the new characters of this lesson. The first time you read a sentence, focus special attention on the characters and words that are new to you, reminding yourself of their pronunciation and meaning. The second time, aim to comprehend the overall meaning of the sentence.

一、那個東西我先去找一下兒，要是沒有，我們可以在裏面問一下兒。

二、坐在高先生左邊的那個小姐是誰？高太太在哪兒呢？

三、你要是找我們，我們不是在上面，就是在下面。

四、我上個星期去西安了，這個星期要去成都，下個星期要回天津。

五、我不知道這個公司裏頭有多少人，可是我知道不少。

六、你的名片就在你左邊的那個位子上。

七、這個飯店裏有多少工人？好像今天有很多沒來，是不是？

八、那個大鐘下頭是什麼東西？

九、那三個人裏頭一個是我的老師，一個是我的同學，一個是我的學生。

十、王大海在裏邊找，在外邊找，在上邊找，在下邊找，在左邊找，在右邊找，可是都沒有。

B. CONVERSATIONS

Read out loud the following conversations, including the name or role of the person speaking. If possible, find a partner or partners and each of you play a role. Then switch roles, so you get practice reading all of the lines.

一、
邊外山：這邊兒的位子上有東西，我們去右邊兒坐吧。
金文明：右邊兒的位子上也有東西。我們去哪兒呢？
邊外山：裏邊兒的位子上好像沒有東西，我們去裏邊兒坐吧。

二、
方大年：你去哪兒？
左明生：我去裏頭找開關。
方大年：開關不是在外頭嗎？
左明生：我不知道。謝謝你！
方大年：哪裏，哪裏。

三、
王：小李，我問你一下兒，這是一台五八六嗎？裏面有多少RAM？
李：對，是一台五八六。裏面有一百二十八個。
王：是你的嗎？
李：不是我的，是我的同屋小何的。
王：開關在右邊吧？
李：好像開關在左邊，不過請你不要開。

C. CHARACTER DIFFERENTIATION DRILLS

Distinguish carefully the following similar-looking characters, pronouncing each one out loud and thinking of its meaning.

一、外外外名名名
二、外外外多多多
三、外名外多名外多
四、左左左右右右
五、左左左在在在
六、左左左不不不
七、左右不在不在左右
八、下下下不不不
九、下下下上上上
十、下不上不上不下
十一、面面面回回回
十二、面面面兩兩兩
十三、面面面西西西
十四、面回面西面兩面

D. NARRATIVE

Read the following narrative, paying special attention to punctuation and overall structure. The first time you read the narrative, read it out loud; the second time, read silently and try to gradually increase your reading speed. Always think of the meaning of what you're reading.

上個月我的同事老金第一次去廣州。在廣州他先去了中大，就是中山大學。那邊的學生很多，差不多八萬四千人，也有不少美國學生。老師有八千一百多位。中大裏邊、外邊都有很多飯店可以住，不過外邊的飯店比較貴。吃飯也不難，可以在大學裏面吃，也可以在外面吃，可是在中大裏面吃比較好。老金很高興他去了廣州，也很高興他住在中山大學的飯店裏。下個月十五號他要第二次去廣州，這次他的太太也去。

E. SUPPLEMENT: A HANDWRITTEN NOTE

(see Simplified Characters section)

Notes

A2. 坐在高先生左边的那个小姐 (坐在高先生左邊的那個小姐) "that young lady sitting to the left of Mr. Gao."

A3. The pattern 不是……就是…… means "if not…then…."

A6. 你的名片就在你左边的那个位子上 (你的名片就在你左邊的那個位子上) "Your name cards are located at the seat to your left." The 就 means "exactly, precisely," but in English we would probably not say this.

A9. 那三个人里头 (那三個人裏頭) "Of those three people" or "Among those three people." 里头 (裏頭) usually means "in" or "inside," but sometimes it can be translated as "of" or "among."

A10. 可是都没有 (可是都沒有) "but it was nowhere" (lit. "but in all cases it was not present."

B2a. 开关不是在外头吗？(開關不是在外頭嗎？) "Isn't the switch outside?" This is a rhetorical question that indicates the speaker believes the switch is outside.

B2b. Given the context, 我不知道 here doesn't mean "I don't know" but rather means "I didn't know (the fact that the switch is outside)." In Chinese one could not say *我没知道 (*我沒知道), since 没 can only be used with action verbs.

B3. 不是我的，是我的同屋小何的 "It's not mine, it's my roommate, Little He's" or "It's not mine, it belongs to my roommate, Little He."

E1. 同学们 (同學們) "The classmates." The pluralizing suffix 们 (們), which you have so far only seen suffixed to personal pronouns like 我们 (我們), 你们 (你們), and 他们 (他們) can also be suffixed to a small number of nouns denoting people. 同学 (同學) is one of those nouns. Be careful not to add 们 (們) to a noun denoting people unless you are certain you have heard or seen it so used by native speakers.

E2. 吃个饭 (吃個飯) "eat a meal"

E3. 在天津西路158号的 "成都饭店" (在天津西路158號的「成都飯店」) "at the Chengdu Hotel, which is at 158 Tianjin West Road."

Hong Kong street sign

UNIT 6

Biographical Information (I)

COMMUNICATIVE OBJECTIVES

Once you've mastered this unit, you'll be able to use Chinese to read and write:

1. Where someone is from, where they were born and grew up, and where they live now.
2. About people's family members: "son," "daughter," "older brother," "younger brother," "little brother," etc.
3. About people's rank among their siblings: "oldest," "second-oldest," "third-oldest," etc.
4. About how people look: "young" or "old."
5. The reason why someone does or doesn't do something or why something is as it is.
6. About different levels of the educational system: "elementary school," "university," etc.
7. About one's grade or year in different educational institutions: "first grade in elementary school," "senior year of college," etc.
8. Intermediate directions: "northeast," "northwest," "southeast," and "southwest."
9. Sentences, conversations, and passages about the act of forgetting.
10. A simple essay about the meaning of friendship.
11. A humorous story.
12. An e-mail.
13. A child's rhyme.
14. Characters with multiple pronunciations.

PART 1

Conversation with a Six-year-old

New Characters and Words

Study the six characters below and the common words written with them, paying careful attention to each character's pronunciation, meaning, and structure, as well as similar-looking characters. After you've studied a character, turn to the *Practice Essentials* volume and practice writing it on the practice sheet, making sure to follow the correct stroke order and direction as you pronounce it out loud and think of its meaning.

169 喜 **xǐ** like, happy, joy

The radical, at the very bottom, is 口 **kǒu** "mouth." This radical is referred to colloquially as 口字底 **kǒuzìdǐ** "bottom made up of the character 口." The component making up the top half of the character is 吉 **jí** "lucky" [**BF**]. When one is "lucky" and "likes" something, one uses one's "mouth" to shout for "joy."

170 欢(歡) **huān** happy

Radical of the simplified form is 又 **yòu** "again." Radical of the traditional form is 欠 **qiàn** "owe." Phonetic of the traditional form is 雚 **guàn** "heron" [**BF**]. The explanation is that when a "heron" swallows a fish, it "owes" the fish thanks and is "happy." Contrast 欢(歡) with 难(難) **nán** (65).

喜欢(喜歡) **xǐhuan** like [**V/AV**]

171 朋 **péng** friend

Radical is 月 **yuè** "moon." The colloquial name for this radical is 月字旁 **yuèzìpáng** "side made up of the character 月." The whole character can serve as a phonetic, e.g., in 棚 **péng** as in 棚子 **péngzi** "shed," 崩 **bēng** as in 山崩 **shānbēng** "landslide," and 蹦 **bèng** "jump." Contrast 朋 with 明 **míng** (15).

172 友 **yǒu** friend

又 **yòu** "again" is both the radical and the phonetic. Contrast 友 with 在 **zài** (149), 左 **zuǒ** (165), and 右 **yòu** (166).

朋友	**péngyou**	friend [N]
男朋友	**nánpéngyou**	boyfriend [N]
女朋友	**nǚpéngyou**	girlfriend [N]

173 真 **zhēn** real, really

Radical is 目 **mù** "eye" [BF]. This character has an alternate traditional form 眞 .

真	**zhēn**	really [A]

174 级(級) **jí** rank, grade

Radical is 丝(絲) **sī** "silk." When at the left side of a character, this radical is referred to colloquially as 绞丝旁(絞絲旁) **jiǎosīpáng** "side made up of twisted silk" and is written as 纟(糹). Phonetic is 及 **jí** "and." Contrast 级(級) with 纪(紀) **jì** (105). Be especially careful to contrast the words 年级(年級) **niánjí** and 年纪(年紀) **niánji** "age."

年级(年級)	**niánjí**	grade (in school) [N]
几年级(幾年級)	**jǐniánjí**	which grade?
一年级(一年級)	**yīniánjí**	first grade

New Words in BSC 6-1 Written with Characters You Already Know

好吃	**hǎochī**	be good to eat [SV]
上	**shàng**	go to, attend [V]
小学(小學)	**xiǎoxué**	elementary school [PW]
上小学(上小學)	**shàng xiǎoxué**	attend elementary school
中学(中學)	**zhōngxué**	middle school [PW]
高中	**gāozhōng**	senior high school [PW]
高一	**gāoyī**	sophomore year of high school [TW]
高二	**gāo'èr**	junior year of high school [TW]
高三	**gāosān**	senior year of high school [TW]
大一	**dàyī**	first year in college [TW]
大二	**dà'èr**	sophomore year in college [TW]
大三	**dàsān**	junior year in college [TW]
大四	**dàsì**	senior year in college [TW]

Junior high school in Taiwan

Reading Exercises (Simplified Characters)

Now practice reading the new characters and words for this lesson in context in sentences, conversations, and narratives. Be sure to refer to the Notes at the end of this lesson, and make use of the accompanying audio disc to hear and practice correct pronunciation, phrasing, and intonation.

A. SENTENCES

Read out loud each of the following sentences, which include all the new characters of this lesson. The first time you read a sentence, focus special attention on the characters and words that are new to you, reminding yourself of their pronunciation and meaning. The second time, aim to comprehend the overall meaning of the sentence.

一、我喜欢北京，可是我的朋友都比较喜欢上海。

二、我们要是没事儿，喜欢去北京饭店吃饭，那儿的饭真好吃。

三、我有两个高中同学，一个叫王安，一个叫万安，他们都是我很好的朋友。

四、朋友，你喜欢吃中国饭吗？里边的东西可好吃了，来吧！

五、要是好吃你就多吃一点儿，要是不好吃你就少吃一点儿。

六、金山大一那年，没有朋友。他今年大四，朋友可真多！

七、明年我要上大二，我的女朋友要上大三。

八、这位同学，你多大了？你上几年级？

九、我的同屋是大一的学生，她的男朋友是大四的学生。

十、大海上大学四年级，文文上高中三年级。

B. CONVERSATIONS

Read out loud the following conversations, including the name or role of the person speaking. If possible, find a partner or partners and each of you play a role. Then switch roles, so you get practice reading all of the lines.

一、

美国太太　：小朋友，你叫什么名字？

中国小朋友：我叫小明。

美国太太　：小明，你几岁了？

中国小朋友：六岁了。

美国太太　：你上小学了吧？
中国小朋友：对，上一年级了。
美国太太　：来，这是你的。你喜欢不喜欢？
中国小朋友：我很喜欢，谢谢！真好吃！

二、
男：你有没有男朋友？
女：我有男的朋友，可是没有男朋友。
男：你喜欢我吗？
女：你别问我这个！

"Double happiness"

C. CHARACTER DIFFERENTIATION DRILLS

Distinguish carefully the following similar-looking characters, pronouncing each one out loud and thinking of its meaning.

一、友 友 友 右 右 右
二、友 友 友 左 左 左
三、友 友 友 在 在 在
四、友 在 左 右 左 右 友 在
五、级 级 级 纪 纪 纪
六、年级，年纪，年级，年纪
七、欢 欢 欢 难 难 难
八、欢 难 难 欢 欢 难 欢

Taiwanese bookstore

D. NARRATIVES

Read the following narratives, paying special attention to punctuation and overall structure. The first time you read a narrative, read it out loud; the second time, read silently and try to gradually increase your reading speed. Always think of the meaning of what you're reading.

一、什么叫"好朋友"？你有事儿可以去找他，他有事儿也可以来找你，这个叫好朋友。坐在那边的那个人就是我的好朋友小王。他的名字叫王大川，他是天津人，今年三十岁。我们小学、中学都是同学。上了大学，大一、大二、大四我们是同屋。我很喜欢小王，小王也很喜欢我。我们两个是好朋友！

二、我去老李的公司找老李，可是老李不在。我问老钱老李在哪儿，可是老钱也不知道老李去什么地方了。老钱要我先在他们公司里吃饭。他们公司的饭真好吃！

Reading Exercises (Traditional Characters)

A. SENTENCES

Read out loud each of the following sentences, which include all the new characters of this lesson. The first time you read a sentence, focus special attention on the characters and words that are new to you, reminding yourself of their pronunciation and meaning. The second time, aim to comprehend the overall meaning of the sentence.

一、我喜歡北京，可是我的朋友都比較喜歡上海。

二、我們要是沒事兒，喜歡去北京飯店吃飯，那兒飯真好吃。

三、我有兩個高中同學，一個叫王安，一個叫萬安，他們都是我很好的朋友。

四、朋友，你喜歡吃中國飯嗎？裏邊的東西可好吃了，來吧！

五、要是好吃你就多吃一點兒，要是不好吃你就少吃一點兒。

六、金山大一那年，沒有朋友。他今年大四，朋友可真多！

七、明年我要上大二，我的女朋友要上大三。

八、這位同學，你多大了？你上幾年級？

九、我的同屋是大一的學生，她的男朋友是大四的學生。

十、大海上大學四年級，文文上高中三年級。

B. CONVERSATIONS

Read out loud the following conversations, including the name or role of the person speaking. If possible, find a partner or partners and each of you play a role. Then switch roles, so you get practice reading all of the lines.

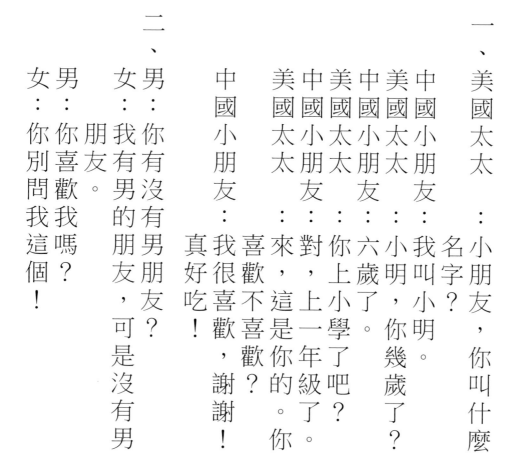

一、

美國太太：小朋友，你叫什麼名字？

中國小朋友：我叫小明。

美國太太：小明，你幾歲了？

中國小朋友：六歲了。

美國太太：你上小學了吧？

中國小朋友：對，上一年級了。

美國太太：來，這是你的。你喜歡不喜歡？

中國小朋友：我很喜歡，謝謝！真好吃！

二、

男：你有沒有男朋友？

女：我有男的朋友，可是沒有男朋友。

男：你喜歡我嗎？

女：你別問我這個！

C. CHARACTER DIFFERENTIATION DRILLS

Distinguish carefully the following similar-looking characters, pronouncing each one out loud and thinking of its meaning.

一、友友友右右右

二、友友友左左左

三、友友友在在在

四、友在左右左右友在

五、級級級紀紀紀

六、年級，年紀，年級，年紀

七、歡歡歡難難難

八、歡難難歡歡難歡

Middle school in Beijing

D. NARRATIVES

Read the following narratives, paying special attention to punctuation and overall structure. The first time you read a narrative, read it out loud; the second time, read silently and try to gradually increase your reading speed. Always think of the meaning of what you're reading.

一、

什麼叫「好朋友」？你有事兒可以去找他，他有事兒也可以來找你，這個叫好朋友。坐在那邊的那個人就是我的好朋友，小王。他的名字叫王大川，他是天津人，今年三十歲。我們小學、中學都是同學，上了大學，大一、大二、大四我們是同屋。我很喜歡小王，小王也很喜歡我。我們兩個是好朋友！

二、

我去老李的公司找老李，可是老李不在。我問老錢老李在哪兒，可是老錢也不知道老李去什麼地方了。老錢要我先在他們公司裏吃飯。他們公司的飯真好吃！

"Buffet and lunch boxes" (written from right to left)

Notes

A4a. 朋友 is here used as a vocative. That is, it is addressed to someone and said to attract their attention, much as in English we might say "Hey, friend, could you do me a favor?"

A4b. 里边 (裏邊) "inside" here probably refers to "inside" a restaurant.

A4c. 东西 (東西) "things" can be used to refer to food; in fact, 吃的东西 (吃的東西) is a common way to say "things to eat" or "food."

A5a. 要是……就…… means "if...then...."

A5b. 多吃一点儿 (多吃一點兒) means "eat a little more." Similarly, 少吃一点儿 (少吃一點兒), which occurs later in this same sentence, means "eat a little less."

A6a. 金山大一那年 should be parsed as follows: 金山 + 大一 + 那年. Hints: 金山 is a person's name, and 大一 is an abbreviation of 大学一年级 (大學一年級).

A6b. 他今年大四，朋友可真多！"He's a senior this year, and he has really many friends!" (lit. "He this year university fourth grade, friends indeed really many!")

A8. 这位同学 (這位同學), literally "This classmate," is here said to address the student concerned and attract her or his attention. The best English equivalent might be "Excuse me, young lady" or "Excuse me, young man." 这位同学 (這位同學) could be said by anybody (e.g., a visitor to the school), not only by a fellow classmate.

B1. 小朋友, literally "Little friend," is often used to address children whose name one doesn't know, much like English "Little boy" or "Little girl."

B2. For many Chinese speakers, there is a distinction between 男朋友 "boyfriend" and 男的朋友 "male friend," or between 女朋友 "girlfriend" and 女的朋友 "female friend."

D1a. 你有事儿可以去找他 (你有事兒可以去找他) "When you have something (you need help with, you) can go seek him out."

D1b. 坐在那边的那个人 (坐在那邊的那個人) "That person (who is) sitting over there."

D2. 老钱要我先在他们公司里吃饭 (老錢要我先在他們公司裏吃飯) "Old Qian wants me to eat in their company first." Regarding 他们公司里 (他們公司裏), note that there is often no 的 between a personal pronoun and the word 公司, because the connection between a person and her or his company is considered so close. Also, in China many larger companies have dining rooms or canteens for their employees, so it's sometimes possible to invite a person from the outside to join one for a meal in one's company.

"It's strictly prohibited to jump down from the (train station) platform"

PART 2

Chat at the Chiang Kai-shek Memorial

你看起来很年轻！
(你看起來很年輕！)
我今年二十九岁。
(我今年二十九歲。)

New Characters and Words

Study the six characters below and the common words written with them, paying careful attention to each character's pronunciation, meaning, and structure, as well as similar-looking characters. After you've studied a character, turn to the *Practice Essentials* volume and practice writing it on the practice sheet, making sure to follow the correct stroke order and direction as you pronounce it out loud and think of its meaning.

175 长(長) **cháng** long
zhǎng grow

This character can itself serve as a radical. It can also serve as a phonetic, e.g., in 怅 (悵) **chàng** as in 惆怅 (惆悵) **chóuchàng** "disconsolate," 张 (張) **Zhāng** (surname), 涨 (漲) **zhǎng** as in 涨价 (漲價) **zhǎngjià** "rise in price," 帐 (帳) **zhàng** as in 蚊帐 (蚊帳) **wénzhàng** "mosquito net," 账 (賬) **zhàng** as in 账单 (賬單) **zhàngdān** "bill," and 胀 (脹) **zhàng** as in 通货膨胀 (通貨膨脹) **tōnghuò péngzhàng** "inflation." This character was originally a pictograph showing "long" and "growing" hair. Since hair was generally not cut in ancient times, the older someone was, the more their hair had "grown" and the "longer" it was. Contrast the simplified form 长 with 老 **lǎo** (61) and 片 **piàn** (91). Also note carefully this character's two different pronunciations.

长 (長)	**cháng**	be long [SV]
长 (長)	**zhǎng**	grow [V]
长大 (長大)	**zhǎngdà**	grow up [RC]

176 看 **kàn** look, see

Radical is 目 **mù** "eye" [BF]. The other component is 手 **shǒu** "hand." If you put your "hand" over your "eyes," you can "see" better (since you can obstruct the sun's rays).

看	**kàn**	look, see [**V**]
好看	**hǎokàn**	be good-looking [**SV**]
看看	**kànkan**	take a look
吃吃看	**chīchi kàn**	try and eat, try eating
问问看 (問問看)	**wènwen kàn**	try and ask, try asking

177 起 **qǐ** rise, begin

Radical is 走 **zǒu** "walk." The colloquial name for this radical is 走字旁 **zǒuzìpáng** "side made up of the character 走." Note that when 走 serves as the radical in another character, its last stroke is lengthened, with the component on the right side placed above the last stroke of 走. Phonetic is 己 **jǐ** "oneself" [**BF**]. In some fonts, the last stroke is lengthened like this: 起

对不起 (對不起)	**duìbuqǐ**	"excuse me" [**IE**]
起来 (起來)	**-qilai**	in the VERBing [**RE**]
看起来 (看起來)	**kànqilai**	in the looking [**RC**]
学起来 (學起來)	**xuéqilai**	in the learning [**RC**]

178 轻 (輕) **qīng** light (not heavy)

Radical is 车 (車) **chē** "vehicle." Phonetic is 巠 **jīng** "underground stream."

年轻 (年輕)	**niánqīng**	be young [**SV**]

179 出 **chū** out, go out

Radical is 凵 **kǎn** "receptacle" [**BF**]. The primitive version of this character was a picture of a grass sprout (屮 **chè**, a rare character not in use today) growing "out" of the ground. Contrast 出 and 山 **shān** (14).

出生	**chūshēng**	be born [**V**]

180 还 (還) **hái** still

Radical is 辶 **chuò** "walk, go" [**BF**]. The colloquial name for this radical is 走之 **zǒu zhī** "the walking 之," because of its meaning "walk" and its resemblance to the particle 之. This character has another pronunciation and meaning, **huán** "return," to which the radical and phonetic are related. Later, the character was borrowed to represent the unrelated word **hái** "still, yet, in addition." Contrast 还 (還) with 过 (過) **guò** (136) and 这 (這) **zhè/zhèi-** (96).

还 (還)	**hái**	still [**A**]
还可以 (還可以)	**hái kéyi**	still be O.K., not too bad
还是 (還是)	**hái shi**	still is
还是…好了 (還是…好了)	**hái shi...hǎole**	it would be better if... [**PT**]

New Words in BSC 6-2 Written with Characters You Already Know

金	**jīn**	gold [**BF**]

金	**Jīn**	Jin (or Kim, in Korean) [SN]
大	**-dà**	big [RE] (as in 长大 (長大) "grow up")
这里 (這裡)	**zhèli**	here [PW]
那里 (那裡)	**nàli**	there [PW]
哪里 (哪裡)	**náli**	where? [QW]
儿子 (兒子)	**érzi**	son [N]
女儿 (女兒)	**nǚ'ér**	daughter [N] (note that in this word, unlike most words that contain a final 儿 (兒), the 儿 (兒) is NOT combined with the previous syllable)

Reading Exercises (Simplified Characters)

Now practice reading the new characters and words for this lesson in context in sentences, conversations, and narratives. Be sure to refer to the Notes at the end of this lesson, and make use of the accompanying audio disc to hear and practice correct pronunciation, phrasing, and intonation.

A. SENTENCES

Read out loud each of the following sentences, which include all the new characters of this lesson. The first time you read a sentence, focus special attention on the characters and words that are new to you, reminding yourself of their pronunciation and meaning. The second time, aim to comprehend the overall meaning of the sentence.

一、你们的女儿长大了，也长高了。她很好看！
二、那个年轻人还是学生，还没有名片。
三、好像左边的位子比较好，您先在那儿坐坐看吧。
四、这个地方看起来不太好看，可是住起来还可以。
五、她是女的，不过看起来好像是男的。
六、何先生、何太太的女儿是在中国出生的，儿子是在美国出生的。
七、那个饭店，里面、外面都很好看，可是饭吃起来真难吃。
八、我不知道这个地方对不对，你还是先问问看吧。
九、我不知道那个东西在哪里，我先找找看吧。
十、王大海今年22岁，还年轻，很多事他还不知道。

B. CONVERSATIONS

Read out loud the following conversations, including the name or role of the person speaking. If possible, find a partner or partners and each of you play a role. Then switch roles, so you get practice reading all of the lines.

一、
美国人：你是哪里人？
中国人：我在西安出生，在成都长大的。
美国人：你看起来很年轻。你还没有三十岁吧？
中国人：还没有。我今年二十九。

二、
李太太：方小姐，今天您就住在我这里吧！
方小姐：好，真谢谢您！
李太太：方小姐，您的东西都带来了吗？
方小姐：都带来了。不过，您别叫我“方小姐”，好吗？我叫方文明，还是叫名字好了！
李太太：好，好。您还没吃饭吧？来，我们先吃一点儿东西吧。这个你吃吃看。
方小姐：真好吃！……都很好吃。我还真没吃过这么好吃的饭！
李太太：哪里，哪里。好吃就多吃一点儿。

C. CHARACTER DIFFERENTIATION DRILLS

Distinguish carefully the following similar-looking characters, pronouncing each one out loud and thinking of its meaning.

一、出 出 出 山 山 山
二、出 山 出 出 山 山 出
三、长 长 长 老 老 老
四、长 长 长 片 片 片
五、长 老 长 片 长 老 片 长
六、还 还 还 这 这 这
七、还 还 还 过 过 过
八、还 过 这 还 这 还 过
九、还 还 还 不 不 不
十、还 不 不 还 不 还 还

Hong Kong street sign

D. NARRATIVES

Read the following narrative, paying special attention to punctuation and overall structure. The first time you read the narrative, read it out loud; the second time, read silently and try to gradually increase your reading speed. Always think of the meaning of what you're reading.

林东生是一个美国大学一年级的学生。他在高中学过三年中文，今年在大学上中文二年级。林东生去过中国，他知道中国有很多好看的地方，也有很多很好吃的东西。中文学起来比较难，不过林东生很喜欢学。他还很年轻，还有很多年可以学中文。大三那年他要去北京住一年。林东生一天学两、三个钟头的中文，很忙。他真是一个好学生。

E. SUPPLEMENT: CHILDREN'S RHYME

Read out loud the following children's rhyme, which is popular in both mainland China and Taiwan.

一二三四五六七，我的朋友在哪里？
在这里，在这里，我的朋友在这里！

Reading Exercises (Traditional Characters)

A. SENTENCES

Read out loud each of the following sentences, which include all the new characters of this lesson. The first time you read a sentence, focus special attention on the characters and words that are new to you, reminding yourself of their pronunciation and meaning. The second time, aim to comprehend the overall meaning of the sentence.

一、你們的女兒長大了，也長高了。她很好看！

二、那個年輕人還是學生，還沒有名片。

三、好像左邊的位子比較好，您先在那兒坐坐看吧。

四、這個地方看起來不太好看，可是住起來還可以。

五、她是女的，不過看起來好像是男的。

六、何先生、何太太的女兒是在中國出生的，兒子是在美國出生的。

七、那個飯店，裏面、外面都很好看，可是飯吃起來真難吃。

八、我不知道這個地方對不對，你還是先問問看吧。

九、我不知道那個東西在哪裏，我先找找看吧。

十、王大海今年二十二歲，還年輕，很多事他還不知道。

B. CONVERSATIONS

Read out loud the following conversations, including the name or role of the person speaking. If possible, find a partner or partners and each of you play a role. Then switch roles, so you get practice reading all of the lines.

一、美國人：你是哪裏人？

中國人：我在西安出生，在成都長大的。

美國人：你看起來很年輕。你還沒有三十歲吧？

中國人：還沒有。我今年二十九。

二、李太太：方小姐，今天您就住在我這裏吧！

方小姐：好，真謝謝您！

李太太：方小姐，您的東西都帶來了嗎？

方小姐：都帶來了。不過，您別叫我「方小姐」，好嗎？我叫方文明，還是叫名字好了！

李太太：好，好。您還沒吃飯吧？來，我們先吃一點兒東西吧。這個你吃吃看。

方小姐：真好吃！……都很好吃。我還真沒吃過這麼好吃的飯！

李太太：哪裏，哪裏。好吃就多吃一點兒。

C. CHARACTER DIFFERENTIATION DRILLS

Distinguish carefully the following similar-looking characters, pronouncing each one out loud and thinking of its meaning.

一、出出出山山山

二、出山出出山山出

三、長長長老老老

四、長長長片片片

五、長老長片長老片長

六、還還還這這這

七、還還還過過過

八、還過這還這還過

九、還還還不不不 (simplified only)

十、還不不還不還還 (simplified only)

D. NARRATIVE

Read the following narrative, paying special attention to punctuation and overall structure. The first time you read the narrative, read it out loud; the second time, read silently and try to gradually increase your reading speed. Always think of the meaning of what you're reading.

林東生是一個美國大學一年級的學生。他在高中學過三年中文，今年在大學上中文二年級。林東生去過中國，他知道中國有很多好看的地方，也有很多很好吃的東西。中文學起來比較難，不過林東生很喜歡學。他還很年輕，還有很多年可以學中文。大三那年他要去北京住一年。林東生一天學兩、三個鐘頭的中文，很忙。他真是一個好學生。

A Hong Kong girl arrives at her middle school

E. SUPPLEMENT: CHILDREN'S RHYME

Read out loud the following children's rhyme, which is popular in both mainland China and Taiwan.

一二三四五六七，
我的朋友在哪裏？
在這裏，在這裏，
我的朋友在這裏！

Shanghai restaurant in Hong Kong

Notes

A1a. **CHARACTERS WITH MULTIPLE PRONUNCIATIONS.** In this line, note the character 长 (長), which is used to write **cháng** "be long" and is also used to write **zhǎng** "grow." Actually, we've seen a case like this before: 都, which is pronounced **dū** in 成都 **Chéngdū** "Chengdu", but which can also write the word **dōu** "both, all." This phenomenon, where two different words have the same written representation, is not unusual in either Chinese or English. In English such words are called heteronyms; consider "minute" ("a minute of your time" vs. "a minute quantity"), "number" ("a prime number" vs. "my mouth got number and number"), and "tear" ("shed a tear" vs. "tear up a sheet of paper"). In Chinese a character that has two or more different pronunciations and meanings is called a 多音字 **duōyīnzì** (some Chinese use the term 破音字 **pòyīnzì**). There are in Chinese fairly many characters with two pronunciations, a much smaller number with three, and at least one character that has four! In some cases, the pronunciations and meanings may differ by only a little, but in other cases they may be quite different. In reading Chinese, it's important to pay careful attention to the context so you know which word is meant. Occasionally there can be ambiguities, but usually the meaning is clear. From now on, whenever we encounter a new 多音字 **duōyīnzì**, we'll bring it to your attention. See also the "Characters with Multiple Pronunciations" list on the disc.

A1b. 长高 (長高) **zhǎnggāo** "grow tall" is a resultative compound that is grammatically similar to 长大 (長大) **zhǎngdà** "grow up."

A4. 这个地方看起来不太好看，可是住起来还可以 (這個地方看起來不太好看，可是住起來還可以) "This place doesn't look very nice, but it's O.K. to stay at" (lit. "This place in the looking at not very good-looking, but in the staying at still can.").

A7. 饭吃起来真难吃 (飯吃起來真難吃) "the food tastes really awful" (lit. "food in the eating of it really hard to eat").

A8. 我不知道这个地方对不对 (我不知道這個地方對不對) "I don't know whether this place is right or not."

A9. 我不知道那个东西在哪里 (我不知道那個東西在哪裏) "I don't know where that thing is." First, be aware that 这里 (這裏), 那里 (那裏), and 哪里 (哪裏) are much more common in standard written Chinese than their northern-style, spoken counterparts 这儿 (這兒), 那儿 (那兒), and 哪儿 (哪兒). Second, remember that in older writings -- and even today in the writing of some people, the character 那 can stand for either 那 or 哪. Had this sentence been written 我不知道那个东西在那里

(我不知道那個東西在那裏), you should have considered the possibility that the 那里 (那裏) was in fact an old-fashioned version of modern standard 哪里 (哪裏).

B2. 我还真没吃过这么好吃的饭！(我還真沒吃過這麼好吃的飯！) "I've really never eaten such good food before!" Instead of meaning "still" as it usually does, the 还 (還) in this sentence expresses emphasis.

D1. 林东生一天学两、三个钟头的中文 (林東生一天學兩、三個鐘頭的中文) "Lin Dongsheng studies two or three hours of Chinese every day." Note that 一天 "on one day" is a common way to express "every day," "each day," or "per day."

D2. Notice the 的 in 两、三个钟头的中文 (兩、三個鐘頭的中文) "two or three hours of Chinese." As is usually the case with 的, this 的 indicates that what precedes the 的 describes what follows the 的. So what about the Chinese that Lin Dongsheng is studying? It's "two or three hours' worth" of Chinese.

Major thoroughfare in Beijing near Tiananmen Square

Chat at the Chiang Kai-shek Memorial (cont.)

PART 3

你儿子、女儿上学了吗？
(你兒子、女兒上學了嗎？)
没有。他们因为还小，所以还没上学。
(沒有。他們因為還小，所以還沒上學。)

New Characters and Words

Study the six characters below and the common words written with them, paying careful attention to each character's pronunciation, meaning, and structure, as well as similar-looking characters. After you've studied a character, turn to the *Practice Essentials* volume and practice writing it on the practice sheet, making sure to follow the correct stroke order and direction as you pronounce it out loud and think of its meaning.

181 因 **yīn** because

Radical is 囗 **wéi** "enclose" [**BF**]. This radical is referred to colloquially as 围字框（圍字框）**wéizìkuàng** "frame of the character 围（圍）." The other component is 大 **dà** (13). 因 is itself a common phonetic, e.g., in 姻 **hūn** as in 婚姻 **hūnyīn** "marriage," 烟 **yān** "smoke," 咽 **yàn** "swallow," and 恩 **ēn** as in 恩惠 **ēnhuì** "mercy." Contrast 因 with 口 **kǒu** (140), 日 **rì** (132), and 回 **huí** (161).

182 为（為） **wèi** for, because of

Radical of the simplified form is 丶 **zhǔ** "dot" [**BF**]. Radical of the traditional form is 火 **huǒ** "fire." Notice that the "fire radical" is written 灬 and is referred to colloquially as 四点火（四點火）**sìdiǎn huǒ** "four dots of fire" when it occurs at the bottom of a character. There is an alternate form of the traditional character 為 that one also sees frequently, 爲, and its radical is 爪 **zhuǎ** "claw" [**BF**]. Traditional 爲 was originally the picture of a monkey, which was borrowed to represent this word. The whole character 为（為）can function as a phonetic in some characters, e.g., 伪（偽）**wěi** "false" [**BF**].

因为（因為）	**yīnwei**	because [**CJ**]
为什么（為什麼）	**wèishenme**	why? (pronounced **wèishemme**) [**QW**]

183 所 **suǒ** that which

Radical is 戶/户 **hù** "door" [BF]. The other component is 斤 **jīn** "catty."

所以	**suóyi**	therefore, so [CJ]
因为…所以…(因為…所以…)	**yīnwei...suóyi...**	because... [PT]

184 作 **zuò** do, make

Radical is 人 **rén** "person," since it is "people" who "do" or "make" things. This radical is written 亻 when occurring at the left side of a character so as not to get in the way of the component at the right. The colloquial name for this radical is 人字旁 **rénzìpáng** "side made up of the character 人." Phonetic is 乍 **zhà** "suddenly" [BF]. Contrast 作 with 所 **suǒ** (183).

工作	**gōngzuò**	work [N/V]

185 校 **xiào** school

Radical is the pictograph 木 **mù** "tree" [BF], since schoolhouses are often made of wood. This radical is referred to colloquially as 木字旁 **mùzìpáng** "side made up of the character 木." Note that when 木 is written at the left of a character as a radical, its last stroke is shortened so that it doesn't collide with the component to its right. The phonetic in 校 is 交 **jiāo** "hand over."

学校(學校)	**xuéxiào**	school [N]
台北美国学校(台北美國學校)	**Táiběi Měiguo Xuéxiào**	Taipei American School [PW]
校长(校長)	**xiàozhǎng**	school principal [N]

186 能 **néng** be able to, can

Radical is 肉 **ròu** "meat," which is usually written 月 when occurring as a component of a character. 能 was originally a picture of a bear ("bear" is now written with four dots at the bottom as 熊 **xióng**). A bear, even minus the four dots, "can" do almost anything. Contrast 能 with 比 **bǐ** (143) and 北 **běi** (16).

能	**néng**	be able to, can [AV]

New Words in BSC 6-3 Written with Characters You Already Know

东南(東南)	**dōngnán**	southeast [PW]
东北(東北)	**dōngběi**	northeast [PW]
西南	**xī'nán**	southwest [PW]
西北	**xīběi**	northwest [PW]
上学(上學)	**shàngxué**	attend school [VO]
没有(沒有)	**méiyou**	(indicates past negative of action verbs) [AV]

Reading Exercises (Simplified Characters)

Now practice reading the new characters and words for this lesson in context in sentences, conversations, and narratives. Be sure to refer to the Notes at the end of this lesson, and make use of the accompanying audio disc to hear and practice correct pronunciation, phrasing, and intonation.

A. SENTENCES

Read out loud each of the following sentences, which include all the new characters of this lesson. The first time you read a sentence, focus special attention on the characters and words that are new to you, reminding yourself of their pronunciation and meaning. The second time, aim to comprehend the overall meaning of the sentence.

一、这是学校的大事，我真不知道我们的校长为什么没有来。

二、台北美国学校不在台北市外边，在台北市里边。

三、你的男朋友在哪儿工作？一个月有多少钱？

四、我因为太忙，所以没能去你们的学校看你们的校长。

五、谢小姐因为下星期一要去香港，比较忙，所以今天不能来。

六、王校长因为在学校里还有一点事，所以先走了。

七、请看，河北省在中国的北边，四川省在中国的西南边。

八、我喜欢中文，可是我不知道为什么中文学起来那么难。

九、你的同屋能不能在饭店里面找一个工作？

十、王大海在他朋友的公司里工作了一、两年，有了一点钱，开了一个小公司。

B. CONVERSATIONS

Read out loud the following conversations, including the name or role of the person speaking. If possible, find a partner or partners and each of you play a role. Then switch roles, so you get practice reading all of the lines.

一、

边太太：你儿子、女儿上学了吗？

方太太：没有，他们还小。儿子三岁，女儿九个月大，所以还没有上学。

边太太：你在哪里工作？

方太太：我在台北美国学校工作。不过，因为儿子、女儿还小，所以我工作半天。

二、
安老师：我们太忙了！为什么我们的工作这么多？
司老师：我们的工作太多是因为学生太多。
安老师：对，对。我们的学生是太多了，工作也太多了，可是钱太少了……
司老师：校长来了，校长来了。我们走吧！

C. CHARACTER DIFFERENTIATION DRILLS

Distinguish carefully the following similar-looking characters, pronouncing each one out loud and thinking of its meaning.

一、作 作 作 所 所 所
二、作 所 所 作 作 作 所
三、能 能 能 比 比 比
四、能 能 能 北 北 北
五、能 比 北 能 能 北 比 能

D. NARRATIVE

Read the following narrative, paying special attention to punctuation and overall structure. The first time you read the narrative, read it out loud; the second time, read silently and try to gradually increase your reading speed. Always think of the meaning of what you're reading.

李大海是美国学生，今年住在广东省广州市。因为他上的学校在广州的西南边，工作的地方在广州的东南边，住的地方在广州的西北边，所以他要走很长的路，很忙，很忙。不过广州的什么街在哪儿，什么地方有什么吃的，李大海都知道。所以他在广州的中国朋友都叫他“半个广州人”。

Reading Exercises (Traditional Characters)

A. SENTENCES

Read out loud each of the following sentences, which include all the new characters of this lesson. The first time you read a sentence, focus special attention on the characters and words that are new to you, reminding yourself of their pronunciation and meaning. The second time, aim to comprehend the overall meaning of the sentence.

一、這是學校的大事，我真不知道我們的校長為什麼沒有來。

二、台北美國學校不在台北市外邊，在台北市裏邊。

三、你的男朋友在哪兒工作？一個月有多少錢？

四、我因為太忙，所以沒能去你們的學校看你們的校長。

五、謝小姐因為下星期一要去香港，比較忙，所以今天不能來。

六、王校長因為在學校裏還有一點事，所以先走了。

七、請看，河北省在中國的北邊，四川省在中國的西南邊。

八、我喜歡中文，可是我不知道為什麼中文學起來那麼難。

九、你的同屋能不能在飯店裏面找一個工作？

十、王大海在他朋友的公司裏工作了一、兩年，有了一點錢，開了一個小公司。

B. CONVERSATIONS

Read out loud the following conversations, including the name or role of the person speaking. If possible, find a partner or partners and each of you play a role. Then switch roles, so you get practice reading all of the lines.

一、邊太太：你兒子、女兒上學了嗎？
方太太：沒有，他們還小。兒子三歲，女兒九個月大，所以還沒有上學。
邊太太：你在哪裏工作？
方太太：我在台北美國學校工作。不過，因為兒子、女兒還小，所以我工作半天。

二、安老師：我們太忙了！為什麼我們的工作這麼多？
司老師：我們的工作太多是因為學生太多。
安老師：對，對。我們的學生是太多了，工作也太多了，可是錢太少了……
司老師：校長來了，校長來了。我們走吧！

C. CHARACTER DIFFERENTIATION DRILLS

Distinguish carefully the following similar-looking characters, pronouncing each one out loud and thinking of its meaning.

一、作作作所所所
二、作所所作作作所
三、能能能比比比
四、能能能北北北
五、能比北能能北比能

"Everyone is responsible for protecting cultural relics, carving and drawing strictly prohibited, violators will be fined"

D. NARRATIVE

Read the following narrative, paying special attention to punctuation and overall structure. The first time you read the narrative, read it out loud; the second time, read silently and try to gradually increase your reading speed. Always think of the meaning of what you're reading.

李大海是美國學生，今年住在廣東省廣州市。因為他上的學校在廣州的西南邊，工作的地方在廣州的東南邊，住的地方在廣州的西北邊，所以他要走很長的路，很忙，很忙。不過廣州的什麼街在哪兒，什麼地方有什麼吃的，李大海都知道。所以他在廣州的中國朋友都叫他「半個廣州人」。

Notes

A1. 大事, literally "big thing," could here be translated as "important issue" or "major event."

A4. Besides meaning "look" or "see," the verb 看 can also sometimes, as here, mean "visit."

A5. 谢小姐因为下星期一要去香港，比较忙，所以今天不能来 (謝小姐因為下星期一要去香港，比較忙，所以今天不能來) "Because Ms. Xie is going to Hong Kong next Monday and (because she) is relatively busy, therefore she can't come today."

A8. According to the latest Chinese standards for punctuation, a period is required at the end of this sentence, but traditionally many writers of Chinese would put a question mark at the end of indirect questions such as this, and write: 我喜欢中文，可是我不知道为什么中文学起来那么难？(我喜歡中文，可是我不知道為什麼中文學起來那麼難？).

A10. 工作了一、两年 (工作了一、兩年) "worked for one or two years."

B2. 我们的学生是太多了 (我們的學生是太多了) "We do have too many students." Normally, there would be no 是 in a sentence with a stative verb like 多. The reason for the 是 here is emphasis; the speaker is emphatically agreeing with the other speaker, who just made this point.

D1. 他上的学校 (他上的學校) "the school he attends."

D2. 工作的地方 "the place where (he) works."

D3. 住的地方 "the place where (he) lives."

D4. 他要走很长的路 (他要走很長的路) "he has to walk a long way" (lit. "he needs to walk a long road").

D5. 广州的什么街在哪儿，什么地方有什么吃的，李大海都知道 (廣州的什麼街在哪兒，什麼地方有什麼吃的，李大海都知道) "Li Dahai knows the location of all of Guangzhou's streets and where you can get different foods" (lit. "What street of Guangzhou's is where, what place has what things to eat, Li Dahai knows it all.")

D6. 他在广州的中国朋友 (他在廣州的中國朋友) "his Chinese friends in Guangzhou."

D7. The expression 半个广州人 (半個廣州人) translates literally as "half a native of Guangzhou." This means "almost like a native of Guangzhou" or "a semi-native of Guangzhou." Expressions using 半个 (半個) in this way are not uncommon, for example, 半个上海人 (半個上海人), 半个台湾人 (半個台灣人), and 半个中国人 (半個中國人).

Hong Kong street sign

Chat at the Chiang Kai-shek Memorial (cont.)

New Characters and Words

Study the six characters below and the common words written with them, paying careful attention to each character's pronunciation, meaning, and structure, as well as similar-looking characters. After you've studied a character, turn to the *Practice Essentials* volume and practice writing it on the practice sheet, making sure to follow the correct stroke order and direction as you pronounce it out loud and think of its meaning.

187 哥 **gē** older brother

Radical is 口 **kǒu** "mouth." This radical is referred to colloquially as 口字旁 **kǒuzìpáng** "side made up of the character 口." Phonetic is 可 **kě** "may" [**BF**] (145), which is here written twice. Contrast 哥 with 可 (145), 何 (19), and 司 (95).

哥哥	**gēge**	older brother [**N**]
大哥	**dàgē**	oldest brother [**N**]

---

188 弟 **dì** younger brother

Radical is 弓 **gōng** "bow." This character is itself a phonetic, e.g., in 第 **dì-** (133) and 递（遞）**dì** as in 递给（遞給）**dìgěi** "give to." Contrast 弟 and 第 **dì-** (133).

弟弟	**dìdi**	younger brother [**N**]
大弟弟	**dà dìdi**	older younger brother [**N**]
小弟	**xiǎodì**	little brother [**N**]

189 妹 **mèi** younger sister

Radical is 女 **nǚ** "woman" [**BF**]. This radical is referred to colloquially as 女字旁 **nǚzìpáng** "side made up of the character 女." Note that when 女 is written at the left of a character as a radical, its last stroke is shortened so that it doesn't collide with the component to its right. Phonetic is 未 **wèi** "not yet" [**BF**]. A "younger sister" may sometimes be thought of by her family members as "not yet" a fully matured "woman."

妹妹	**mèimei**	younger sister [**N**]
大妹	**dàmèi**	older younger sister [**N**]
小妹	**xiǎomèi**	little sister [**N**]
姐妹	**jiěmèi**	older and younger sisters [**N**]

190 忘 **wàng** forget

Radical is 心 **xīn** "heart." This radical is referred to colloquially as 心字底 **xīnzìdǐ** "bottom made up of the character 心." Phonetic is 亡 **wáng** "flee" [**BF**]. If a matter has "fled" from your "heart," it has been "forgotten."

忘	**wàng**	forget [**V**]
我忘了。	**Wǒ wàngle.**	I forgot.

191 家 **jiā** family, home; (for companies, hotels, etc.)

Radical is 宀 **mián** "roof" [**BF**]. This radical is referred to colloquially as 宝盖头 (寶蓋頭) **bǎogàitóu** "top made up of a canopy." The other component is 豕 **shǐ** "pig" [**BF**]. A "pig" under a "roof" represents "home," since pigs were often raised at home in ancient China, as they gave off warmth and served as natural heating.

家	**jiā**	family, home [**PW**]; (for companies, factories, hotels, stores) [**M**]
我家里 (我家裏)	**wǒ jiāli**	in my family
我们家 (我們家)	**wǒmen jiā**	our family
回家	**huíjiā**	return to one's home [**VO**]
一家公司	**yìjiā gōngsī**	a company

192 给 (給) **gěi** give; for

Radical is 丝 (絲) **sī** "silk." When at the left side of a character, this radical is referred to colloquially as 绞丝旁 (絞絲旁) **jiǎosīpáng** "side made up of twisted silk" and is written as 纟 (糹). Phonetic is 合 **hé** "shut." In China it's common to "give" "silk" as a gift.

给 (給)	**gěi**	give [**V/PV**]; for [**CV**]

New Words in BSC 6-4 Written with Characters You Already Know

大姐	**dàjiě**	oldest sister [**N**]
老	**lǎo-**	(indicates one's rank among one's siblings) [**BF**]
老大	**lǎodà**	oldest (among siblings) [**N**]

Reading Exercises (Simplified Characters)

Now practice reading the new characters and words for this lesson in context in sentences, conversations, and narratives. Be sure to refer to the Notes at the end of this lesson, and make use of the accompanying audio disc to hear and practice correct pronunciation, phrasing, and intonation.

A. SENTENCES

Read out loud each of the following sentences, which include all the new characters of this lesson. The first time you read a sentence, focus special attention on the characters and words that are new to you, reminding yourself of their pronunciation and meaning. The second time, aim to comprehend the overall meaning of the sentence.

一、我大哥今年五十八岁，我大姐五十五岁。

二、哥哥、姐姐、弟弟、妹妹我都没有，可是我有很多好朋友。

三、我差一点儿忘了明天是我弟弟的生日！

四、对不起，您能不能给我那个钟？我要看看。谢谢！

五、你今天去哪家公司？你可别忘了带你的名片。

六、我忘了今天是星期一，那家公司星期一不开门。

七、我家左边有一家公司，右边有一家饭店。

八、我大哥在一家公司工作，很忙，不过我不太知道他在那儿做什么。

九、因为星期六我小妹京京要来看我，所以我星期五就不回家了。

十、王大海在他们家是老二，他上面有一个姐姐，下面有一个妹妹。

B. CONVERSATIONS

Read out loud the following conversations, including the name or role of the person speaking. If possible, find a partner or partners and each of you play a role. Then switch roles, so you get practice reading all of the lines.

一、

台湾人：我在我们家是老大。我有一个弟弟、两个妹妹。

美国人：他们都住在台北吗？

台湾人：我大妹住在台北。

美国人：对不起，我忘了我还有一点事，先走了。我姓高，高大文。这是我的名片。

台湾人：谢谢您，高先生。我姓何。我也给您我的名片。

二、
林先生：您贵姓？
谢小姐：我姓谢。您贵姓？
林先生：我姓林，这是我的名片。您能给我您的名片吗？
谢小姐：对不起，我今天忘了带了。下次给您，好吗？

C. CHARACTER DIFFERENTIATION DRILLS

Distinguish carefully the following similar-looking characters, pronouncing each one out loud and thinking of its meaning.

一、哥 哥 哥 可 可 可
二、哥 哥 哥 何 何 何
三、哥 哥 哥 司 司 司
四、哥 哥 哥 同 同 同
五、哥 可 哥 何 哥 司 哥 同

D. NARRATIVE

Read the following narrative, paying special attention to punctuation and overall structure. The first time you read the narrative, read it out loud; the second time, read silently and try to gradually increase your reading speed. Always think of the meaning of what you're reading.

中国有一个小学生，姓高，名字叫明山，今年十岁。他们家住在西安。高明山不是好学生，学校的老师问他的事，他差不多都不知道，所以老师不太喜欢他。有一天，是星期一，有一位老师问他：

老师：高明山，中国有多少人口？你知道不知道？忘了吧？
高明山：我没忘，中国有1,300,000,001个人。
老师：不对！上个星期我们不是学过中国有1,300,000,000人吗？

高明山：可是老师，您还不知道吧？星期六我的小妹妹出生了，所以中国的人口多了一个，今天中国有1,300,000,001个人了！

E. SUPPLEMENT: AN E-MAIL

Read out loud the following e-mail. Be prepared to answer questions from your instructor and/or classmates on the content: From whom is it? To whom? When was it sent? What is the problem? What is the reason for the problem?

发件人：金文美 <wenmei@263.net.cn>
发送时间：2011年3月10日星期四21:18
收件人：金文山 <wenshan928@sina.com>
主题：对不起

大哥：

你好！我上次说这个星期六要请你、大姐、小弟和小妹吃美国饭。
真对不起，因为今天校长要我这个星期六去天津，下星期三回家，所以不知道我们可不可以下星期六（3月19日）吃饭？
也请你问问他们，好吗？谢谢！

二妹

Reading Exercises (Traditional Characters)

A. SENTENCES

Read out loud each of the following sentences, which include all the new characters of this lesson. The first time you read a sentence, focus special attention on the characters and words that are new to you, reminding yourself of their pronunciation and meaning. The second time, aim to comprehend the overall meaning of the sentence.

一、我大哥今年五十八歲，我大姐五十五歲。

二、哥哥、姐姐、弟弟、妹妹我都沒有，可是我有很多好朋友。

三、我差一點兒忘了明天是我弟弟的生日！

四、對不起，您能不能給我那個鐘？我要看看。謝謝！

五、你今天去哪家公司？你可別忘了帶你的名片。

六、我忘了今天是星期一，那家公司星期一不開門。

七、我家左邊有一家公司，右邊有一家飯店。

八、我大哥在一家公司工作，很忙，不過我不太知道他在那兒做什麼。

九、因為星期六我小妹京京要來看我，所以我星期五就不回家了。

十、王大海在他們家是老二，他上面有一個姐姐，下面有一個妹妹。

B. CONVERSATIONS

Read out loud the following conversations, including the name or role of the person speaking. If possible, find a partner or partners and each of you play a role. Then switch roles, so you get practice reading all of the lines.

一、台灣人：我在我們家是老大。我有一個弟弟、兩個妹妹。

美國人：他們都住在台北嗎？

台灣人：我大妹住在台北。

美國人：對不起，我忘了我還有一點事，先走了。我姓高，高大文。這是我的名片。

台灣人：謝謝您，高先生。我姓何。我也給您我的名片。

二、林先生：您貴姓？

謝小姐：我姓謝。您貴姓？

林先生：我姓林，這是我的名片。您能給我您的名片嗎？

謝小姐：對不起，我今天忘了帶了。下次給您，好嗎？

C. CHARACTER DIFFERENTIATION DRILLS

Distinguish carefully the following similar-looking characters, pronouncing each one out loud and thinking of its meaning.

一、哥哥哥可可可

二、哥哥哥何何何

三、哥哥哥司司司

四、哥哥哥同同同

五、哥可哥何哥司哥同

Sign at Hong Kong flower show

D. NARRATIVE

Read the following narrative, paying special attention to punctuation and overall structure. The first time you read the narrative, read it out loud; the second time, read silently and try to gradually increase your reading speed. Always think of the meaning of what you're reading.

中國有一個小學生，姓高，名字叫明山，今年十歲。他們家住在西安。高明山不是好學生，學校的老師問他的事，他差不多都不知道，所以老師不太喜歡他。有一天，是星期一，有一位老師問他：

老師　：高明山，中國有多少人口？你知道不知道？忘了吧？

高明山：我沒忘，中國有 1,300,000,001 個人。

老師　：不對！上個星期我們不是學過中國有 1,300,000,000 人嗎？

高明山：可是老師，您還不知道吧？星期六我的小妹妹出生了，所以中國的人口多了一個，今天中國有 1,300,000,001 個人了！

Taipei street sign

E. SUPPLEMENT: AN E-MAIL

Read out loud the following e-mail. Be prepared to answer questions from your instructor and/or classmates on the content: From whom is it? To whom? When was it sent? What is the problem? What is the reason for the problem?

發件人：金文美 <wenmei@263.net.cn>
發送時間：2011年3月10日星期四21:18
收件人：金文山 <wenshan928@sina.com>
主題：對不起

大哥：

你好！我上次說這個星期六要請你、大姐、小弟和小妹吃美國飯。
真對不起，因爲今天校長要我這個星期六去天津，下星期三回家，所以不知道我們可不可以下星期六（3月19日）吃飯?
也請你問問他們，好嗎？謝謝！

二妹

Notes

A3. 我差一点儿忘了明天是我弟弟的生日！(我差一點兒忘了明天是我弟弟的生日！) "I nearly forgot that tomorrow is my younger brother's birthday!" Remember that the basic meaning of the verb 差 (差) is "lack." 差一点儿 (差一點兒) means "lacking by (only) a little," in other words, "nearly" or "almost." The structure and meaning of 差一点儿 (差一點兒) and 差不多 (差不多) "almost, about" are similar.

A4. 您能不能给我那个钟？(您能不能給我那個鐘？) "Can you give me that clock?" Just as in English, this is not a question asking whether the other person is able to give the speaker a clock, but rather a polite request asking him or her to do so.

A8. 我不太知道 "I'm not too clear" (lit. "I don't too much know").

A9. 所以我星期五就不回家了 "so Friday I won't be going home (after all, as it now turns out)." The implication of the 就 "then" and the changed situation 了 is that since circumstances have changed, the speaker has changed her or his plans.

D2a. 上个星期我们不是学过中国有1,300,000,000人吗？(上個星期我們不是學過中國有1,300,000,000人嗎？) "Didn't we learn last week that China has one billion three hundred million people?" This is a rhetorical question being used not to ask a real question but to emphasize a fact.

D2b. 所以中国的人口多了一个 (所以中國的人口多了一個) "So China's population has increased by one." The verb 多 here literally means "become more."

E1. There is no need for you to learn the following words from the e-mail header now, but in case you're curious, here are the Pinyin transcriptions and English meanings:

发件人 (發件人)	**fājiànrén**	sender
发送时间 (發送時間)	**fāsòng shíjiān**	transmission time
收件人	**shōujiànrén**	addressee
主题 (主題)	**zhǔtí**	subject

Road in Chaoyang District, Beijing

UNIT 7

Biographical Information (II)

COMMUNICATIVE OBJECTIVES

Once you've mastered this unit, you'll be able to use Chinese to read and write:

1. About when and with whom someone arrived in a certain place.
2. What languages people know and where they learned them.
3. How well people speak, read, and write Chinese and other languages.
4. Passages that contrast different time periods and discuss the order of events: "before," "after," "in the beginning," "originally," "formerly," "later," etc.
5. Several amusing stories.
6. Some Chinese book titles.
7. A song about learning Chinese.

PART 1

More Questions About One's Family

New Characters and Words

Study the six characters below and the common words written with them, paying careful attention to each character's pronunciation, meaning, and structure, as well as similar-looking characters. After you've studied a character, turn to the *Practice Essentials* volume and practice writing it on the practice sheet, making sure to follow the correct stroke order and direction as you pronounce it out loud and think of its meaning.

193 表 **biǎo** (indicates cousins of a different surname)

Radical is 衣 **yī** "clothing" [**BF**]. 表 is itself a phonetic, e.g., in 表 (錶) **biǎo** "watch," 裱 **biǎo** "mount a picture," and 婊 **biǎo** as in 婊子 **biǎozi** "whore."

表哥	**biǎogē**	older male cousin of different surname [**N**]
表姐	**biǎojiě**	older female cousin of different surname [**N**]
表弟	**biǎodì**	younger male cousin of different surname [**N**]
表妹	**biǎomèi**	younger female cousin of different surname [**N**]

194 县(縣) **xiàn** county

Radical of the simplified form is 厶 **sī** "private." Radical of the traditional form is 糸 (alternate form of traditional 絲) **sī** "silk." This character is itself a phonetic, e.g., in 悬 (懸) **xuán** "hang." Contrast simplified 县 with 真 **zhēn** (173). The traditional form of the character has a common alternate form 縣 .

县 (縣)	**xiàn**	county [**N**]
东明县 (東明縣)	**Dōngmíng Xiàn**	Dongming County (in Shandong Province) [**PW**]
广河县 (廣河縣)	**Guǎnghé Xiàn**	Guanghe County (in Gansu Province) [**PW**]
林口县 (林口縣)	**Línkǒu Xiàn**	Linkou County (in Heilongjiang Province) [**PW**]

文安县(文安縣)	**Wén'ān Xiàn**	Wenan County (in Hebei Province) [PW]

195 城 **chéng** city

Radical is 土 **tǔ** "earth." The colloquial name for this radical is 土字旁 **tǔzìpáng** "side made up of the character 土." Notice that the top horizontal line of 土 is shorter than the bottom line. Also notice that when used as a radical, the bottom line of 土 slants up toward the right, so as not to get in the way of the other component. Phonetic is 成 **chéng** "become." "Earth" "becomes" a "city." Formerly, 城 meant "city wall" but in time, the "wall" around a city defined the "city." 城 is a relatively colloquial word; 市 **shì** (47), also "city," is more formal.

城	**chéng**	city [N]
北京城	**Běijīng chéng**	the city of Beijing
城里(城裏)	**chéngli**	in the city
城里头(城裏頭)	**chéng lǐtou**	in the city
长城(長城)	**Cháng Chéng**	Great Wall [PW]
长城饭店(長城飯店)	**Cháng Chéng Fàndiàn**	Great Wall Hotel [PW]

196 原 **yuán** original

Radical is 厂 **ān** "thatched hut" [BF], which is referred to colloquially as 厂字头(厰字頭) **chǎngzìtóu** "top made up of the character 厂." The other component is 泉 **quán** "spring" [BF]. 原 can itself serve as a phonetic, e.g., in 源 **yuán** as in 来源(來源) **láiyuán** "source" and 愿(願) **yuàn** as in 愿意(願意) **yuànyi** "be willing."

原来(原來)	**yuánlái**	originally, formerly [A]
太原	**Tàiyuán**	Taiyuan (capital of Shanxi Province) [PW]

197 厂(廠) **chǎng** factory

Radical of the simplified form is 厂 **ān** "thatched hut" [BF], which is referred to colloquially as 厂字头(厰字頭) **chǎngzìtóu** "top made up of the character 厂." Radical of the traditional form is 广 **yǎn** "eaves" [BF], which is referred to colloquially as 广字头(廣字頭) **guǎngzìtóu** "top made up of the character 广." The other component in traditional 廠 is 敞 **chǎng** "spacious" [BF]. The explanation of the traditional form is "factories" are "spacious" and have "eaves." Contrast 厂(廠) with 广(廣) **guǎng** (27).

厂(廠)	**chǎng**	factory [N]
工厂(工廠)	**gōngchǎng**	factory [PW]

198 现(現) **xiàn** appear; current, present

Radical is 玉 **yù** "jade," but notice that as a radical, the last stroke of 玉 is dropped, so that the radical then looks like 王 **wáng** "king." For that reason, the colloquial name for this radical is 王字旁 **wángzìpáng** "side made up of the character 王." Notice also that when used as a radical, the bottom line of 王 slants up toward the right, so as not to get in the way of the other component. Phonetic is 见(見) **jiàn** "see." From "something that has just appeared," the meaning has been extended to "current" or "now."

现在(現在)	**xiànzài**	now [A]

New Words in BSC 7-1 Written with Characters You Already Know

还 (還) **hái** in addition [A]
呢 **ne** (indicates a pause) [P]
口 **kǒu** (for people) [M]

Reading Exercises (Simplified Characters)

Now practice reading the new characters and words for this lesson in context in sentences, conversations, and narratives. Be sure to refer to the Notes at the end of this lesson, and make use of the accompanying audio disc to hear and practice correct pronunciation, phrasing, and intonation.

A. SENTENCES

Read out loud each of the following sentences, which include all the new characters of this lesson. The first time you read a sentence, focus special attention on the characters and words that are new to you, reminding yourself of their pronunciation and meaning. The second time, aim to comprehend the overall meaning of the sentence.

一、中国有两千多个县。
二、我原来是工人，在太原的一家工厂工作，可是现在老了，不工作了。
三、我表弟原来在长城饭店工作，现在他开公司了。
四、您知道不知道那个工人现在是不是还在那家工厂工作？
五、我们家有五口人，我们一家五口都住在广东省台山县。
六、我们很喜欢现在住的地方。
七、我知道长城饭店在北京城里头，不过我忘了在什么路上。
八、我们家原来住在台中县，现在住在台中市了。
九、那家工厂原来在北京城里头，现在在北京城外头了。
十、王大海在中国有两个表哥，在台湾还有一个表弟、一个表妹。

B. CONVERSATIONS

Read out loud the following conversations, including the name or role of the person speaking. If possible, find a partner or partners and each of you play a role. Then switch roles, so you get practice reading all of the lines.

一、
表妹：表姐，你们家住在哪儿？
表姐：我们住在大兴县，在北京城的南边儿。
表妹：那，你们家都有什么人？
表姐：我们家有三口人：你表哥、你二表姐还有我。
表妹：表姐，您在哪儿工作？
表姐：我原来在一家工厂工作。因为他们给的钱太少，所以呢，现在在一家比较小的公司工作，可是钱很多。

二、
关小文：何老师，去年这个学校学中文的学生多不多？
何老师：我原来在第43中学工作，所以不知道。
关小文：现在在这里学中文的学生是男生多？是女生多？
何老师：好像一半一半吧。

C. CHARACTER DIFFERENTIATION DRILLS

Distinguish carefully the following similar-looking characters, pronouncing each one out loud and thinking of its meaning.

一、厂 厂 厂 广 广 广
二、厂 广 广 厂 厂 广 厂
三、县 县 县 真 真 真
四、县 真 县 真 县 真 县

D. NARRATIVE

Read the following narrative, paying special attention to punctuation and overall structure. The first time you read the narrative, read it out loud; the second time, read silently and try to gradually increase your reading speed. Always think of the meaning of what you're reading.

高文公先生是南京人。他家里有三口人：高先生、高太太，还有一个儿子小明。高家一家三口都住在南京市东山街五十五号。高先生开工厂，他的工厂在南京城外头。我忘了那个地方叫什么名字，好像叫南口县。高先生原来在一家美国公司工作。他在那儿工作了五、六年，可是因为他们给的钱太少，所以他开了这家工厂。高先生开工厂差不多一年半了。高先生的表弟林明原来也在这家工厂工作，可是现在他去南京市里的一家公司工作了。

Reading Exercises (Traditional Characters)

A. SENTENCES

Read out loud each of the following sentences, which include all the new characters of this lesson. The first time you read a sentence, focus special attention on the characters and words that are new to you, reminding yourself of their pronunciation and meaning. The second time, aim to comprehend the overall meaning of the sentence.

一、中國有兩千多個縣。
二、我原來是工人，在太原的一家工廠工作，可是現在老了，不工作了。
三、我表弟原來在長城飯店工作，現在他開公司了。
四、您知道不知道那個工人現在是不是還在那家工廠工作？
五、我們家有五口人，我們一家五口都住在廣東省台山縣。
六、我們很喜歡現在住的地方。
七、我知道長城飯店在北京城裏頭，不過我忘了在什麼路上。
八、我們家原來住在台中縣，現在住在台中市了。
九、那家工廠原來在北京城裏頭，現在在北京城外頭了。
十、王大海在中國有兩個表哥，在台灣還有一個表弟、一個表妹。

B. CONVERSATIONS

Read out loud the following conversations, including the name or role of the person speaking. If possible, find a partner or partners and each of you play a role. Then switch roles, so you get practice reading all of the lines.

一、

表妹：表姐，你們家住在哪兒？

表姐：我們住在大興縣，在北京城的南邊兒。

表妹：那，你們家都有什麼人？

表姐：我們家有三口人：你表哥、你二表姐還有我。

表妹：表姐，您在哪兒工作？

表姐：我原來在一家工廠工作。因為他們給的錢太少，所以呢，現在在一家比較小的公司工作，可是錢很多。

二、

關小文：何老師，去年這個學校學中文的學生多不多？

何老師：我原來在第43中學工作，所以不知道。

關小文：現在在這裏學中文的學生是男生多是女生多？

何老師：好像一半一半吧。

C. CHARACTER DIFFERENTIATION DRILLS

Distinguish carefully the following similar-looking characters, pronouncing each one out loud and thinking of its meaning.

一、廠廠廠廣廣廣

二、廠廣廣廠廠廣廠

三、縣縣縣真真真

四、縣真縣真縣真縣

D. NARRATIVE

Read the following narrative, paying special attention to punctuation and overall structure. The first time you read the narrative, read it out loud; the second time, read silently and try to gradually increase your reading speed. Always think of the meaning of what you're reading.

高文公先生是南京人。

他家裏有三口人：高先生、高太太，還有一個兒子小明。高家一家三口都住在南京市東山街五十五號。高先生開工廠，他的工廠在南京城外頭。我忘了那個地方叫什麼名字，好像叫南口縣。高先生原來在一家美國公司工作。他在那兒工作了五、六年，可是因為他們給的錢太少，所以他開了這家工廠。高先生開工廠差不多一年半了，還可以。高先生的表弟林明原來也在這家工廠工作，可是現在他去南京市裏的一家公司工作了。

Notes

A1a. As you will have noticed, as of this lesson the Chinese font size has again been reduced. You will need to become accustomed to reading Chinese written in various fonts and sizes, as well as handwritten Chinese.

A1b. It's not so easy to count the total number of counties in China, since besides the traditional counties, the term 县 (縣) also encompasses so-called autonomous counties, county-level cities, and yet other administrative divisions that are equivalent to counties. Furthermore, the total number tends to change every few years. But it's safe to say there are well over two thousand counties in China.

A4. 那个工人现在是不是还在那家工厂工作？(那個工人現在是不是還在那家工廠工作？) A literal translation would be: "That worker, is it or is it not the case that he/she is now still working at that factory?" In smoother English, we could say: "Is that worker now still working at that factory?"

A5. 一家五口 "all five of us in our family" (lit. "whole family five members"). The number 一 can sometimes mean "whole." Other examples are 一天 "the whole day long" and 一路 "the whole road -- all along the way."

B2. 是男生多？是女生多？"Are there more male students or female students?" (lit. "Is it that male students are many? Is it that female students are many?") This is another example of a Choice-type Question with Choice Implied (cf. 4-3: B2b, 4-4: B5).

D1. 开工厂 (開工廠) "operate a factory," "run a factory."

D2. 开工厂差不多一年半了 (開工廠差不多一年半了) "has been operating a factory for about a year and a half." The implication is that Mr. Gao is still operating the factory now (or as of the time of the writing of this passage). In sentences indicating duration of time, a sentence-final particle 了 at the end of the sentence indicates that the action of the verb has been continuing for a period of time up to and including the present (cf. 4-1: A5).

PART 2

"You Can Speak Chinese!"

您好！您会
说中国话！
(您好！您會
說中國話！)
会一点儿。
(會一點兒。)

New Characters and Words

Study the six characters below and the common words written with them, paying careful attention to each character's pronunciation, meaning, and structure, as well as similar-looking characters. After you've studied a character, turn to the *Practice Essentials* volume and practice writing it on the practice sheet, making sure to follow the correct stroke order and direction as you pronounce it out loud and think of its meaning.

199 会(會) **huì** know how to, can

Radical of the simplified form is 人 **rén** "person," which is here spread out across the top of the character and known as 人字头 (人字頭) **rénzìtóu** "top made up of the character 人." Radical of the traditional form is 曰 **yuē** "say" [**BF**]. 会 (會) is itself a phonetic, e.g., in 绘 (繪) **huì** "draw" and 烩 (燴) **huì** "braise." Contrast simplified 会 with 公 **gōng** (94), 今 **jīn** (106), and 全 (全) **quán** (203).

会 (會)	**huì**	know how to, can [**AV**]

200 说(說) **shuō** say, speak

Radical is 讠 (言) **yán** "word" or "speech" [**BF**]. The colloquial name for this radical is 言字旁 **yánzìpáng** "side made up of the character 言." Phonetic is 兑 (兌) **duì** "exchange" [**BF**]. The explanation is that one "speaks" out and "exchanges" "words." As regards the traditional form 說, be aware that in some font styles and when handwritten, the first two strokes of the right-hand component, 兌, are written as 兑.

说 (說)	**shuō**	say, speak [**V**]
就是说 (就是說)	**jiù shi shuō**	that is to say

201 话(話) **huà** word, language [N]

Radical is 讠(言) **yán** "speech" [BF]. The colloquial name for this radical is 言字旁 **yánzìpáng** "side made up of the character 言." The other component is 舌 **shé** "tongue" [BF]. The explanation is that if you use your "tongue" to "speak," you produce a "word."

说话(說話)	**shuōhuà**	speak words, speak [VO]
中国话(中國話)	**Zhōngguo huà**	spoken Chinese [PH]
说中国话(說中國話)	**shuō Zhōngguo huà**	speak Chinese
广东话(廣東話)	**Guǎngdōng huà**	Cantonese dialect [PH]
上海话(上海話)	**Shànghǎi huà**	Shanghainese dialect [PH]
台湾话(台灣話)	**Táiwān huà**	Taiwanese dialect [PH]

202 写(寫) **xiě** write

Radical of the simplified form is 冖 **mì** "cover" [BF]. Radical of the traditional form is 宀 **mián** "roof" [BF], which is referred to colloquially as 宝盖头(寶蓋頭) **bǎogàitóu** "top made up of a canopy." The whole character can serve as a phonetic, e.g., in 泻(瀉) **xiè** as in 泻肚(瀉肚) **xièdù** "have diarrhea."

写(寫)	**xiě**	write [V]
写字(寫字)	**xiězì**	write characters, write [VO]
写中国字(寫中國字)	**xiě Zhōngguo zì**	write Chinese characters, write Chinese

203 全(全) **quán** completely

Radical of the simplified form is 人 **rén** "person," which is called 人字头(人字頭) **rénzìtóu** "top made up of the character 人" when occurring at the top of a character. Radical of the traditional form is 入 **rù** "enter" [BF]. The other component of 全(全) is 王 **wáng** "king" (6). The whole character can serve as a phonetic, e.g., 痊(痊) **quán** as in 痊愈(痊愈) **quányù** "cure" and 诠(詮) **quán** as in 诠释(詮釋) **quánshì** "annotation." Most writers of traditional characters ignore the fact that the traditional radical should be 入 **rù** "enter" [BF] and write this character as if its radical were 人, that is, the same as the simplified form. Contrast 全(全) with 金 **jīn** (46) and 会(會) **huì** (199).

全(全)	**quán**	completely [A]

204 得 **děi** must
-de (verb suffix that indicates manner)

Radical is 彳 **chì** "short and slow step" [BF]. This radical is referred to colloquially as 双立人(雙立人) **shuānglìrén** "double standing person." Contrast 得 with 们(們) **men** (57) and 很 **hěn** (58). Note that 得 is a 多音字 **duōyīnzì** (cf. 6-2, note A1a).

得	**děi**	must [AV]
得	**-de**	(verb suffix that indicates manner, e.g., 说得很好(說得很好) **shuōde hěn hǎo** "speak very well") [P]

New Words in BSC 7-2 Written with Characters You Already Know

几 (幾)	**jǐ-**	a few, several [NU]
几百个 (幾百個)	**jǐbǎige**	several hundred
字	**zì**	character, word [N]
中国字 (中國字)	**Zhōngguo zì**	Chinese character [PH]
有的	**yǒude**	some [AT/PR]
有的...有的...	**yǒude...yǒude...**	some...others... [PT]

Reading Exercises (Simplified Characters)

Now practice reading the new characters and words for this lesson in context in sentences, conversations, and narratives. Be sure to refer to the Notes at the end of this lesson, and make use of the accompanying audio disc to hear and practice correct pronunciation, phrasing, and intonation.

A. SENTENCES

Read out loud each of the following sentences, which include all the new characters of this lesson. The first time you read a sentence, focus special attention on the characters and words that are new to you, reminding yourself of their pronunciation and meaning. The second time, aim to comprehend the overall meaning of the sentence.

一、那个美国人会说中国话，可是不会写中国字。
二、他中国话说得很好，不过中国字写得不太好，他还得学几年。
三、你写的中文全对，你的中文写得真好！
四、你说得对，我这儿真的有几百块钱，可是为什么全得给你呢？
五、我的朋友有的是男的，有的是女的。
六、有的中国人在美国住了几十年，中国字差不多全忘了。
七、有的人说中国话很难说，有的人说中国字很难写。你说呢？
八、中国字看起来很好看，不过写起来不太好写。
九、老王会写几百个字，小何会写几十个，我会写几个。你呢？你会写几个？
十、王大海说他得走了，好像他家里还有一点儿事。

B. CONVERSATIONS

Read out loud the following conversations, including the name or role of the person speaking. If possible, find a partner or partners and each of you play a role. Then switch roles, so you get practice reading all of the lines.

一、
北京人：您会说中国话！
美国人：会一点儿。
北京人：您说得很好。是在哪儿学的？
美国人：原来我在美国学过一点儿，现在在北京的一个学校学。
北京人：您会写中国字儿吗？
美国人：我会几百个中国字。有的会写，有的不会。
北京人：您还会说什么话？
美国人：我学过一点儿广东话，可是现在全忘了。

二、
李明山：大安，这个地方是不是你的学校？
何大安：对，这就是台北美国学校。
李明山：这里的学生都会中文吗？
何大安：有的会说，也会写；有的会说，不会写；还有的不会说也不会写。

C. CHARACTER DIFFERENTIATION DRILLS

Distinguish carefully the following similar-looking characters, pronouncing each one out loud and thinking of its meaning.

一、会 会 会 全 全 全
二、会 会 会 金 金 金
三、会 金 全 会 全 金 全 会
四、说 说 说 话 话 话
五、说 话 话 说 话 说 话
六、得 得 得 很 很 很
七、得 很 得 很 很 得 很
八、会 会 会 今 今 今
九、会 会 会 公 公 公
十、会 今 会 公 会 今 公 会

D. NARRATIVE

Read the following narrative, paying special attention to punctuation and overall structure. The first time you read the narrative, read it out loud; the second time, read silently and try to gradually increase your reading speed. Always think of the meaning of what you're reading.

住在我们家后面的林老太太可真喜欢说话！上个星期日七点钟我去看她，她说她儿子现在在一个学校学日文。她说她儿子是很好的儿子，也是很好的学生，日文差不多全会说了，日文的字也会写不少了。她还说她女儿也是好女儿，会说很多地方的话—台湾话、广东话、台山话、上海话都说得很好。差不多九点钟我说："林老太太，对不起，我还有事儿，得走了，"不过她不要我走，她说她还有很多的话还没说。九点半我说："林老太太，对不起，现在我真得走了，"不过林老太太还要说话！十点多钟她还要说话，我很不高兴，走了。在她家外面的大街上，她说请我下个星期日还来。有人说女人都很喜欢说话，我不知道这个话对不对，不过我知道林老太太这个人真的太喜欢说话了！

E. SUPPLEMENT: BOOK TITLES

Read out loud the following book titles.

一、《中国可以说不》
二、《中国还是能说不》
三、《中国不高兴》

Reading Exercises (Traditional Characters)

A. SENTENCES

Read out loud each of the following sentences, which include all the new characters of this lesson. The first time you read a sentence, focus special attention on the characters and words that are new to you, reminding yourself of their pronunciation and meaning. The second time, aim to comprehend the overall meaning of the sentence.

一、那個美國人會說中國話，可是不會寫中國字。

二、他中國話說得很好，不過中國字寫得不太好，他還得學幾年。

三、你寫的中文全對，你的中文寫得真好！

四、你說得對，我這兒真的有幾百塊錢，可是為什麼全得給你呢？

五、我的朋友有的是男的，有的是女的。

六、有的中國人在美國住了幾十年，中國字差不多全忘了。

七、有的人說中國話很難說，有的人說中國字很難寫。你說呢？

八、中國字看起來很好看，不過寫起來不太好寫。

九、老王會寫幾百個字，小何會寫幾十個，我會寫幾個。你呢？你會寫幾個？

十、王大海說他得走了，好像他家裏還有一點兒事。

B. CONVERSATIONS

Read out loud the following conversations, including the name or role of the person speaking. If possible, find a partner or partners and each of you play a role. Then switch roles, so you get practice reading all of the lines.

一、北京人：您會說中國話！

美國人：會一點兒。

北京人：您說得很好。是在哪兒學的？

美國人：原來我在美國學過一點兒，現在在北京的一個學校學。

北京人：您會寫中國字兒嗎？

美國人：我會幾百個中國字。有的會寫，有的不會。

北京人：您還會說什麼話？

美國人：我學過一點兒廣東話，可是現在全忘了。

二、李明山：大安，這個地方是不是你的學校？

何大安：對，這就是台北美國學校。

李明山：這裏的學生都會中文嗎？

何大安：有的會說，也會寫；有的會說，不會寫；還有的不會說也不會寫。

C. CHARACTER DIFFERENTIATION DRILLS

Distinguish carefully the following similar-looking characters, pronouncing each one out loud and thinking of its meaning.

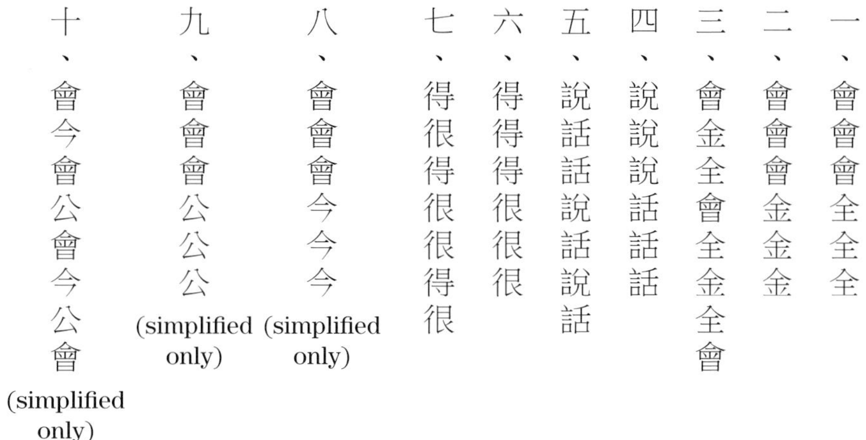

一、會會會全全全

二、會會會金金金

三、會金全會全金全會

四、說說說話話話

五、說話話說話說話

六、得得得很很很

七、得很得很很得很

八、會會會今今今 (simplified only)

九、會會會公公公 (simplified only)

十、會今會公會今公會 (simplified only)

D. NARRATIVE

Read the following narrative, paying special attention to punctuation and overall structure. The first time you read the narrative, read it out loud; the second time, read silently and try to gradually increase your reading speed. Always think of the meaning of what you're reading.

住在我們家後面的林老太太可真喜歡說話！上個星期日七點鐘我去看她，她說她兒子現在在一個學校學日文。她說她兒子是很好的兒子，也是很好的學生，日文差不多全會說了，日文的字也會寫不少了。她還說她女兒也是好女兒，會說很多地方的話——台灣話、廣東話、台山話、上海話都說得很好。差不多九點鐘我說：「林老太太，對不起，我還有事兒，得走了」，不過她不要我走，她說她還有很多的話還沒說。九點半我說：「林老太太，對不起，現在我真得走了」，不過林老太太還要說話！十點多鐘她還要說話，我很不高興，走了。在她家外面的大街上，她說請我下個星期日還來。有人說女人都很喜歡說話，我不知道這個話對不對，不過我知道林老太太這個人真的太喜歡說話了！

Hong Kong street sign

E. SUPPLEMENT: BOOK TITLES

Read out loud the following book titles.

一、《中國可以說不》
二、《中國還是能說不》
三、《中國不高興》

Notes

A6. 几十年 (幾十年) "several tens of years" or "several decades."

A9. 我会写几个。你呢？你会写几个？(我會寫幾個。你呢？你會寫幾個？) "I can write a few. How about you? How many can you write?" Be careful about how you interpret 几个 (幾個); does it mean "a few, several" or does it mean "how many?" In speech, intonation and stress help clarify the meaning; in writing, punctuation marks often help. Of course, you should always consider the grammatical structure and overall context.

B2. 有的……有的……还有的…… (有的……有的……還有的……) "Some...others... and still others...."

E1. This is your first example of《 》or 书名号 (書名號) **shūmínghào**. These brackets are used to indicate book and article titles, or sometimes the names of newspapers or journals.

E1-3. These three best-selling books are ultra nationalist volumes highly critical of the U.S. and Japan as well as certain aspects of modern Chinese society. The first two were published in 1996 while the third appeared in 2008. To be sure, huge numbers of books about America and other Western countries have been published in China in the last century and the great majority of them have been quite positive.

Chinese book cover (see section E above)

The Nosy Professor

PART 3

New Characters and Words

Study the six characters below and the common words written with them, paying careful attention to each character's pronunciation, meaning, and structure, as well as similar-looking characters. After you've studied a character, turn to the *Practice Essentials* volume and practice writing it on the practice sheet, making sure to follow the correct stroke order and direction as you pronounce it out loud and think of its meaning.

205 到 **dào** arrive, reach; to

Radical is 刀 **dāo** "knife," which is written 刂 when occurring at the right-hand side of a character and is referred to colloquially as 立刀 **lìdāo** "standing knife." In this character, the radical provides a hint as to the approximate pronunciation of the character. The other component is 至 **zhì** "arrive" [**BF**], which gives the meaning.

到	**dào**	arrive, reach [**V**]; to [**CV/PV**]
到...去	**dào...qù**	go to... [**PT**]
到...来 (到…來)	**dào...lái**	come to... [**PT**]
还不到 (還不到)	**hái bú dào**	have not yet reached (e.g., a certain age)

206 时 (時) **shí** time; when; hour, o'clock

Radical is 日 **rì** "sun" [**BF**], which here gives a hint as to the meaning "time." The colloquial name for this radical is 日字旁 **rìzìpáng** "side made up of the character 日." Phonetic of the traditional form is 寺 **sì** "temple" [**BF**]. The other component of the simplified form is 寸 **cùn** "inch."

时 (時)	**shí**	hour, o'clock (written Chinese) [**BF**]
三时半 (三時半)	**sān shí bàn**	three thirty (the equivalent of 三点半 (三點半) in spoken Chinese)

207 候 **hòu** wait

Radical is 人 **rén** "person." Phonetic is 侯 **hóu** "nobleman" [BF]. In this character, the phonetic includes the radical within it, which is rather unusual.

时候 (時候)	**shíhou**	time [N]
什么时候 (什麼時候)	**shénme shíhou**	what time? (pronounced **shémme shíhou**)
有的时候 (有的時候)	**yǒude shíhou**	sometimes [PH]

208 始 **shǐ** begin

Radical is 女 **nǚ** "woman" [BF]. This radical is referred to colloquially as 女字旁 **nǚzìpáng** "side made up of the character 女." Note that when 女 is written at the left of a character as a radical, its last stroke is shortened so that it doesn't collide with the component to its right. The other component in 始 is 台 **tái** (18).

开始 (開始)	**kāishǐ**	begin [V]; in the beginning [TW]

209 和 **hé** and, with; peace, harmony

Radical is 口 **kǒu** "mouth," here on the right, which is unusual. Phonetic is 禾 **hé** "growing grain" [BF]. Contrast 和 with 何 **Hé** (19) and 知 **zhī** (147).

和	**hé**	and [CJ]; with [CV]
和…一起	**hé...yìqǐ**	together with… [PT]

210 又 **yòu** again

This character is itself a radical. It is also a phonetic, e.g., in 友 **yǒu** as in 朋友 **péngyou** "friend." Originally 又 was a picture of a hand. When eating, the "hand" goes to the mouth "again" and "again." Contrast 又 with 文 **wén** (21), simplified 对 **duì** (108), and 友 **yǒu** (172).

又	**yòu**	again [A]

New Words in BSC 7-3 Written with Characters You Already Know

一起	**yìqǐ**	together [NU]
那么 (那麼)	**nàme**	like that, so [A] (pronounced **nèmme**)
一个人 (一個人)	**yíge rén**	by oneself, alone [PH]

Reading Exercises (Simplified Characters)

Now practice reading the new characters and words for this lesson in context in sentences, conversations, and narratives. Be sure to refer to the Notes at the end of this lesson, and make use of the accompanying audio disc to hear and practice correct pronunciation, phrasing, and intonation.

A. SENTENCES

Read out loud each of the following sentences, which include all the new characters of this lesson. The first time

you read a sentence, focus special attention on the characters and words that are new to you, reminding yourself of their pronunciation and meaning. The second time, aim to comprehend the overall meaning of the sentence.

一、我表哥谢文和的工作可真好！钱那么多，事儿又那么少！
二、老路星期一来找我，星期二又来找我，星期三又来找我……我开始有一点儿不喜欢他了。
三、因为她开始工作了，所以现在比较忙了。
四、我第一次到中国去是我高一那年，今年又要去了，真高兴！
五、我有的时候和我的女朋友一起吃饭，有的时候一个人吃饭。
六、公司星期一到星期五九点开门，五点半关门；星期六九点开门，十二点关门。
七、王太太还没来，我也不知道她什么时候来。
八、小金的男朋友没有钱又不好看，可是人好，所以小金那么喜欢他。
九、这个太好吃了，所以我吃了那么多。
十、王大海看起来很年轻，有一次有一个女同学问他，是不是还不到二十岁？

B. CONVERSATIONS

Read out loud the following conversations, including the name or role of the person speaking. If possible, find a partner or partners and each of you play a role. Then switch roles, so you get practice reading all of the lines.

一、
中国人：你什么时候到北京的？
美国人：我是今年二月到的。
中国人：你一个人来的吗？
美国人：不，和我太太一起来的。
中国人：你在哪儿学的中文？是不是在中国学过？
美国人：开始是在美国学的。我大学三年级那年又在台湾学了几个月。
中国人：你的中国话说得真好！
美国人：哪里，哪里。我的中文还很差呢。

二、
住在美国的中国人：你的中文说得这么好，什么时候开始学的？
美国人：我大一那年就开始了。
住在美国的中国人：去过中国吗？
美国人：去过十几次了，我上个月去了，下个月又要去了。

C. CHARACTER DIFFERENTIATION DRILLS

Distinguish carefully the following similar-looking characters, pronouncing each one out loud and thinking of its meaning.

一、又 又 又 文 文 文
二、又 又 又 友 友 友
三、又 友 又 文 又 友 又
四、又 又 又 对 对 对
五、又 又 又 欢 欢 欢
六、又 对 又 欢 又 对 又 欢

D. NARRATIVES

Read the following narratives, paying special attention to punctuation and overall structure. The first time you read a narrative, read it out loud; the second time, read silently and try to gradually increase your reading speed. Always think of the meaning of what you're reading.

一、在中国，七月中到八月三十一号，学生不上学。我在那个时候和我的高中同学去过很多地方。我们去过天津、西安、上海和南京，也去过山西、湖北、四川、广东、广西和海南。

二、李安国老先生是四川人，说的是一口四川话。他原来不住在台湾，他原来住在四川。他是一九四九年和家人一起到台湾去的，住在台北，到现在有六十多年了。开始，他不太喜欢台湾，可是现在喜欢了。有的时候有人问他是什么地方的人，他就说："我是四川人，不过我在台湾住了这么多年了，你也能说我现在是半个台湾人了！"

E. SUPPLEMENT: A CHINESE SONG

Below is a song about learning Chinese that has been sung at some Chinese language programs in the U.S. The song, which is titled 我学中文 (我學中文), is based on the Chinese children's song 两只老虎 (兩隻老虎) **Liǎngzhī Lǎohǔ** "Two Tigers," which in turn is sung to the tune of the well-known French nursery melody *Frère Jacques* (in English known as "Are you sleeping, Brother John?"). You've already learned all the words in this song except for these two: 快 **kuài** "be fast" and 奇怪 **qíguài** "be strange." Now read the song aloud. After you've read it aloud once or twice, try singing it!

我学中文，我学中文，学得快，学得快，
一天就会说话，两天就会写字，真奇怪，真奇怪！

Reading Exercises (Traditional Characters)

A. SENTENCES

Read out loud each of the following sentences, which include all the new characters of this lesson. The first time you read a sentence, focus special attention on the characters and words that are new to you, reminding yourself of their pronunciation and meaning. The second time, aim to comprehend the overall meaning of the sentence.

一、我表哥謝文和的工作可真好！錢那麼多，事兒又那麼少！

二、老路星期一來找我，星期二又來找我，星期三又來找我：……我開始有一點兒不喜歡他了。

三、因為她開始工作了，所以現在比較忙了！

四、我第一次到中國去是我高一那年，今年又要去了，真高興！

五、我有的時候和我的女朋友一起吃飯，有的時候一個人吃飯。

六、公司星期一到星期五九點開門，五點半關門；星期六九點開門，十二點關門。

七、王太太還沒來，我也不知道她什麼時候來。

八、小金的男朋友沒有錢又不好看，可是人好，所以小金那麼喜歡他。

九、這個太好吃了，所以我吃了那麼多。

十、王大海看起來很年輕，有一次有一個女同學問他，是不是還不到二十歲？

B. CONVERSATIONS

Read out loud the following conversations, including the name or role of the person speaking. If possible, find a partner or partners and each of you play a role. Then switch roles, so you get practice reading all of the lines.

一、中國人：你什麼時候到北京的？

美國人：我是今年二月到的。

中國人：你一個人來的嗎？

美國人：不，和我太太一起來的。

中國人：你在哪兒學的中文？是不是在中國學過？

美國人：開始是在美國學的。我大學三年級那年又在台灣學了幾個月。

中國人：你的中國話說得真好！

美國人：哪裏，哪裏。我的中文還很差呢。

二、住在美國的中國人：你的中文說得這麼好，什麼時候開始學的？

美國人：我大一那年就開始了。

住在美國的中國人：去過中國嗎？

美國人：去過十幾次了，我上個月去了，下個月又要去了。

C. CHARACTER DIFFERENTIATION DRILLS

Distinguish carefully the following similar-looking characters, pronouncing each one out loud and thinking of its meaning.

一、又又又文文文

二、又又又友友友

三、又友又文又友又

四、又又又對對對 (simplified only)

五、又又又歡歡歡 (simplified only)

六、又對又歡又對又歡 (simplified only)

D. NARRATIVES

Read the following narratives, paying special attention to punctuation and overall structure. The first time you read a narrative, read it out loud; the second time, read silently and try to gradually increase your reading speed. Always think of the meaning of what you're reading.

一、在中國，七月中到八月三十一號，學生不上學。我在那個時候和我的高中同學去過很多地方。我們去過天津、西安、上海和南京，也去過山西、湖北、四川、廣東、廣西和海南。

二、李安國老先生是四川人，說的是一口四川話。他原來不住在台灣，他原來住在四川。他是一九四九年和家人一起到台灣去的，住在台北，到現在有六十多年了。開始，他不太喜歡台灣，可是現在喜歡了。有的時候有人問他是什麼地方的人，他就說：「我是四川人，不過我在台灣住了這麼多年了，你也能說我現在是半個台灣人了！」

E. SUPPLEMENT: A CHINESE SONG

Below is a song about learning Chinese that has been sung at some Chinese language programs in the U.S. The song, which is titled 我学中文 (我學中文), is based on the Chinese children's song 两只老虎 (兩隻老虎) **Liǎngzhī Lǎohǔ** "Two Tigers," which in turn is sung to the tune of the well-known French nursery melody *Frère Jacques* (in English known as "Are you sleeping, Brother John?"). You've already learned all the words in this song except for these two: 快 **kuài** "be fast" and 奇怪 **qíguài** "be strange." Now read the song aloud. After you've read it aloud once or twice, try singing it!

我學中文，我學中文，學得快，學得快，
一天就會說話，兩天就會寫字，真奇怪，真奇怪！

Notes

A2. 我开始有一点儿不喜欢他了(我開始有一點兒不喜歡他了) "I began to not like him so much anymore" or "I began to somewhat dislike him." The pattern 有一点儿 (有一點兒) occurs before some verbs to indicate that something is "a little" something or "somewhat" something. The meaning is usually negative. This pattern will be taken up in greater detail in a future lesson.

A8. 小金的男朋友没有钱又不好看 (小金的男朋友沒有錢又不好看) "Little Jin's boyfriend has no money and he's also not good-looking" or "Little Jin's boyfriend neither has money nor is good-looking." Here 又, literally "again," is best translated "and also" or "and in addition."

D1. 七月中 "mid July."

D2. 说的是一口四川话 (說的是一口四川話) means literally "what he speaks is a mouthful of Sichuan speech." In more idiomatic English, we could translate this as "he speaks Sichuan dialect." 口, literally "mouthful," can serve as a measure for languages and dialects.

Conversation with a Waitress

请问，你是从
中国来的吗？
(請問，你是從
中國來的嗎？)
是。你去过中国吗？
(是。你去過中國嗎？)

New Characters and Words

Study the six characters below and the common words written with them, paying careful attention to each character's pronunciation, meaning, and structure, as well as similar-looking characters. After you've studied a character, turn to the *Practice Essentials* volume and practice writing it on the practice sheet, making sure to follow the correct stroke order and direction as you pronounce it out loud and think of its meaning.

211 从(從) **cóng** from; follow

Radical of the simplified form is 人 **rén** "person." Notice that the second stroke of the radical 人, on the left, is abbreviated and does not go all the way down, so as to leave room for the other 人, on the right. Radical of the traditional form is 彳 **chì** "short and slow step" [BF], which is referred to colloquially as 双立人(雙立人) **shuānglìrén** "double standing person." The simplified form -- which is actually the ancient form of the character -- is a compound ideograph showing two people "following" each other. Contrast simplified 从 with 人 **rén** (30) and 以 **yǐ** (146). Contrast traditional 從 with traditional 後 **hòu** (213).

从(從)	**cóng**	from [CV]
从…来(從…來)	**cóng...lái**	come from... [PT]

212 前 **qián** in front, front; before

Radical is 刀 **dāo** "knife," here in the form 刂. The character 前 is itself a phonetic, e.g., in 煎 **jiān** "pan-fry," 剪 **jiǎn** "cut with scissors," and **jiàn** 箭 "arrow."

前	**qián**	in front, front [L]
以前	**yǐqián**	before, formerly [MA]
…以前	**...yǐqián**	before... [PT]

前边（前邊）	**qiánbian**	in front; front [PW]
前面	**qiánmian**	in front; front [PW]
前头（前頭）	**qiántou**	in front; front [PW]
从前（從前）	**cóngqián**	in the past, formerly [A]
前天	**qiántiān**	day before yesterday [TW]
前年	**qiánnián**	year before last [TW]

213 后（後） hòu in back, back; after

Radical of the simplified form is 口 **kǒu** "mouth." This radical is referred to colloquially as 口字底 **kǒuzìdǐ** "bottom made up of the character 口." Radical of the traditional form is 彳 **chì** "short and slow step" [BF], which is referred to colloquially as 双立人（雙立人）**shuānglìrén** "double standing person." Contrast simplified 后 with 右 **yòu** (166), 可 **kě** (145), 司 **sī** (95), 同 **tóng** (80), 台 **tái** (18) and 叫 **jiào** (78). Contrast traditional 後 with traditional 從 **cóng** (211).

后（後）	**hòu**	in back, back [L]
以后（以後）	**yǐhòu**	in the future [TW]
…以后（…以後）	**...yǐhòu**	after... [PT]
后边（後邊）	**hòubian**	in back, back [PW]
后面（後面）	**hòumian**	in back, back [PW]
后头（後頭）	**hòutou**	in back, back [PW]
后来（後來）	**hòulái**	afterwards, later [A]
后天（後天）	**hòutiān**	day after tomorrow [TW]
后年（後年）	**hòunián**	year after next [TW]

214 之 zhī (particle in written-style Chinese, often equivalent to 的 in spoken-style Chinese)

Radical is 丶 **zhǔ** "dot" [BF]. 之 is a phonetic, e.g., 芝 **zhī** as in 芝麻 **zhīma** "sesame."

…之前	**...zhīqián**	before..., ...ago [PT]
…之后（…之後）	**...zhīhòu**	after..., in [PT]

215 听（聽） tīng listen, hear

Radical of the simplified form is 口 **kǒu** "mouth," which is referred to colloquially as 口字旁 **kǒuzìpáng** "side made up of the character 口." Radical of the traditional form is 耳 **ěr** "ear" [BF], which is a pictograph of the inside and outside of a human ear. The explanation of the simplified form is that one "listens" to what is said with the "mouth." The explanation of the traditional form is that one "listens" with the "ear."

听（聽）	**tīng**	listen, hear [V]
听说（聽說）	**tīngshuō**	hear of, hear it said that [V]
好听（好聽）	**hǎotīng**	be nice to listen to, pretty (of music, voices, sounds) [SV]

216 觉(覺) **jué** feel

Radical is 见(見) **jiàn** "see." Contrast 觉(覺) with 学(學) **xué** (153), 字 **zì** (84), and 兴(興) **xìng** (90).

觉得(覺得)	**juéde**	feel [V]

New Words in BSC 7-4 Written with Characters You Already Know

就	**jiù**	only [A]
就是	**jiù shi**	it's only that
差(差)	**chà**	be lacking, deficient [SV]

Reading Exercises (Simplified Characters)

Now practice reading the new characters and words for this lesson in context in sentences, conversations, and narratives. Be sure to refer to the Notes at the end of this lesson, and make use of the accompanying audio disc to hear and practice correct pronunciation, phrasing, and intonation.

A. SENTENCES

Read out loud each of the following sentences, which include all the new characters of this lesson. The first time you read a sentence, focus special attention on the characters and words that are new to you, reminding yourself of their pronunciation and meaning. The second time, aim to comprehend the overall meaning of the sentence.

一、前天我听说你的表姐要从广州来看你。
二、小林来这家公司之前，在哪里工作？
三、你听我说，从前，在中国有一个老人，住在山里头，他一百二十岁了，可是看起来好像六十几岁。
四、你听谁说我有两个哥哥？我就有一个哥哥！
五、我觉得这里的中国饭不好吃，以后我们不要来这家饭店了。
六、你是谁？你从什么地方来？你到什么地方去？
七、那个中国学生说他到了美国之后，去了很多地方，真的学了不少东西。
八、前边、后边都有人坐，没有位子了，我们走吧。
九、上大学以前，我没学过中文。我是上大学以后开始学中文的。
十、王大海，为什么你中国话说得那么好，可是中国字写得那么差呢？

B. CONVERSATIONS

Read out loud the following conversations, including the name or role of the person speaking. If possible, find a partner or partners and each of you play a role. Then switch roles, so you get practice reading all of the lines.

一、
美国人：请问，你是从中国来的吗？
中国人：是。你去过中国吗？你的中国话说得很好！
美国人：哪里。你家在中国什么地方？
中国人：西安。你听说过吗？

美国人：听说过。来美国之前，你在哪里工作？
中国人：来美国以前，我在一家工厂工作。

二、
美国学生　　　　　：请问，您是从北京来的吗？
住在美国的北京人：是的。有什么事儿？
美国学生　　　　　：您说的中国话真好听！
住在美国的北京人：谢谢你！你是美国人，你的中文说得也不差！

三、
美国学生：在美国学中文很难！
台湾学生：你们学校有没有从中国来的学生？
美国学生：有。
台湾学生：那OK了。

C. CHARACTER DIFFERENTIATION DRILLS

Distinguish carefully the following similar-looking characters, pronouncing each one out loud and thinking of its meaning.

一、觉 觉 觉 学 学 学
二、觉 觉 觉 兴 兴 兴
三、觉 学 觉 兴 觉 学 觉
四、从 从 从 后 后 后
五、从 后 从 从 后 后 从
六、从 从 从 以 以 以
七、从 以 以 以 从 从 从 以

D. NARRATIVES

Read the following narratives, paying special attention to punctuation and overall structure. The first time you read a narrative, read it out loud; the second time, read silently and try to gradually increase your reading speed. Always think of the meaning of what you're reading.

一、我来中国以前，不会说中国话，也不会写中国字。"一二三"、"你好"、"谢谢"我都不会。可是来了三年之后，中国话差不多都会说了，中国字写得也不差。我还有一个中国女朋友，北京人，人很好，她说的北京话可真好听。我觉得中国真好！

二、从前有一个姓王的，叫王大。因为王大很喜欢吃饭，所以很多人都叫他"吃饭大王"。后来王大老了，看起来好像一个钟那么大。他得在家里，不能工作，也不能到街上去看看，所以他的朋友也就很少了。

Reading Exercises (Traditional Characters)

A. SENTENCES

Read out loud each of the following sentences, which include all the new characters of this lesson. The first time you read a sentence, focus special attention on the characters and words that are new to you, reminding yourself of their pronunciation and meaning. The second time, aim to comprehend the overall meaning of the sentence.

一、前天我聽說你的表姐要從廣州來看你。

二、小林來這家公司之前，在哪裏工作？

三、你聽我說，從前，在中國有一個老人，住在山裏頭，他一百二十歲了，可是看起來好像六十幾歲。

四、你聽誰說我有兩個哥哥？我就有一個哥哥！

五、我覺得這裏的中國飯不好吃，以後我們不要來這家飯店了。

六、你是誰？你從什麼地方來？你到什麼地方去？

七、那個中國學生說他到了美國之後，去了很多地方，真的學了不少東西。

八、前邊、後邊都有人坐，沒有位子了，我們走吧。

九、上大學以前，我沒學過中文。我是上大學以後開始學中文的。

十、王大海，為什麼你中國話說得那麼好，可是中國字寫得那麼差呢？

B. CONVERSATIONS

Read out loud the following conversations, including the name or role of the person speaking. If possible, find a partner or partners and each of you play a role. Then switch roles, so you get practice reading all of the lines.

一、美國人：請問，你是從中國來的嗎？
中國人：是。你去過中國嗎？你的中國話說得很好。
美國人：哪裏。你家在中國什麼地方？
中國人：西安。你聽說過嗎？
美國人：聽說過。來美國之前，你在哪裏工作？
中國人：來美國以前，我在一家工廠工作。

二、美國學生：請問，您是從北京來的嗎？
住在美國的北京人：是的。有什麼事兒？
美國學生：您說的中國話真好聽！
住在美國的北京人：謝謝你！你是美國人，你的中文說得也不差！

三、美國學生：在美國學中文很難！
台灣學生：你們學校有沒有從中國來的學生？
美國學生：有。
台灣學生：那ＯＫ了。

C. CHARACTER DIFFERENTIATION DRILLS

Distinguish carefully the following similar-looking characters, pronouncing each one out loud and thinking of its meaning.

一、覺覺覺學學學

二、覺覺覺興興興

三、覺學覺興覺學覺

四、從從從後後後

五、從後從從後後從

六、從從從以以以 (simplified only)

七、從以以以從從從以 (simplified only)

D. NARRATIVES

Read the following narratives, paying special attention to punctuation and overall structure. The first time you read a narrative, read it out loud; the second time, read silently and try to gradually increase your reading speed. Always think of the meaning of what you're reading.

一、我來中國以前，不會說中國話，也不會寫中國字。「一二三」、「你好」、「謝謝」我都不會。可是來了三年之後，中國話差不多都會說了，中國字寫得也不差。我還有一個中國女朋友，北京人，人很好，她說的北京話可真好聽。我覺得中國真好！

二、從前有一個姓王的，叫王大。因為王大很喜歡吃飯，所以很多人都叫他「吃飯大王」。後來王大老了，看起來好像一個鐘那麼大。他得在家裏，不能工作，也不能到街上去看看，所以他的朋友也就很少了。

Notes

A3. 你听我说 (你聽我說) "Listen" (lit. "Listen to me speak").

A7. 学了不少东西 (學了不少東西) "learned lots of things."

B3. 那OK了。The Taiwanese student here means that, so long as there are some students from China at the American student's campus in the U.S. with whom the American student can practice Chinese, then there shouldn't be that much of a problem learning Chinese in America.

D2. 吃饭大王 (吃飯大王) "great king of eating." This involves word play, since the person's name is 王大, which is the exact reverse of 大王 "great king."

House number plate in Yangming Mountain area near Taipei

Going-out-of-business sale at Macau clothing store

UNIT 8

Getting Around Beijing (I)

COMMUNICATIVE OBJECTIVES

Once you've mastered this unit, you'll be able to use Chinese to read and write:

1. About how to get to a certain place.
2. About the four cardinal directions: "north," "south," "east," and "west."
3. Passages discussing if a certain place is near or far from where you are, or if a certain place is near or far from some other place, and how long it takes to get from one place to another.
4. Passages about taking taxis in China: calling a taxi company and giving appropriate instructions to the taxi company or driver such as from where to where, when, how many people, how many pieces of luggage, complaining if the taxi you requested has not yet arrived, discussing alternate routes if traffic should be congested, etc.
5. Several humorous stories.
6. About Beijing and Taipei's positions on the question of whether there is only one China.
7. A telephone message.
8. Name cards from mainland China, Hong Kong, and Taiwan.

PART 1

"How Do I Get to the Beijing Hotel?"

去北京饭店
怎么走？
(去北京飯店
怎麼走？)
往前走，过了
天安门就到了。
(往前走，過了
天安門就到了。)

New Characters and Words

Study the six characters below and the common words written with them, paying careful attention to each character's pronunciation, meaning, and structure, as well as similar-looking characters. After you've studied a character, turn to the *Practice Essentials* volume and practice writing it on the practice sheet, making sure to follow the correct stroke order and direction as you pronounce it out loud and think of its meaning.

217 怎 **zěn** how

Radical is 心 **xīn** "heart." This radical is referred to colloquially as 心字底 **xīnzìdǐ** "bottom made up of the character 心." Phonetic is 乍 **zhà** "suddenly." If something happens "suddenly," the "heart" might ask "how" it happened. Contrast 怎 with 作 **zuò** (184) and 所 **suǒ** (183).

怎么 (怎麼)	**zěnme**	how (pronounced **zěmme**) [QW]
去…怎么走 (去…怎麼走)	**qù...zěnme zǒu**	how do you get to… [PT]

218 往 **wǎng** go toward; to, toward

Radical is 彳 **chì** "short and slow step" [BF]. This radical is referred to colloquially as 双立人 (雙立人) **shuānglìrén** "double standing person." Phonetic is 王 **wáng** "king" (6). Contrast 往 with 住 **zhù** (138).

往	**wǎng/wàng**	to, toward [CV]
往东走 (往東走)	**wàng dōng zǒu**	go toward the east
往西开 (往西開)	**wàng xī kāi**	drive toward the west

219 离(離) **lí** leave; distant from, from

Radical of the simplified form is 禸 **róu** "rump." Radical of the traditional form is 隹 **zhuī** "short-tailed bird" [BF]. The phonetic is 离 **lí**, which can itself serve as a phonetic in other characters, e.g., 璃 **lí** as in 玻璃 **bōli** "glass" and 篱 **lí** as in 篱笆 **líba** "fence." The traditional form was formerly used to represent a bird, the Chinese oriole. It's said that when this bird was heard or seen in the spring, it was taken as a sign that unmarried daughters should "leave" their homes and find the house of their future husband. Eventually, another character was adopted for "oriole" and 離 was given its present meaning of "leave" or "be distant from."

离 (離)	**lí**	be distant from, from [CV]

220 远(遠) **yuǎn** far away

Radical is 辶 **chuò** "walk, go" [BF]. The colloquial name for this radical is 走之 **zǒu zhī** "the walking 之," because of its meaning "walk" and its resemblance to the particle 之. Phonetic of the simplified form is 元 **yuán**. Phonetic of the traditional form is 袁 **Yuán** [SN]. Contrast simplified 远 with simplified 过 **guò** (136) and simplified 边 **biān** (159). Contrast traditional 遠 with traditional 還 **hái** (180).

远 (遠)	**yuǎn**	be far away [SV]
离…很远 (離…很遠)	**lí...hěn yuǎn**	be far from... [PT]

221 近 **jìn** close, near

Radical is 辶 **chuò** "walk, go" [BF]. The colloquial name for this radical is 走之 **zǒu zhī** "the walking 之," because of its meaning "walk" and its resemblance to the particle 之. Phonetic is 斤 **jīn** "catty." Contrast 近 with simplified 这 **zhè/zhèi-** (96) and simplified 听 **tīng** (215).

近	**jìn**	be close, near [SV]
离…很近 (離…很近)	**lí...hěn jìn**	be close to... [PT]

222 概 **gài** approximate, general

Radical is the pictograph 木 **mù** "tree" [BF]. This radical is referred to colloquially as 木字旁 **mùzìpáng** "side made up of the character 木." Note that when 木 is written at the left of a character as a radical, its last stroke is shortened so that it doesn't collide with the component to its right. The rest of the character, which here serves as the phonetic, is 既 **jì** "since" [BF]. Note that there is an alternate form of the traditional character that is printed as 槪.

大概	**dàgài**	probably, about [A]

New Words in BSC 8-1 Written with Characters You Already Know

开 (開)	**kāi**	drive, operate a vehicle [V]
过 (過)	**guò**	pass, go by [V]
天安门 (天安門)	**Tiān'ānmén**	Tiananmen [PW]
北京饭店 (北京飯店)	**Běijīng Fàndiàn**	Beijing Hotel [PW]
走	**zǒu**	go, walk [V]
走路	**zǒulù**	walk [VO]

...的话 (…的話)	**...-de huà**	if... [PT]
左右	**zuǒyòu**	about, approximately [PW]
南	**nán**	south [L]
西	**xī**	west [L]
北	**běi**	north [L]
东方 (東方)	**dōngfāng**	east, the East [PW]
南方	**nánfāng**	south, the South [PW]
西方	**xīfāng**	west, the West [PW]
北方	**běifāng**	north, the North [PW]
东方人 (東方人)	**Dōngfāng rén**	Asian person [PH]
南方人	**nánfāng rén**	southerner [PH]
西方人	**Xīfāng rén**	Western person [PH]
北方人	**běifāng rén**	northerner [PH]
南方话 (南方話)	**nánfāng huà**	southern speech [PH]
北方话 (北方話)	**běifāng huà**	northern speech [PH]

"No parking"

Reading Exercises (Simplified Characters)

Now practice reading the new characters and words for this lesson in context in sentences, conversations, and narratives. Be sure to refer to the Notes at the end of this lesson, and make use of the accompanying audio disc to hear and practice correct pronunciation, phrasing, and intonation.

A. SENTENCES

Read out loud each of the following sentences, which include all the new characters of this lesson. The first time you read a sentence, focus special attention on the characters and words that are new to you, reminding yourself of their pronunciation and meaning. The second time, aim to comprehend the overall meaning of the sentence.

一、先生，请问，去天安门怎么走？离这儿还远吗？
二、你往前走差不多一刻钟，过了北京饭店就到了。
三、小李的家离我的家很近，可是老王的家离我的家很远。
四、我要是知道那么远的话，我大概就不走路来了！
五、北方人说北方话，南方人说南方话。
六、他是西方人，不过他有很多朋友是东方人。
七、大学离我的家不远，走半个钟头左右就可以到。
八、我的公司离我住的地方很近，走一刻钟就可以到。
九、我的生日是八月三号，今天是三月八号，所以离我的生日还很远。
十、王大海说他很不高兴，因为他的生日过了，朋友都没给他东西；我说他们大概太忙了，所以忘了。

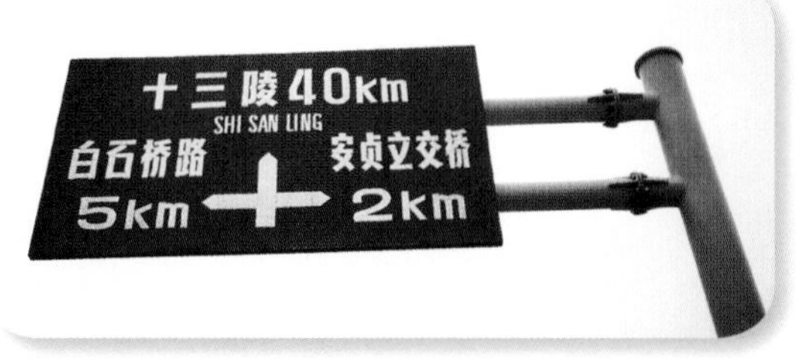

B. CONVERSATIONS

Read out loud the following conversations, including the name or role of the person speaking. If possible, find a partner or partners and each of you play a role. Then switch roles, so you get practice reading all of the lines.

一、
美国人：请问，去北京饭店怎么走？
北京人：北京饭店是吗？往前走，过了天安门就到了。
美国人：离这儿还远吗？
北京人：离这儿比较远。走路的话，大概要半个钟头左右吧。
美国人：好，谢谢您！

二、
东方人：你的中国话说得太好了！
西方人：哪里，哪里。我的中文不好，还差得很远……

三、(on the telephone)
小姐：先生，你好像是北方人吧？
先生：是的，我是北方人，你怎么知道的？
小姐：我听你说话就觉得你大概是北方人。
先生：可是我不是中国的北方人，我是美国的北方人！

"Driving after alcohol strictly prohibited"

C. CHARACTER DIFFERENTIATION DRILLS

Distinguish carefully the following similar-looking characters, pronouncing each one out loud and thinking of its meaning.

一、往 往 往 住 住 住
二、往 住 往 往 住 住 往
三、怎 怎 怎 作 作 作
四、怎 作 怎 怎 作 作 怎
五、近 近 近 听 听 听
六、近 听 近 听 听 近 听 近
七、远 远 远 近 近 近
八、远 远 远 边 边 边
九、远 远 远 过 过 过
十、远 远 远 这 这 这
十一、远 近 远 边 远 过 远 这 远 近

"Long live the great unity of the world's peoples"

"Long live the People's Republic of China"

D. NARRATIVES

Read the following narratives, paying special attention to punctuation and overall structure. The first time you read a narrative, read it out loud; the second time, read silently and try to gradually increase your reading speed. Always think of the meaning of what you're reading.

一、有一位老先生姓钱。他是北方人，可是说的是一口南方话。我前天问他天安门怎么走？他先说得往东走，后来又说不对，得往西走。我问他天安门离北京饭店远不远。他说天安门离北京饭店很近，可是又说北京饭店离天安门很远！钱老先生大概忘了天安门在哪儿了吧。

二、我家住在北京西长安街55号，离天安门、北京饭店都很近。我家的后面是南长街。从南长街往北走不远有一家饭店名字叫海南大饭店。我觉得那家饭店还可以，不太贵，他们的海南饭也很好吃。我很喜欢和我们公司的同事在那家饭店吃中饭。你的美国朋友谢小姐可以住在那里。要是谢小姐不要住那家，南长街还有很多其他的饭店可以去看看。

Reading Exercises (Traditional Characters)

A. SENTENCES

Read out loud each of the following sentences, which include all the new characters of this lesson. The first time you read a sentence, focus special attention on the characters and words that are new to you, reminding yourself of their pronunciation and meaning. The second time, aim to comprehend the overall meaning of the sentence.

一、先生，請問，去天安門怎麼走？離這兒還遠嗎？

二、你往前走差不多一刻鐘，過了北京飯店就到了。

三、小李的家離我的家很近，可是老王的家離我的家很遠。

四、我要是知道那麼遠的話，我大概就不走路來了！

五、北方人說北方話，南方人說南方話。

六、他是西方人，不過他有很多朋友是東方人。

七、大學離我的家不遠，走半個鐘頭左右就可以到。

八、我的公司離我住的地方很近，走一刻鐘就可以到。

九、我的生日是八月三號，今天是三月八號，所以離我的生日還很遠。

十、王大海說他很不高興，因為他的生日過了，朋友都沒給他東西；我說他們大概太忙了，所以忘了。

B. CONVERSATIONS

Read out loud the following conversations, including the name or role of the person speaking. If possible, find a partner or partners and each of you play a role. Then switch roles, so you get practice reading all of the lines.

一、

美國人：請問，去北京飯店怎麼走？

北京人：北京飯店是嗎？往前走，過了天安門就到了。

美國人：離這兒還遠嗎？

北京人：離這兒比較遠。走路的話，大概要半個鐘頭左右吧。

美國人：好，謝謝您！

二、

東方人：你的中國話說得太好了！

西方人：哪裏，哪裏。我的中文不好，還差得很遠……

三、

小姐：先生，你好像是北方人吧？

先生：是的，我是北方人，你怎麼知道的？

小姐：我聽你說話就覺得你大概是北方人。

先生：可是我不是中國的北方人，我是美國的北方人！

C. CHARACTER DIFFERENTIATION DRILLS

Distinguish carefully the following similar-looking characters, pronouncing each one out loud and thinking of its meaning.

一、往往往住住住

二、往住往往住住往

三、怎怎怎作作作

四、怎作怎怎作作怎

五、近近近聽聽聽 (simplified only)

六、近聽近聽聽近聽近 (simplified only)

七、遠遠遠近近近

八、遠遠遠邊邊邊

九、遠遠遠過過過

十、遠遠遠這這這

十一、遠近遠邊遠過遠這遠近

"Toilets to the north"

D. NARRATIVES

Read the following narrative, paying special attention to punctuation and overall structure. The first time you read the narrative, read it out loud; the second time, read silently and try to gradually increase your reading speed. Always think of the meaning of what you're reading.

一、有一位老先生姓錢。他是北方人，可是說的是一口南方話。我前天問他天安門怎麼走？他先說得往東走，後來又說不對，得往西走。我問他天安門離北京飯店遠不遠。他說天安門離北京飯店很近，可是又說北京飯店離天安門很遠！錢老先生大概忘了天安門在哪兒了吧。

二、我家住在北京西長安街55號，離天安門、北京飯店都很近。我家的後面是南長街。從南長街往北走不遠有一家飯店名字叫海南大飯店。我覺得那家飯店還可以，不太貴，他們的海南飯也很好吃。我很喜歡和我們公司的同事在那家飯店吃中飯。你的美國朋友謝小姐可以住在那裏。要是謝小姐不要住那家，南長街還有很多其他的飯店可以去看看。

Notes

D1a. 说的是一口南方话 (說的是一口南方話) means literally "what he speaks is a mouthful of southern speech." In more idiomatic English, we could translate this as "he speaks southern dialect" or just "he speaks southern" (cf. 7-3: D2).

D1b. Note that in the clause 他先说得往东走 (他先說得往東走), the character 得 is pronounced **děi** and means "must."

D2a. 从南长街往北走不远有一家饭店名字叫海南大饭店 (從南長街往北走不遠有一家飯店名字叫海南大飯店) "Going north from Nanchang Street, not far away there is a hotel named the Hainan Hotel."

D2b. 吃中饭 (吃中飯) "eat lunch." Be sure to distinguish 吃中饭 (吃中飯) from 吃中国饭 (吃中國飯) "eat Chinese food"!

Taipei street sign

Calling for a Taxi to the Airport

PART 2

我要车去首都机场。
(我要車去首都機場。)
您现在在哪儿？
(您現在在哪兒？)

New Characters and Words

Study the six characters below and the common words written with them, paying careful attention to each character's pronunciation, meaning, and structure, as well as similar-looking characters. After you've studied a character, turn to the *Practice Essentials* volume and practice writing it on the practice sheet, making sure to follow the correct stroke order and direction as you pronounce it out loud and think of its meaning.

223 汽 **qì** steam, vapor, gas

Radical is 水 **shuǐ** "water." Notice that this radical is written 氵 and is referred to colloquially as 三点水 (三點水) **sāndiǎn shuǐ** "three drops of water" when it occurs at the left-hand side of a character. Phonetic is 乞 **qǐ** "beg" [**BF**].

224 车(車) **chē** wheeled machine, vehicle

This character is itself a common radical. The traditional form of this character is a picture of a cart: two wheels (二) and a body (日) connected by an axle (一). It has here been turned upright to save space. Contrast 车(車) with 东(東) **dōng** (29), 年 **nián** (104), and 来(來) **lái** (135).

车(車)	**chē**	vehicle (car, taxi, bus, bicycle) [**N**]
车(車)	**Chē**	Che (also Cha or Tcha, a common Korean surname) [**SN**]
车子(車子)	**chēzi**	car, vehicle [**N**]
汽车(汽車)	**qìchē**	car, vehicle [**N**]
汽车公司(汽車公司)	**qìchē gōngsī**	car company, taxi company [**PH**]

225 首 **shǒu** head; chief, capital

This character is itself a radical. Contrast 首 with 道 **dào** (148).

首都	**shǒudū**	capital (city) [N] (note that 都 is a 多音字 **duōyīnzì**, cf. 6-2, note A1a; 都 is usually pronounced **dōu** and then means "all, both," but here it's pronounced **dū** and means "city")

226 机(機) **jī** opportunity; machine

Radical is the pictograph 木 **mù** "tree" [BF]. This radical is referred to colloquially as 木字旁 **mùzìpáng** "side made up of the character 木." Note that when 木 is written at the left of a character as a radical, its last stroke is shortened so that it doesn't collide with the component to its right. Phonetic is 几(幾) **jǐ** (97) "how many, few." The first machines were looms, constructed of wood. A "few" pieces of "wood" can be assembled to create a "machine." Contrast 机(機) with 几(幾) **jǐ** (97).

机会(機會)	**jīhui**	opportunity, chance [N]

227 场(場) **chǎng** place

Radical is 土 **tǔ** "earth." The colloquial name for this radical is 土字旁 **tǔzìpáng** "side made up of the character 土." Notice that the top horizontal line of 土 is shorter than the bottom line. Also notice that when used as a radical, the bottom line of 土 slants up toward the right, so as not to get in the way of the other component. Phonetic of 场(場) is the whole component on the right side, which is fairly common in various characters and here pronounced **chǎng** but elsewhere usually pronounced **shāng**. The traditional form 場 has an alternate form 塲 that is encountered occasionally.

机场(機場)	**jīchǎng**	airport [N]
首都机场(首都機場)	**Shǒudū Jīchǎng**	Capital Airport [PW]

228 等 **děng** wait

Radical is 竹 **zhú** "bamboo" [BF]. The colloquial name for this radical is 竹字头(竹字頭) **zhúzìtóu** "top made up of the character 竹." Notice that, when it is a radical, the third and sixth strokes of 竹 are shortened. The other component is 寺 **sì** "temple" [BF]. "Waiting" under the "bamboo" by the "temple." Contrast 等 with 第 **dì** (133).

等	**děng**	wait, wait for [V]

New Words in BSC 8-2 Written with Characters You Already Know

好的	**hǎode**	"all right," "O.K." [IE]
门口(門口)	**ménkǒu**	doorway, entrance [N]
姓名	**xìngmíng**	first and last name [N]
北外	**Běiwài**	(abbreviation for Beijing Foreign Studies University) [PW]
外国(外國)	**wàiguo**	foreign country [N]
外国人(外國人)	**wàiguo rén**	foreigner [PH]
外国话(外國話)	**wàiguo huà**	foreign language [PH]

Reading Exercises (Simplified Characters)

Now practice reading the new characters and words for this lesson in context in sentences, conversations, and narratives. Be sure to refer to the Notes at the end of this lesson, and make use of the accompanying audio disc to hear and practice correct pronunciation, phrasing, and intonation.

A. SENTENCES

Read out loud each of the following sentences, which include all the new characters of this lesson. The first time you read a sentence, focus special attention on the characters and words that are new to you, reminding yourself of their pronunciation and meaning. The second time, aim to comprehend the overall meaning of the sentence.

一、听说坐汽车去机场要一个钟头左右。
二、我们明天七点要坐老何的车子去首都机场。
三、要是有机会的话，我要到上海去看我的一个外国朋友。
四、一九二八年到一九四九年，中国的首都在南京，不在北京。
五、您是外国人，请您写您的中文姓名，还有您的外国姓名。
六、我觉得外国话都很难学，也很难听，你觉得呢？
七、她是中国人，在金门出生的，可是她的先生是外国人。
八、有的住在美国的中国人叫美国人"外国人"。
九、"首都汽车公司：八时开门，五时半关门"
十、王大海要我们半个钟头以后到北外门口等他。

B. CONVERSATIONS

Read out loud the following conversations, including the name or role of the person speaking. If possible, find a partner or partners and each of you play a role. Then switch roles, so you get practice reading all of the lines.

一、

汽车公司的人：您好！北京汽车公司。
外国人：你好。我要个车去首都机场。
汽车公司的人：您现在在哪儿？
外国人：在北京大学。
汽车公司的人：几个人？
外国人：就我一个人。
汽车公司的人：什么时候要车？
外国人：现在就要。
汽车公司的人：行。您贵姓？
外国人：我是美国人，我的中文姓名是司开来。
汽车公司的人：好的。您在北大门口儿等吧。

二、

车太太：女儿，你在你的大学有机会说中国话吗？
女儿：有，说中国话的机会很多。
车太太：那么，有没有机会学写中国字？
女儿：也有，不过学中国字的机会比较少。

C. CHARACTER DIFFERENTIATION DRILLS

Distinguish carefully the following similar-looking characters, pronouncing each one out loud and thinking of its meaning.

一、车 车 车 东 东 东
二、车 车 车 来 来 来
三、车 东 车 东 来 车 来 东 车
四、首 首 首 道 道 道
五、首 道 道 首 首 道 道 首
六、机 几 几 机 机 几 几 机
七、等 等 等 第 第 第
八、等 第 第 等 等 第 等 第

"Love and protect the lawn, please do not enter"

D. NARRATIVES

Read the following narratives, paying special attention to punctuation and overall structure. The first time you read a narrative, read it out loud; the second time, read silently and try to gradually increase your reading speed. Always think of the meaning of what you're reading.

一、我家离首都机场很近，从这儿坐半个钟头的车就可以到首都机场。我住在东山街四十五号，真的不难找，我的姓名写在大门上。

二、王先生从美国带来的车子真好看。现在在中国有美国汽车的人还不太多，所以王先生很高兴。王先生在首都机场工作，以前因为家离工作的地方太远，所以他一个星期就回家一次。现在有了汽车，他可以开车回家，开半个多钟头就可以到家了。

Reading Exercises (Traditional Characters)

A. SENTENCES

Read out loud each of the following sentences, which include all the new characters of this lesson. The first time you read a sentence, focus special attention on the characters and words that are new to you, reminding yourself of their pronunciation and meaning. The second time, aim to comprehend the overall meaning of the sentence.

一、聽說坐汽車去機場要一個鐘頭左右。

二、我們明天七點要坐老何的車子去首都機場。

三、要是有機會的話，我要到上海去看我的一個外國朋友。

四、一九二八年到一九四九年，中國的首都在南京，不在北京。

五、您是外國人，請您寫您的中文姓名，還有您的外國姓名。

六、我覺得外國話都很難學，也很難聽，你覺得呢？

七、她是中國人，在金門出生的，可是她的先生是外國人。

八、有的住在美國的中國人叫美國人「外國人」。

九、「首都汽車公司：八時開門，五時半關門」

十、王大海要我們半個鐘頭以後到北外門口等他。

B. CONVERSATIONS

Read out loud the following conversations, including the name or role of the person speaking. If possible, find a partner or partners and each of you play a role. Then switch roles, so you get practice reading all of the lines.

一、汽車公司的人：您好！北京汽車公司。
外國人：你好。我要個車去首都機場。
汽車公司的人：您現在在哪兒？
外國人：在北京大學。
汽車公司的人：幾個人？
外國人：就我一個人。
汽車公司的人：什麼時候要車？
外國人：現在就要。
汽車公司的人：行。您貴姓？
外國人：我是美國人，我的中文姓名是司開來。
汽車公司的人：好的。您在北大門口兒等吧。

二、車太太：女兒，你在你的大學有機會說中國話嗎？
女兒：有，說中國話的機會很多。
車太太：那麼，有沒有機會學寫中國字？
女兒：也有，不過學中國字的機會比較少。

C. CHARACTER DIFFERENTIATION DRILLS

Distinguish carefully the following similar-looking characters, pronouncing each one out loud and thinking of its meaning.

一、車車車東東東
二、車車車來來來
三、車東車東來車來東車
四、首首首道道道
五、首道道首首道道首
六、機幾幾機機幾幾機
七、等等等第第第
八、等第第等等第等第

Hong Kong street sign

D. NARRATIVES

Read the following narratives, paying special attention to punctuation and overall structure. The first time you read a narrative, read it out loud; the second time, read silently and try to gradually increase your reading speed. Always think of the meaning of what you're reading.

一、我家離首都機場很近，從這兒坐半個鐘頭的車就可以到首都機場。我住在東山街四十五號，真的不難找，我的姓名寫在大門上。

二、王先生從美國帶來的車子真好看。現在在中國有美國汽車的人還不太多，所以王先生很高興。王先生在首都機場工作，以前因為家離工作的地方太遠，所以他一個星期就回家一次。現在有了汽車，他可以開車回家，開半個多鐘頭就可以到家了。

Notes

A6a. 我觉得外国话都很难学，也很难听 (我覺得外國話都很難學，也很難聽) "I feel that foreign languages are all hard to learn, and also don't sound nice." The two 难 (難) in this sentence are rather different. The first one means "be difficult" while the second one means "be unpleasant". Compare 难吃 (難吃) "be unpleasant to eat, bad-tasting" and 难看 (難看) "be unpleasant to look at, ugly."

A6b. 你觉得呢？(你覺得呢？) "What do you think?" (lit. "And you feel...?").

A9. This line is from a sign and was composed in written-style Chinese. In spoken-style Chinese, this would be said as八点开门，五点半关门 (八點開門，五點半關門).

A10. 王大海要我们半个钟头以后到北外门口等他 (王大海要我們半個鐘頭以後到北外門口等他) "Wang Dahai wants us to go to the entrance to Beijing Foreign Studies University to wait for him in half an hour." Here, 半个钟头以后 (半個鐘頭以後) literally means "after half an hour," but when describing future events, we would usually translate 以后 (以後) into English as "in...."

B2. 说中国话的机会很多 (說中國話的機會很多) "There are many opportunities to speak Chinese" (lit. "Opportunities to speak Chinese are many").

D1. 我的姓名写在大门上 (我的姓名寫在大門上) "My name is written on the front door." Notice how the postverb construction 写在 (寫在) "write on" or (as in this sentence) "be written on" is used. Also, note that 大门 (大門) means "front door" (lit. "big door" or "main door").

D2a. 王先生从美国带来的车子真好看 (王先生從美國帶來的車子真好看) "The car that Mr. Wang brought from the U.S. looks really nice." Private individuals would not normally be allowed to import vehicles into China, unless they worked in foreign embassies or had special connections.

D2b. 他一个星期就回家一次 (他一個星期就回家一次) "He returns home only once a week" (lit. "He one week only returns home one time").

Calling for a Taxi to the Airport (cont.)

PART 3

我半个小时以前打电话要
过车，怎么到现在还没来？
（我半個小時以前打電話要
過車，怎麼到現在還沒來？）

New Characters and Words

Study the six characters below and the common words written with them, paying careful attention to each character's pronunciation, meaning, and structure, as well as similar-looking characters. After you've studied a character, turn to the *Practice Essentials* volume and practice writing it on the practice sheet, making sure to follow the correct stroke order and direction as you pronounce it out loud and think of its meaning.

229 打 **dǎ** hit, beat

Radical is 手 **shǒu** "hand," which at the left side of a character is written as 扌 and is referred to colloquially as 提手 **tíshǒu** "raised hand." The radical here gives a rough indication of the meaning, since one "hits" with one's "hand." The other component is 丁 **Dīng** [SN].

打	**dǎ**	hit, beat [V]
打的	**dǎdī**	take a taxi [VO] (note that the character 的 is a 多音字 **duōyīnzì**, cf. 6-2, note A1a; 的 is most commonly pronounced **-de**, but in the expression 打的 it's pronounced **dī**)

230 电（電） **diàn** electricity; lightning

Radical of the simplified form is 田 **tián** "field" [BF]. Radical of the traditional form is 雨 **yǔ** "rain," which often indicates meteorological phenomena. The colloquial name for this radical is 雨字头（雨字頭） **yǔzitóu** "top made up of the character 雨." Notice that, as a radical, 雨 is written wider but is squeezed together at the top, so as to leave room for the component below. Also, depending on the writer or font designer's preference, the "four drops of rain" in 雨 may be straight, slant downwards, or some slant upwards and others slant downwards. As always, follow your instructor or mentor's model or the models on the character practice sheets in *Basic Written Chinese Practice Essentials.*

电话（電話）	**diànhuà**	telephone [N]

打电话(打電話)	**dǎ diànhuà**	make a telephone call [PH]

231 班 **bān** class; shift

Radical is 玉 **yù** "jade," but notice that as a radical the last stroke (the dot) is dropped, so that the radical then looks like 王 **wáng** "king." For that reason, the colloquial name for this radical is 王字旁 **wángzìpáng** "side made up of the character 王." Notice also that when used as a radical, the bottom line of 王 slants up toward the right, so as not to get in the way of the other component. The phonetic in 班 is 玨 **jué** "two pieces of jade"[BF], which as a phonetic provides the pronunciation **bān**. This phonetic is also unusual in that the remaining component of the character in which it occurs is inserted into its middle, as is the case in 班 or in 斑 **bān** as in 斑点(斑點) **bāndiǎn** "spot."

班	**Bān**	Ban [SN]
班	**bān**	class [N]
班上	**bānshang**	in a class
中文班	**Zhōngwén bān**	Chinese class [PH]
上班	**shàngbān**	go to work, work [VO]
下班	**xiàbān**	get off from work [VO]

232 间(間) **jiān** between, during; space or time in between

Radical is 门(門) **mén** "door." This radical is referred to colloquially as 门字框(門字框) **ménzìkuàng** "frame of the character 门(門)." The other component is 日 **rì** "sun" [BF]. This character is a picture of the "sun" shining through the "space" between "doors." 间(間) can itself serve as a phonetic, e.g., in 简(簡) **jiǎn** as in 简单(簡單) **jiǎndān** "simple." Contrast 间(間) with 问(問) **wèn** (75), 开(開) **kāi** (122), 门(門) **mén** (123), and 关(關) **guān** (124).

时间(時間)	**shíjiān**	time [N]
上下班时间(上下班時間)	**shàngxiàbān shíjiān**	the time when one goes to or gets off from work [N]

233 交 **jiāo** hand over; intersect

Radical is 亠 **tóu** "head" [BF]. The other component is 父 **fù** "father" [BF]. 交 serves as a phonetic in several other characters, e.g., in 郊 **jiāo** as in 郊区(郊區) **jiāoqū** "suburbs," 饺 **jiǎo** as in 饺子(餃子) **jiǎozi** "dumplings," 较(較) **jiào** (144) as in 比较(比較) **bǐjiào** "comparatively," and 校 **xiào** (185) as in 学校(學校) **xuéxiào** "school." The earliest form of 交 was a pictograph showing a person with her or his legs crossed or "intersecting." Contrast 交 with 文 **wén** (21), 较(較) **jiào** (144), and 校 **xiào** (185).

234 通 **tōng** through, open; connect

Radical is 辶 **chuò** "walk, go" [BF]. The colloquial name for this radical is 走之 **zǒu zhī** "the walking 之," because of its meaning "walk" and its resemblance to the particle 之. Phonetic is 甬 **yǒng**, with the secondary phonetic being 用 **yòng**. Contrast 通 with traditional 過 **guò** (136).

交通	**jiāotōng**	traffic [N]
通知	**tōngzhī**	notify [V]
通县(通縣)	**Tōng Xiàn**	Tong County [PW] (located to the east of downtown Beijing; now known as 通州 **Tōngzhōu** District of Beijing)

New Words in BSC 8-3 Written with Characters You Already Know

司机 (司機)	**sījī**	driver, chauffeur [N]
小时 (小時)	**xiǎoshí**	hour [N]
要	**yào**	need to, have to [AV]; request [V]
怎么 (怎麼)	**zěnme**	how come, why (pronounced **zěmme**) [QW]
上	**shàng**	go to, come to [V]
去	**-qù**	(indicates motion away from the speaker, as in 带去 (帶去) "take along") [RE]
会 (會)	**huì**	be likely to, will [AV]
一会儿 (一會兒)	**yìhuǐr**	a while [N]; note that 会 (會) is a 多音字 **duōyīnzì**, cf. 6-2, note A1a; it's usually pronounced **huì**, as in the previous item in this list, but is here pronounced **huǐ**)

Reading Exercises (Simplified Characters)

Now practice reading the new characters and words for this lesson in context in sentences, conversations, and narratives. Be sure to refer to the Notes at the end of this lesson, and make use of the accompanying audio disc to hear and practice correct pronunciation, phrasing, and intonation.

A. SENTENCES

Read out loud each of the following sentences, which include all the new characters of this lesson. The first time you read a sentence, focus special attention on the characters and words that are new to you, reminding yourself of their pronunciation and meaning. The second time, aim to comprehend the overall meaning of the sentence.

一、要是你觉得走路太远的话，可以打个的，一会儿就到。
二、钱太太家里好像没有电话，我们怎么通知她呢？
三、我在这儿等了一个多小时了，李东山怎么还没来？
四、我一会儿就会给司机打电话，通知他我们今天六点下班。
五、他在电话公司上班，九点上班，五点下班，一天工作八小时。
六、现在是下班时间，交通大概会很不好吧？
七、她在交通大学的中文班上有八个同学：一半是男生，一半是女生。
八、原来的河北省通县现在叫“北京市通州”了。
九、台北市的交通比较差，上下班时间车子太多。
十、王大海说他半个小时以前要过车，怎么到现在还没来？

B. CONVERSATIONS

Read out loud the following conversations, including the name or role of the person speaking. If possible, find a partner or partners and each of you play a role. Then switch roles, so you get practice reading all of the lines.

一、
汽车公司的人：你好！北京汽车公司。
外国人　　　：我半个小时以前打电话要过车，怎么到现在还没来？
汽车公司的人：对不起，现在是上下班时间。

外国人　　　：还要等多长时间？
汽车公司的人：一会儿就会到。
外国人　　　：好吧。

二、
万国明：好像今年北京的交通比较好了。
班安太：不过上下班儿时间还是很差。
万国明：要是打的的话，从北京饭店到首都机场得要一个小时吗？
班安太：要是上下班儿的时候，大概要吧。

C. CHARACTER DIFFERENTIATION DRILLS

Distinguish carefully the following similar-looking characters, pronouncing each one out loud and thinking of its meaning.

一、间 间 间 问 问 问
二、间 间 间 门 门 门
三、间 问 门 间 门 问 间
四、间 间 间 开 开 开 (traditional only)
五、间 间 间 关 关 关 (traditional only)
六、间 问 开 间 关 间 门 问 间 (traditional only)

D. NARRATIVE

Read the following narrative, paying special attention to punctuation and overall structure. The first time you read the narrative, read it out loud; the second time, read silently and try to gradually increase your reading speed. Always think of the meaning of what you're reading.

班大明是司机，在上海大饭店上班。他六点上班，九点下班，一天得工作十五个小时，很忙。班先生的车子是美国车，车上还有电话，所以给饭店的汽车公司打电话不难。现在上海市打的的人很多。有的时候班先生在上海大饭店等人，有的时候他得到机场等人。上下班时间，上海的交通不太好。路上车子太多，人也太多，所以班先生很不喜欢在那个时候开车。

E. SUPPLEMENT: CHINESE NAME CARDS

Read out loud the information on the Chinese name cards below. Be prepared to answer questions from your instructor and/or classmates on the person's name, place of work, address, phone number, etc.

一、

李 一 山
大东海公司
中国北京市天津大街四十四号　电话：0086-21-62832817
FAX: 0086-21-62832818　E-mail: yishan@mail.com.cn

二、

香港中山学会　会长
张 大 安
香港湾仔港湾道三百五十六号　电话：二八三六一七七五

三、

司 文
校长

台南美国学校

709台湾台南市长和路八十八号
电话：(+886-06) 2223492
e-mail: s22022@ttas.edu.tw

Reading Exercises (Traditional Characters)

A. SENTENCES

Read out loud each of the following sentences, which include all the new characters of this lesson. The first time you read a sentence, focus special attention on the characters and words that are new to you, reminding yourself of their pronunciation and meaning. The second time, aim to comprehend the overall meaning of the sentence.

一、要是你覺得走路太遠的話，可以打個的，一會兒就到。

二、錢太太家裏好像沒有電話，我們怎麼通知她呢？

三、我在這兒等了一個多小時了，李東山怎麼還沒來？

四、我一會兒就會給司機打電話，通知他我們今天六點下班。

五、他在電話公司上班，九點上班，五點下班，一天工作八小時。

六、現在是下班時間，交通大概會很不好吧？

七、她在交通大學的中文班上有八個同學：一半是男生，一半是女生。

八、原來的河北省通縣現在叫「北京市通州」了。

九、台北市的交通比較差，上下班時間車子太多。

十、王大海說他半個小時以前要過車，怎麼到現在還沒來？

"Public telephone"

B. CONVERSATIONS

Read out loud the following conversations, including the name or role of the person speaking. If possible, find a partner or partners and each of you play a role. Then switch roles, so you get practice reading all of the lines.

一、汽車公司的人：您好！北京汽車公司。
外國人：我半個小時以前打電話要過車，怎麼到現在還沒來？
汽車公司的人：對不起，現在是上下班時間。
外國人：還要等多長時間？
汽車公司的人：一會兒就會到。
外國人：好吧。

二、萬國明：好像今年北京的交通比較好了。
班安太：不過上下班兒時間還是很差。
萬國明：要是打的的話，從北京飯店到首都機場得要一個小時嗎？
班安太：要是上下班兒的時候，大概要吧。

C. CHARACTER DIFFERENTIATION DRILLS

Distinguish carefully the following similar-looking characters, pronouncing each one out loud and thinking of its meaning.

一、間間間問問問
二、間間間門門門
三、間問門間門問間
四、間間間開開開
五、間間間關關關
六、間問開間關間門問間

Hong Kong taxi

D. NARRATIVE

Read the following narrative, paying special attention to punctuation and overall structure. The first time you read the narrative, read it out loud; the second time, read silently and try to gradually increase your reading speed. Always think of the meaning of what you're reading.

班大明是司機，在上海大飯店上班。他六點上班，九點下班，一天得工作十五個小時，很忙。班先生的車子是美國車，車上還有電話，所以給飯店的汽車公司打電話不難。現在上海市打的的人很多。有的時候班先生在上海大飯店等人，有的時候他得到機場等人。上下班時間，上海的交通不太好。路上車子太多，人也太多，所以班先生很不喜歡在那個時候開車。

"No visitors during working hours"

E. SUPPLEMENT: CHINESE NAME CARDS

Read out loud the information on the Chinese name cards below. Be prepared to answer questions from your instructor and/or classmates on the person's name, place of work, address, phone number, etc.

一、

大東海公司

李一山

中國北京市天津大街四十四號　電話：0086-21-62832817

FAX: 0086-21-62832818　E-mail: yishan@mail.com.cn

二、

香港中山學會　會長

張大安

香港灣仔港灣道三百五十六號　電話：二八三六一七七五

三、

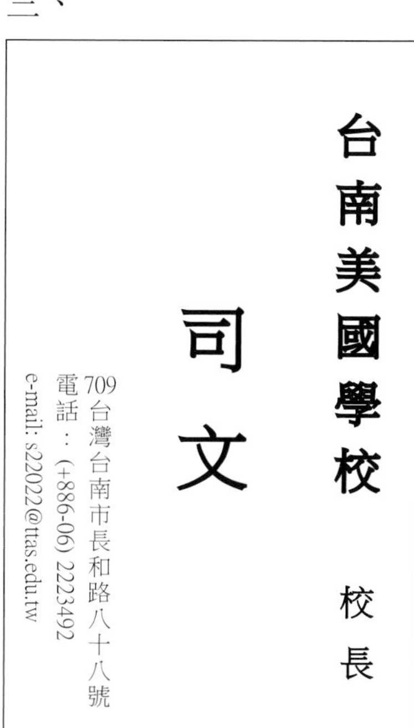

台南美國學校　校長
司文
709台灣台南市長和路八十八號
電話：(+886-06) 2223492
e-mail: s22022@ttas.edu.tw

Notes

A3. 我在这儿等了一个多小时了（我在這兒等了一個多小時了）"I've been waiting here for more than an hour." 小时（小時）can be said or written, but 钟头（鐘頭）is a spoken word that seldom occurs in standard written Chinese.

A5. One could say, or write, either 八小时（八小時）or 八个小时（八個小時）.

E1. Names and contact information on this and the next two name cards are fictitious, though based on real name cards. Some mainland Chinese name cards are printed in traditional characters. The format for name cards in mainland China and Taiwan may be either vertical or horizontal.

E2a. Remember that 中山 refers to Dr. Sun Yat-sen, the founder of the Republic of China (cf. BWC B-3: D2).

E2b. 学会（學會）means "academic society" or "institute."

E2c. 会长（會長）is a title that here means the head of a 学会（學會）. We might translate this as "President" or "Director."

E2d. 湾子（灣仔）, pronounced **Wānzǐ** in Mandarin, is one of the 18 districts of Hong Kong. (You haven't learned the character 仔 yet, but you should be able to guess the pronunciation from 子, which you have learned.)

E2e. 道 means "road" (cf. character presentation for 道 in BWC 5-1, no. 148).

Calling for a Taxi to the Airport (cont.)

New Characters and Words

Study the six characters below and the common words written with them, paying careful attention to each character's pronunciation, meaning, and structure, as well as similar-looking characters. After you've studied a character, turn to the *Practice Essentials* volume and practice writing it on the practice sheet, making sure to follow the correct stroke order and direction as you pronounce it out loud and think of its meaning.

235 件 **jiàn** (for pieces of luggage, matters, etc.)

Radical is 人 **rén** "person," which is written 亻 when occurring at the left side of a character so as not to get in the way of the component at the right. The colloquial name for this radical is 人字旁 **rénzìpáng** "side made up of the character 人." The other component is 牛 **niú** "ox."

件	**jiàn**	(for pieces of luggage, matters, etc.) **[M]**
一件事	**yíjiàn shì**	a matter, a thing (abstract)

236 行 **xíng** walk, go; all right, O.K.

This character, which is itself a radical, is a picture of two footsteps (彳 **chì** on the left and 亍 **chù** on the right). After taking two "steps," one has begun to "walk." 行 is the radical of several characters relating to motion, the phonetic being inserted in the middle, e.g., 街 **jiē** (42) and 衍 **yǎn** as in 敷衍 **fūyǎn** "go through the motion." Contrast 行 with 件 **jiàn** (235), 往 **wǎng** (218), 得 **děi** (204), 很 **hěn** (58), and 街 **jiē** (42).

行	**xíng**	be all right, be O.K. **[V]**
不行	**bù xíng**	it won't do; no
行不行？	**Xíng bu xíng?**	Is it O.K. or is it not O.K.?
行李	**xíngli**	luggage, baggage **[N]**
一件行李	**yíjiàn xíngli**	a piece of luggage

237 需 **xū** need

Radical is 雨 **yǔ** "rain," which often indicates meteorological phenomena. The colloquial name for this radical is 雨字头 (雨字頭) **yǔzìtóu** "top made up of the character 雨." Notice that, as a radical, 雨 is written wider but is squeezed together at the top, so as to leave room for the component below. Also, depending on the writer or font designer's preference, the "four drops of rain" in 雨 may be straight, slant downwards, or some slant upwards and others slant downwards. As always, follow your instructor or mentor's model or the models on the character practice sheets in *Basic Written Chinese Practice Essentials*. The other component in 需 is 而 **ér** "moreover." Contrast 需 with 要 **yào** (137) and 電 **diàn** (230).

需要	**xūyào**	need [V/AV]

238 只 **zhǐ** only

Radical is 口 **kǒu** "mouth." The other component is 八 **bā** "eight." As a mnemonic, you might wish to remember: "only" "eight" "mouths," not nine! Contrast 只 with 八 **bā** (9) and 口 **kǒu** (140).

只	**zhǐ**	only [A]
只好	**zhǐhǎo**	have no choice but, can only [A]

239 换(換) **huàn** change, exchange

Radical is 手 **shǒu** "hand," which at the left side of a character is written as 扌 and is referred to colloquially as 提手 **tíshǒu** "raised hand." Phonetic is 奂 (奐) **huàn**.

换 (換)	**huàn**	change, change to, exchange [V]
换车 (換車)	**huàn chē**	change (to other) buses, change trains
换工作 (換工作)	**huàn gōngzuò**	change jobs
换钱 (換錢)	**huàn qián**	change money
换人 (換人)	**huàn rén**	change (to other) people

240 条(條) **tiáo** long and narrow piece of something

Radical is 木 **mù** "wood" [BF]. The other component of the simplified form is 夂 **zhǐ** "go" [BF], while the other component of the traditional form is 攸 **yōu** "related to" [BF].

条 (條)	**tiáo**	(for streets, alleys) [M]
一条路 (一條路)	**yìtiáo lù**	a road
换一条别的路 (換一條別的路)	**huàn yìtiáo biéde lù**	change to another road
条子 (條子)	**tiáozi**	note (written on a strip of paper) [N]

New Words in BSC 8-4 Written with Characters You Already Know

轻 (輕)	**qīng**	be light (not heavy) [SV]
找	**zhǎo**	give in change [V]
找钱 (找錢)	**zhǎoqián**	give (sb.) change [VO]
别的 (別的)	**biéde**	other, another [AT]

开车 (開車)	**kāichē**	drive a car [VO]
半天	**bàntiān**	"half the day," a long time [NU + M]
从...到... (從…到…)	**cóng...dào...**	from...to... [PT]

Reading Exercises (Simplified Characters)

Now practice reading the new characters and words for this lesson in context in sentences, conversations, and narratives. Be sure to refer to the Notes at the end of this lesson, and make use of the accompanying audio disc to hear and practice correct pronunciation, phrasing, and intonation.

A. SENTENCES

Read out loud each of the following sentences, which include all the new characters of this lesson. The first time you read a sentence, focus special attention on the characters and words that are new to you, reminding yourself of their pronunciation and meaning. The second time, aim to comprehend the overall meaning of the sentence.

一、先生，对不起，您好像还没找钱给我呢！
二、这件行李怎么这么轻？是不是里头没有东西？
三、我开车开了半天了，我们换个人开，行不行？
四、李先生，我有一件事需要找您，您现在有没有时间？
五、你行李太多了！去外国好像一个人只能带两件行李。
六、你的男朋友给你的条子上写了什么？
七、这条路车子太多了，我们只好换一条别的路走了。
八、请问，从西安开车到成都需要多长时间？
九、要是需要换钱的话，是不是在机场就可以换？
十、这件事儿，要是王大海也不行，我们只好换人。

B. CONVERSATIONS

Read out loud the following conversations, including the name or role of the person speaking. If possible, find a partner or partners and each of you play a role. Then switch roles, so you get practice reading all of the lines.

一、
司机　：是您要车到首都机场吗？
外国人：对，是我。
司机　：就这两件行李吗？
外国人：对。从这儿到机场需要多少时间？
司机　：一个小时左右吧。这条路车子太多，我们只好换条别的路走了。
外国人：多少钱？
司机　：一百二十八块四。
外国人：给您一百五十块。您找我二十块就好了。
司机　：谢谢！
外国人：没事儿。

二、
外国人：司机先生，您看，路上车子这么多，我们是不是换条别的路走比较好？
司机　：您要换别的路也行，不过现在是下班儿时间，走别的路也差不多。

C. CHARACTER DIFFERENTIATION DRILLS

Distinguish carefully the following similar-looking characters, pronouncing each one out loud and thinking of its meaning.

一、只 只 只 口 口 口
二、只 只 只 八 八 八
三、只 口 只 八 只 口 八 口 只

D. NARRATIVES

Read the following narratives, paying special attention to punctuation and overall structure. The first time you read a narrative, read it out loud; the second time, read silently and try to gradually increase your reading speed. Always think of the meaning of what you're reading.

一、从我家到我的学校只有一条路比较好走，叫南京东路。别的路都有很多车，不过南京东路的交通还行。坐半个多小时的车就可以到，也不需要换车。

二、你说有几个中国？从1949年到现在，北京说："只有一个中国，没有两个中国。"从1949年到现在，台北也说："只有一个中国，没有两个中国。"

三、我是美国大三的学生。我很高兴，下个月就要去北京大学学中文了。我要去中国住一年，所以得带很多东西。不过，机场的人说去外国，一个人只能带两件行李，所以我只好少带东西。中国离美国很远；从我家到北京需要二十四个小时左右，时间太长了！有很多事我还不知道：怎么从机场到北京大学？在哪儿换钱？怎么打电话回家？可是，我去以前大概可以问我这边的中国同学吧。

E. SUPPLEMENT: A TELEPHONE MESSAGE

(see Traditional Characters section)

Reading Exercises (Traditional Characters)

A. SENTENCES

Read out loud each of the following sentences, which include all the new characters of this lesson. The first time you read a sentence, focus special attention on the characters and words that are new to you, reminding yourself of their pronunciation and meaning. The second time, aim to comprehend the overall meaning of the sentence.

一、先生，對不起，您好像還沒找錢給我呢！
二、這件行李怎麼這麼輕？是不是裏頭沒有東西？
三、我開車開了半天了，我們換個人開，行不行？
四、李先生，我有一件事需要找您，您現在有沒有時間？
五、你行李太多了！去外國好像一個人只能帶兩件行李。
六、你的男朋友給你的條子上寫了什麼？
七、這條路車子太多了，我們只好換一條別的路走了。
八、請問，從西安開車到成都需要多長時間？
九、要是需要換錢的話，是不是在機場就可以換？
十、這件事兒，要是王大海也不行，我們只好換人。

B. CONVERSATIONS

Read out loud the following conversations, including the name or role of the person speaking. If possible, find a partner or partners and each of you play a role. Then switch roles, so you get practice reading all of the lines.

一、司機：是您要車到首都機場嗎？
外國人：對，是我。
司機：就這兩件行李嗎？
外國人：對。從這兒到機場需要多少時間？
司機：一個小時左右吧。這條路車子太多，我們只好換條別的路走了。
外國人：多少錢？
司機：一百二十八塊四。
外國人：給您一百五十塊。您找我二十塊就好了。
司機：謝謝！
外國人：沒事兒。

二、外國人：司機先生，您看，路上車子這麼多，我們是不是換條別的路走比較好？
司機：您要換別的路也行，不過現在是下班兒時間，走別的路也差不多。

C. CHARACTER DIFFERENTIATION DRILLS

Distinguish carefully the following similar-looking characters, pronouncing each one out loud and thinking of its meaning.

一、只 只 只 口 口 口
二、只 只 只 八 八 八
三、只 口 只 八 只 口 八 口 只

D. NARRATIVES

Read the following narratives, paying special attention to punctuation and overall structure. The first time you read a narrative, read it out loud; the second time, read silently and try to gradually increase your reading speed. Always think of the meaning of what you're reading.

一、從我家到我的學校只有一條路比較好走，叫南京東路。別的路都有很多車，不過南京東路的交通還行。坐半個多小時的車就可以到，也不需要換車。

二、你說有幾個中國？從一九四九年到現在，北京說：「只有一個中國，沒有兩個中國。」

三、我是美國大三的學生。我很高興，下個月就要去北京大學學中文了。我去中國住一年，所以得帶很多東西。不過機場的人說去外國，一個人只能帶兩件行李，所以我只好少帶東西。中國離美國很遠；從我家到北京需要二十四個小時左右，時間太長了！有很多事我還不知道：怎麼從機場到北京大學？在哪兒換錢？怎麼打電話回家？可是，我去以前大概可以問我這邊的中國同學吧。

E. SUPPLEMENT: A TELEPHONE MESSAGE

Read out loud the following telephone message given to an American guest by a clerk at the front desk of the Taipei hotel at which she is staying. (There are a few unfamiliar characters in it, but you should be able to figure out most of the details.) Be prepared to answer questions from your instructor and/or classmates on the content of the note.

友星大飯店 Friends Hotel

留言條 MESSAGE

日期 Date 1/12 From 美國先生

房號 Room No. 818 To 司小姐

電話號碼 Phone No. 386-677-0943

☑來過電話 Called お電話がございました

☐來　訪 Visited in person おいでになりました

☑請回電話 Please call back お電話を下さい

留言 Message 時間 Time 10:56

家裡有事，請回電話.

CLERK 李

Notes

A10. 要是王大海也不行 "If Wang Dahai also won't do" or "If Wang Dahai also doesn't work out." There are two possible interpretations: the first is "several other people have already not worked out"; the second is "Wang Dahai has already not worked out when it came to several other matters, so if he again doesn't work out as regards this matter...."

B2a. 司机先生 (司機先生), literally "driver sir," is a very polite way to refer to a cab driver or chauffeur.

B2b. 我们是不是换条别的路走比较好？(我們是不是換條別的路走比較好？) "Might it be better if we took a different road?" (lit. "As for us, is it or is it not a situation where changing to a different road to go on would be relatively better?") 是不是 is often used in this manner to make polite suggestions.

B2c. 您要换别的路也行 (您要換別的路也行) "If you want to change to another road that also would work" or, in better English, "We could change to a different road."

B2d. 走别的路也差不多 (走別的路也差不多) "Going by way of another road would be about the same."

D1a. 只有一条路比较好走 (只有一條路比較好走) "there is only one road that is comparatively easy to take."

D1b. 坐半个多小时的车就可以到 (坐半個多小時的車就可以到) "(if you) take a bus for (a little) more than half an hour then (that soon) you can arrive (at my school)." The 就 here implies "as early as."

UNIT 9 Getting Around Beijing (II)

PART 1

Lost in Beijing

请问，和平饭店怎么走？
(請問，和平飯店怎麼走？)
对不起，我不是本地人，
我也不太清楚。
(對不起，我不是本地人，
我也不太清楚。)

New Characters and Words

Study the six characters below and the common words written with them, paying careful attention to each character's pronunciation, meaning, and structure, as well as similar-looking characters. After you've studied a character, turn to the *Practice Essentials* volume and practice writing it on the practice sheet, making sure to follow the correct stroke order and direction as you pronounce it out loud and think of its meaning.

241 平 **píng** even, balanced, flat; calm, peaceful

Radical is 干 **gān** "shield" [BF]. Notice how the components of 平 are "even," "balanced," and "at peace" with one another. Contrast 平 with 半 **bàn** (117) and 十 **shí** (11).

平	**Píng**	Ping [SN]
和平	**hépíng**	peace [N]
和平东路 (和平東路)	**Hépíng Dōng Lù**	Heping East Road [PW]

242 本 **běn** root; this

Radical is the pictograph 木 **mù** "tree" [BF]. The short line (一) across the bottom of 木 represents the ground level and focuses attention on the "root" of the tree, which is found below the ground.

本地	**běndì**	this place, here [N]
本地人	**běndì rén**	person from "this area," a local person [PH]
日本	**Rìběn**	Japan [PW]
日本人	**Rìběn rén**	Japanese person [PH]
日本话 (日本話)	**Rìběn huà**	Japanese language [PH]

243 直 **zhí** straight

Radical is 目 **mù** "eye" [BF]. Phonetic is 十 **shí** (11). This whole character can itself serve as a phonetic, e.g., in 值 **zhí** as in 价值 (價值) **jiàzhí** "value," 殖 **zhí** as in 繁殖 **fánzhí** "reproduce," 植 **zhí** as in 种植 (種植) **zhòngzhí** "grow," and 置 **zhì** as in 处置 (處置) **chǔzhì** "handle." In ancient China, before the advent of surveying tools, "ten" "eyes" (i.e., five people) would be called upon to ascertain whether a line was "straight." Contrast 直 with 真 **zhēn** (173).

一直	**yìzhí**	straight [A]

---

244 分 **fēn** divide; minute; cent, fen

Radical is 刀 **dāo** "knife." The other component is 八 **bā** (9), which is here spread out across the top of the character. A "knife" has here "divided" the character 八 into two separate parts. Contrast 分 with simplified 万 **wàn** (142) and 方 **fāng** (158).

分	**fēn**	minute; cent, fen (unit of currency) [M]
一分钟 (一分鐘)	**yìfēn zhōng**	one minute
一分钱 (一分錢)	**yìfēn qián**	one cent, one penny, one fen

---

245 清 **qīng** clear; Qing (Dynasty)

Radical is 水 **shuǐ** "water." Notice that this radical is written 氵 and is referred to colloquially as 三点水 (三點水) **sāndiǎn shuǐ** "three drops of water" when it occurs at the left-hand side of a character. Phonetic is 青 **qīng** "blue, green." Contrast 清 and 请 (請) **qǐng** (67).

---

246 楚 **chǔ** clear

Radical is the pictograph 木 **mù** "tree" [BF]. The whole character itself can serve as a phonetic in some characters, e.g., traditional 礎 **chǔ** as in 基础 (基礎) **jīchǔ** "foundation."

楚	**Chǔ**	Chu [SN]
清楚	**qīngchu**	be clear, be clear about [SV]

New Words in BSC 9-1 Written with Characters You Already Know

路口	**lùkǒu**	intersection [N]

Reading Exercises (Simplified Characters)

Now practice reading the new characters and words for this lesson in context in sentences, conversations, and narratives. Be sure to refer to the Notes at the end of this lesson, and make use of the accompanying audio disc to hear and practice correct pronunciation, phrasing, and intonation.

A. SENTENCES

Read out loud each of the following sentences, which include all the new characters of this lesson. The first time you read a sentence, focus special attention on the characters and words that are new to you, reminding yourself of their pronunciation and meaning. The second time, aim to comprehend the overall meaning of the sentence.

一、您往前走，一直走到前面那个路口，就到和平饭店了。
二、从1928年一直到1949年，北京不叫“北京”，叫“北平”。
三、小妹妹，你真有钱！你说，你那儿有几分钱？
四、（电话里）平小姐，我十分钟就到您那儿，您等我一下！
五、本地的日本饭真好吃，也不贵。
六、明明，你听我说，这个路口车很多，我们得先左右看一下。
七、对不起，我写得不太清楚，这是一个“平”字，不是“半”。
八、我问你，要是一个人一分钟能写三十个字的话，那么十分钟能写多少字？
九、日本的首都叫东京；听说东京人说的日本话真好听。
十、王大海需要换钱，可是他不太清楚到什么地方去换钱。

B. CONVERSATIONS

Read out loud the following conversations, including the name or role of the person speaking. If possible, find a partner or partners and each of you play a role. Then switch roles, so you get practice reading all of the lines.

一、
钱海文：请问，和平饭店离这儿有多远？
王金平：对不起，我不是本地人，我也不太清楚。
钱海文：请问，和平饭店离这儿有多远？
安中天：要走差不多十分钟吧。
钱海文：一直走就可以到吗？
安中天：不是，你得在下一个路口往东走。
钱海文：我知道了，谢谢！

二、
高老师：请问，机场在哪里？
林小明：对不起，我不是本地人，这个我不太清楚。您问那位先生吧。
高老师：先生，请问机场在哪里？
山口　：我不是中国人，我是日本人。您说机场？对不起，我也不清楚。
高老师：先生，请问，您知道不知道机场在哪里？
王京生：机场，是吗？机场在城外头，离这儿很远。不过，我也要去机场，我车上还有一个位子，你可以和我一起去。

C. CHARACTER DIFFERENTIATION DRILLS

Distinguish carefully the following similar-looking characters, pronouncing each one out loud and thinking of its meaning.

一、平 平 平 半 半 半
二、平 半 平 平 半 半 平
三、直 直 直 真 真 真
四、直 直 直 县 县 县
五、直 真 直 县 真 直 县 直
六、分 分 分 万 万 万
七、分 万 分 万 分 分 万

Taipei street sign

D. NARRATIVES

Read the following narratives, paying special attention to punctuation and overall structure. The first time you read a narrative, read it out loud; the second time, read silently and try to gradually increase your reading speed. Always think of the meaning of what you're reading.

一、前天有一个人问我和平饭店在哪里？我因为不是本地人，所以我说对不起，我也不清楚。今天又有两个人问我和平饭店在哪里。为什么这么多人要找这家饭店呢？

二、楚先生的儿子不是一个好学生，很多事他都不知道。他就知道一年有十二个月，一个月有三十天，别的事他都不太清楚。你问他这个月是几月？他说是一号了。你问他今天几号了？他说是星期一。你问他今年是哪年？他说他忘了。你问他为什么不知道？他说学校里的老师没说。

Reading Exercises (Traditional Characters)

A. SENTENCES

Read out loud each of the following sentences, which include all the new characters of this lesson. The first time you read a sentence, focus special attention on the characters and words that are new to you, reminding yourself of their pronunciation and meaning. The second time, aim to comprehend the overall meaning of the sentence.

一、您往前走，一直走到前面那個路口，就到和平飯店了。

二、從一九二八年一直到一九四九年，北京不叫「北京」，叫「北平」。

三、小妹妹，你真有錢！你說，你那兒有幾分錢？

四、（電話裏）平小姐，我十分鐘就到您那兒，您等我一下！

五、本地的日本飯真好吃，也不貴。

六、明明，你聽我說，這個路口車很多，我們得先左右看一下。

七、對不起，我寫得不太清楚，這是一個「平」字，不是「半」。

八、我問你，要是一個人一分鐘能寫三十個字的話，那麼十分鐘能寫多少字？

九、日本的首都叫東京；聽說東京人說的日本話真好聽。

十、王大海需要換錢，可是他不太清楚到什麼地方去換錢。

Taipei street sign

B. CONVERSATIONS

Read out loud the following conversations, including the name or role of the person speaking. If possible, find a partner or partners and each of you play a role. Then switch roles, so you get practice reading all of the lines.

一、錢海文：請問，和平飯店離這兒有多遠？

王金平：對不起，我不是本地人，我也不太清楚。

錢海文：請問，和平飯店離這兒有多遠？

安中天：要走差不多十分鐘吧。

錢海文：一直走就可以到嗎？

安中天：不是，你得在下一個路口往東走。

錢海文：我知道了，謝謝！

二、高老師：請問，機場在哪裏？

林小明：對不起，我不是本地人，這個我不太清楚。您問那位先生吧。

高老師：先生，請問機場在哪裏？

山口：我不是中國人，我是日本人。您說機場？對不起，我也不清楚。

高老師：先生，請問，您知道不知道機場在哪裏？

王京生：機場，是嗎？機場在城外頭，離這兒很遠。不過，我也要去機場，我車上還有一個位子，你可以和我一起去。

C. CHARACTER DIFFERENTIATION DRILLS

Distinguish carefully the following similar-looking characters, pronouncing each one out loud and thinking of its meaning.

一、平平平半半半

二、平半平平半半平

三、直直直真真真

四、直直直縣縣縣

五、直真直縣真直縣直

六、分分分萬萬萬

七、分萬分萬分分萬

"This lane not open—blind alley" (first character is missing a stroke)

"All types of vehicles prohibited from entering"

D. NARRATIVES

Read the following narratives, paying special attention to punctuation and overall structure. The first time you read a narrative, read it out loud; the second time, read silently and try to gradually increase your reading speed. Always think of the meaning of what you're reading.

一、前天有一個人問我和平飯店在哪裏？我因為不是本地人，所以我說對不起，我也不清楚。今天又有兩個人問我和平飯店在哪裏。為什麼這麼多人要找這家飯店呢？

二、楚先生的兒子不是一個好學生，很多事他都不知道。他就知道一年有十二個月，一個月有三十天，別的事他都不太清楚。你問他這個月是幾月？他說是一號了。你問他今天幾號了？他說是星期一。你問他今年是哪年？他說他忘了。你問他為什麼不知道？他說學校裏的老師沒說。

Beijing street sign

Notes

A2a. 从……一直到……(從……一直到……) is a common pattern that means "from...straight up to..." or "from...all the way until...."

A2b. In 1928, the government of the Republic of China moved the capital of China from Beijing to Nanjing. Since Beijing 北京 literally means "Northern Capital," it was decided to change the name Beijing to Beiping 北平, meaning "Northern Peace."

A10. 他不太清楚到什么地方去换钱（他不太清楚到什麼地方去換錢）"He wasn't very clear about where he should go to change money." Note that the stative verb 清楚 "be clear about..." can, as here, be followed by a clause.

B1. Observe what Qian Haiwen asks here: 和平饭店离这儿有多远？(和平飯店離這兒有多遠？) "How far away from here is the Peace Hotel?" Be sure you understand and can use the pattern:

A	离（離）	B	有	多遠？

"How far away from B is A?"

D1. Notice the question mark in the indirect question 前天有一个人问我和平饭店在哪里？(前天有一個人問我和平飯店在哪裏？) "The day before yesterday a person asked me where the Peace Hotel was." Chinese purists may argue that this is improper punctuation, but the fact is that writers of Chinese frequently use question marks for indirect questions like this.

Sign on building in Beijing housing development

By Bus and Street Car to the Summer Palace

PART 2

公車
对不起，请问，去动物园坐几路车？(對不起，請問，去動物園坐幾路車？)
您先坐323路公共汽车，然后换电车。(您先坐323路公共汽車，然後換電車。)

New Characters and Words

Study the six characters below and the common words written with them, paying careful attention to each character's pronunciation, meaning, and structure, as well as similar-looking characters. After you've studied a character, turn to the *Practice Essentials* volume and practice writing it on the practice sheet, making sure to follow the correct stroke order and direction as you pronounce it out loud and think of its meaning.

247 共 **gòng** altogether

Radical is 八 **bā** "eight." The whole character itself is a common phonetic, e.g., in 龚 (龔) **Gōng** (surname), 供 **gōng** as in 供给 (供給) **gōngjǐ** "provide," 恭 **gōng** as in 恭敬 **gōngjìng** "respectful," 烘 **hōng** as in 烘干 (烘乾) **hōnggān** "to dry," and 洪 **hóng** as in 洪水 **hóngshuǐ** "flood." 共 is a pictograph showing four hands working "all together." Contrast 共 with simplified 兴 **xìng** (90) and 半 **bàn** (117).

公共	**gōnggòng**	public [AT]
公共汽车 (公共汽車)	**gōnggòng qìchē**	public bus, bus [PH]
一共	**yígòng**	in all [A]

248 站 **zhàn** station, stop

Radical is 立 **lì** "to stand" [BF]. Phonetic is 占 **zhān** "to divine." We have seen this phonetic before in 点 (點) **diǎn** (115) and 店 **diàn** (162).

站	**zhàn**	station, stop [N/M]
车站 (車站)	**chēzhàn**	bus stop [N]
北京站	**Běijīng Zhàn**	Beijing Railway Station
北京西站	**Běijīng Xī Zhàn**	Beijing West Railway Station

249 然 **rán** thus

Radical is 火 **huǒ** "fire." Notice that this radical is written 灬 and is referred to colloquially as 四点火（四點火）**sìdiǎn huǒ** "four dots of fire" when it occurs at the bottom of a character. The whole character can serve as a phonetic, e.g., in 燃 **rán** as in 燃烧（燃燒）**ránshāo** "burn."

然后（然後）	**ránhòu**	afterward, then [MA]
先…然后…（先…然後…）	**xiān...ránhòu...**	first...then... [PT]

250 动（動） **dòng** move

Radical is 力 **lì** "power." Phonetic in the traditional form is 重 **zhòng** "heavy." If one applies enough "power" to "heavy" objects, they will "move."

251 物 **wù** thing, matter

Radical is 牛 **niú** "ox," which at the left side of a character is written as 牜 and is referred to colloquially as 牛字旁 **niúzìpáng** "side made up of the character 牛." Be careful not to confuse the radical 牜 with the radical 扌（提手 **tíshǒu** "raised hand"）. Phonetic is 勿 **wù** "don't" [BF].

动物（動物）	**dòngwù**	animal (lit. "moving thing") [N]

252 园（園） **yuán** garden, park, orchard

Radical is 囗 **wéi** "enclose" [BF]. This radical is referred to colloquially as 围字框（圍字框）**wéizìkuàng** "frame of the character 围（圍）." Phonetic of the simplified form is 元 **yuán**, while phonetic of the traditional form is 袁 **Yuán** [SN]. Contrast 园（園）and 远（遠）**yuǎn** (220).

动物园（動物園）	**dòngwùyuán**	zoo (lit. "animal garden") [PW]
动物园（動物園）	**Dòngwùyuán**	Zoo (name of a major bus and street car station near the Beijing Zoo) [PW]

New Words in BSC 9-2 Written with Characters You Already Know

电车（電車）	**diànchē**	street car, trolley, tram [N]
上车（上車）	**shàngchē**	get on a vehicle [VO]
路	**lù**	(for bus routes or lines) [M]

Reading Exercises (Simplified Characters)

Now practice reading the new characters and words for this lesson in context in sentences, conversations, and narratives. Be sure to refer to the Notes at the end of this lesson, and make use of the accompanying audio disc to hear and practice correct pronunciation, phrasing, and intonation.

A. SENTENCES

Read out loud each of the following sentences, which include all the new characters of this lesson. The first time you read a sentence, focus special attention on the characters and words that are new to you, reminding yourself of their pronunciation and meaning. The second time, aim to comprehend the overall meaning of the sentence.

一、65路公共汽车是从北京西站到动物园的。
二、我们先去北京大学看一位老师，然后去北京动物园看动物。
三、从北京西站到天安门坐什么车好？坐公车好？坐电车好？打的好？
四、广州动物园里头一共有多少动物，谁知道？
五、你要是太忙了，没时间从家里打电话，就等一会儿从公共电话打给我也行。
六、请问，去动物园要坐几站？
七、前面那个车站是公车站？是电车站？我是外国人，我不太清楚。
八、我的同屋下个月要先去香港，然后去台湾，一共要走差不多一个星期。
九、请问，去动物园是坐公共汽车比较好呢？是坐电车比较好呢？
十、王大海很喜欢和他的女朋友一起去动物园看动物，听说他们去年一共去了十几次。

B. CONVERSATIONS

Read out loud the following conversations, including the name or role of the person speaking. If possible, find a partner or partners and each of you play a role. Then switch roles, so you get practice reading all of the lines.

一、
外国人：对不起，请问，去长城大饭店坐几路车？
中国人：长城大饭店，是吗？您先坐二〇三路公共汽车，然后换一一六路电车。
外国人：那，我坐到哪儿换一一六路呢？
中国人：坐到电话公司换车。
外国人：谢谢！
中国人：没事儿。车来了，上车吧！

"Personnel not from this unit please do not enter"

二、
关明山：请问，去北京动物园要坐几路公共汽车？
边海清：我看看。去动物园……坐27路、601 路都行。
关明山：在哪儿上车？
边海清：前面就是车站。
关明山：那，在哪儿下车呢？
边海清：在动物园站下车。那站就叫“动物园”。
关明山：谢谢您！
边海清：不谢，不谢。

C. CHARACTER DIFFERENTIATION DRILLS

Distinguish carefully the following similar-looking characters, pronouncing each one out loud and thinking of its meaning.

一、园 园 园 远 远 远
二、园 远 园 园 远 远 园

Beijing bus stop

D. NARRATIVES

Read the following narratives, paying special attention to punctuation and overall structure. The first time you read a narrative, read it out loud; the second time, read silently and try to gradually increase your reading speed. Always think of the meaning of what you're reading.

一、我的男朋友很喜欢去动物园。他一个星期要去一、两次。他说他很喜欢动物，有时候他觉得人没有动物好呢。我问他为什么这么说，他说他也不太清楚。今天我原来要和他一起去饭店吃一点东西，可是他说十点钟又要带我去动物园了！

二、今天六点半，我的儿子小安就说他要去动物园。我说："我今天带你去动物园，可是我们得先去买一点儿东西，然后去动物园，好不好？"小安听了很不高兴，因为他不能等。我们只好不买东西，去动物园了。今天是星期天，很多车往动物园去，所以交通不太好。在公共汽车站等车的人也很多，上了公共汽车，也没有位子坐。不过小安很高兴！

E. SUPPLEMENT: BEIJING BUS ROUTES

Below are excerpts from a guide to Beijing bus routes. First read out loud the numbers of the various bus routes and their starting and ending points. Then be prepared to answer questions from your instructor and/or classmates on which bus route you should take to get to a certain place, or from where to where particular bus routes go.

7路	动物园 — 和平门
9路	金台路 — 前门
20路	北京南站 — 北京站
54路	北京南站 — 北京站
102路	动物园 — 北京南站
103路	动物园 — 北京站
106路	东直门外 — 北京南站
309路	广安门北站 — 二七厂
359路	东直门 — 首都机场
360路	动物园 — 香山

Hong Kong school bus stop

Taipei bus stop

Reading Exercises (Traditional Characters)

A. SENTENCES

Read out loud each of the following sentences, which include all the new characters of this lesson. The first time you read a sentence, focus special attention on the characters and words that are new to you, reminding yourself of their pronunciation and meaning. The second time, aim to comprehend the overall meaning of the sentence.

一、65路公共汽車是從北京西站到動物園的。

二、我們先去北京大學看一位老師，然後去北京動物園看動物。

三、從北京西站到天安門坐什麼車好？坐公車好？坐電車好？打的好？

四、廣州動物園裏頭一共有多少動物，誰知道？

五、你要是太忙了，沒時間從家裏打電話，就等一會兒從公共電話打給我也行。

六、請問，去動物園要坐幾站？

七、前面那個車站是公車站？是電車站？我是外國人，我不太清楚。

八、我的同屋下個月要先去香港，然後去台灣，一共要走差不多一個星期。

九、請問，去動物園是坐公共汽車比較好呢？是坐電車比較好呢？

十、王大海很喜歡和他的女朋友一起去動物園看動物，聽說他們去年一共去了十幾次。

B. CONVERSATIONS

Read out loud the following conversations, including the name or role of the person speaking. If possible, find a partner or partners and each of you play a role. Then switch roles, so you get practice reading all of the lines.

一、

外國人：對不起，請問，去長城大飯店坐幾路車？

中國人：長城大飯店，是嗎？您先坐二〇三路公共汽車，然後換一一六路電車。

外國人：那，我坐到哪兒換一一六路呢？

中國人：坐到電話公司換車。

外國人：謝謝！

中國人：沒事兒。車來了，上車吧！

二、

關明山：請問，去北京動物園要坐幾路公共汽車？

邊海清：我看看。去動物園……坐二七路、六〇一路都行。

關明山：在哪兒上車？

邊海清：前面就是車站。

關明山：那，在哪兒下車呢？

邊海清：在動物園站下車。那站就叫「動物園」。

關明山：謝謝您！

邊海清：不謝，不謝。

C. CHARACTER DIFFERENTIATION DRILLS

Distinguish carefully the following similar-looking characters, pronouncing each one out loud and thinking of its meaning.

一、園園園遠遠遠

二、園遠園園遠遠園

"Public toilet"

D. NARRATIVES

Read the following narratives, paying special attention to punctuation and overall structure. The first time you read a narrative, read it out loud; the second time, read silently and try to gradually increase your reading speed. Always think of the meaning of what you're reading.

一、我的男朋友很喜歡去動物園。他一個星期要去一、兩次。他說他很喜歡動物，有時候他覺得人沒有動物好呢。我問他為什麼這麼說，他說他也不太清楚。今天我原來要和他一起去飯店吃一點東西，可是他說十點鐘又要帶我去動物園了！

二、今天六點半，我的兒子小安就說他要去動物園。我說：「我今天帶你去動物園，可是我們得先去買一點兒東西，然後去動物園，好不好？」小安聽了很不高興，因為他不能等。我們只好不買東西，去動物園了。今天是星期天，很多車往動物園去，所以交通不太好。在公共汽車站等車的人也很多，上了公共汽車，也沒有位子坐。不過小安很高興！

"Fire prevention and safety committee"

E. SUPPLEMENT: BEIJING BUS ROUTES

Below are excerpts from a guide to Beijing bus routes. First read out loud the numbers of the various bus routes and their starting and ending points. Then be prepared to answer questions from your instructor and/or classmates on which bus route you should take to get to a certain place, or from where to where particular bus routes go.

360路	359路	309路	106路	103路	102路	54路	20路	9路	7路
動物園—香山	東直門—首都機場	廣安門北站—二七廠	東直門外—北京南站	動物園—北京站	動物園—北京南站	北京南站—北京站	北京南站—北京站	金台路—前門	動物園—和平門

"Beijing electrical appliance factory"

Notes

A1. 65路公共汽车是从北京西站到动物园的（65路公共汽車是從北京西站到動物園的）"Public bus number 65 is from Beijing West Railway Station to Zoo." The pattern 是……的 here emphasizes that "that's the way it is." Though the following wouldn't normally be said, the underlying structure of the previous sentence could be analyzed as this: 65路公共汽车是从北京西站到动物园的公共汽车（65路公共汽車是從北京西站到動物園的公共汽車）"Public bus number 65 is a public bus that from Beijing West Railway Station goes to Zoo."

A3. 公车（公車）"public bus, bus" is a common abbreviation of 公共汽车（公共汽車）.

B2. 不谢（不謝）"You're welcome" (lit. "Don't thank") is a common response to expressions of thanks. It is often said twice, as here.

D1. 有时候他觉得人没有动物好（有時候他覺得人沒有動物好）"Sometimes he feels people aren't as good as animals." The pattern A 没有 B C means "A is/are not as C as B." The "kernel" of this sentence is: 人没有动物好 "People aren't as good as animals" (lit. "People don't have animals good"). You'll learn more about this pattern in BSC 10-4.

D2. 今天六点半，我的儿子小安就说他要去动物园（今天六點半，我的兒子小安就說他要去動物園）"Today at 6:30, my son, Little An, already said he wanted to go to the zoo." This 就 means "as early as" a given time.

PART 3

By Bus and Street Car to the Summer Palace (cont.)

一张到动物园儿的。
(一張到動物園兒的。)
有买票的吗？
没票的买票！
(有買票的嗎？
沒票的買票！)

New Characters and Words

Study the six characters below and the common words written with them, paying careful attention to each character's pronunciation, meaning, and structure, as well as similar-looking characters. After you've studied a character, turn to the *Practice Essentials* volume and practice writing it on the practice sheet, making sure to follow the correct stroke order and direction as you pronounce it out loud and think of its meaning.

253 买(買) **mǎi** buy

Radical of the simplified form is 大 **dà** (13), while radical of the traditional form is 貝 **bèi** "cowrie shell" [**BF**]. Shells were used as money in earlier times to "buy" things with. Contrast the simplified form 买 with simplified 头 **tóu** (120) and simplified 兴 **xìng** (90). Contrast traditional 買 and traditional 貴 **guì** (85).

买(買)	**mǎi**	buy [**V**]

---

254 卖(賣) **mài** sell

Radical of the simplified form is 十 (11), while radical of the traditional form is 貝 **bèi** "cowrie shell" [**BF**]. Shells were used as money in earlier times to "sell" things with. Note that 卖(賣) is the same as 买(買) **mǎi** "buy" (253) except that for the simplified form there is a 十 on top and for the traditional form there is a 士 **shì** "scholar" [**BF**] on top. Be sure to distinguish 买(買) and 卖(賣) carefully in speech and in writing!

卖(賣)	**mài**	sell [**V**]
买卖(買賣)	**mǎimài**	buying and selling, business [**N**]

255 票 **piào** ticket

Radical is 示 **shì** "show" [BF]. The whole character is a common phonetic, e.g., in 漂 **piào** as in 漂亮 **piàoliang** "pretty," 飘 (飄) **piāo** as in 飘游 (飄游) **piāoyóu** "float gently," and 标 (標) **biāo** as in 目标 (目標) **mùbiāo** "goal." Contrast 票 and 要 **yào** (137).

票	**piào**	ticket [N]

---

256 张(張) **zhāng** (for flat objects like tables, name cards)

Radical is 弓 **gōng** "bow." Phonetic is 长 (長) **zhǎng** "grow." Contrast 张 (張) and 长 (長) **cháng/zhǎng** (175).

张 (張)	**Zhāng**	Zhang, Chang (also Jhang or Gang, a common Korean surname) [SN]
张 (張)	**zhāng**	(for flat objects like tables, name cards) [M]
一张票 (一張票)	**yìzhāng piào**	a ticket
这张名片 (這張名片)	**zhèizhāng míngpiàn**	this business card

---

257 刚(剛) **gāng** just now

Radical is 刀 **dāo** "knife," which is written 刂 when occurring at the right-hand side of a character. The phonetic is 冈 (岡) **gāng**.

刚 (剛)	**gāng**	just now, just [A]
刚刚 (剛剛)	**gānggāng**	just now, just [A]

---

258 毛 **máo** hair, fur; ten cents

This character, which can serve both as radical and (rarely) as phonetic, is a pictograph of hairs on a person's head. Contrast 毛 with 七 **qī** (8) and 也 **yě** (52).

毛	**Máo**	Mao [SN]
毛	**máo**	ten cents, dime [M]
一毛钱 (一毛錢)	**yìmáo qián**	ten cents, a dime

New Words in BSC 9-3 Written with Characters You Already Know

没 (沒)	**méi**	not to have [V]
叫	**jiào**	call (someone) [V]
上	**shàng**	get on (a vehicle, etc.) [V]

Reading Exercises (Simplified Characters)

Now practice reading the new characters and words for this lesson in context in sentences, conversations, and narratives. Be sure to refer to the Notes at the end of this lesson, and make use of the accompanying audio disc to hear and practice correct pronunciation, phrasing, and intonation.

A. SENTENCES

Read out loud each of the following sentences, which include all the new characters of this lesson. The first time you read a sentence, focus special attention on the characters and words that are new to you, reminding yourself of their pronunciation and meaning. The second time, aim to comprehend the overall meaning of the sentence.

一、以前北京的公车票一张只要五毛钱，可是现在好像要一块了。
二、美国人说“十五分钱”，中国人说“一毛五分钱”。
三、我刚刚给你一张我的名片，你还说我没给你！
四、王小姐，我没叫您，我叫的是文小姐。她今天在不在？
五、听说买票得到公共汽车公司去买了，不能在公车上买了，是真的吗？
六、我刚从机场来，为什么现在又要去机场呢？
七、张南生，毛老师刚叫了你的名字，你怎么还不去？
八、我没钱买公共汽车票，一毛都没有，只好走路。
九、我刚买了两张车票，来，给你一张，我们一起坐车。
十、大海刚卖了他的汽车，他说以后要坐公车、电车。

B. CONVERSATIONS

Read out loud the following conversations, including the name or role of the person speaking. If possible, find a partner or partners and each of you play a role. Then switch roles, so you get practice reading all of the lines.

一、
公车小姐：有买票的吗？没票的买票！
外国人　：一张到动物园儿的。
公车小姐：您是在哪儿上的？
外国人　：刚上的。
公车小姐：一块。
外国人　：给您钱。

二、
毛太太：老张！这几天买卖还行吧？
老张　：不是很好，不过还可以。
毛太太：我买一张公车票。
老张　：好，五毛钱。
毛太太：谢谢你！
老张　：没事儿。

三、
毛子文：这张CD是谁的？
张东山：是我的，我刚买的。
毛子文：我能听听吗？
张东山：可以，可以。

Hong Kong gas station

C. CHARACTER DIFFERENTIATION DRILLS

Distinguish carefully the following similar-looking characters, pronouncing each one out loud and thinking of its meaning.

一、张 张 张 长 长 长

二、张 长 张 长 张 张 长
三、买 买 买 卖 卖 卖
四、卖 卖 卖 贵 贵 贵
五、买 卖 贵 买 贵 卖 买 卖
六、毛 毛 毛 也 也 也
七、毛 毛 毛 七 七 七
八、毛 也 毛 七 也 毛 也 七
九、头 买 兴 卖 买 头 兴 卖

D. NARRATIVES

Read the following narratives, paying special attention to punctuation and overall structure. The first time you read a narrative, read it out loud; the second time, read silently and try to gradually increase your reading speed. Always think of the meaning of what you're reading.

一、我表姐小平下个月从香港来美国，她要我给她买一张从我家到Chicago的票。我买了以后，她说我买的时间不好，所以我只好去换票。我买了第二张票以后，她还是不高兴，说我买的票太贵。我以后不给她买票了。

二、我们都叫老毛"五毛"。他去哪儿都只带五毛钱。老毛以前说是因为没钱，可是他现在是买卖人，很有钱了。不知道为什么，老毛还是只带五毛钱！

E. SUPPLEMENT: A CHINESE CHARACTER RIDDLE

Read the following riddle out loud and answer orally if you can. 它 is the character for the pronoun **tā** "it." See the end of the Notes section for the correct answer.

"人"有它是大，"天"没它也是大。请问，这是什么字？

Reading Exercises (Traditional Characters)

A. SENTENCES

Read out loud each of the following sentences, which include all the new characters of this lesson. The first time you read a sentence, focus special attention on the characters and words that are new to you, reminding yourself of their pronunciation and meaning. The second time, aim to comprehend the overall meaning of the sentence.

一、以前北京的公車票一張只要五毛錢，可是現在好像要一塊了。

二、美國人說「十五分錢」，中國人說「一毛五分錢」。

三、我剛剛給你一張我的名片，你還說我沒給你！

四、王小姐，我沒叫您，我叫的是文小姐。她今天在不在？

五、聽說買票得到公共汽車公司去買了，不能在公車上買了，是真的嗎？

六、我剛從機場來，為什麼現在又要去機場呢？

七、張南生，毛老師剛叫了你的名字，你怎麼還不去？

八、我沒錢買公共汽車票，一毛都沒有，只好走路。

九、我剛買了兩張車票，來，給你一張，我們一起坐車。

十、大海剛賣了他的汽車，他說以後要坐公車、電車。

B. CONVERSATIONS

Read out loud the following conversations, including the name or role of the person speaking. If possible, find a partner or partners and each of you play a role. Then switch roles, so you get practice reading all of the lines.

一、公車小姐：有買票的嗎？沒票的買票！
外國人：一張到動物園兒的。
公車小姐：您是在哪兒上的？
外國人：剛上的。
公車小姐：一塊。
外國人：給您錢。

二、毛太太：老張！這幾天買賣還行吧？
老張：不是很好，不過還可以。
毛太太：我買一張公車票。
老張：好，五毛錢。
毛太太：謝謝你！
老張：沒事兒。

三、毛子文：這張CD是誰的？
張東山：是我的，我剛買的。
毛子文：我能聽聽嗎？
張東山：可以，可以。

C. CHARACTER DIFFERENTIATION DRILLS

Distinguish carefully the following similar-looking characters, pronouncing each one out loud and thinking of its meaning.

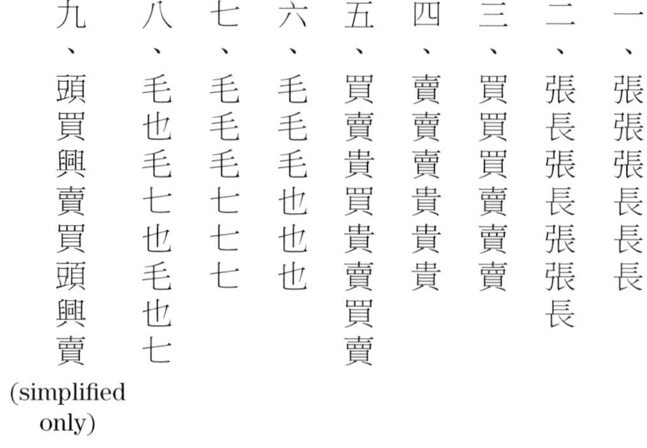

一、張張張長長長
二、張長張長張張長
三、買買買賣賣賣
四、賣賣賣貴貴貴
五、買賣貴買貴賣買賣
六、毛毛毛也也也
七、毛毛毛七七七
八、毛也毛七也毛也七
九、頭買興賣買頭興賣 (simplified only)

D. NARRATIVES

Read the following narratives, paying special attention to punctuation and overall structure. The first time you read a narrative, read it out loud; the second time, read silently and try to gradually increase your reading speed. Always think of the meaning of what you're reading.

一、我表姐小平下個月從香港來美國，她要我給她買一張從我家到Chicago的票。我買了以後，她說我買的時間不好，所以我只好去換票。我買了第二張票以後，她還是不高興，說我買的票太貴。我以後不給她買票了。

二、我們都叫老毛「五毛」。他去哪兒都只帶五毛錢。老毛以前說是因為沒錢，可是他現在是買賣人，很有錢了。不知道為什麼，老毛還是只帶五毛錢！

E. SUPPLEMENT: A CHINESE CHARACTER RIDDLE

Read the following riddle out loud and answer orally if you can. 它 is the character for the pronoun **tā** "it". See the end of the Notes section for the correct answer.

「人」有它是大，
「天」沒它也是大。
請問，這是什麼字？

Hong Kong MTR station

Notes

A1. **WRITTEN-STYLE TERMS FOR DIFFERENT DENOMINATIONS OF MONEY.** In BWC 4-2: A1, we discussed some differences between spoken-style and written-style Chinese. In sentence A1 in the present lesson, 毛 is the character for the spoken-style word for "ten cents" or "dime." You needn't memorize this yet but you should be aware that in written-style Chinese, a different word is used for "ten cents," namely, 角 **jiǎo**. There is also a different word in written-style Chinese for spoken-style 块 (塊) **kuài** "dollar," namely, 元 **yuán**. As you can imagine, the character 元 is extremely common on advertisements and signs (you've come across 元 before as a phonetic in the simplified characters 园 **yuán** and 远 **yuǎn**). Study the following table comparing spoken and written-style terms for different denominations of money, and be sure you learn this information before going to a country where Chinese is used:

SPOKEN STYLE	WRITTEN STYLE	ENGLISH
分 **fēn**	分 **fēn**	penny, cent, fen
毛 **máo**	角 **jiǎo**	dime, ten cents
块 (塊) **kuài**	元 **yuán**	dollar, yuan

A3. 我刚刚给你一张我的名片，你还说我没给你！(我剛剛給你一張我的名片，你還說我沒給你！) "I just gave you one of my name cards, and you actually say that I didn't give you any!" This 还 (還) expresses emphasis and can be translated as "even," "still," or "actually."

A4. 我叫的是文小姐 "The one I called (for) is Ms. Wen."

A8. 我……一毛都没有 (我……一毛都沒有) "I don't have even a dime."

D2. 他去哪儿都只带五毛钱 (他去哪兒都只帶五毛錢) "Wherever he goes, he only takes along 50 cents." When question words are followed by 都, they often take on an indefinite sense of "wherever," "whoever," "whatever," etc. This will be explained in more detail later in the course.

E. Chinese people are very fond of character riddles. Given the complexities of the Chinese writing system, there are many opportunities for them to have a bit of fun. As regards the character riddle in this Supplement, the answer to the riddle is: "the character 一." This is because if the character 一 is added to the character 人, then it becomes the character 大; and if 天 doesn't have the stroke 一 in it, it also becomes the character 大.

PART 4

By Bus and Street Car to the Summer Palace (cont.)

New Characters and Words

Study the six characters below and the common words written with them, paying careful attention to each character's pronunciation, meaning, and structure, as well as similar-looking characters. After you've studied a character, turn to the *Practice Essentials* volume and practice writing it on the practice sheet, making sure to follow the correct stroke order and direction as you pronounce it out loud and think of its meaning.

259 早 **zǎo** be early

Radical is 日 "sun" [**BF**] (132). The other component is 十 (11), which here represents the horizon. If one sees the "sun" rising over the horizon, it must be "early." This character also serves as a phonetic, e.g., in 草 **cǎo** "grass." Contrast 早 with 中 **zhōng** (23) and 千 **qiān** (114).

早	**zǎo**	be early [**SV**]
早上	**zǎoshang**	in the morning [**TW**]
早饭 (早飯)	**zǎofàn**	breakfast [**N**]

260 着 (着) **-zháo** (indicates action of verb is realized)
-zhe (indicates continuous aspect)

Radical is 目 **mù** "eye" [**BF**]. The other constituent of the simplified character is 羊 **yáng** "sheep." Note the slight difference—a reduction by one stroke—in the simplified version 着 as compared with the traditional version 着. In practice, most people when handwriting the traditional version write it identically with the simplified version. Also, note there is a common alternate form of the traditional character, 著. Contrast 着 (着) with 差 (差) **chà** (118) and 看 **kàn** (176). Finally, note that 着 (着) is a 多音字 **duōyīnzì** , since it represents both **-zháo** and **-zhe** (cf. 6-2, note A1a).

着 (着/著)	**-zháo**	(indicates action of verb is realized) [**RE**]

找着（找着/找著）	**zhǎozháo**	look for and find, find [RC]
找不着（找不着/找不著）	**zhǎobuzháo**	look for and can't find, can't find [RC]
着（着/著）	**-zhe**	(indicates continuous aspect) [P]
早着呢（早着呢/早著呢）	**zǎozhe ne**	it's still early

261 记（記） **jì** remember; record

Radical is 讠（言）**yán** "speech" [BF]. The colloquial name for this radical is 言字旁 **yánzìpáng** "side made up of the character 言." Phonetic is 己 **jǐ** "oneself" [BF]. If one "records" "speech" "oneself," then one will "remember" it better. Contrast 记（記）with 纪（紀）**jì** (105).

记得（記得）	**jìde**	remember [V]

262 心 **xīn** heart, mind

This character, 心 **xīn** "heart," is itself a common radical and a rather rare phonetic. When at the left side of a character, 心 as radical is referred to colloquially as 心字旁 **xīnzìpáng** "side made up of the character 心" and is written as 忄. 心 is a pictograph, representing the four ventricles of the heart.

小心	**xiǎoxīn**	be careful (lit. "make the heart small") [SV]
中心	**zhōngxīn**	center [N]
中文中心	**Zhōngwén zhōngxīn**	Chinese language center

263 准（準） **zhǔn** be accurate

Radical of the simplified form is 冫 **bīng** "ice." This radical is referred to colloquially as 两点水（兩點水）**liǎngdiǎn shuǐ** "two drops of water." The other component of the simplified form is 隹 **zhuī** "short-tailed bird" [BF]. Radical of the traditional form is 水 **shuǐ** "water." Notice that this radical is written 氵 and is referred to colloquially as 三点水（三點水）**sāndiǎn shuǐ** "three drops of water" when it occurs at the left-hand side of a character. The other components of the traditional form are 隹 **zhuī** "short-tailed bird" [BF] and 十 **shí** (11).

264 备（備） **bèi** prepare

Radical of the simplified form is 田 **tián** "field" [BF], with the other component being 夂 **pū** "tap." Radical of the traditional form is 人 **rén** "person," which is written 亻 when occurring at the left side of a character so as not to get in the way of the component at the right. The colloquial name for this radical is 人字旁 **rénzìpáng** "side made up of the character 人."

准备（準備）	**zhǔnbèi**	prepare, get ready; plan, intend [V]

New Words in BSC 9-4 Written with Characters You Already Know

呢	**ne**	(indicates continuous aspect) [P]
看	**kàn**	read [V]
车票（車票）	**chēpiào**	bus ticket [N]
月票	**yuèpiào**	monthly ticket [N]
下车（下車）	**xiàchē**	get off a vehicle [VO]

到	**-dào**	(indicates action of verb is attained) [RE]
找到	**zhǎodào**	look for and find, find [RC]

Reading Exercises (Simplified Characters)

Now practice reading the new characters and words for this lesson in context in sentences, conversations, and narratives. Be sure to refer to the Notes at the end of this lesson, and make use of the accompanying audio disc to hear and practice correct pronunciation, phrasing, and intonation.

A. SENTENCES

Read out loud each of the following sentences, which include all the new characters of this lesson. The first time you read a sentence, focus special attention on the characters and words that are new to you, reminding yourself of their pronunciation and meaning. The second time, aim to comprehend the overall meaning of the sentence.

一、老毛，你现在就要走了吗？还早着呢，多坐一会儿吧。
二、请您别准备早饭，我知道吃早饭比较好，可是我们家里早上不吃早饭。
三、从1929年在中国北方找到的“北京人”可以知道，很早以前，那个地方就有人住了。
四、这条路车子太多了，你要记得，走路要很小心！
五、你的名片我记得我有两张，可是不知道为什么，现在找不着了。
六、我们还吃着早饭呢，请她等一会儿，还早着呢。
七、我准备九月先去香港，然后去台湾。
八、有中国人的地方就听得到中国话，吃得到中国饭。
九、你要是找不着小张的话，可以给他写一个条子。他会看中文吧？
十、大海前天给他的女朋友准备了早饭，可是不太好吃，她不喜欢。

B. CONVERSATIONS

Read out loud the following conversations, including the name or role of the person speaking. If possible, find a partner or partners and each of you play a role. Then switch roles, so you get practice reading all of the lines.

一、
外国人　：到了吧？
公车小姐：早着呢，还有五站，到时候我叫您。（过了几分钟以后）这位先生，下一站就是动物园儿了，您要准备下车了。
外国人　：好，谢谢您……对不起，我的票找不着了！
公车小姐：我记得您买过票了，以后可得小心点儿。
外国人　：好的，真对不起。

二、
姐姐：弟弟，你怎么还没去上学？
弟弟：早着呢，我还有时间吃早饭呢。
姐姐：东西都准备好了吗？
弟弟：都准备好了。
姐姐：弟弟，今天第一天上学，你得小心一点儿。别忘了在第五站下车。你听到了吗？
弟弟：听到了，我会记得的。

C. CHARACTER DIFFERENTIATION DRILLS

Distinguish carefully the following similar-looking characters, pronouncing each one out loud and thinking of its meaning.

一、着 着 着 看 看 看
二、着 着 着 差 差 差
三、着 看 差 着 差 看 着
四、早 早 早 中 中 中
五、早 早 早 千 千 千
六、早 中 早 千 早 中 早

D. NARRATIVE

Read the following narrative, paying special attention to punctuation and overall structure. The first time you read the narrative, read it out loud; the second time, read silently and try to gradually increase your reading speed. Always think of the meaning of what you're reading.

北京有一个地方叫"京广中心"，"京"是"北京"的京，"广"是"广州"的广，在北京市的东边。这个地方北京人都知道，从1990年开到现在有20多年了。京广中心很高也很大，里面有一家很好的饭店、几十家公司，还有卖东西的地方和人住的地方，所以有的人说京广中心是"城里面的城"。不过在京广中心住很贵，一个月大概要一万五千块到两万五千块。不少外国买卖人在京广中心开了公司，也在那儿上班，也在那儿住。京广中心交通还行，外头就有很多车站，离北京站也不远，早上五、六点钟打的去首都机场也只要半小时左右就到了。有一家美国大学开的中文中心离京广中心比较近。要是你是外国人，住在京广中心的话，你大概可以在那儿学中文。

E. SUPPLEMENT: A HANDWRITTEN NOTICE

Read out loud the following handwritten notice that was posted on the bulletin board of a large Chinese language center for foreign students in Beijing. Be prepared to answer questions from your instructor and/or classmates on the content of the note.

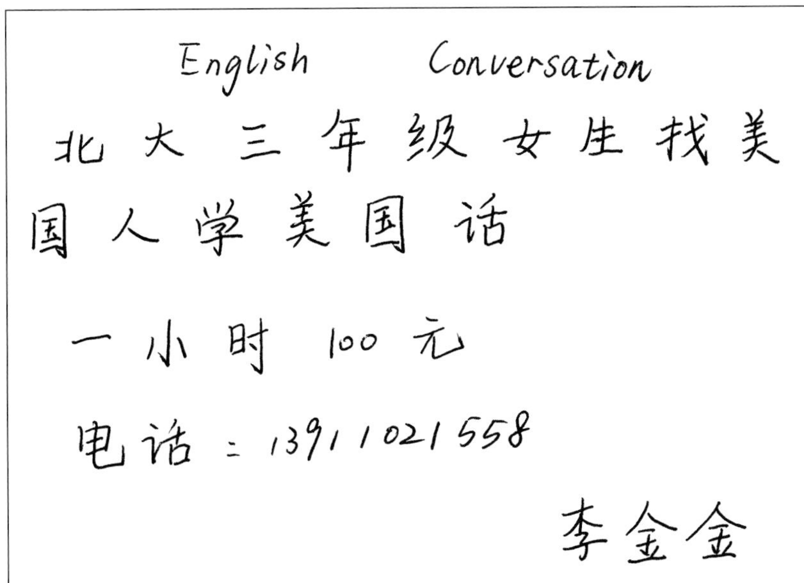
English Conversation
北大三年级女生找美国人学美国话
一小时 100 元
电话：13911021558
李金金

Reading Exercises (Traditional Characters)

A. SENTENCES

Read out loud each of the following sentences, which include all the new characters of this lesson. The first time you read a sentence, focus special attention on the characters and words that are new to you, reminding yourself of their pronunciation and meaning. The second time, aim to comprehend the overall meaning of the sentence.

一、老毛，你現在就要走了嗎？還早着呢，多坐一會兒吧。

二、請您別準備早飯，我知道吃早飯比較好，可是我們家裏早上不吃早飯。

三、從一九二九年在中國北方找到的「北京人」可以知道，很早以前，那個地方就有人住了。

四、這條路車子太多了，你要記得，走路要很小心！

五、你的名片我記得我有兩張，可是不知道為什麼，現在找不着了。

六、我們還吃着早飯呢，請她等一會兒，還早着呢。

七、我準備九月先去香港，然後去台灣。

八、有中國人的地方就聽得到中國話，吃得到中國飯。

九、你要是找不着小張的話，可以給他寫一個條子。他會看中文吧？

十、大海前天給他的女朋友準備了早飯，可是不太好吃，她不喜歡。

B. CONVERSATIONS

Read out loud the following conversations, including the name or role of the person speaking. If possible, find a partner or partners and each of you play a role. Then switch roles, so you get practice reading all of the lines.

一、外國人：到了吧？

公車小姐：早着呢，還有五站，到時候我叫您。（過了幾分鐘以後）這位先生，下一站就是動物園兒了，您要準備下車了。

外國人：好，謝謝您……對不起，我的票。找不着了！

公車小姐：我記得您買過票了，以後可得小心點兒。

外國人：好的，真對不起。

二、姐姐：弟弟，你怎麼還沒去上學？

弟弟：早着呢，我還有時間吃早飯呢。

姐姐：東西都準備好了嗎？

弟弟：都準備好了。

姐姐：弟弟，今天第一天上學，你得小心一點兒。別忘了在第五站下車。你聽到了嗎？

弟弟：聽到了，我會記得的。

C. CHARACTER DIFFERENTIATION DRILLS

Distinguish carefully the following similar-looking characters, pronouncing each one out loud and thinking of its meaning.

一、着着着看看看

二、着着着差差差

三、着看差着差看着

四、早早早中中中

五、早早早千千千

六、早中早千早中早

Taipei bus advertisement

D. NARRATIVE

Read the following narrative, paying special attention to punctuation and overall structure. The first time you read the narrative, read it out loud; the second time, read silently and try to gradually increase your reading speed. Always think of the meaning of what you're reading.

北京有一個地方叫「京廣中心」，「京」是「北京」的京，「廣」是「廣州」的廣，在北京市的東邊。這個地方北京人都知道，從一九九〇年開到現在有二十多年了。京廣中心很高也很大，裏面有一家很好的飯店、幾十家公司，還有賣東西的地方和人住的地方，所以有的人說京廣中心是「城裏面的城」。不過在京廣中心住很貴，一個月大概要一萬五千塊到兩萬五千塊。不少外國買賣人在京廣中心開了公司，也在那兒上班，也在那兒住。京廣中心交通還行，外頭就有很多車站，離北京站也不遠，早上五、六點鐘打的去首都機場也只要半小時左右就到了。有一家美國大學開的中文中心離京廣中心比較近。要是你是外國人，住在京廣中心的話，你大概可以在那兒學中文。

E. SUPPLEMENT: A HANDWRITTEN NOTICE

(see Simplified Characters section)

Notes

A1a. 你现在就要走了吗？(你現在就要走了嗎？) "You're leaving right now?" The pattern 就要……了 means "be about to...," so 你现在就要走了吗？(你現在就要走了嗎？) literally means "You now are about to leave?"

A1b. 还早着呢，多坐一会儿吧 (還早着呢，多坐一會兒吧) "It's still early, why don't you sit a while longer?" The phrase 多坐一会儿 (多坐一會兒) literally means "more sit a while." This will be explained and practiced in more detail later in the course.

A3a. Be sure you understand that the coverb 从 (從) "from" does NOT go with the year "1929" that follows it (as would often be the case in other sentences), but rather goes with the noun 北京人 that comes later in the sentence. So the "skeleton" of the first phrase is: 从 "北京人" 可以知道 (從「北京人」可以知道) "from 'Peking Man' we can know that...."

A3b. 很早以前，那个地方就有人住了 (很早以前，那個地方就有人住了) "Long ago, there were already people living in that place." 很早以前 "long ago, a long time ago" is a common and useful phrase that you should memorize as a "chunk." The 就 later in this sentence means "as early as then" or "already."

A3c. Here, 北京人 refers to "Peking Man," that is, fossils from the early human known as Homo erectus pekinensis discovered in the vicinity of Beijing in 1923.

A4. 要 is a verb of many meanings. In 你要记得 (你要記得), 要 indicates necessity, so we could translate this phrase as "you need to remember," "you should remember," or "you must remember."

A6. 我们还吃着早饭呢，请她等一会儿，还早着呢 (我們還吃着早飯呢，請她等一會兒，還早着呢) "We're still eating breakfast; ask her to wait a while, it's still early." In both the first and the last clauses of this sentence, the combination of 着 (着) plus 呢 indicates continuous aspect, in other words, that the action of eating and the state of being early are still continuing and have not yet been completed.

A7. Although the meaning of 准备 (準備) is often "prepare" or "get ready," in this sentence it means "plan" or "intend."

A8. 有中国人的地方就听得到中国话，吃得到中国饭 (有中國人的地方就聽得到中國話，吃得到中國飯) "Wherever there are Chinese people, you can hear the Chinese language and you can eat Chinese food" (lit. "Places where there are Chinese people, can hear Chinese speech, can eat Chinese food").

B1. 过了几分钟以后 (過了幾分鐘以後) "after a few minutes had passed."

B2. 我会记得的 (我會記得的) "I'll remember." This 会 (會) means "will." In the speech and writing of many Chinese, especially those from southern China and Taiwan, it is often followed at the end of the sentence by an optional 的.

D1. 京广中心交通还行，外头就有很多车站 (京廣中心交通還行，外頭就有很多車站) "Transportation at the Jingguang Centre is fairly convenient, there being many bus stops right outside." The 就 in 外头就有 (外頭就有) here means "as close as that" or "that close."

E1. 美国话 (美國話) is not a particularly common term, but can be used to mean "American English" as opposed to, for example, British English.

E2. 一小时100元 (一小時100元) "one hundred dollars per hour." Do you remember the character 元 **yuán** that was mentioned in the Notes for BWC 9-3? Even though 元 isn't officially introduced in this volume, you should try to learn it now. As we mentioned in the previous lesson, 元 is commonly used in written-style Chinese as the equivalent of spoken-style 块 (塊) **kuài** to mean "dollar."

UNIT 10 Weather

PART 1

A Weather Forecast

早！今天外头多少度？
(早！今天外頭多少度？)
我看看。今天最高温是28度，最低温是24度。

New Characters and Words

Study the six characters below and the common words written with them, paying careful attention to each character's pronunciation, meaning, and structure, as well as similar-looking characters. After you've studied a character, turn to the *Practice Essentials* volume and practice writing it on the practice sheet, making sure to follow the correct stroke order and direction as you pronounce it out loud and think of its meaning.

265 越 **yuè** exceed

Radical is 走 **zǒu** "walk." The colloquial name for this radical is 走字旁 **zǒuzìpáng** "side made up of the character 走." Note that when 走 serves as the radical in another character, its last stroke is lengthened, with the component on the right side placed above the last stroke of 走. The phonetic in 越 is 戉 **yuè** "battle-axe."

越来越 (越來越)	**yuè lái yuè**	more and more [**PT**]
越南	**Yuènán**	Vietnam [**PW**]
越南文	**Yuènánwén**	written Vietnamese language [**N**]
越南话 (越南話)	**Yuènán huà**	spoken Vietnamese language [**PH**]
越南人	**Yuènán rén**	Vietnamese person [**PH**]

266 最 **zuì** most

Radical is 曰 **yuē** "say" [**BF**]. Be sure to distinguish 曰 from 日 **rì** "sun" [**BF**] (132), which can also serve as a radical. Besides 曰, the other component in 最 is 取 **qǔ** "obtain."

最	**zuì**	most [**A**]
最近	**zuìjìn**	recently; in the near future [**MA**]
最后 (最後)	**zuìhòu**	in the end, finally [**MA**]

267 温 **wēn** warm, mild

Radical is 水 **shuǐ** "water." Notice that this radical is written 氵 and is referred to colloquially as 三点水 (三點水) **sāndiǎn shuǐ** "three drops of water" when it occurs at the left-hand side of a character. In traditional characters, there is a common alternate form of 温 printed as 溫; however, even when writing traditional characters, most people handwrite the character as 温.

温	**Wēn**	Wen [SN]
最高温	**zuìgāowēn**	high(est) temperature [N]
温州	**Wēnzhōu**	(important city in Zhejiang Province) [PW]
温州街	**Wēnzhōu Jiē**	Wenzhou Street (well-known street in downtown Taipei) [PH]

268 低 **dī** low

Radical is 人 **rén** "person," which is written 亻 when occurring at the left side of a character so as not to get in the way of the component at the right. The colloquial name for this radical is 人字旁 **rénzìpáng** "side made up of the character 人." Phonetic is 氐 **Dī**, the name of an ancient barbarian tribe. In some fonts, the dot that constitutes the last stroke of the character looks like a horizontal line: 低.

低	**dī**	be low [SV]
最低温	**zuìdīwēn**	low(est) temperature [N]

269 度 **dù** degree (of temperature)

Radical is 广 **yǎn** "eaves" [BF]. This radical is referred to colloquially as 广字头 (廣字頭) **guǎngzìtóu** "top made up of the character 广." This character is itself a phonetic, e.g., in 渡 **dù** as in 渡河 **dùhé** "cross a river" and 镀 (鍍) **dù** as in 镀金 (鍍金) **dùjīn** "gold-plate." Contrast 度 with 麼 **me** (128).

度	**dù**	degree (of temperature) [M]
几度 (幾度)	**jǐdù**	how many degrees?
二十八度	**èrshibādù**	twenty-eight degrees
温度	**wēndù**	temperature [N]
最高温度	**zuì gāo wēndù**	high(est) temperature [PH]
最低温度	**zuì dī wēndù**	low(est) temperature [PH]

270 定 **dìng** settle, determine

Radical is 宀 **mián** "roof" [BF]. This radical is referred to colloquially as 宝盖头 (寶蓋頭) **bǎogàitóu** "top made up of a canopy." Contrast 定 with 走 **zǒu** (70) and 是 **shì** (76).

一定	**yídìng**	definitely [A]
不一定	**bù yídìng**	not necessarily [PH]

New Words in BSC 10-1 Written with Characters You Already Know

所以说 (所以說)	**suóyi shuō**	so, therefore [PH]
早	**zǎo**	"good morning" [IE]

可能	**kěnéng**	be possible [AV]
成	**chéng**	into [PV]
准 (準)	**zhǔn**	be accurate [SV]
天	**tiān**	sky [N]
从...开始 (從⋯開始)	**cóng...kāishǐ**	starting from... [PT]

Reading Exercises (Simplified Characters)

Now practice reading the new characters and words for this lesson in context in sentences, conversations, and narratives. Be sure to refer to the Notes at the end of this lesson, and make use of the accompanying audio disc to hear and practice correct pronunciation, phrasing, and intonation.

A. SENTENCES

Read out loud each of the following sentences, which include all the new characters of this lesson. The first time you read a sentence, focus special attention on the characters and words that are new to you, reminding yourself of their pronunciation and meaning. The second time, aim to comprehend the overall meaning of the sentence.

一、你的中文说得越来越准，可是我的中文好像越来越差！
二、你最喜欢吃什么？最不喜欢吃什么？
三、你会不会觉得最近温度好像越来越低了？
四、本地的最高温大概几度？最低温几度？
五、我们不一定得去动物园，你不要去我们就不去了！
六、这个我以前还真没听说过，不可能吧！
七、小心！有一个小动物离你越来越近了！
八、我开始上班以后，不知道为什么，越来越没钱。
九、那个人不一定是中国人，可能是越南人吧。
十、王大海那个人真好，早上看到人，一定说“早，您好”。

B. CONVERSATIONS

Read out loud the following conversations, including the name or role of the person speaking. If possible, find a partner or partners and each of you play a role. Then switch roles, so you get practice reading all of the lines.

一、
王先生：李开来，早！
李先生：王定和，早！你最近还好吧？
王先生：我最近越来越忙。
李先生：可是你最近钱越来越多，不是吗？
王先生：不是。我越来越忙，不过钱越来越少！
李先生：那你可能得换一个工作！

二、
弟弟：最贵的车子一定是最好的车子吧？
哥哥：不一定。
弟弟：那么，最好的车子一定是最贵的车子吧？
哥哥：那也不一定。弟弟，你听我说，有的时候最贵的东西不一定是最好的，最好的也不一定是最贵的。现在清楚了吧？

三、
温州人：你知道中国去年的GDP是多少吗？
上海人：我只知道中国的GDP最近几年越来越高，可是说真的，我不太清楚去年是多少。

C. CHARACTER DIFFERENTIATION DRILLS

Distinguish carefully the following similar-looking characters, pronouncing each one out loud and thinking of its meaning.

一、定 定 定 走 走 走
二、定 定 定 是 是 是
三、定 走 是 定 定 走 是 定
四、度 度 度 广 广 广
五、度 度 度 么 么 么
六、度 度 度 厂 厂 厂
七、度 广 度 广 么 度 厂 度

Taipei street sign

D. NARRATIVES

Read the following narratives, paying special attention to punctuation and overall structure. The first time you read a narrative, read it out loud; the second time, read silently and try to gradually increase your reading speed. Always think of the meaning of what you're reading.

一、有一个外国人在中国住了很长时间了，中文原来很好，不过不知道为什么，他的中文最近越来越差。他的中国同事说"请坐"，他听成了"请走"，他觉得同事大概不喜欢外国人。他要问他的中国朋友"你最近好不好？"，可是他不小心，说成了"你最近老不老？"。"左"字他看成了"右"字，"十"字他写成了"千"字。最后他觉得中文太难太难了，就回国去了。

二、中国一共有多少姓？北京有一个"姓名中心"，那儿的人说他们最近找到了四千一百多个中国人的姓。他们说北京人姓王的最多，姓张的第二多，姓李的第三多。王、张、李这三个姓都是中国人的"大姓"。他们还说，十个北京人里头就有一个姓王。有一位中国大学老师说，最近在中国，三个字的姓名越来越多。原来在中国三个字的姓名很多，可是从1960年到1990年出生的中国人，两个字的姓名的比较多。不过，从差不多2000年开始，三个字的姓名又多起来了。最后那位老师还说，中国人有的时候说"两个姓李的人五百年以前是一家人"，这么说不一定对。

E. SUPPLEMENT: A CHINESE JOKE

Read out loud the following joke, including the reference to the person speaking. If possible, find a partner and each of you play one of the roles. Then switch roles, so you get practice reading all the lines.

女：你最喜欢的人是谁？
男：就是你。
女：那么，你最不喜欢的人是谁呢？
男：就是你的男朋友！

Reading Exercises (Traditional Characters)

A. SENTENCES

Read out loud each of the following sentences, which include all the new characters of this lesson. The first time you read a sentence, focus special attention on the characters and words that are new to you, reminding yourself of their pronunciation and meaning. The second time, aim to comprehend the overall meaning of the sentence.

一、你的中文說得越來越準，可是我的中文好像越來越差！

二、你最喜歡吃什麼？最不喜歡吃什麼？

三、你會不會覺得最近温度好像越來越低了？

四、本地的最高温大概幾度？最低温幾度？

五、我們不一定得去動物園，你不要去我們就不去了！

六、這個我以前還真沒聽說過，不可能吧！

七、小心！有一個小動物離你越來越近了！

八、我開始上班以後，不知道為什麼，越來越沒錢。

九、那個人不一定是中國人，可能是越南人吧。

十、王大海那個人真好，早上看到人，一定說「早，您好」。

B. CONVERSATIONS

Read out loud the following conversations, including the name or role of the person speaking. If possible, find a partner or partners and each of you play a role. Then switch roles, so you get practice reading all of the lines.

一、王先生：李開來，早！

李先生：王定和，早！你最近還好吧？

王先生：我最近越來越忙。

李先生：可是你最近錢越來越多，不是嗎？

王先生：不是。我越來越忙，不過錢越來越少！

李先生：那你可能得換一個工作！

二、弟弟：最貴的車子一定是最好的車子吧？

哥哥：不一定。

弟弟：那麼，最好的車子一定是最貴的車子吧？

哥哥：那也不一定。弟弟，你聽我說，有的時候最貴的東西不一定是最好的，最好的也不一定是最貴的。現在清楚了吧？

三、温州人：你知道中國去年的ＧＤＰ是多少嗎？

上海人：我只知道中國的ＧＤＰ最近幾年越來越高，可是說真的，我不太清楚去年是多少。

C. CHARACTER DIFFERENTIATION DRILLS

Distinguish carefully the following similar-looking characters, pronouncing each one out loud and thinking of its meaning.

一、定定定走走走

二、定定定是是是

三、定走是定定走是定

四、度度度廣廣廣

五、度度度麼麼麼

六、度度度廠廠廠

七、度廣度廣麼度廠度

D. NARRATIVES

Read the following narrative, paying special attention to punctuation and overall structure. The first time you read the narrative, read it out loud; the second time, read silently and try to gradually increase your reading speed. Always think of the meaning of what you're reading.

一、有一個外國人在中國住了很長時間了，中文原來很好，不過不知道為什麼，他的中文最近越來越差。他的中國同事說「請坐」，他聽成了「請走」，他覺得同事大概不喜歡外國人。他要問他的中國朋友「你最近好不好？」，可是他不小心，說成了「你最近老不老？」，「左」字他看成了「右」字，「十」字他寫成了「千」字。最後他覺得中文太難太難了，就回國去了。

二、中國一共有多少姓？北京有一個「姓名中心」，那兒的人說他們最近找到了四千一百多個中國人的姓。他們說北京人姓王的最多，姓張的第二多，姓李的第三多。王、張、李這三個姓都是中國人的「大姓」。他們還說，十個北京人裏頭就有一個姓王。有一位中國大學老師說，最近在中國，三個字的姓名越來越多。原來在中國三個字的姓名很多，可是從一九六〇年到一九九〇年出生的中國人，兩個字的姓名的比較多。不過，從差不多二〇〇〇年開始，三個字的姓名又多起來了。最後那位老師還說，中國人有的時候說「兩個姓李的人五百年以前是一家人」，這麼說不一定對。

E. SUPPLEMENT: A CHINESE JOKE

Read out loud the following joke, including the reference to the person speaking. If possible, find a partner and each of you play one of the roles. Then switch roles, so you get practice reading all the lines.

女：你最喜歡的人是誰？
男：就是你。
女：那麼，你最不喜歡的人是誰呢？
男：就是你的男朋友！

Notes

A3. 你会不会觉得 (你會不會覺得) literally means "Would you be likely to feel that...?" However, in actual use, it's just an equivalent of English "Do you feel that...?"

A5. 你不要去我们就不去了 (你不要去我們就不去了) here means "If you don't want to go, then we won't go!"

A6. 这个我以前还真没听说过 (這個我以前還真沒聽說過) "This I really have never heard of before." The 还 (還) here means "really," "even," or "actually" and serves to strengthen the negative sense of the verb.

A10. 早上看到人 "In the morning when he sees people." 看到 means "see" (someone or something).

D1. "左"字他看成了"右"字，"十"字他写成了"千"字 (「左」字他看成了「右」字，「十」字他寫成了「千」字) "He read the character for 'left' as the character for 'right,' and he wrote the character for 'ten' as the character for 'thousand.'" Notice how characters are quoted in Chinese: "左" 字 "the character **zuǒ**", etc.

D2a. 多起来了 (多起來了) here means "became many" or "increased."

D2b. 两个姓李的人五百年以前是一家人 (兩個姓李的人五百年以前是一家人) "500 years ago, two people with the surname Li were members of the same family." This is commonly said and believed but, as this narrative points out, is not actually true.

E. Note the use of the characters 男 and 女 alone to stand for 男人 and 女人 or 男的 and 女的. Such abbreviations are very common in written-style Chinese.

"Diligently study the new traffic regulations"

PART 2

Beijing Weather

这么说，我来得正是时候了。
(這麼說，我來得正是時候了。)
对！
(對！)

New Characters and Words

Study the six characters below and the common words written with them, paying careful attention to each character's pronunciation, meaning, and structure, as well as similar-looking characters. After you've studied a character, turn to the *Practice Essentials* volume and practice writing it on the practice sheet, making sure to follow the correct stroke order and direction as you pronounce it out loud and think of its meaning.

271 气(氣) **qì** gas, air

Simplified 气 **qì** "gas, air" is itself its own radical; and it's the radical in the traditional form 氣. Phonetic in both is 乞 **qǐ** "beg" as in 乞丐 **qǐgài** "beggar"; you've seen this phonetic previously in 吃 **chī** (151). The other part of the traditional character is 米 **mǐ** "rice." "Rice" gives off "air" when cooked. Contrast 气 (氣) and 汽 **qì** "steam, vapor" (223).

天气 (天氣)	**tiānqi**	be weather [N]
生气 (生氣)	**shēngqì**	get angry [VO]

272 冷 **lěng** cold

Radical is 冫 **bīng** "ice." This radical is referred to colloquially as 两点水 (兩點水) **liǎngdiǎn shuǐ** "two drops of water." Phonetic is 令 **lìng** "command, order." Contrast 冷 with 今 **jīn** (106) and 会 (會) **huì** (199).

冷	**lěng**	be cold [SV]

273 热(熱) **rè** hot

Radical is 火 **huǒ** "fire." Notice that this radical is written 灬 and is referred to colloquially as 四点火(四點火) **sìdiǎn huǒ** "four dots of fire" when it occurs at the bottom of a character. Phonetic is 執(执) **zhí** "hold" [BF]. If you "hold" "fire," your hand will become very "hot."

热(熱)	**rè**	be hot [SV]

274 死 **sǐ** die

Radical is 歹 **dǎi** "bad" [BF]. According to one source, 匕 is an inversion of 人 **rén** "person." In that case, this character can be explained as: "dying" is something "bad" that happens to "people."

死	**sǐ**	die [V]
热得要死(熱得要死)	**rède yào sǐ**	so hot one will die, be very hot

275 干(乾) **gān** dry

Radical of the simplified form is 干 **gān** "shield" [BF]. 干 can also serve as a phonetic, e.g., in 肝 **gān** "liver," 杆 **gān** as in 杆子 **gānzi** "pole," 刊 **kān** as in 期刊 **qīkān** "periodical," and in 岸 **àn** "coast" (283). Radical of the traditional form is 乙 **yǐ** "second of the ten Celestial Stems." Contrast the simplified form 干 with 十 **shí** (11), 千 **qiān** (114), 半 **bàn** (117), 子 **zǐ** (155), and 平 **píng** (241).

干(乾)	**gān**	be dry [SV]

276 正 **zhèng** just

Radical is 止 **zhǐ** "stop" [BF]. Contrast 正 with 五 **wǔ** (5), 王 **wáng** (6), and 上 **shàng** (25).

正	**zhèng**	just [A]

New Words in BSC 10-2 Written with Characters You Already Know

要	**yào**	if [MA]
很少	**hěn shǎo**	seldom [PH]
又...又...	**yòu...yòu...**	both...and... [PT]
不...也不...	**bù...yě bù...**	neither...nor... [PT]
这么说(這麼說)	**zhème shuō**	saying it like this; then [PH] (pronounced **zhèmme shuō**)

Reading Exercises (Simplified Characters)

Now practice reading the new characters and words for this lesson in context in sentences, conversations, and narratives. Be sure to refer to the Notes at the end of this lesson, and make use of the accompanying audio disc to hear and practice correct pronunciation, phrasing, and intonation.

A. SENTENCES

Read out loud each of the following sentences, which include all the new characters of this lesson. The first time

you read a sentence, focus special attention on the characters and words that are new to you, reminding yourself of their pronunciation and meaning. The second time, aim to comprehend the overall meaning of the sentence.

一、有的人比较喜欢热的天气，有的人比较喜欢冷的天气。
二、那儿的天气不冷也不热，就是太干了。
三、今天外面真是冷得要死。
四、你们来得正是时候，不冷也不热。
五、广州的天气要是不这么热就好了。
六、那个地方不是热得要死就是冷得要死，怎么能住呢？
七、现在是七月，天气怎么这么冷？这儿七月很少这么冷。
八、这条路又难走，车子又多，我们换条别的路走吧。
九、你说你不是学生，这么说，你是老师吧？
十、王大海又要去动物园了。他的女朋友很少生气，不过这次她真的生气了。

B. CONVERSATIONS

Read out loud the following conversations, including the name or role of the person speaking. If possible, find a partner or partners and each of you play a role. Then switch roles, so you get practice reading all of the lines.

一、
方国兴：小王，早！
王外山：小方，早！今天天气好吗？
方国兴：太热了，真是热得要死！
王外山：你知道现在外面有多少度？
方国兴：我也不太清楚，可是听说今天最高气温是四十一度。

二、
金小姐：何小姐，你来得正是时候！
何小姐：是吗？为什么呢？
金小姐：我们这里十月的天气最好。
何小姐：那太好了。我上次来真是热死了。
金小姐：你上次是什么时候来的？
何小姐：好像是七月吧。

C. CHARACTER DIFFERENTIATION DRILLS

Distinguish carefully the following similar-looking characters, pronouncing each one out loud and thinking of its meaning.

一、冷 冷 冷 今 今 今
二、冷 今 冷 冷 今 今 冷
三、正 正 正 五 五 五
四、正 正 正 王 王 王
五、正 王 正 五 正 五 王 正
六、干 干 干 千 千 千
七、干 千 干 干 千 千 干

Hong Kong street sign

D. NARRATIVES

Read the following narrative, paying special attention to punctuation and overall structure. The first time you read the narrative, read it out loud; the second time, read silently and try to gradually increase your reading speed. Always think of the meaning of what you're reading.

一、我觉得最近几年，本地的天气越来越好。从前这儿不是太冷就是太热。一月冷得要死，八月又热得要死，天气也很干。可是现在很少那么干，温度不高也不低，天气不冷也不热。正好！

二、我们都知道，有的人很喜欢生气，还有的人很少生气。我有一个朋友，老毛，他很少生气。不过，要是老毛生气的话，他可真的会生很大的气。老毛是一个……等一下儿，什么事儿？是不是老毛生气了？我们小心一点儿，离他远点儿比较好。走吧！

E. SUPPLEMENT: HIGH AND LOW TEMPERATURES

The tables below give high and low temperatures for each month for three major Chinese cities. Read out loud the information in each table and then, based on the tables, answer questions from your instructor or classmates. (see Notes for important information)

北京												
	1月	2月	3月	4月	5月	6月	7月	8月	9月	10月	11月	12月
最高温	2	4	11	20	26	31	31	29	26	19	10	3
最低温	-9	-7	-1	7	13	18	22	21	14	7	-1	-7

上海												
	1月	2月	3月	4月	5月	6月	7月	8月	9月	10月	11月	12月
最高温	8	9	13	18	23	27	32	32	27	22	17	11
最低温	1	2	5	11	16	20	25	24	21	14	9	3

香港												
	1月	2月	3月	4月	5月	6月	7月	8月	9月	10月	11月	12月
最高温	18.6	18.6	21.5	25.1	28.4	30.4	31.3	31.1	30.2	27.7	24.0	20.3
最低温	14.1	14.4	16.9	20.6	23.9	26.1	26.7	26.4	25.6	23.4	19.4	15.7

Reading Exercises (Traditional Characters)

A. SENTENCES

Read out loud each of the following sentences, which include all the new characters of this lesson. The first time you read a sentence, focus special attention on the characters and words that are new to you, reminding yourself of their pronunciation and meaning. The second time, aim to comprehend the overall meaning of the sentence.

一、有的人比較喜歡熱的天氣，有的人比較喜歡冷的天氣。

二、那兒的天氣不冷也不熱，就是太乾了。

三、今天外面真是冷得要死。

四、你們來得正是時候，不冷也不熱。

五、廣州的天氣要是不這麼熱就好了。

六、那個地方不是熱得要死就是冷得要死，怎麼能住呢？

七、現在是七月，天氣怎麼這麼冷？這兒七月很少這麼冷。

八、這條路又難走，車子又多，我們換條別的路走吧。

九、你說你不是學生，這麼說，你是老師吧？

十、王大海又要去動物園了。他的女朋友很少生氣，不過這次她真的生氣了。

B. CONVERSATIONS

Read out loud the following conversations, including the name or role of the person speaking. If possible, find a partner or partners and each of you play a role. Then switch roles, so you get practice reading all of the lines.

一、

方國興：小王，早！

王外山：小方，早！今天天氣好嗎？

方國興：太熱了，真是熱得要死！

王外山：你知道現在外面有多少度？

方國興：我也不太清楚，可是聽說今天最高氣温是四十一度。

二、

金小姐：何小姐，你來得正是時候！

何小姐：是嗎？為什麼呢？

金小姐：我們這裏十月的天氣最好。

何小姐：那太好了。我上次來真是熱死了。

金小姐：你上次是什麼時候來的？

何小姐：好像是七月吧。

Park in Taipei

C. CHARACTER DIFFERENTIATION DRILLS

Distinguish carefully the following similar-looking characters, pronouncing each one out loud and thinking of its meaning.

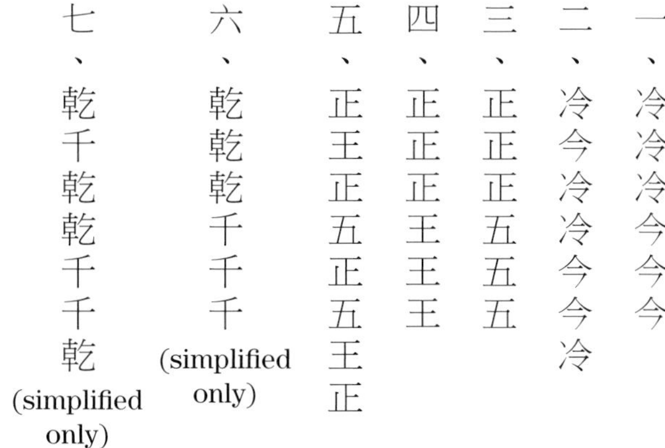

一、冷冷冷今今今

二、冷今冷冷今今冷

三、正正正五五五

四、正正正王王王

五、正王正五正五王正

六、乾乾乾千千千 (simplified only)

七、乾千乾乾千千乾 (simplified only)

D. NARRATIVES

Read the following narrative, paying special attention to punctuation and overall structure. The first time you read the narrative, read it out loud; the second time, read silently and try to gradually increase your reading speed. Always think of the meaning of what you're reading.

一、我覺得最近幾年，本地的天氣越來越好。從前這兒不是太冷就是太熱。一月冷得要死，八月又熱得要死，天氣也很乾。可是現在很少那麼乾，溫度不高也不低，天氣不冷也不熱。正好！

二、我們都知道，有的人很喜歡生氣，還有的人很少生氣。我有一個朋友，老毛，他很少生氣。不過，要是老毛生氣的話，他可真的會生很大的氣。老毛是一個……等一下兒，什麼事兒？是不是老毛生氣了？我們小心一點兒，離他遠點兒比較好。走吧！

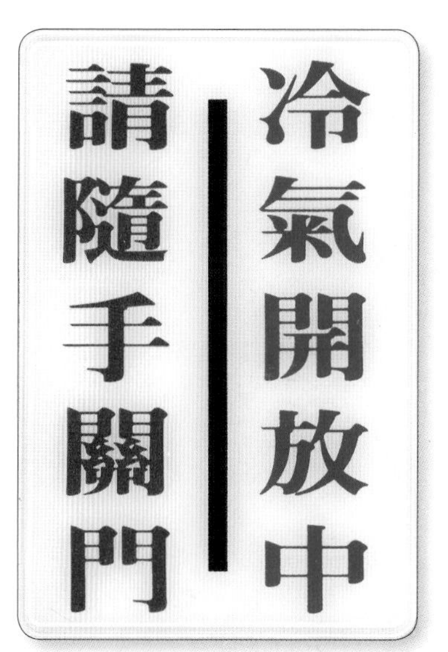

"Air conditioning on, please keep door closed"

E. SUPPLEMENT: HIGH AND LOW TEMPERATURES

(see Simplified Characters section)

Notes

B1. In BWC 2-3, you learned that the character 兴 (興) in the word 高兴 (高興) is pronounced **xìng**. However, be aware that 兴 (興) is a 多音字 **duōyīnzì** "character with multiple pronunciations" (cf. BWC 6-2: A1a). In personal and geographical names, 兴 (興) is usually pronounced **xīng**. Therefore, the personal name 方国兴 (方國興) should be pronounced **Fāng Guóxīng**.

D1. 从前这儿不是太冷就是太热 (從前這兒不是太冷就是太熱) "Formerly, if it wasn't too cold here then it was too hot" or "Formerly, it was either too cold here or it was too hot." Learn the pattern 不是A就是B "if it isn't A, then it's B" or "it's either A or B."

D2a. 生很大的气 (生很大的氣) "get very angry."

D2b. 等一下儿，什么事儿？(等一下兒，什麼事兒？) "Wait a second, what's the matter?"

D2c. 离他远点儿比较好 (離他遠點兒比較好) "it would be better to get further away from him."

E. All the temperatures in the tables are given in Centigrade or 摄氏 (攝氏) **Shèshì**, as is customary in China. When reading the temperatures out loud, be sure to add the measure 度 **dù** "degrees" after each temperature. The expression for "below zero" is 〇下 **líng xià**, so -9º would be said as 〇下九度 **líng xià jiŭ dù**. Also, the decimal point is pronounced as 点 (點) **diăn**, so 18.6º would be said as 十八点六度 (十八點六度) **shíbā diăn liùdù**.

Hong Kong street sign

PART 3

Taiwan Weather

是不是又要下雨了？
对。其实，现在就在下。
(對。其實，現在就在下。)

New Characters and Words

Study the six characters below and the common words written with them, paying careful attention to each character's pronunciation, meaning, and structure, as well as similar-looking characters. After you've studied a character, turn to the *Practice Essentials* volume and practice writing it on the practice sheet, making sure to follow the correct stroke order and direction as you pronounce it out loud and think of its meaning.

277 样(樣) **yàng** kind, variety; way, manner

Radical is the pictograph 木 **mù** "tree" [BF]. This radical is referred to colloquially as 木字旁 **mùzìpáng** "side made up of the character 木." Note that when 木 is written at the left of a character as a radical, its last stroke is shortened so that it doesn't collide with the component to its right. Phonetic is 羊 **yáng** "sheep." The other component in the traditional form is 永 **yǒng** "permanent" [BF].

样子(樣子)	**yàngzi**	way, appearance [N]
这样(這樣)	**zhèiyang**	this way, like this [MA] (also **zhèyang**)
这样子(這樣子)	**zhèiyangzi**	this way, like this [MA] (also **zhèyangzi**)
那样(那樣)	**nèiyang**	that way, like that [MA] (also **nàyang**)
那样子(那樣子)	**nèiyangzi**	that way, like that [MA] (also **nàyangzi**)
怎么样(怎麼樣)	**zěnmeyàng**	how, in what way [QW] (pronounced **zěmmeyàng**)
好像…的样子 (好像…的樣子)	**hǎoxiàng... -de yàngzi**	it seems like... [PT]

278 进(進) **jìn** enter, go forward, advance

Radical is 辶 **chuò** "walk, go" [BF]. The colloquial name for this radical is 走之 **zǒu zhī** "the walking 之," because of its meaning "walk" and its resemblance to the particle 之. The phonetic of the simplified form is 井 **jǐng** "well" [BF]. The other component in the traditional form is 隹 **zhuī** "short-tailed bird" [BF]. When a "bird" "goes" somewhere, it always flies forward, thereby "advancing." Contrast simplified 进 and 近 **jìn** (221). Contrast traditional 進 and 誰 **shéi** (121).

进(進)	**jìn**	enter [V]
请进(請進)	**qǐng jìn**	"please come in" [IE]
进来(進來)	**jìnlái**	come in [RC/RE]
进去(進去)	**jìnqu**	go in [RC]
走进来(走進來)	**zǒujìnlái**	come walking in [RC]
走进去(走進去)	**zǒujìnqu**	go walking in [RC]

279 雨 **yǔ** rain

This character is itself a radical and occurs in a number of terms having to do with meteorological phenomena. The horizontal stroke at the top represents the sky, with the four short strokes below representing rain drops. You've seen 雨 before in traditional 電 **diàn** "lightning" (230). Notice that, depending on the writer or font designer's preference, the "four drops of rain" in 雨 may be straight, slant downwards, or some slant upwards and others slant downwards. As always, follow your instructor or mentor's model or the models on the character practice sheets in *Basic Written Chinese Practice Essentials*. Contrast 雨 with 西 **xī** (35), 两(兩) **liǎng-** (99), and 面 **miàn** (168).

雨	**yǔ**	rain [N]
下雨	**xiàyǔ**	rain [VO]
毛毛雨	**máomáoyǔ**	light rain [N]
下毛毛雨	**xià máomáoyǔ**	drizzle [PH]

280 但 **dàn** but

Radical is 人 **rén** "person," which is written 亻 when occurring at the left side of a character so as not to get in the way of the component at the right. The colloquial name for this radical is 人字旁 **rénzìpáng** "side made up of the character 人." Phonetic is 旦 **dàn** "dawn." Contrast 但 with 早 **zǎo** (259) and 日 **rì** (132).

但是	**dànshi**	but [CJ]
不但	**búdàn**	not only [A]

281 其 **qí** its, his, her, their

Radical is 八 **bā** "eight." 其 itself is a common phonetic, e.g., in 期 **qī/qí** (126) as in 星期, 旗 **qí** as in 旗子 **qízi** "flag," 棋 **qí** as in 下棋 **xiàqí** "play chess," and 欺 **qī** as in 欺负(欺負) **qīfu** "bully." Contrast 其 and 期 **qí/qī** (126).

其他	**qítā**	other [AT]

282 实(實) **shí** real, solid, true

Radical is 宀 **mián** "roof" [BF]. This radical is referred to colloquially as 宝盖头 (寶蓋頭) **bǎogàitóu** "top made up of a canopy." The other component of the simplified form is 头 **tóu** (120), while the other component of the traditional form is 贯 (貫) **guàn** "pass through" [BF]. If something can "pass through" a "roof," then it's "real" and "solid" enough. Contrast 实 (實) with 头 (頭) **tóu** (120), 买 (買) **mǎi** (253), 兴 (興) **xìng** (90), and 卖 (賣) **mài** (254).

其实 (其實)	**qíshí**	actually [MA]
实在 (實在)	**shízài**	really, truly [A]

New Words in BSC 10-3 Written with Characters You Already Know

在	**zài**	(indicates progressive aspect) [P]
天天	**tiāntiān**	every day [M+M]
出门 (出門)	**chūmén**	go outside, go out [VO]
出去	**chūqu**	go out [RC/RE]
出来 (出來)	**chūlái**	come out [RC/RE]
看出来 (看出來)	**kànchūlái**	know something by looking [RC]
看不出来 (看不出來)	**kànbuchūlái**	can't tell by looking [RC]
上	**-shang**	up, on [RE]; as in 换上 (換上) "change into and put on (clothes)" or 写上 (寫上) "write (something) on (something)"

Reading Exercises (Simplified Characters)

Now practice reading the new characters and words for this lesson in context in sentences, conversations, and narratives. Be sure to refer to the Notes at the end of this lesson, and make use of the accompanying audio disc to hear and practice correct pronunciation, phrasing, and intonation.

A. SENTENCES

Read out loud each of the following sentences, which include all the new characters of this lesson. The first time you read a sentence, focus special attention on the characters and words that are new to you, reminding yourself of their pronunciation and meaning. The second time, aim to comprehend the overall meaning of the sentence.

一、其他的人都出来了，只有小何还没出来。你进去看看，好吗？
二、今天外头不但冷，听说还会下大雨，你别出去了。
三、您六十岁了？实在看不出来！看您的样子，最多四十五岁吧。
四、其实，外面正在下雨，但是因为是毛毛雨，所以看不出来。
五、你进来坐坐吧，外头实在太冷了。不但冷，还在下雨呢。
六、我看不太清楚，但是外面看起来好像在下毛毛雨的样子。
七、林进明天天早上六点钟就出门。你呢？你几点出门？
八、这班学生里头只有一个同学天天都来，其他的有的时候来，有的时候不来。
九、好像要下雨的样子，我们进去吧！

十、因为下雨了，所以我们都要回家，只有王大海一定要去动物园。

B. CONVERSATIONS

Read out loud the following conversations, including the name or role of the person speaking. If possible, find a partner or partners and each of you play a role. Then switch roles, so you get practice reading all of the lines.

一、
谢太太：是不是又要下雨了？
边太太：对。其实，现在就在下，但是因为是毛毛雨，所以你可能看不出来。
谢太太：我这次来台北，天天都下雨，都不能出门！
边太太：对。不但这样，天气也很冷。下次我们去台中吧。

二、
钱大安：小李，是你吗？请进！……最近怎么样？
李平　：还是老样子。小钱，你看，下雨了！下得越来越大了。我真不喜欢这样儿的天气。
钱大安：但是我喜欢。我最喜欢下雨。
李平　：真的吗？那我得问你，你喜欢下大雨？喜欢下毛毛雨？
钱大安：下大雨，下毛毛雨我都喜欢。

三、
中国学生：在中国，你要进一个好大学，一定要上一个好中学。
美国学生：其实，在美国也是这样。

C. CHARACTER DIFFERENTIATION DRILLS

Distinguish carefully the following similar-looking characters, pronouncing each one out loud and thinking of its meaning.

一、雨 雨 雨 两 两 两
二、雨 雨 雨 面 面 面
三、雨 雨 雨 西 西 西
四、雨 面 雨 两 雨 西 雨 面
五、但 但 但 早 早 早
六、但 早 早 但 但 早 但
七、其 其 其 期 期 期
八、其 期 其 期 期 其 其
九、进 进 进 谁 谁 谁
十、实 实 实 头 头 头
十一、实 实 实 卖 卖 卖
十二、实 实 实 买 买 买
十三、实 头 实 卖 实 买 实

"Train station entrance"

D. NARRATIVES

Read the following narratives, paying special attention to punctuation and overall structure. The first time you read a narrative, read it out loud; the second time, read silently and try to gradually increase your reading speed. Always think of the meaning of what you're reading.

一、这个地方又干又热，很少下雨，也很少会冷。最高温差不多四十度，最低温差不多二十五度，天天都是这样。最近两个月一次也没下雨。看样子，明后天也不会下雨。但是有人说明天会下大雨。可能吗？实在看不出来。我们等等看吧！

二、有一次，一个住在美国的中国人和他的美国朋友一起去买东西。那个中国人找到了他要的东西，最后问他的美国朋友："好吃吗？"美国人说："这个可不能吃！"中国人说："我不是要吃，我是要知道这个东西卖多少钱。你们美国话'多少钱'不是叫'HAO CHI MA'吗？"过了一会儿，他又说："对不起，其实，我要说的是'HAO MA CHI'，不是'HAO CHI MA'，我外国话不好，我要问卖东西的人'多少钱'"。

E. SUPPLEMENT: SEVERAL HANDWRITTEN NOTES

Read out loud the following handwritten notes. Be prepared to answer questions from your instructor and/or classmates on the content of each note and the likely relationship of the author to the recipient.

一、

林老师：

校长找您有事

李 3:40

二、

写得还可以，错字不多。不过下次中国字要写得清楚一点！

三、

欢欢：

我今天早上来看你但是你不在，所以只好给你写这张条子。

同学们那里有一件事需要你来，没有你不行。请看到这张条子以后一定要给我打电话，8939-6534. 我在家等你的电话，不出门。

谢谢！

文文

3月11日

Reading Exercises (Traditional Characters)

A. SENTENCES

Read out loud each of the following sentences, which include all the new characters of this lesson. The first time you read a sentence, focus special attention on the characters and words that are new to you, reminding yourself of their pronunciation and meaning. The second time, aim to comprehend the overall meaning of the sentence.

一、其他的人都出來了，只有小何還沒出來。你進去看看，好嗎？

二、今天外頭不但冷，聽說還會下大雨，你別出去。

三、您六十歲了？實在看不出來！看您的樣子，最多四十五歲吧。

四、其實，外面正在下雨，但是因為是毛毛雨，所以看不出來。

五、你進來坐坐吧，外頭實在太冷了。不但冷，還在下雨呢。

六、我看不太清楚，但是外面看起來好像在下毛毛雨的樣子。

七、林進明天天早上六點鐘就出門。你呢？你幾點出門？

八、這班學生裏頭只有一個同學天天都來，其他的有的時候來，有的時候不來。

九、好像要下雨的樣子，我們進去吧！

十、因為下雨了，所以我們都要回家，只有王大海一定要去動物園。

B. CONVERSATIONS

Read out loud the following conversations, including the name or role of the person speaking. If possible, find a partner or partners and each of you play a role. Then switch roles, so you get practice reading all of the lines.

一、謝太太：是不是又要下雨了？
邊太太：對。其實，現在就在下，但是因為是毛毛雨，所以你可能看不出來。
謝太太：我這次來台北，天天都下雨，都不能出門！
邊太太：對。不但這樣，天氣也很冷。下次我們去台中吧。

二、錢大安：小李，是你嗎？請進！……最近怎麼樣？
李平：還是老樣子。小錢，你看，下雨了！下得越來越大了。我真不喜歡這樣兒的天氣。
錢大安：但是我喜歡。我最喜歡下雨。
李平：真的嗎？那我得問你，你喜歡下大雨？喜歡下毛毛雨？
錢大安：下大雨，下毛毛雨我都喜歡。

三、中國學生：在中國，你要進一個好大學，一定要上一個好中學。
美國學生：其實，在美國也是這樣。

"May you strike it rich" (consists of four characters combined into one)

C. CHARACTER DIFFERENTIATION DRILLS

Distinguish carefully the following similar-looking characters, pronouncing each one out loud and thinking of its meaning.

一、雨雨雨兩兩兩
二、雨雨雨面面面
三、雨雨雨西西西
四、雨面雨兩雨西雨面
五、但但但早早早
六、但早早但但早但
七、其其其期期期
八、其期其期期其其
九、進進進誰誰誰
十、實實實頭頭頭 (simplified only)
十一、實實實賣賣賣
十二、實實實買買買
十三、實頭實賣實買實

D. NARRATIVES

Read the following narratives, paying special attention to punctuation and overall structure. The first time you read a narrative, read it out loud; the second time, read silently and try to gradually increase your reading speed. Always think of the meaning of what you're reading.

一、這個地方天氣又乾又熱，很少下雨，也很少會冷。最高温差不多四十度，最低温差不多二十五度，天天都是這樣。最近兩個月一次也沒下雨。看樣子，明後天也不會下雨。但是有人說明天會下大雨。可能嗎？實在看不出來。我們等等看吧！

二、有一次，一個住在美國的中國人和他的美國朋友一起去買東西。那個中國人找到了他要的東西，最後問他的美國朋友：「好吃嗎？」美國人說：「這個可不能吃！」中國人說：「我不是要吃，我是要知道這個東西賣多少錢。你們美國話『多少錢』不是叫‘HAO CHI MA’嗎？」過了一會兒，他又說：「對不起，其實，我要說的是‘HAO MA CHI’，不是‘HAO CHI MA’。我外國話不好，我要問賣東西的人『多少錢』」。

E. SUPPLEMENT: SEVERAL HANDWRITTEN NOTES

(see Simplified Characters section)

Notes

A3. 看您的样子 (看您的樣子) "Looking at your appearance" or, in better English, "From the way you look."

A6. 我看不太清楚，但是外面看起来好像在下毛毛雨的样子 (我看不太清楚，但是外面看起來好像在下毛毛雨的樣子) "I can't see very clearly, but outside, from looking at it, it appears to be drizzling." Note particularly 看不太清楚. This is the negative potential resultative compound 看不清楚 "can't see clearly" (cf. BSC 9-4: 5) with an additional 太 infixed into it: 看不太清楚 "not be able to see too clearly" or "can't see very clearly."

A7. 林进明天天早上六点钟就出门 (林進明天天早上六點鐘就出門) "Lin Jinming goes out every morning at 6:00, that early." The 就 means "that early" or "as early as that."

A8. 这班学生里头只有一个同学天天都来 (這班學生裏頭只有一個同學天天都來) "In this class of students there is only one classmate who comes every day." Note the 都 after 天天.

B1. 是不是又要下雨了？ "Is it going to rain again?" Normally, 又 is used for past events, e.g., 老毛又生气了 "Old Mao got angry again." However, for events that take place on a regular basis (such as rain), 又 can be used when discussing the future.

D1a. 很少下雨，也很少会冷 (很少下雨，也很少會冷) "It seldom rains, and it'll seldom get cold."

D1b. 最近两个月一次也没下雨 (最近兩個月一次也沒下雨) "The last two months it hasn't rained even once." The pattern 一次也没 + VERB means "didn't VERB even once." This pattern will be explained in more detail in a future lesson.

D1c. 看样子 (看樣子) "The way it looks" (lit. "Looking at appearance").

D1d. 明後天 means "tomorrow or the day after tomorrow." 明 is here an abbreviation for 明天. What do you think the expression 明後年, which also exists, would mean?

D2a. 这个可不能吃 (這個可不能吃) "This you certainly can't eat." Remember that 可 can function as an adverb meaning "certainly, indeed."

D2b. 过了一会儿 (過了一會兒) "after a while."

E2. 错字 (錯字) **cuòzì** means "wrong characters." The character 错 (錯) **cuò** "be wrong" is introduced in the next lesson (character number 284).

"Entrance" (note the incorrect reversed "N" in the Pinyin)

PART 4

Talking About the Weather in Your Hometown

你家在美国什么地方？
(你家在美國什麼地方？)
在美国西岸，离
San Francisco不远。
(在美國西岸，離
San Francisco不遠。)
OHIO STATE

New Characters and Words

Study the six characters below and the common words written with them, paying careful attention to each character's pronunciation, meaning, and structure, as well as similar-looking characters. After you've studied a character, turn to the *Practice Essentials* volume and practice writing it on the practice sheet, making sure to follow the correct stroke order and direction as you pronounce it out loud and think of its meaning.

283 岸 **àn** coast, shore, bank

Radical is 山 **shān** "mountain." Phonetic is 干 **gān** "shield," which is also the simplified form for traditional 乾 **gān** "dry" (275).

东岸（東岸）	**dōngàn**	east coast **[PW]**
西岸	**xī'àn**	west coast **[PW]**
两岸（兩岸）	**liǎng'àn**	the two shores (term for the two sides of the Taiwan Straits, i.e., mainland China and Taiwan) **[N]**

284 错（錯） **cuò** mistake, wrong

Radical is 金 **jīn** "gold, metal" [**BF**]. This radical is referred to colloquially as 金字旁 **jīnzìpáng** "side made up of the character 金." When used as a radical in writing simplified characters, the sixth and seventh strokes of 金 are deleted, so that the radical is then simplified to 钅. When writing traditional characters, the last stroke of 金 slants up toward the right, so as not to get in the way of the other component. Phonetic is 昔 **xī** "former times." Contrast 错（錯）with 钱（錢）**qián** (111).

错（錯）	**cuò**	be wrong **[SV]**; wrong **[RE]**
说错（說錯）	**shuōcuò**	say something wrong **[RC]**
不错（不錯）	**bú cuò**	"not bad," "quite good" **[IE]**

285 阳(陽) **yáng** sun

Radical is 阜 **fù** "mound" [BF], which is written 阝 when occurring at the left-hand side of a character. This radical is referred to colloquially as 左耳旁 **zuǒ'ěrpáng** "side made up of a left ear." Contrast 阳(陽) with 日 **rì** (132) and 场(場) **chǎng** (227).

太阳(太陽)	**tàiyáng**	sun [N]
出太阳(出太陽)	**chū tàiyáng**	the sun comes/is out [PH]
阳明山(陽明山)	**Yángmíng Shān**	Yangming Mountain [PW]
贵阳(貴陽)	**Guìyáng**	Guiyang (capital of Guizhou Province) [PW]

286 晚 **wǎn** evening; late

Radical is 日 **rì** "sun" [BF]. The colloquial name for this radical is 日字旁 **rìzìpáng** "side made up of the character 日." Phonetic is 免 **miǎn** "avoid." The idea is that "evening" is a time when the "sun" is "avoided."

晚	**wǎn**	be late [SV]
晚上	**wǎnshang**	in the evening [TW]
晚饭(晚飯)	**wǎnfàn**	dinner, evening meal [N]

287 已 **yǐ** already

Radical is 己 **jǐ** "self." Note that 已 cannot be used alone in speech, but is often used together with 经(經) **jīng** (288) to form the adverb 已经(已經) **yǐjīng** "already."

288 经(經) **jīng** pass through

Radical is 丝(絲) **sī** "silk." When at the left side of a character, this radical is referred to colloquially as 绞丝旁(絞絲旁) **jiǎosīpáng** "side made up of twisted silk" and is then written as 纟(糹). Phonetic is 巠 **jīng** "underground stream,"as you saw previously in 轻(輕) **qīng** "be light" (178). Contrast 经(經) and 轻(輕) **qīng** (178).

已经(已經)	**yǐjīng**	already [A]

New Words in BSC 10-4 Written with Characters You Already Know

气候(氣候)	**qìhou**	climate [N]
美	**měi**	be beautiful [SV]
难过(難過)	**nánguò**	be sad [SV]
差不多(差不多)	**chàbuduō**	not lack much, be good enough [IE]
比	**bǐ**	compare [CV/V]
...的时候(…的時候)	**...-de shíhou**	when... [PT]
A比B C	**A bǐ B C**	A is more C than B [PT]
A没有B这么C (A沒有B這麼C)	**A méiyou B zhème C**	A is not as C as B [PT]

Reading Exercises (Simplified Characters)

Now practice reading the new characters and words for this lesson in context in sentences, conversations, and narratives. Be sure to refer to the Notes at the end of this lesson, and make use of the accompanying audio disc to hear and practice correct pronunciation, phrasing, and intonation.

A. SENTENCES

Read out loud each of the following sentences, which include all the new characters of this lesson. The first time you read a sentence, focus special attention on the characters and words that are new to you, reminding yourself of their pronunciation and meaning. The second time, aim to comprehend the overall meaning of the sentence.

一、我觉得美国东岸的气候比西岸好，但是小李觉得东岸的气候没有西岸那么好。
二、对不起，实在对不起，我听错了，所以就说错话了！
三、他已经学了半年的中文了，已经会说不少东西了。
四、今天早上太阳出来的时候实在太美了，你说是不是？
五、我觉得北京饭店不但比和平饭店贵，饭也没有和平饭店的那么好吃。
六、我小的时候喜欢去阳明山，现在太忙了，已经很多年没去了。
七、今天出大太阳了，明天的天气大概也不错。
八、你的表哥走了，别太难过了，我们早晚都会死……
九、我刚来的时候，不太喜欢东岸的气候，但是现在喜欢了。
十、“大海，你别难过”，王大海的女朋友说：“要是你今天晚上一定要去动物园看动物的话，我可以和你一起去”。

B. CONVERSATIONS

Read out loud the following conversations, including the name or role of the person speaking. If possible, find a partner or partners and each of you play a role. Then switch roles, so you get practice reading all of the lines.

一、
中国人：你家在美国什么地方？
美国人：在美国的西岸，离San Francisco不太远。
中国人：那儿的气候怎么样？
美国人：那儿的气候还不错。比北京好，也没有这儿这么干。

二、
万太太：弟弟，晚饭你要吃什么？
儿子　：我要吃早饭！
万太太：什么？是你说错了？是我听错了？你要吃早饭？！
儿子　：我没说错，你也没听错。我晚上就是喜欢吃早饭。现在美国年轻人都是这样，你不知道吗？

三、
外国学生：老师，您觉得我的中文怎么样？
中文老师：比以前好。不过，这个字你看错了。不是“要不要”的“要”，这是“车票”的“票”。还有，“年轻”的“轻”，你写成“已经”的“经”了。
外国学生：对不起，是我的错。谢谢老师。

C. CHARACTER DIFFERENTIATION DRILLS

Distinguish carefully the following similar-looking characters, pronouncing each one out loud and thinking of its meaning.

一、经 经 经 轻 轻 轻
二、经 轻 轻 经 经 轻 经 轻
三、阳 阳 阳 场 场 场 (traditional only)
四、阳 场 场 阳 阳 场 (traditional only)
五、阳 阳 阳 日 日 日
六、阳 日 日 阳 日 阳 日

D. NARRATIVES

Read the following narrative, paying special attention to punctuation and overall structure. The first time you read the narrative, read it out loud; the second time, read silently and try to gradually increase your reading speed. Always think of the meaning of what you're reading.

一、我有一个老同事姓高，他是贵阳人。他跟他太太有一个女儿，名字叫“兴”。她的全名叫“高兴”。要是有人问她叫什么名字，她就说“高兴”。要是高先生、高太太找女儿的时候，他们就叫：“高兴！高兴！”他们家里从早到晚都有人叫：“高兴！高兴！高兴！”所以这一家人真的都很高兴。

二、我是北京人，现在给你们说一说我老家北京的气候吧。从三月到五月，北京的天气还不错，不是太冷也不是太热，有时候下一点儿雨。从六月开始，天气越来越热，七月和八月有时候雨也很大。七、八月的时候，最高温度差不多四十度，最低温度差不多二十度。最近几年，北京好像越来越热，有时候热得要死。九月、十月是北京天气最好的时候，人人都喜欢。那个时候不冷也不热，出太阳的时候多。这个时候很多外国人到北京来看天安门、后海、北京动物园、香山和长城，还有很多别的地方。这正是来北京的好时候。从十二月到二月天气又干又冷，很少下雨，那个时候来北京的外国人也比较少。所以说，要是你有机会到北京来，还是九月、十月那个时候来最好！

E. SUPPLEMENT: FOUR-CHARACTER EXPRESSIONS

Chinese people love the rhythm, succinctness, and erudition of 成语（成語）**chéngyǔ** "four-character expressions." Can you guess what the following 成语（成語）mean? They're all written with characters that you've learned in the twelve units of this book. For English translations, see the Notes at the end of this lesson.

一、不三不四
二、不大不小
三、不多不少
四、不中不西
五、七上八下
六、人山人海
七、一字千金

Reading Exercises (Traditional Characters)

A. SENTENCES

Read out loud each of the following sentences, which include all the new characters of this lesson. The first time you read a sentence, focus special attention on the characters and words that are new to you, reminding yourself of their pronunciation and meaning. The second time, aim to comprehend the overall meaning of the sentence.

一、我覺得美國東岸的氣候比西岸好，但是小李覺得東岸的氣候沒有西岸那麼好。

二、對不起，實在對不起，我聽錯了，所以就說錯話了！

三、他已經學了半年的中文了，已經會說不少東西了。

四、今天早上太陽出來的時候實在太美了，你說是不是？

五、我覺得北京飯店不但比和平飯店貴，飯也沒有和平飯店的那麼好吃。

六、我小的時候喜歡去陽明山，現在太忙了，已經很多年沒去了。

七、今天出大太陽了，明天的天氣大概也不錯。

八、你的表哥走了，別太難過了，我們早晚都會死……

九、我剛來的時候，不太喜歡東岸的氣候，但是現在喜歡了。

十、「大海，你別難過」，王大海的女朋友說：「要是你今天晚上一定要去動物園看動物的話，我可以和你一起去」。

B. CONVERSATIONS

Read out loud the following conversations, including the name or role of the person speaking. If possible, find a partner or partners and each of you play a role. Then switch roles, so you get practice reading all of the lines.

一、中國人：你家在美國什麼地方？

美國人：在美國的西岸，離 San Francisco 不太遠。

中國人：那兒的氣候怎麼樣？

美國人：那兒的氣候還不錯。比北京好，也沒有這兒這麼乾。

二、萬太太：弟弟，晚飯你要吃什麼？

兒子：我要吃早飯！

萬太太：什麼？你說錯了？是我聽錯了？你要吃早飯？！

兒子：我沒說錯，你也沒聽錯。我晚上就是喜歡吃早飯。現在美國年輕人都是這樣，你不知道嗎？

三、外國學生：老師，您覺得我的中文怎麼樣？

中文老師：比以前好。不過，這個字你看錯了。不是「要不要」的「要」，這是「車票」的「票」。還有，「年輕」的「輕」，你寫成「已經」的「經」了。

外國學生：對不起，是我的錯。謝謝老師。

C. CHARACTER DIFFERENTIATION DRILLS

Distinguish carefully the following similar-looking characters, pronouncing each one out loud and thinking of its meaning.

一、經經經輕輕輕

二、經輕輕經經輕經輕

三、陽陽陽場場場

四、陽場場陽陽場

五、陽陽陽日日日 (simplified only)

六、陽日日陽日陽日 (simplified only)

D. NARRATIVES

Read the following narrative, paying special attention to punctuation and overall structure. The first time you read the narrative, read it out loud; the second time, read silently and try to gradually increase your reading speed. Always think of the meaning of what you're reading.

一、

我有一個老同事姓高，他是貴陽人。他跟他太太有一個女兒，名字叫「興」。她的全名叫「高興」。要是有人問她叫什麼名字，她就說：「高興」。要是高先生、高太太找女兒的時候，他們就叫：「高興！高興！」他們家裏從早到晚都有人叫「高興！高興！高興！」所以這一家人真的都很高興。

二、

我是北京人，現在給你們說一說我老家北京的氣候吧。從三月到五月，北京的天氣還不錯，不是太冷也不是太熱，有時候下一點兒雨。從六月開始，天氣越來越熱，七月和八月有時候雨也很大。七、八月的時候，最高温度差不多四十度，最低温度差不多二十度。最近幾年，北京好像越來越熱，有時候熱得要死。九月、十月是北京天氣最好的時候，人人都喜歡。那個時候不冷也不熱，出太陽的時候多。這個時候很多外國人到北京來看天安門、後海、北京動物園、香山和長城，還有很多別的地方。這正是來北京的好時候。從十二月到二月天氣又乾又冷，很少下雨，那個時候來北京的外國人也比較少。所以說，要是你有機會到北京來，還是九月、十月那個時候來最好！

E. SUPPLEMENT: FOUR-CHARACTER EXPRESSIONS

(see Simplified Characters section)

Notes

A2. 说错话 (說錯話) means "say the wrong thing."

A3. 他已经学了半年的中文了 (他已經學了半年的中文了) means "He has already been studying Chinese for half a year." The implication is that he's still studying Chinese now. In BSC 11-1 we'll formally take up the use of sentence-final particle 了 at the end of a sentence to indicate that the action of a verb has been continuing for a period of time up to and including the present.

A6. The 了 at the end of 已经很多年没去了 (已經很多年沒去了) indicates that the situation has been continuing for a period of time up to and including the present (cf. note A3 above). An English translation would be "haven't gone (there) for many years."

A8a. 走了 "has gone" is here a euphemism for "has died."

A8b. 早晚 (lit. "early late") is a very common and useful expression that means "sooner or later."

B3. In the last line of this conversation, 是我的错 (是我的錯) means "It's my mistake" or "It's my fault."

D1. In sentence 5, 从早到晚 (從早到晚) means "from morning until evening."

D2a. In sentence 6 of this narrative, 人人都喜欢 (人人都喜歡) means "everyone likes it." Note the adverb 都 after 人人; it's very common to have a 都 after reduplicated forms like 人人 "everyone," 天天 "every day," or 年年 "every year."

D2b. In sentence 8, 后海 (後海) **Hòuhǎi** is a lake in central Beijing famous for its attractive scenery and lively night life. By day one can take boat rides and shop in the many small boutiques, while at night one can enjoy the many restaurants, pubs, teahouses, and cafes.

E1. 不三不四 "Neither 3 nor 4—neither fish nor fowl."

E2. 不大不小 "Neither big nor small."

E3. 不多不少 "Neither many nor few."

E4. 不中不西 "Neither Chinese nor Western."

E5. 七上八下 "Seven up eight down—be flustered, perturbed, upset."

E6. 人山人海 "A huge crowd of people."

E7. 一字千金 "One character is worth a thousand pieces of gold—not one word may be changed."

E. Character Index

This character index includes in it all the characters—both simplified and traditional—that are introduced in *Basic Written Chinese*. The index is arranged by the total number of strokes in a character, so all you need to do to look up a character is count the number of strokes. This index will be useful when you want to look up the pronunciation of a character you learned earlier in this volume that you have fogotten, or when you want to find out in which lesson a given character was introduced, so that you can review the information in this book about it.

In the character index below, the character is listed first, followed by its pronunciation in Pinyin and its character number in this course. Within each group of characters having the same number of strokes, characters are arranged by alphabetical order of the Pinyin romanization (and then, if necessary, by tone). When a character is different in its official simplified and traditional forms, the traditional form is enclosed by parentheses and—in this index only—the simplified form is enclosed by brackets. In this way, you'll always be clear about whether a given character is traditional, simplified, or the same in both systems.

1 Stroke

一 **yī** (1)

2 Strokes

八 **bā** (9)
[厂] **chǎng** (197)
[儿] **ér** (156)
二 **èr** (2)
[几] **jǐ-** (97)
九 **jiǔ** (10)
了 **le** (71)
七 **qī** (8)
人 **rén** (30)
十 **shí** (11)
又 **yòu** (210)

3 Strokes

川 **chuān** (38)
大 **dà** (13)
[干] **gān** (275)
[个] **ge** (87)
工 **gōng** (154)
[广] **guǎng** (27)
口 **kǒu** (140)
[么] **me** (128)
[门] **mén** (123)
女 **nǚ** (101)
千 **-qiān** (114)
三 **sān** (3)
山 **shān** (14)
上 **shàng** (25)
[万] **-wàn** (142)
下 **xià** (167)
小 **xiǎo** (24)
也 **yě** (52)
已 **yǐ** (287)
之 **zhī** (214)
子 **zǐ** (155)

4 Strokes

比 **bǐ** (143)
不 **bù** (63)
[长] **cháng/zhǎng** (175)
[车] **chē** (224)
[从] **cóng** (211)
方 **fāng** (158)
分 **fēn** (244)
公 **gōng** (94)
今 **jīn** (106)
[开] **kāi** (122)
六 **liù** (7)
毛 **máo** (258)
片 **piàn** (91)
[气] **qì** (271)
日 **rì** (132)
少 **shǎo** (110)
什 **shén** (127)
太 **tài** (64)
天 **tiān** (33)
王 **wáng** (6)
文 **wén** (21)
五 **wǔ** (5)
心 **xīn** (262)
以 **yǐ** (146)
友 **yǒu** (172)
月 **yuè** (130)
中 **zhōng** (23)

5 Strokes

半 **bàn** (117)
北 **běi** (16)
本 **běn** (242)
[边] **biān** (159)
出 **chū** (179)
打 **dǎ** (229)
[电] **diàn** (230)
[东] **dōng** (29)
[对] **duì** (108)
[号] **hào** (131)
[记] **jì** (261)
叫 **jiào** (78)
可 **kě** (145)
[们] **men** (57)
平 **píng** (241)
去 **qù** (53)
生 **shēng** (22)
市 **shì** (47)
司 **sī** (95)
四 **sì** (4)
他 **tā** (55)
台 **tái** (18)
[头] **tóu** (120)
外 **wài** (164)
位 **wèi** (98)
[写] **xiě** (202)
右 **yòu** (166)
正 **zhèng** (276)
只 **zhǐ** (238)
左 **zuǒ** (165)

6 Strokes

安 **ān** (37)
百 **-bǎi** (113)
[场] **chǎng** (227)
成 **chéng** (31)
吃 **chī** (151)
次 **cì** (134)
地 **dì** (157)
[动] **dòng** (250)
多 **duō** (103)
[刚] **gāng** (257)
共 **gòng** (247)
[关] **guān** (124)
[过] **-guo** (136)
好 **hǎo** (50)
[后] **hòu** (213)
[欢] **huān** (170)
回 **huí** (161)
[会] **huì** (199)
[机] **jī** (226)
[级] **jí** (174)
[纪] **jì** (105)
件 **jiàn** (235)
交 **jiāo** (233)
她 **tā** (56)
老 **lǎo** (61)
[吗] **ma** (60)
[买] **mǎi** (253)
忙 **máng** (59)
名 **míng** (83)
那 **nà/nèi-** (109)
年 **nián** (104)
(全) **quán** (203)
[全] **quán** (203)
[师] **shī** (102)
死 **sǐ** (274)
[岁] **suì** (107)
同 **tóng** (80)
[问] **wèn** (75)
西 **xī** (35)
先 **xiān** (69)
行 **xíng** (236)
[兴] **xìng** (90)
[阳] **yáng** (285)
因 **yīn** (181)
有 **yǒu** (139)
[园] **yuán** (252)
在 **zài** (149)
早 **zǎo** (259)
州 **zhōu** (28)
字 **zì** (84)

7 Strokes

吧 **ba** (89)
(別) **bié** (82)
[别] **bié** (82)
(車) **chē** (224)
但 **dàn** (280)
低 **dī** (268)
弟 **dì** (188)
[饭] **fàn** (152)
[还] **hái** (180)
何 **hé** (19)
[间] **jiān** (232)
近 **jìn** (221)
[进] **jìn** (278)
[块] **kuài** (112)
[来] **lái** (135)
冷 **lěng** (272)
李 **lǐ** (20)
[里] **lǐ** (163)
[两] **liǎng-** (99)
(沒) **méi** (92)

F. Chinese-English Glossary

This glossary of characters and words introduced in *Basic Written Chinese* is arranged by Pinyin romanization. It will be especially useful when you have forgotten the characters for something that you remember how to say, when you have forgotten the meaning of a character or characters that you can pronounce, or when you remember how to pronounce the first character of a word but have forgotten the characters that follow.

The following information is included for each entry: the Chinese word, spelled in Pinyin, printed in **bold**; the Chinese character(s), first in simplified characters and then, if different, in traditional characters (enclosed in parentheses); one or more English glosses; the word class of the Chinese word [in brackets]; and the numbers of the unit and part where the Chinese word was introduced (in parentheses). For example:

Pinyin	Characters	English, Word Class, and Unit-Part
zhōngtóu	钟头 (鐘頭)	hour [N] (3-4)

The entries are arranged in alphabetical order of the Pinyin spellings, spelled one syllable at a time, with the vowel **u** preceding **ü**. Syllables are listed in order of tone, i.e., in the order Tone One, Tone Two, Tone Three, Tone Four, followed by Neutral Tone. For entries consisting of more than one syllable, we go through the first syllable tone by tone before considering the second syllable. For example:

bā bá báyuè bǎ bà ba -bǎi bān bānjiā bàngōngshì bāng bāngmáng

Hyphens (-), apostrophes ('), and periods (...) are disregarded for purposes of alphabetization. In the case of two entries with identical spelling, order is determined based on order of introduction in the textbook. If two or more different items are spelled identically and are written with the same character(s), they are treated as different usages of one entry rather than as two separate entries.

The purpose of this glossary is to refresh your memory of words that have previously been introduced but which you may have forgotten. Since each entry includes the number of the unit and part in the textbook where the item first occurred, you are encouraged to refer back to that part for more detailed information. Don't try to learn new words from this glossary; keep in mind that a Chinese word means something only in a certain grammatical and semantic context and that English translations can be misleading.

A

Ān 安 An [SN] (B-3)

B

bā 八 eight [NU] (A-2)

bāyuè 八月 August [TW] (4-2)

ba 吧 (indicates supposition) [P] (2-3); (indicates suggestions) [P] (3-3)

-bǎi 百 hundred [NU] (3-3)

-bǎiwàn 百万 (百萬) million [NU] (4-4)

Bān 班 Ban [SN] (8-3)

bān 班 class [N] (8-3)

bàn 半 half [NU] (3-4)

bàntiān 半天 a long time [NU + M] (8-4)

běi 北 north [L] (8-1)

běibiān 北边 (北邊) in the north [PW] (5-3)

Běidà 北大 Peking University [PW] (5-2)

běifāng 北方 north, the North [PW] (8-1)

běifāng huà 北方话 (北方話) northern speech [PH] (8-1)

běifāng rén 北方人 northerner [PH] (8-1)

Běijīng 北京 Beijing [PW] (A-3)

Běijīng Fàndiàn 北京饭店 (北京飯店) Beijing Hotel [PW] (8-1)

Běijīng rén 北京人 person from Beijing [PH] (B-1)

Běijīng Shì 北京市 Beijing City [PH] (B-4)

Běiwài 北外 Beijing Foreign Studies University [PW] (8-2)

běndì 本地 this place, here [N] (9-1)

běndì rén 本地人 local person [PH] (9-1)

bǐ 比 compare [CV/V] (10-4)

bǐjiào 比较 (比較) comparatively, relatively [A] (4-4)

Biān 边 (邊) Bian [SN] (5-3)

biǎodì 表弟 younger male cousin of different surname [N] (7-1)

biǎogē 表哥 older male cousin of different surname [N] (7-1)

biǎojiě 表姐 older female cousin of different surname [N] (7-1)

biǎomèi 表妹 younger female cousin of different surname [N] (7-1)

bié 别 (別) don't [AV] (2-2)

biéde 别的 (别的) other, another [AT] (8-4)
bú cuò 不错 (不錯) "not bad," "quite good" [IE] (10-4)
búdàn 不但 not only [A] (10-3)
búguò 不过 (不過) however [CJ] (5-1)
búyào 不要 don't [AV] (4-3)
bù 不 not [A] (1-3)
bù dōu 不都 not all [PT] (2-1)
bù...yě bù 不…也不 neither...nor [PT] (10-2)
bù yídìng 不一定 not necessarily [PH] (10-1)

C

chà 差 (差) lack [V] (3-4); be lacking, deficient [SV] (7-4)
chàbuduō 差不多 (差不多) almost, about [A] (3-4); not lack much, be good enough [IE] (10-4)
cháng 长 (長) be long [SV] (6-2)
Cháng Chéng 长城 (長城) Great Wall [PW] (7-1)
Cháng Chéng Fàndiàn 长城饭店 (長城飯店) Great Wall Hotel [PW] (7-1)
chǎng 厂 (廠) factory [N] (7-1)
Chē 车 (車) Che [SN] (8-2)
chē 车 (車) vehicle (car, taxi, bus, bicycle) [N] (8-2)
chēpiào 车票 (車票) bus ticket [N] (9-4)
chēzhàn 车站 (車站) bus stop [N] (9-2)
chēzi 车子 (車子) car, vehicle [N] (8-2)
chéng 城 city [N] (7-1)
chéng 成 into [PV] (10-1)
Chéngdū 成都 Chengdu [PW] (B-2)
chī 吃 eat [V] (5-2)
chīfàn 吃饭 (吃飯) eat food, eat [VO] (5-2)
chūlái 出来 (出來) come out [RC/RE] (10-3)
chūmén 出门 (出門) go outside, go out [VO] (10-3)
chūqu 出去 go out [RC/RE] (10-3)
chūshēng 出生 be born [V] (6-2)
chū tàiyáng 出太阳 (出太陽) the sun comes/is out [PH] (10-4)
Chǔ 楚 Chu [SN] (9-1)
cì 次 time [M] (4-3)
cóng 从 (從) from [CV] (7-4)
cóng...dào 从…到 (從…到) from... to [PT] (8-4)
cóng...kāishǐ 从…开始 (從…開始) starting from [PT] (10-1)
cóng...lái 从…来 (從…來) come from [PT] (7-4)
cóngqián 从前 (從前) in the past, formerly [A] (7-4)
cuò 错 (錯) be wrong [SV]; wrong [RE] (10-4)

D

dǎ 打 hit, beat [V] (8-3)
dǎdī 打的 take a taxi [VO] (8-3)
dǎ diànhuà 打电话 (打電話) make a telephone call [PH] (8-3)
dà 大 be big, large, great [SV] (A-3); be old (of people) [SV] (3-2)
-dà 大 big [RE] (6-2)
dà dìdi 大弟弟 older younger brother [N] (6-4)
dà'èr 大二 sophomore year in college [TW] (6-1)
dàgài 大概 probably, about [A] (8-1)
dàgē 大哥 oldest brother [N] (6-4)
dàjiē 大街 main street, avenue [N] (B-3)
dàjiě 大姐 oldest sister [N] (6-4)
dàmèi 大妹 older younger sister [N] (6-4)
dàsān 大三 junior year in college [TW] (6-1)
dàsì 大四 senior year in college [TW] (6-1)
dàxué 大学 (大學) university, college [N] (5-2)
dàxuéshēng 大学生 (大學生) college student [N] (5-2)
dàyī 大一 first year in college [TW] (6-1)
dài 带 (帶) take along, take, bring [V] (2-4)
dànshi 但是 but [CJ] (10-3)
dào 到 arrive, reach [V]; to [CV/PV] (7-3)
-dào 到 (indicates action of verb is attained) [RE] (9-4)
dào...lái 到…来 (到…來) come to [PT] (7-3)
dào...qù 到…去 go to [PT] (7-3)
-dao 到 to [PV] (5-3)
-de 的 (possession) [P] (2-2); (what precedes describes what follows) [P] (2-4)
-de 得 (verb suffix that indicates manner) [P] (7-2)
-de huà 的话 (的話) if [PT] (8-1)
-de shíhou 的时候 (的時候) when [PT] (10-4)
děi 得 must [AV] (7-2)
děng 等 wait, wait for [V] (8-2)
dī 低 be low [SV] (10-1)
dì- 第 (forms ordinal numbers) [SP] (4-3)
dìdi 弟弟 younger brother [N] (6-4)
dìfang 地方 place [N] (5-3)
diǎn 点 (點) o'clock [M] (3-4)
diànchē 电车 (電車) street car, trolley, tram [N] (9-2)
diànhuà 电话 (電話) telephone [N] (8-3)
dōng 东 (東) east [L] (4-2)
dōngàn 东岸 (東岸) east coast [PW] (10-4)
dōngběi 东北 (東北) northeast [PW] (6-3)
dōngbiān 东边 (東邊) in the east [PW] (5-3)
dōngfāng 东方 (東方) east, the East [PW] (8-1)
Dōngfāng rén 东方人 (東方人) Asian person [PH] (8-1)
Dōngjīng 东京 (東京) Tokyo [PW] (B-1)
Dōngmíng Xiàn 东明县 (東明縣) Dongming County [PW] (7-1)
dōngnán 东南 (東南) southeast [PW] (6-3)
dòngwù 动物 (動物) animal [N] (9-2)
Dòngwùyuán 动物园 (動物園) Zoo (bus station) [PW] (9-2)
dòngwùyuán 动物园 (動物園) zoo [PW] (9-2)
dōngxi 东西 (東西) thing [N] (5-4)
dōu 都 all, both [A] (1-2)
dōu bù 都不 all not, none [PT] (2-1)
Dū 都 Du [SN] (B-2)
dù 度 degree (of temperature) [M] (10-1)
duì 对 (對) be correct [SV] (3-2)
duìbuqǐ 对不起 (對不起) "excuse me" [IE] (6-2)

duō 多 be many, much, more [SV] (4-4)
duō 多 how [QW] (3-2)
duōshǎo 多少 how much, how many [QW] (3-3)
duó 多 how [QW] (3-2)

E

érzi 儿子 (兒子) son [N] (6-2)
èr 二 two [NU] (A-1)
èryuè 二月 February [TW] (4-2)

F

fàn 饭 (飯) cooked rice, food [N] (5-2)
fàndiàn 饭店 (飯店) hotel [PW] (5-3)
Fāng 方 Fang [SN] (5-3)
fēn 分 minute; cent, fen (unit of currency) [M] (9-1)

G

gān 干 (乾) be dry [SV] (10-2)
gāng 刚 (剛) just now, just [A] (9-3)
gānggāng 刚刚 (剛剛) just now, just [A] (9-3)
Gāo 高 Gao, Kao [SN] (1-3)
gāo 高 be tall, high [SV] (1-3)
gāo'èr 高二 junior year of high school [TW] (6-1)
gāosān 高三 senior year of high school [TW] (6-1)
gāoxìng 高兴 (高興) be happy [SV] (2-3)
gāoyī 高一 sophomore year of high school [TW] (6-1)
gāozhōng 高中 senior high school [PW] (6-1)
gēge 哥哥 older brother [N] (6-4)
ge 个 (個) (general measure) [M] (2-3)
gěi 给 (給) give [V/PV]; for [CV] (6-4)
gōngchǎng 工厂 (工廠) factory [N] (7-1)
gōnggòng 公共 public [AT] (9-2)
gōnggòng qìchē 公共汽车 (公共汽車) public bus, bus [PH] (9-2)
gōngrén 工人 worker, laborer [N] (5-2)
gōngsī 公司 company, firm [N] (2-4)
gōngzuò 工作 work [N/V] (6-3)
Guān 关 (關) Guan [SN] (4-1)
guān 关 (關) close (not open) [V] (4-1)
guānmén 关门 (關門) close a door, close [VO] (4-1)
Guǎngdōng 广东 (廣東) Guangdong (province) [PW] (B-1)
Guǎngdōng huà 广东话 (廣東話) Cantonese dialect [PH] (7-2)
Guǎngdōng rén 广东人 (廣東人) person from Guangdong [PH] (B-1)
Guǎnghé Xiàn 广河县 (廣河縣) Guanghe County [PW] (7-1)
Guǎngxī 广西 (廣西) Guangxi (province) [PW] (B-2)
Guǎngzhōu 广州 (廣州) Guangzhou [PW] (B-1)
Guǎngzhōu Shì 广州市 (廣州市) Guangzhou City [PH] (B-4)
Guì 贵 (貴) Gui [SN] (2-3)
guì 贵 (貴) be expensive [SV] (3-3)
guìxìng 贵姓 (貴姓) "what's your honorable surname?" [IE] (2-3)
Guìyáng 贵阳 (貴陽) Guiyang (capital of Guizhou Province) [PW] (10-4)
Guìzhōu 贵州 (貴州) Guizhou (province) [PW] (2-3)
guò 过 (過) pass, go by [V] (8-1)
-guo 过 (過) (indicates experience) [P] (4-3)

H

hái 还 (還) still [A] (6-2); in addition [A] (7-1)
hái shi...hǎole 还是…好了 (還是…好了) it would be better if [PT] (6-2)
Hǎikǒu 海口 Haikou (capital of Hainan Province) [PW] (4-4)
Hǎinán 海南 Hainan (province) [PW] (B-3)
hào 号 (號) number; day of the month (in speech) [M] (4-2)
hǎo 好 be good [SV] (1-2); "all right," "O.K." [IE] (2-2)
hǎochī 好吃 be good to eat [SV] (6-1)
hǎode 好的 "all right," "O.K." [IE] (8-2)
hǎokàn 好看 be good-looking [SV] (6-2)
hǎotīng 好听 (好聽) be nice to listen to, pretty [SV] (7-4)
hǎoxiàng 好像 apparently, it seems to me [A] (4-4)
hǎoxiàng...-de yàngzi 好像…的样子 (好像…的樣子) it seems like [PT] (10-3)
Hé 何 He, Ho [SN] (A-4)
hé 和 and [CJ]; with [CV] (7-3)
hé...yìqǐ 和…一起 together with [PT] (7-3)
Héběi 河北 Hebei (province) [PW] (B-4)
Héběi Shěng 河北省 Hebei Province [PH] (B-4)
Hé'nán 河南 Henan (province) [PW] (B-4)
Hé'nán Shěng 河南省 Henan Province [PH] (B-4)
hépíng 和平 peace [N] (9-1)
Hépíng Dōng Lù 和平东路 (和平東路) Heping East Road [PW] (9-1)
hěn 很 very [A] (1-2)
hěn shǎo 很少 seldom [PH] (10-2)
hòu 后 (後) in back, back [L] (7-4)
hòubian 后边 (後邊) in back, back [PW] (7-4)
hòulái 后来 (後來) afterwards, later [MA] (7-4)
hòumian 后面 (後面) in back, back [PW] (7-4)
hòunián 后年 (後年) year after next [TW] (7-4)
hòutiān 后天 (後天) day after tomorrow [TW] (7-4)
hòutou 后头 (後頭) in back, back [PW] (7-4)
Húběi 湖北 Hubei (province) [PW] (B-4)
Húběi Shěng 湖北省 Hubei Province [PH] (B-4)
Hú'nán 湖南 Hunan (province) [PW] (B-4)
Hú'nán Shěng 湖南省 Hunan Province [PH] (B-4)
huàn 换 (換) change, change to, exchange [V] (8-4)
huí 回 go back to [V]; time [M] (5-3)
huì 会 (會) know how to, can [AV] (7-2); be likely to, will [AV] (8-3)
huíjiā 回家 return to one's home [VO] (6-4)

J

jīchǎng 机场 (機場) airport [N] (8-2)
jīhui 机会 (機會) opportunity, chance [N] (8-2)
jǐ- 几 (幾) how many [QW] (3-1); a few, several [NU] (7-2)

jǐhào 几号 (幾號) which day of the month [QW] (4-2)
jǐyuè 几月 (幾月) which month [QW] (4-2)
jìde 记得 (記得) remember [V] (9-4)
jiā 家 family, home [PW]; (for companies, etc.) [M] (6-4)
jiàn 件 (for pieces of luggage, matters, etc.) [M] (8-4)
jiāotōng 交通 traffic [N] (8-3)
jiào 叫 be named [EV] (2-1); call someone a name [V] (2-2); call [V] (9-3)
jiē 街 street [N] (B-3)
jiějie 姐姐 older sister [N] (3-2)
jiěmèi 姐妹 older and younger sisters [N] (6-4)
Jīn 金 Jin, Chin [SN] (B-4)
jīn 金 gold [BF] (6-2)
Jīnmén 金门 (金門) Quemoy [PW] (4-1)
jīnnián 今年 this year [TW] (3-2)
jìn 近 be close, near [SV] (8-1)
jìn 进 (進) enter [V] (10-3)
jìnlái 进来 (進來) come in [RC/RE] (10-3)
jìnqu 进去 (進去) go in [RC] (10-3)
Jīnshān 金山 district in Shanghai; town in Taiwan [PW] (B-4)
jīntiān 今天 today [TW] (4-2)
Jīngdū 京都 Kyoto [PW] (B-2)
jiǔ 九 nine [NU] (A-2)
jiǔyuè 九月 September [TW] (4-2)
jiù 就 then; precisely, exactly [A] (4-2); only [A] (7-4)
juéde 觉得 (覺得) feel [V] (7-4)

K

kāi 开 (開) open; depart (of train, etc.) [V] (4-1); drive, operate vehicle [V] (8-1)
kāichē 开车 (開車) drive a car [VO] (8-4)
kāiguān 开关 (開關) on-off switch [N] (5-4)
kāimén 开门 (開門) open a door, open [VO] (4-1)
kāishǐ 开始 (開始) begin [V]; in the beginning [TW] (7-3)
kàn 看 look, see [V] (6-2); read [V] (9-4)
kànbuchūlái 看不出来 (看不出來) can't tell by looking [RC] (10-3)
kànchūlái 看出来 (看出來) know something by looking [RC] (10-3)
kànqilai 看起来 (看起來) in the looking [RC] (6-2)
kéyi 可以 may, can [AV]; be O.K. [SV] (5-1)
kě 可 indeed, certainly [A] (5-3)
kěnéng 可能 be possible [AV] (10-1)
kěshi 可是 but [CJ] (5-1)
kè 刻 quarter of an hour [M] (3-4)
kǒu 口 (for people) [M] (7-1)
kuài 块 (塊) dollar (monetary unit) [M] (3-3)

L

lái 来 (來) come [V] (4-3)
Lǎo 老 Lao, Lau [SN] (1-3)
lǎo 老 be old [SV] (1-3)
lǎo- 老 (indicates rank among siblings) [BF] (6-4)
lǎodà 老大 oldest (among siblings) [N] (6-4)
lǎoshī 老师 (老師) teacher [N] (3-1)
le 了 (indicates changed situation) [P] (1-4)
-le 了 (indicates completed action) [P] (2-4)
lěng 冷 be cold [SV] (10-2)
lí 离 (離) be distant from, from [CV] (8-1)
lí...hěn jìn 离…很近 (離…很近) be close to [PT] (8-1)
lí...hěn yuǎn 离…很远 (離…很遠) be far from [PT] (8-1)
Lǐ 李 Li, Lee [SN] (A-4)
lǐ 里 (裏) in, inside [L] (5-4)
lǐbian 里边 (裏邊) in, inside [PW] (5-4)
lǐmiàn 里面 (裏面) in, inside [PW] (5-4)
lǐtou 里头 (裏頭) in, inside [PW] (5-4)
liǎng- 两 (兩) two [NU] (3-1)
liǎng'àn 两岸 (兩岸) mainland China and Taiwan [N] (10-4)
Lín 林 Lin, Lam, Lum, Lim [SN] (A-2)
Línkǒu Xiàn 林口县 (林口縣) Linkou County [PW] (7-1)
líng 〇 zero [NU] (3-3)
liù 六 six [NU] (A-2)
liùyuè 六月 June [TW] (4-2)
Lù 路 Lu [SN] (B-2)
lù 路 road [N] (B-2); (for bus routes or lines) [M] (9-2)
lùkǒu 路口 intersection [N] (9-1)

M

ma 吗 (嗎) (indicates questions) [P] (1-2)
mǎi 买 (買) buy [V] (9-3)
mǎimài 买卖 (買賣) buying and selling, business [N] (9-3)
mài 卖 (賣) sell [V] (9-3)
máng 忙 be busy [SV] (1-2)
Máo 毛 Mao [SN] (9-3)
máo 毛 ten cents, dime [M] (9-3)
máomáoyǔ 毛毛雨 light rain [N] (10-3)
méi 没 (沒) (past negative of action verbs) [AV] (2-4); not to have [V] (9-3)
méi shìr 没事儿 (沒事兒) "it's nothing," "never mind" [IE] (5-3)
méiyou 没有 (沒有) not have [V] (4-4); (past negative of action verbs) [AV] (6-3)
méiyou...zhème A 没有 B 这么 C (A 沒有 B 這麼 C) A is not as C as B [PT] (10-4)
měi 美 be beautiful [SV] (10-4)
Měiguo 美国 (美國) America [PW] (2-1)
Měiguo rén 美国人 (美國人) American, native of America [PH] (2-1)
mèimei 妹妹 younger sister [N] (6-4)
Mén 门 (門) Men [SN] (4-1)
mén 门 (門) door, gate [N] (4-1)
ménkǒu 门口 (門口) doorway, entrance [N] (8-2)
ménr 门儿 (門兒) door, gate [N] (5-2)
míng 明 bright [BF] (A-3)
míngnián 明年 next year [TW] (4-2)
míngpiàn 名片 name card [N] (2-4)
míngtiān 明天 tomorrow [TW] (4-2)
míngzi 名字 name [N] (2-2)

N

náli 哪里 (哪裏) not at all [IE] (5-4); where [QW] (6-2)
nǎ- 哪 which [QW] (2-1)
nà 那 that [PR/SP]; in that case, so [CJ] (3-3)
nàli 那里 (那裏) there [PW] (6-2)

nàme 那么 (那麼) then, in that case [A] (4-2); like that, so [A] (7-3)
Nán 南 Nan [SN] (B-3)
nán 南 south [L] (8-1)
nán 难 (難) be difficult, hard [SV] (1-3)
nánbiān 南边 (南邊) in the south [PW] (5-3)
nánde 男的 man, male [N] (3-1)
nánfāng 南方 south, the South [PW] (8-1)
nánfāng huà 南方话 (南方話) southern speech [PH] (8-1)
nánfāng rén 南方人 southerner [PH] (8-1)
nánguò 难过 (難過) be sad [SV] (10-4)
Nánjīng 南京 Nanjing [PW] (B-3)
nánlǎoshī 男老师 (男老師) male teacher [N] (3-1)
nánpéngyou 男朋友 boyfriend [N] (6-1)
nánshēng 男生 male student [N] (3-1)
nánxuésheng 男学生 (男學生) male student [N] (5-2)
nǎr 哪儿 (哪兒) where [QW] (5-2)
nàr 那儿 (那兒) there [PW] (5-2)
ne 呢 what about [P] (1-1); (pause) [P] (7-1); (continuous aspect) [P] (9-4)
něi- 哪 which [QW] (2-1)
něibiān 哪边 (哪邊) what side, where [QW] (5-3)
něiguó 哪国 (哪國) which country [QW] (2-1)
nèi- 那 that [PR/SP] (3-3)
nèibian 那边 (那邊) that side, there [PW] (5-3)
nèiyang 那样 (那樣) that way, like that [MA] (10-3)
nèiyangzi 那样子 (那樣子) that way, like that [MA] (10-3)
néng 能 be able to, can [AV] (6-3)
nǐ 你 you [PR] (1-1)
nǐ hǎo 你好 "how are you?" [IE] (1-1)
nǐmen 你们 (你們) you (plural) [PR] (1-4)
Nián 年 Nian [SN] (3-2)
nián 年 year [M] (4-2)
niánjí 年级 (年級) grade (in school) [N] (6-1)
niánji 年纪 (年紀) age [N] (3-2)
niánqīng 年轻 (年輕) be young [SV] (6-2)
nín 您 you (polite) [PR] (2-3)
nǚde 女的 woman, female [N] (3-1)
nǚ'ér 女儿 (女兒) daughter [N] (6-2)
nǚlǎoshī 女老师 (女老師) female teacher [N] (3-1)
nǚpéngyou 女朋友 girlfriend [N] (6-1)
nǚshēng 女生 female student [N] (3-1)
nǚxuésheng 女学生 (女學生) female student [N] (5-2)

P

péngyou 朋友 friend [N] (6-1)
piào 票 ticket [N] (9-3)
Píng 平 Ping [SN] (9-1)

Q

qī 七 seven [NU] (A-2)
qīyuè 七月 July [TW] (4-2)
qíshí 其实 (其實) actually [MA] (10-3)
qítā 其他 other [AT] (10-3)
qìchē 汽车 (汽車) car, vehicle [N] (8-2)
qìchē gōngsī 汽车公司 (汽車公司) car company, taxi company [PH] (8-2)
qìhou 氣候 (气候) climate [N] (10-4)
-qilai 起来 (起來) in the VERBing [RE] (6-2)
-qiān 千 thousand [NU] (3-3)
-qiānwàn 千万 (千萬) ten million [NU] (4-4)
Qián 钱 (錢) Qian [SN] (3-3)
qián 钱 (錢) money [N] (3-3)
qián 前 in front, front [L] (7-4)
qiánbian 前边 (前邊) in front; front [PW] (7-4)
qiánmian 前面 in front; front [PW] (7-4)
qiánnián 前年 year before last [TW] (7-4)
qiántiān 前天 day before yesterday [TW] (7-4)
qiántou 前头 (前頭) in front; front [PW] (7-4)
qīng 轻 (輕) be light (not heavy) [SV] (8-4)
qīngchu 清楚 be clear, be clear about [SV] (9-1)
qǐng 请 (請) "please" [IE] (1-4)
qǐng jìn 请进 (請進) "please come in" [IE] (10-3)
qǐng wèn 请问 (請問) "excuse me," "may I ask" [IE] (2-1)
qǐng zuò 请坐 (請坐) "please sit down" [IE] (1-4)
qù 去 go, go to [V] (1-1)
-qù 去 (indicates motion away from the speaker) [RE] (8-3)
qùnián 去年 last year [TW] (4-2)
qù...zěnme zǒu 去…怎么走 (去…怎麼走) how do you get to [PT] (8-1)
quán 全 (全) completely [A] (7-2)

R

ránhòu 然后 (然後) afterward, then [MA] (9-2)
rè 热 (熱) be hot [SV] (10-2)
rén 人 person [N] (B-1)
rénkǒu 人口 population [N] (4-4)
rì 日 day; day of the month (in writing) [BF] (4-2)
Rìběn 日本 Japan [PW] (9-1)
Rìběn huà 日本话 (日本話) Japanese language [PH] (9-1)
Rìběn rén 日本人 Japanese person [PH] (9-1)
Rìwén 日文 Japanese (especially written Japanese) [N] (4-2)

S

sān 三 three [NU] (A-1)
sānyuè 三月 March [TW] (4-2)
shān 山 mountain, hill [N] (A-3)
Shāndōng 山东 (山東) Shandong (province) [PW] (B-1)
Shānxī 山西 Shanxi (province) [PW] (B-2)
Shānxī Shěng 山西省 Shanxi Province [PH] (B-4)
shàng 上 on [L] (5-4); go to [V] (6-1); get on (a vehicle, etc.) [V] (9-3)
shàng- 上 last [SP] (3-2)
shàngbān 上班 go to work, work [VO] (8-3)
shàngbian 上边 (上邊) on top, on [PW] (5-4)
shàngchē 上车 (上車) get on a vehicle [VO] (9-2)
Shànghǎi 上海 Shanghai [PW] (B-1)
Shànghǎi huà 上海话 (上海話) Shanghainese dialect [PH] (7-2)

Shànghǎi rén 上海人 person from Shanghai [PH] (B-1)
shàngmian 上面 on top, on, above [PW] (5-4)
shàngtou 上头 (上頭) on top, on [PW] (5-4)
shàngxué 上学 (上學) attend school [VO] (6-3)
-shang 上 up, on [RE] (10-3)
shǎo 少 be few, less [SV] (4-4)
shéi 谁 (誰) who [QW] (4-1)
shénme 什么 (什麼) what [QW] (4-2)
shēng 生 be born, give birth to [V] (A-4)
shēngqì 生气 (生氣) get angry [VO] (10-2)
shēngrì 生日 birthday [N] (4-2)
shěng 省 province [N] (B-4)
shí 十 ten [NU] (A-2)
shí 时 (時) hour, o'clock (written Chinese) [BF] (7-3)
shí'èryuè 十二月 December [TW] (4-2)
shíhou 时候 (時候) time [N] (7-3)
shíjiān 时间 (時間) time [N] (8-3)
shíwàn 十万 (十萬) hundred thousand [NU] (4-4)
shíyīyuè 十一月 November [TW] (4-2)
shíyuè 十月 October [TW] (4-2)
shízài 实在 (實在) really, truly [A] (10-3)
shì 市 city, municipality [BF] (B-4)
shì 是 be [EV] (2-1)
shì 事 matter, thing (abstract) [N] (5-3)
shì...de 是…的 (indicates time or place of known past actions) [PT] (4-2)
shǒudū 首都 capital (city) [N] (8-2)
Shǒudū Jīchǎng 首都机场 (首都機場) Capital Airport [PW] (8-2)
shuō 说 (說) say, speak [V] (7-2)
shuōcuò 说错 (說錯) say something wrong [RC] (10-4)
shuōhuà 说话 (說話) speak words, speak [VO] (7-2)
Sī 司 Si [SN] (2-4)
sījī 司机 (司機) driver, chauffeur [N] (8-3)
sǐ 死 die [V] (10-2)
sì 四 four [NU] (A-1)
Sìchuān 四川 Sichuan (province) [PW] (B-3)
Sìchuān Shěng 四川省 Sichuan Province [PH] (B-4)
sìyuè 四月 April [TW] (4-2)
suì 岁 (歲) year of age [M] (3-2)
suóyi 所以 therefore, so [CJ] (6-3)
suóyi shuō 所以说 (所以說) so, therefore [PH] (10-1)

T

tā 他 he [PR] (1-2)
tā 她 she [PR] (1-2)
tāmen 他们 (他們) they [PR] (1-2)
tāmen 她们 (她們) they (females only) [PR] (1-2)
tái 台 (for computers, etc.) [M] (5-4)
Táiběi 台北 Taipei [PW] (A-3)
Táiběi Měiguo Xuéxiào 台北美国学校 (台北美國學校) Taipei American School [PW] (6-3)
Táiběi Shì 台北市 Taipei City [PH] (B-4)
Táidōng 台东 (台東) Taitung [PW] (B-1)
Táinán 台南 Tainan [PW] (B-3)
Táishān 台山 Taishan, Toisan [PW] (A-3)
Táiwān 台湾 (台灣) Taiwan [PW] (B-4)
Táiwān huà 台湾话 (台灣話) Taiwanese dialect [PH] (7-2)
Táizhōng 台中 Taichung [PW] (A-4)
tài 太 excessively, too [A] (1-3)
tàitai 太太 Mrs. [N] (1-4); wife [N] (2-3); married woman, lady [N] (2-4)
tàiyáng 太阳 (太陽) sun [N] (10-4)
Tàiyuán 太原 Taiyuan (capital of Shanxi Province) [PW] (7-1)
tiān 天 day [M] (4-1); sky [N] (10-1)
Tiān'ānmén 天安门 (天安門) Tiananmen [PW] (8-1)
Tiānjīn 天津 Tianjin [PW] (B-2)
tiānqi 天气 (天氣) weather [N] (10-2)
tiāntiān 天天 every day [M + M] (10-3)
tiáo 条 (條) (for streets, alleys) [M] (8-4)
tiáozi 条子 (條子) note (written on a strip of paper) [N] (8-4)
tīng 听 (聽) listen, hear [V] (7-4)
tīngshuō 听说 (聽說) hear of, hear it said that [V] (7-4)
tōngzhī 通知 notify [V] (8-3)
Tōng Xiàn 通县 (通縣) Tong County [PW] (8-3)
tóngshì 同事 colleague [N] (5-3)
tóngwū 同屋 roommate [N] (2-2)
tóngwūr 同屋儿 (同屋兒) roommate [N] (5-2)
tóngxué 同学 (同學) classmate [N] (5-2)

W

wài 外 outside [L] (5-4)
wàibian 外边 (外邊) outside [PW] (5-4)
wàiguo 外国 (外國) foreign country [N] (8-2)
wàiguo huà 外国话 (外國話) foreign language [PH] (8-2)
wàiguo rén 外国人 (外國人) foreigner [PH] (8-2)
wàimian 外面 outside [PW] (5-4)
wàitou 外头 (外頭) outside [PW] (5-4)
wǎn 晚 be late [SV] (10-4)
wǎnfàn 晚饭 (晚飯) dinner, evening meal [N] (10-4)
wǎnshang 晚上 in the evening [TW] (10-4)
Wàn 万 (萬) Wan [SN] (4-4)
-wàn 万 (萬) ten thousand [NU] (4-4)
Wáng 王 Wang, Wong, Ong [SN] (A-1)
wǎng 往 to, toward [CV] [BF] (8-1)
wàng 往 to, toward [CV] [BF] (8-1)
wàng 忘 forget [V] (6-4)
wèi 位 (polite measure for people) [M] (3-1)
wèishenme 为什么 (為什麼) why [QW] (6-3)
wèizi 位子 seat, place [N] (5-2)
Wēn 温 Wen [SN] (10-1)
wēndù 温度 temperature [N] (10-1)
Wēnzhōu 温州 important city in Zhejiang Province [PW] (10-1)
Wēnzhōu Jiē 温州街 Wenzhou Street [PH] (10-1)
Wén 文 Wen [SN] (A-4)
Wén'ān Xiàn 文安县 (文安縣) Wenan County [PW] (7-1)
wèn 问 (問) ask [V] (2-1)
wǒ 我 I, me [PR] (1-1)
wǒmen 我们 (我們) we, us [PR] (1-4)
wǔ 五 five [NU] (A-1)
wǔ-bā-liù 五八六 Pentium® (brand of computer) [N] (5-4)

Wǔ Dà Hú 五大湖 Great Lakes [PW] (B-4)
wǔyuè 五月 May [TW] (4-2)

X

xī 西 west [L] (8-1)
Xī'ān 西安 Xian [PW] (B-3)
xī'àn 西岸 west coast [PW] (10-4)
xīběi 西北 northwest [PW] (6-3)
xībiān 西边（西邊）in the west [PW] (5-3)
xīfāng 西方 west, the West [PW] (8-1)
Xīfāng rén 西方人 Western person [PH] (8-1)
xī'nán 西南 southwest [PW] (6-3)
xǐhuan 喜欢（喜歡）like [V/AV] (6-1)
xià 下 on the bottom, under, below [L]; next [SP] (5-4)
xiàbān 下班 get off from work [VO] (8-3)
xiàbian 下边（下邊）on the bottom, under, below [PW] (5-4)
xiàchē 下车（下車）get off a vehicle [VO] (9-4)
xià máomáoyǔ 下毛毛雨 drizzle [PH] (10-3)
xiàmian 下面 on the bottom, under, below [PW] (5-4)
xiàtou 下头（下頭）on the bottom, under, below [PW] (5-4)
xiàyǔ 下雨 rain [VO] (10-3)
xiān 先 first, before someone else [A] (1-4)
xiān...ránhòu 先…然后（先…然後）first...then [PT] (9-2)
xiānsheng 先生 Mr. [N] (1-4); husband [N] (2-3); gentleman [N] (2-4)
xiàn 县（縣）county [N] (7-1)
xiànzài 现在（現在）now [A] (7-1)
xiāng 香 be fragrant, smell good [SV] (5-3)
Xiāng Shān 香山 Fragrant Hills [PW] (B-3)
Xiānggǎng 香港 Hong Kong [PW] (B-3)
Xiānggǎng Zhōngwén Dàxué 香港中文大学（香港中文大學）Chinese University of Hong Kong [PW] (5-2)
xiǎo 小 be small, little, young [SV] (A-4)
xiǎodì 小弟 little brother [N] (6-4)
xiáojie 小姐 Miss, Ms. [N] (1-4); young lady, unmarried lady [N] (2-4)
xiǎomèi 小妹 little sister [N] (6-4)
xiǎoshí 小时（小時）hour [N] (8-3)
xiǎoxīn 小心 be careful [SV] (9-4)
xiǎoxué 小学（小學）elementary school [PW] (6-1)
xiàozhǎng 校长（校長）school principal [N] (6-3)
xiě 写（寫）write [V] (7-2)
xiězì 写字（寫字）write characters, write [VO] (7-2)
Xiè 谢（謝）Xie, Hsieh [SN] (1-3)
xièxie 谢谢（謝謝）"thank you" [IE] (1-3); thank [V] (1-4)
xīngqī 星期 week [N] (4-1)
xīngqī'èr 星期二 Tuesday [TW] (4-1)
xīngqījǐ 星期几（星期幾）which day of the week [QW] (4-1)
xīngqīliù 星期六 Saturday [TW] (4-1)
xīngqīrì 星期日 Sunday [TW] (4-2)
xīngqīsān 星期三 Wednesday [TW] (4-1)
xīngqīsì 星期四 Thursday [TW] (4-1)
xīngqītiān 星期天 Sunday [TW] (4-1)
xīngqīwǔ 星期五 Friday [TW] (4-1)
xīngqīyī 星期一 Monday [TW] (4-1)
xīngqí 星期 week [N] (4-1)
xíng 行 be all right, be O.K. [V] (8-4)
xíngli 行李 luggage, baggage [N] (8-4)
xìng 姓 be surnamed [EV] (2-3)
xìngmíng 姓名 first and last name [N] (8-2)
xūyào 需要 need [V/AV] (8-4)
xué 学（學）study, learn [V] (5-2)
xuéqilai 学起来（學起來）in the learning [RC] (6-2)
xuésheng 学生（學生）student [N] (5-2)
xuéxiào 学校（學校）school [N] (6-3)

Y

Yángmíng Shān 阳明山（陽明山）Yangming Mountain [PW] (10-4)
yàngzi 样子（樣子）way, appearance [N] (10-3)
yāo 一 one (on the telephone) [NU] (5-3)
yào 要 want, cost, take [V]; will [AV] (4-3); need to [AV], request [V] (8-3)
yào 要 if [MA] (10-2)
yàoshi 要是 if [CJ] (5-1)
yě 也 also, too [A] (1-1)
yī 一 one, a [NU] (A-1)
yīyuè 一月 January [TW] (4-2)
yíbànr 一半儿（一半兒）half [NU + NU] (5-2)
yídìng 一定 definitely [A] (10-1)
yíge rén 一个人（一個人）by oneself, alone [PH] (7-3)
yígòng 一共 in all [A] (9-2)
yíxiàr 一下儿（一下兒）(softens the verb) [NU + M] (5-4)
yǐhòu 以后（以後）in the future [TW] (7-4)
yǐhòu 以后（以後）after [PT] (7-4)
yǐjīng 已经（已經）already [A] (10-4)
yǐqián 以前 before, formerly [MA] (7-4)
yǐqián 以前 before [PT] (7-4)
yìdiǎn 一点（一點）a little, some [NU + M] (3-4)
yìdiǎnr 一点儿（一點兒）a little, some [NU + M] (5-2)
yìhuǐr 一会儿（一會兒）a while [N] (8-3)
yìqǐ 一起 together [A] (7-3)
yìzhí 一直 straight [A] (9-1)
yīnwei 因为（因為）because [CJ] (6-3)
yīnwei...suóyi 因为…所以（因為…所以）because [PT] (6-3)
yǒu 有 have; there is, there are [V] (4-4)
yǒude 有的 some [AT/PR] (7-2)
yǒude shíhou 有的时候（有的時候）sometimes [PH] (7-3)
yǒude...yǒude 有的…有的 some... others [PT] (7-2)
yòu 右 right [L] (5-4)
yòu 又 again [A] (7-3)
yòubian 右边（右邊）right side, right [PW] (5-4)
yòu...yòu 又…又 both...and [PT] (10-2)
yǔ 雨 rain [N] (10-3)
yuánlái 原来（原來）originally, formerly [A] (7-1)
yuǎn 远（遠）be far away [SV] (8-1)
yuè 月 month [N] (4-2)
yuè lái yuè 越来越（越來越）more and more [PT] (10-1)
Yuènán 越南 Vietnam [PW] (10-1)

Yuènán huà 越南话 (越南話) spoken Vietnamese language [PH] (10-1)

Yuènánwén 越南文 written Vietnamese language [N] (10-1)

yuèpiào 月票 monthly ticket [N] (9-4)

Z

zài 在 be in, at [V/CV]; be present [V] (5-1); (progressive aspect) [P] (10-3)

-zài 在 at, in, on [PV] (e.g., 住在 "live in") (5-3)

zǎo 早 be early [SV] (9-4); "good morning" [IE] (10-1)

zǎofàn 早饭 (早飯) breakfast [N] (9-4)

zǎoshang 早上 in the morning [TW] (9-4)

zěnme 怎么 (怎麼) how [QW] (8-1); how come, why [QW] (8-3)

zěnmeyàng 怎么样 (怎麼樣) how, in what way [QW] (10-3)

zhàn 站 station, stop [N/M] (9-2)

Zhāng 张 (張) Zhang, Chang [SN] (9-3)

zhāng 张 (張) (for flat objects like tables, name cards) [M] (9-3)

zhǎng 长 (長) grow [V] (6-2)

zhǎngdà 长大 (長大) grow up [RC] (6-2)

-zháo 着 (着) (indicates action of verb is realized) [RE] (9-4)

zhǎo 找 look for [V] (5-1); give in change [V] (8-4)

zhǎobuzháo 找不着 (找不着) look for and can't find, can't find [RC] (9-4)

zhǎodào 找到 look for and find, find [RC] (9-4)

zhǎoqián 找钱 (找錢) give (sb.) change [VO] (8-4)

zhǎozháo 找着 (找着) look for and find, find [RC] (9-4)

zhè 这 (這) this [PR/SP] (2-4)

zhèli 这里 (這裏) here [PW] (6-2)

zhème 这么 (這麼) like this, in this way, so [A] (4-2)

zhème shuō 这么说 (這麼說) saying it like this; then [PH] (10-2)

-zhe 着 (着) (indicates continuous aspect) [P] (9-4)

zhèi- 这 (這) this [SP] (2-4)

zhèibian 这边 (這邊) this side, here [PW] (5-3)

zhèiyang 这样 (這樣) this way, like this [MA] (10-3)

zhèiyangzi 这样子 (這樣子) this way, like this [MA] (10-3)

zhēn 真 really [A] (6-1)

zhèng 正 just [A] (10-2)

zhèr 这儿 (這兒) here [PW] (5-2)

zhīdao 知道 know [V] (5-1)

zhīhòu 之后 (之後) after, in [PT] (7-4)

zhīqián 之前 before, ago [PT] (7-4)

zhǐ 只 only [A] (8-4)

zhǐhǎo 只好 have no choice but, can only [A] (8-4)

zhōng 钟 (鐘) bell; clock [N] (3-4)

zhōngfàn 中饭 (中飯) lunch [N] (5-2)

Zhōngguo 中国 (中國) China [PW] (2-1)

Zhōngguo fàn 中国饭 (中國飯) Chinese food [PH] (5-2)

Zhōngguo huà 中国话 (中國話) spoken Chinese [PH] (7-2)

Zhōngguo rén 中国人 (中國人) Chinese, native of China [PH] (2-1)

Zhōngguo zì 中国字 (中國字) Chinese character [PH] (7-2)

Zhōng-Měi 中美 Sino-American [AT] (2-4)

zhōngtóu 钟头 (鐘頭) hour [N] (3-4)

Zhōngwén 中文 Chinese language [N] (1-3)

Zhōngwén bān 中文班 Chinese class [PH] (8-3)

zhōngxīn 中心 center [N] (9-4)

zhōngxué 中学 (中學) middle school [PW] (6-1)

zhù 住 live (in), stay (in) [V] (4-3)

zhǔn 准 (準) be accurate [SV] (10-1)

zhǔnbèi 准备 (準備) prepare, get ready; plan, intend [V] (9-4)

zì 字 character, word [N] (7-2)

zǒu 走 leave, depart [V] (1-4); go, walk [V] (8-1)

zǒujìnlái 走进来 (走進來) come walking in [RC] (10-3)

zǒujìnqu 走进去 (走進去) go walking in [RC] (10-3)

zǒulù 走路 walk [VO] (8-1)

zuì 最 most [A] (10-1)

zuìdīwēn 最低温 low temperature [N] (10-1)

zuì dī wēndù 最低温度 low temperature [PH] (10-1)

zuìgāowēn 最高温 high temperature [N] (10-1)

zuì gāo wēndù 最高温度 high temperature [PH] (10-1)

zuìhòu 最后 (最後) in the end, finally [MA] (10-1)

zuìjìn 最近 recently [MA] (10-1)

Zuǒ 左 Zuo [SN] (5-4)

zuǒ 左 left [L] (5-4)

zuǒbian 左边 (左邊) left side, left [PW] (5-4)

zuǒyòu 左右 about, approximately [PW] (8-1)

zuò 坐 sit [V] (1-4); travel by, take [V] (3-4)

English Translations, p. 58

1. If it weren't for him, there would be no iPhone. (lit. "There is not him, then there is not iPhone."
2. Get on the street(s)!
3. Beijing FM 106.1 (only black print is translated)
4. Chinese University of Hong Kong
5. October 28 – October 31
6. We're together
7. 8 years, 416 times
8. Last 7 days
9. In ten people one is surnamed Wang (in simplified characters but to be read from top to bottom)
10. Wang is the most common surname in Beijing (lit. "As for Beijing people, those surnamed Wang are the most many")
11. Northern Middle School in Beijing City
12. Shanghai time
13. Why not go to Quemoy
14. Who is it?
15. From the beginning until now
16. One year only 1,290 yuan
17. Chinese workers
18. You must know this (lit. "You cannot not know"; to be read from right to left)
19. "From A to A+"